AREA HANDBOOK
for
PANAMA

Coauthors

Thomas E. Weil

Jan Knippers Black
Howard I. Blutstein
David S. McMorris
Frederick P. Munson
Charles Townsend

Research completed October 1971

Second Edition

Published 1972

(This handbook supersedes DA Pam 550–46, March 1962)

DA Pam 550–46

Library of Congress Catalog Card Number: 72–600052

For sale by the Superintendent of Documents, U.S. Government Printing Office
Washington, D.C. 20402—Price $3.25

FOREWORD

This volume is one of a series of handbooks prepared by Foreign Area Studies (FAS) of The American University, designed to be useful to military and other personnel who need a convenient compilation of basic facts about the social, economic, political, and military institutions and practices of various countries. The emphasis is on objective description of the nation's present society and the kinds of possible or probable changes that might be expected in the future. The handbook seeks to present as full and as balanced an integrated exposition as limitations on space and research time permit. It was compiled from information available in openly published material. An extensive bibliography is provided to permit recourse to other published sources for more detailed information. There has been no attempt to express any specific point of view or to make policy recommendations. The contents of the handbook represent the work of the authors and FAS and do not represent the official view of the United States government.

An effort has been made to make the handbook as comprehensive as possible. It can be expected, however, that the material, interpretations, and conclusions are subject to modification in the light of new information and developments. Such corrections, additions, and suggestions for factual, interpretive, or other changes as readers may have will be welcomed for use in future revisions. Comments may be addressed to—

The Director
Foreign Area Studies
The American University
5010 Wisconsin Avenue, N.W.
Washington, D.C. 20016

PREFACE

The need for a revision of the *Area Handbook for Panama* is underlined not only by the continuing importance of the Republic's location at one of the world's great crossroads but also by new trends in economic development, in education, and in government. Of particular significance are the establishment, in 1968, of the Provisional Junta Government, the subsequent intensification of national consciousness, and renewed discussions with the United States on the status of the Panama Canal Zone.

This book supersedes the *Area Handbook for Panama* published in March 1962, researched and written by Wendell Blanchard, Edwin E. Erickson, Bela C. Maday, Nathan S. Popkin, Suzanne Teleki, and Ernest A. Will, under the chairmanship of Lyman H. Letgers. It represents an effort to provide a compact and objective exposition and analysis of the dominant social, political, and economic characteristics of Panamanian society. It is designed to give readers both within and outside the government an understanding of the dynamics of the elements of the society and an insight into the needs, goals, and achievements of the people. Consultants with firsthand knowledge of the country have provided data not available in printed sources. The authors alone are responsible for the final draft.

English usage follows *Webster's Third New International Dictionary* (unabridged). Spanish words and phrases, used only when adequate English equivalents were lacking, are defined at first appearance. If employed frequently, they are listed in the Glossary. Spanish is based on *Appleton's New Cuyás Dictionary*, fifth edition. Unless otherwise stated, tons used in production and commodity figures are metric tons.

COUNTRY SUMMARY

1. COUNTRY: Republic of Panama (República de Panamá).

2. GOVERNMENT: Under Constitution of 1946, a constitutional republic in form of centralized democracy. In 1971 governed by Provisional Junta Government established after deposition of president in 1968. National Assembly dissolved, and political parties declared "extinct" in 1969, but cabinet, autonomous agencies, and Supreme Court of Justice continued to function.

3. POPULATION: About 1,425,000, as reported in 1970 census. Annual growth rate 1960–70 was 3.04 percent. Urban population 48 percent of total, with some two-thirds concentrated in Panama City. Population about 70 percent mestizo, an amalgam of Spanish, Indian, and Negro. Other groups include 10 percent white, 13 percent Negro, 6 percent Indian, and 1 percent Oriental or Levantine.

4. SIZE: Slightly over 29,000 square miles; country forms narrowest and lowest portion of isthmus linking North and South America.

5. TOPOGRAPHY: Dominant feature of landform in central spine of highlands forming continental divide. Highest elevations in west near Costa Rica and in east near Colombia. Lowest maximum elevations at waist of country where it is crossed by Panama Canal. Most of population concentrated on Pacific side of divide westward from Panama City.

6. LANGUAGES: Spanish, the official language, spoken by nearly all Panamanians. English, a popular and prevalent second tongue, used extensively by Antillean Negroes, and use abetted by the presence of large numbers of North Americans in the Canal Zone. A number of indigenous languages in common use among the tribal Indians, but total number of users of these dialects is small.

7. RELIGION: Though not formally the state religion, Roman Catholic faith recognized by the Constitution as religion of the majority. Religious freedom specifically guaranteed. Some 93 percent of the people Catholic. Protestants of various sects, mostly

Antillean Negroes, represent about 6 percent of the population. Little trace remains of any traditional indigenous religions.

8. EDUCATION: In 1969 about 316,000 students, or over 22 percent of population, enrolled in schools at all levels. Some 95 percent of primary students and a large majority of students at both secondary and higher level were in public schools. All secondary and higher schools are in urban localities.

9. HEALTH: High proportion of medical personnel and facilities, including most of specialized care, concentrated in Panama City. Most of population has ready access to modern medical care of some kind, but folk medical practices survive in parts of interior. The Ministry of Public Health has focused its efforts on tuberculosis, malaria, leprosy, and mental illness.

10. CLIMATE: High temperature and humidity year round, with pleasanter conditions prevailing in highlands and on Pacific side of continental divide. Seasons determined by rainfall rather than by changes in temperature. A dry season extends from December to May in parts of Pacific slope and for shorter periods on Atlantic slope of divide.

11. JUSTICE: Highest court is Supreme Court of Justice, composed of nine magistrates appointed by president with approval of cabinet. Court divided into three chambers—one each for civil, penal, and administrative cases. Lower courts are superior tribunals, circuit courts, and municipal courts. In addition there are customs courts, labor courts, traffic courts, and electoral courts.

12. ADMINISTRATIVE DIVISIONS: In 1971 there were nine political divisions known as provinces. Country bisected in Colón-Panama City area by ten-mile-wide Canal Zone controlled by United States. Country divided into ten National Guard military zones.

13. ECONOMY: Diversified with orientation to servicing transit trade and international commerce. Estimated 1970 gross national product (GNP): US$1 billion. Canal Zone generates as much as 15 percent of GNP.

14. INDUSTRY: Food processing, oil refining, and construction most important.

15. LABOR: Labor force in 1969 estimated 424,000, or about 30 percent of population. Some 27 percent females. Agricultural employment declining but, with nearly 40 percent of total, re-

mained largest sector of employment. Wage and salary earners made up 51 percent of labor force. Union membership small and confined largely to cities of Panama and Colón and to banana plantations.

16. EXPORTS: Bananas, refined petroleum products, and shrimp constitute from 85 to 90 percent of total exports.

17. IMPORTS: Wide range, with consumer goods predominating.

18. CURRENCY: Balboa is unit of currency. One balboa equal to one United States dollar. United States dollar also is legal tender. No exchange restrictions.

19. COMMUNICATIONS: About 74,000 telephones. Government-owned domestic and private international telegraph services.

20. RAILROADS: Four lines—one owned by United States government, one owned by Panamanian government, and two privately owned.

21. ROADS: About 4,150 miles, of which 950 miles are paved.

22. RIVER TRANSPORTATION: Tuira and Bayano rivers used for limited distances by shallow-draft vessels.

23. PORTS AND PORT FACILITIES: Five major ports on Atlantic, two major ports on Pacific, two dozen minor ports.

24. CIVIL AVIATION: Tocumen Airport is principal field. About 240 other airports, airstrips, and landing grounds, of which 115 used commercially. Twenty-one international airlines plus a dozen domestic airlines.

25. MERCHANT MARINE: One of largest in world on paper, but most are foreign owned and never call at Panamanian ports.

26. INTERNATIONAL AGREEMENTS AND MEMBERSHIPS: The country is a party to the Inter-American Treaty of Reciprocal Assistance; the Latin American Nuclear Free Zone Treaty; and the Charter of Punta del Este (Alliance for Progress). Also a member of the Organization of American States, the United Nations and its specialized agencies, the International Monetary Fund, and the Inter-American Development Bank (IDB).

27. AID PROGRAMS: Numerous and varied. Receives aid from United States Agency for International Development, International Bank for Reconstruction and Development (World Bank), IDB, private international banks, and other governments.

28. ARMED FORCES: Only military or paramilitary force is National Guard, which in 1971 numbered about 6,500. About half stationed in Colón-Panama City area. Guard performs police and prison security functions. Maintains small air force and has several coastal patrol vessels. Recruitment by voluntary enlistment. Has capability of maintaining internal security and public order.

PANAMA

TABLE OF CONTENTS

LIST OF ILLUSTRATIONS

LIST OF TABLES

CHAPTER 1

GENERAL CHARACTER OF THE SOCIETY

Living in a land that links the northern and southern hemispheres and provides a transit route between the Atlantic and the Pacific, Panamanians think of their country as "the Bridge of the World." One of the smallest nations in Latin America—in area and population—Panama transcends the limitations of its size by reason of its location. After the sighting of the Pacific Ocean by Vasco Núñez de Balboa in 1513, the isthmus played a vital role in commercial and military operations of the Spanish conquerors. During the nineteenth century, when Panama was part of Colombia, the isthmus continued as an important transit area, as illustrated by the stream of travelers using the route to reach California during the gold rush in the middle of the century and by the building of a transisthmian railway. After establishment of the Republic in 1903, construction of the Panama Canal introduced an element that has deeply affected the economy and the politics of the country ever since.

During the construction of the canal large numbers of English-speaking Negro laborers were brought in from the West Indies—a factor that has had a lasting effect on the makeup of the population. The economy has benefited by payments made by the United States for the use of the Canal Zone, by the purchasing power of zone residents, and by wages paid to Panamanian employees of the canal. Political leaders have invariably made an issue of United States control of the Canal Zone—calling it a "government within a government"—and ties with the United States have dominated Panamanian foreign relations. The interlocking of Panamanian fortunes with foreign decisions on which the Republic has had only limited influence has accounted for an intimate connection between Panamanian nationalism and the United States as a target of criticism and resentment. Through the years the United States has made a number of concessions, and in 1971 negotiations were in progress in the course of which the Panamanians hoped to obtain further modification of the terms under which the United States had maintained control over the Canal Zone.

Most of the people are of mixed Indian, Negro, and white descent, but a number of tribes of pure-blooded Indians inhabit remote parts of Panamanian jungles and islands in the Caribbean. Economic and political power has traditionally been held by a largely white elite. The location of the national center of gravity in the terminal cities of the canal—Colón and Panama City—has in the past minimized the attention given to the rural hinterlands stretching in both directions from the Canal Zone toward Colombia and Costa Rica, respectively. As a result, there has been a deep urban-rural division that has run through all aspects of national life. The government controlled by Brigadier General Omar Torrijos, which assumed power in 1968, initiated programs designed to improve the lot of farmers. The rapidly increasing use of radio receivers has served to stimulate growing political consciousness and cultural interests in isolated areas. The establishment in 1971 of a government radio network and the country's first domestic news service promised further to narrow the gap between the urban and rural populations.

The economy of the cities has been built on a commercial basis that developed early in the country's history to serve travelers and residents occupied with government administration, and in 1971 tourism continued as an important factor in the urban economy. The cities, having absorbed large numbers of migrants from the countryside and towns, face problems of growing needs for housing and social services. Underprivileged city-dwellers have more avenues than their rural cousins for expressing dissatisfaction and a greater inclination to take action in behalf of their own interests.

In 1971 the government followed a policy of stressing political and economic goals favorable to the middle and lower classes and operated programs designed to win the support of these people. Plans for national development announced in 1970 emphasized the need for correcting the imbalances between the poorly developed interior regions and the urbanized area near the Panama Canal. Although the country achieved rapid economic growth during the 1960s, progress was concentrated largely in the urban areas. Approximately 40 percent of the population was engaged in subsistence agriculture and had little contact with the money economy. Furthermore, agricultural income and production have played only a limited role in the country's economy, and the rural areas have not constituted a significant market for industrial products. As a result, the market economy has depended to a substantial degree on demands generated by the Panama Canal and the Canal Zone.

Politically conscious Panamanians have demonstrated their interest in territorial independence ever since breaking away from Spanish rule in 1821, when their territory became a province of

Colombia. They tried unsuccessfully to gain freedom from Colombian rule in 1830, in 1831, and in 1840 and staged as many as fifty uprisings between 1850 and 1903, when they gained their independence. Since then Panamanian political leaders have consistently endeavored to bring about changes in the treaty that granted the United States control over the Canal Zone "in perpetuity."

Panamanian dissatisfaction with the treaty and its amendments came to a head in January 1964, when riots occurred and Panama broke off diplomatic relations with the United States. After reestablishment of relations in April 1964 Panamanian and United States negotiators completed draft treaties dealing with defense matters, the existing lock canal, and a possible sea-level canal in Panama, but in 1970 the Panamanians publicly rejected them. New negotiations were instituted in June 1971.

The determination of the Panamanians to regain control of the territory occupied by the Canal Zone was illustrated by a mass demonstration held in October 1971 to celebrate the third anniversary of the military revolution. Peasants were bussed to Panama City, and a cheering crowd, estimated at 200,000, heard General Torrijos declare that the time might come "for one generation to offer its lives" so that another generation could "live in a free country." A few days later, in a statement to the press, he said he wanted a reduction in the size of the United States military contingent in the zone.

General Torrijos has featured the canal issue in his effort to organize peasants, students, laborers, and the masses in general in opposition to the elite group that has played a leading role in politics since the founding of the Republic. In his anniversary speech he said elections would be held in August 1972 to select an assembly of 500 members who would decide what path the country would follow. At the same time he implied that his authoritarian administration, supported by the National Guard—the only Panamanian armed force in the country—would continue because it was necessary to make sure that the revolution was not "a revolution of only three years." Meanwhile the negotiations with the United States, started in June 1971, progressed.

In 1971 the country continued under a moratorium on political competition imposed in 1968, and the party system, which had consisted of personalistic factions in shifting coalitions, was inoperative. An emerging middle class, for the most part aspiring to upper class status, had yet to develop a distinctive set of goals and values, while the lower classes lacked extensive organization and spokesmen and had been distracted by ethnic antagonism from recognition of common problems.

In 1971 organized interest groups representing agriculturists, professionals, and industrialists undertook to bring pressure to bear on the government, but social contacts and family ties remained the most important factors in the exercise of influence. Although more than 90 percent of the people are professed Roman Catholics, the church, traditionally, has not been a potent political force. In the past it has confined its activities largely to spiritual and cultural matters and has gained the respect and esteem of the people. The society has benefited from schools and hospitals built by the church and, although Roman Catholicism is not officially the state religion, it is regarded as an essential element in the lives of most of the people. In 1971 the church was exhibiting increasing concern for social improvement, and certain churchmen were openly critical of the Torrijos government.

The people's values stem to a large extent from the Hispanic cultural tradition found in most parts of Latin America, but throughout the centuries the country has been subjected to a great many outside cultural influences, and the people have adapted the Hispanic traditions to a developing national temperament of their own. At all social levels the people respect the worth of the individual and his place in society; they believe in family loyalty and in the principle of male predominance and in the past have accepted the tradition of stratification. In 1971 this tradition was being challenged by the efforts of the Torrijos government to mobilize the middle and lower classes to increase their political power. People in urban areas tend to exhibit a stronger sense of nationalism than those in rural areas. Subject to ever-present economic and social pressures, the city dweller is not as apt to be fatalistic as the peasant and is more inclined to take action to improve his lot. The countryman, however, is conditioned to modest hopes and aspirations. He is inclined to face reverses with patience and to accept hardships as the result of forces beyond his control.

The Panamanian thinks of his society in terms of three distinct categories—the Spanish-speaking majority, known as Panameños; the tribal Indians; and the Antillean Negroes. The typical Panamanian may count among his forbears Spanish settlers, indigenous Indians, and Negro slaves brought from Africa in colonial times. Members of the Spanish ruling class, however, have married within their own ethnic group, and white elements have in the past maintained their position at the top of the social structure, and clearly negroid characteristics are more apt to be found at the lower levels.

Friction among members of the three principal groups is traceable to the degree to which the predominant Hispanic culture has been assimilated. Nevertheless, the country's policy is to treat all groups equally, and for practical purposes cultural discrimination has not been worked into regulations and laws. Almost all Panamanians speak Spanish, the official language; and English, spoken widely in the areas adjoining the Canal Zone, is the second tongue. The total number of tribal Indians using indigenous languages is small.

In 1971 schools were available to almost all Panamanians, and more than four-fifths of the people over ten years of age were literate. During the 1960s the governments in power had given priority to expanding and improving the educational system, and enrollments—notably at the secondary and university levels—increased at rates faster than that at which the country's population was growing. In 1971 the government was making a special effort to improve the technical and vocational schools, with a view to attracting more students to these fields.

Progress in education and advances in literacy during the 1950s and 1960s have increased the people's interest in artistic and intellectual expression. Although the country's cultural development has been based on the Hispanic legacy, North American and French influences on Panamanian writers have been substantial. Nationalistic and historical themes have been popular, and literature, poetry, and theatrical productions have reflected the patriotism of the people and pride in their cultural heritage.

CHAPTER 2

HISTORICAL SETTING

Throughout the history of Panama the lives of most of the people have been affected by the importance of the transisthmian route—overland until the early twentieth century and subsequently through the canal. Even before the conquest of Peru, following Vasco Núñez de Balboa's discovery of the short distance between the two oceans in 1513, the feasibility of building a canal was considered; and with the transportation to Spain of the riches of the Inca empire the role of the Isthmus of Panama in history was firmly established.

The transisthmian route early became the focus of development and settlement and virtually the sole source of prosperity. There was, in any case, too little level unforested land to encourage agriculture, and the Spaniards were not interested in tilling the soil as long as fortunes could be made by other means. Precious metals, the source of prosperity in other parts of the newly discovered lands, were scarce and were found only in the wildest parts of the country. Virtually the only continuing source of capital formation, other than the all-important transit traffic, was cattle raising, on which the fortunes of a number of families were based.

When the isthmus became the sole official western terminal and transfer point for shipments to and from Spain for all territories south of Mexico, the importance of the isthmian crossing increased. Panama City became the third richest colonial center of the New World, surpassed only by Lima and Mexico City. With the destruction of Portobelo (on the Caribbean coast) by the English in 1739, however, Spain canceled Panama's port monopoly, and the isthmus entered a relatively depressed period.

United with Colombia after liberation from Spanish rule in 1821, Panama was never satisfied with the association. Geographically isolated (there were no land routes connecting the two), dependent on a trade in which Colombia was neither point of origin nor destination but reaped benefits in customs and fees, and rarely feeling genuine concern for Colombia's continual internal turmoil, Panama seceded temporarily three times during the first twenty years of independence. Separatism became more and more the sentiment of Panamanian leaders of every political persuasion throughout the period of union with Colombia.

Although the Panama Railroad, built by a United States company in 1855, brought new prosperity, this failed to compensate for the increasing involvement in Colombia's incessant civil wars, which by 1902 had nearly ruined Panama. When Colombia rejected a canal treaty in 1903, Panamanian leaders, fully conscious of the strategic potential of their country's location, accepted United States assistance in achieving independence, even though this involved accepting a special status that lasted for over thirty years.

The pattern of Panamanian life has been accentuated, rather than changed, by the canal and the prosperity it has brought to the country. A substantial portion of the population lives within ten miles of the Canal Zone limits, and in mid-1971 the political, economic, and cultural life of the country was concentrated in this area. Most of the Republic east of the zone and nearly all the north coast west of it remain virgin tropical forest. The settled part, south and west, has gained greatly in numbers, but towns are still small—some smaller even than before 1800—and most agriculture continues at a primitive level.

After completion of the canal, national leaders, aware of the country's unique geographical position, were not long in showing dissatisfaction with what seemed to them a disproportionately small share of the proceeds from their only profitable resource. Increasingly, they showed sensitivity over the effect on sovereignty inherent in the phraseology of the canal treaties, even though each renegotiation had resulted in enlarged economic benefits and concessions to national prestige.

In the third quarter of the twentieth century the society continued to mirror vividly its historical background. Most of the country was thinly populated, but a substantial proportion of the people lived near the canal—in Colón on the Caribbean and in Panama City, the capital. The majority were a mixture of white, Negro, and Indian—mainly the result of the Spanish conquest, the importation of African slaves in the early years, and the influx of laborers on the canal in the twentieth century (see ch. 3, Physical Environment and Population).

Politics in Panama was inextricably involved with the canal and with relations with the United States. Political leaders and agitators continued to make an issue of United States political and economic influences that had developed since the beginning of the century. They have not forgotten an agreement under which West Indian Negroes brought in to work on the canal were to be repatriated but were not; they express resentment of privileges of

8

United States citizens living in the Canal Zone and press for an increased annuity from the earnings of the canal (see ch. 9, Political Dynamics and Values; ch. 11, Character and Structure of the Economy).

Because of the global importance of the canal, governments in Panama have been subject to pressures—direct and indirect— from foreign countries other than the United States—notably during World War II and since the establishment of the Castro regime in Cuba. Remembering the example of Egypt's seizure of the Suez Canal and encouraged by outside influences, Panamanians have, through the years, agitated for control of the canal. Despite concessions by the United States, it became evident in the early 1960s that the Panamanians' ultimate goal was complete ownership (see ch. 10, Foreign Relations).

In 1964 feelings over the canal issue exploded in to rioting that resulted in the deaths of both Panamanian and United States soldiers. The Panamanian government broke off diplomatic relations with the United States but found it expedient to resume relations three months later, and negotiations began again. Once more the great significance of the canal to the people became apparent: if the United States were to build a new sea-level canal and turn over the old canal to the Panamanians, the Panamanians would have gained their longstanding demand; but operation of the old canal in competition with a sea-level canal would prove extremely costly and endanger the Panamanian economy.

DISCOVERY, EXPLORATION, AND SETTLEMENT

Rodrigo de Bastidas, sailing from Spain in March 1501, reached the Gulf of Urabá in October, landed briefly in the Darién region, and proceeded an estimated 100 miles farther, thus becoming the first European to see the coast of what is now Panama. A member of his company was Balboa, who remained in Hispaniola.

Problems in the region and in Spain either prevented or cut short further exploration and settlement until 1509, when King Ferdinand, finally in control of both Castile and Aragon, authorized expeditions led by Alonzo de Ojeda and Diego de Nicuesa, neither of which was successful. The followup of the Ojeda expedition was under Martín de Enciso, a prosperous lawyer of Santo Domingo, inexperienced in exploration but ambitious. Among Enciso's 150 prospective colonists was Balboa, whose leadership and enterprise were to make a success of the colony and to lead to the exploration of the eastern part of the isthmus and the discovery of the Pacific.

Balboa's nine-year residence in Hispaniola had earned him nothing but debt, and the authorities had forbidden him to leave the island. He had himself smuggled aboard Enciso's ship, which, in September 1510, reached Urabá, where an abandoned fort and huts had been burned by the Indians. Balboa, drawing upon his recollections of Bastidas' voyage, persuaded the colonists to move across the gulf "where the Indians did not use poisoned arrows." An Indian village, Darién, was taken over in November 1510. The first successful settlement on the mainland, it became the base for all exploration until the founding of the original Panama City, nine years later.

Impatient at the incompetence and arbitrariness of Enciso, the colonists deposed him and elected Balboa one of two chief magistrates. Enciso left, along with two representatives of Balboa, who were to plead the cause of the colony to the king and to ask immediate help and reinforcement from Hispaniola. Help came promptly, with a commission from the governor appointing Balboa as acting captain of the colony. Ferdinand later issued a decree appointing Balboa captain general and acting governor, but this decree did not reach Darién until 1513.

Despite little material assistance during these two years, Balboa made several expeditions to both the east and west. On the second of his trips along the San Blas coast and inland, he visited and made friends with a tribe whose chief's son, Panquiaco, told him of a great ocean only a few days' march to the south, where the tribes had much gold and obtained pearls from nearby islands.

Balboa did not take immediate advantage of this information. The Indians' report of the strength and hostility of the southern tribes was apparently convincing, and the total strength of the Darién settlement was probably less than 200 Spaniards, of which, according to one of Balboa's reports to the king, not over 100 were "fit for war." When the two ships brought 150 men from Hispaniola in 1513, along with the long-delayed royal decree appointing Balboa captain and interim governor, he carried out the postponed transisthmian expedition. Moving south across the isthmus, late in September 1513, he reached a hill from which the Gulf of San Miguel and the Pacific beyond could be seen. On September 29 he reached the gulf and took possession of the ocean, together with all lands it might touch, in the name of the crown of Spain. Because it lay south of his point of observation, he called it the South Sea.

Balboa returned to Darién by a different route, making alliances with, and exacting tribute from, half a dozen chiefs. Throughout his dealings with the Indians, Balboa did not hesitate to use force when opposed but was successful in establishing friendly relations thereafter. He is generally credited with being unique among conquistadores in refraining from wholesale slaughter, torture, and indiscriminate enslavement.

The new governor of Castilla del Oro (as Panama was then called), Pedro Arias de Avila (known as Pedrarias), arrived in June 1514 with a force of more than 2,000 persons, over half of whom were men available for exploration and conquest. With him also came Bishop Quevedo, who founded the first episcopal see on the mainland. Intensely jealous of Balboa's successes and completely unversed in the conditions in the New World, Pedrarias set about discrediting his predecessor and undoing his constructive accomplishments as well—especially in regard to relations with the Indians. Formerly friendly tribes were massacred indiscriminately, and gold and slaves were taken, with the result that the Indians were driven into implacable hostility.

Balboa was kept from performing any useful work for the colony. When the king's decree appointing him *adelantado,* or "advance agent," of the South Sea and governor of the south coast arrived in March 1515, he was prevented from taking possession. When in 1517 Pedrarias finally permitted Balboa to make an expedition into his assigned territory (after learning that he himself would soon be replaced by a new governor), he used the occasion to trump up false charges of treason against Balboa and to have him recalled and executed at Acla in January 1519.

Pedrarias promptly formed an expedition that penetrated to the south coast and, after visiting the islands in the gulf, established Panama City in order to support his claim to the region awarded Balboa. The settlement, officially denoted a city in 1521 and located on the shore about six miles east of the present capital, endured until 1671, when it was attacked by the English pirate Henry Morgan.

The governor's successor arrived at Darién in May 1520 but died aboard ship before he could disembark. Pedrarias went back to Panama and in 1524 was able to persuade the bishop and the residents of Darién to move to his new capital. Exploration and raiding west of Panama had gone on before the death of Balboa and continued thereafter. By land and sea, parties of conquistadores had visited the savanna country on the Gulf of Partita, subjugating the tribes and gathering treasure. The first permanent town west of Panama was founded in 1522. Chiriquí was also penetrated, and a sea expedition explored the Gulf of Montijo and the island of Coiba.

The considerable Indian population of the isthmus declined abruptly during the early years. Tens of thousands were killed in the conquest (Pedrarias was called the Timur of the Indies); many were worked to death as slaves in the fields and mines; and thousands more died of diseases common among white men against which the Indians had developed no resistance. Spaniards in general left agriculture, other than cattle raising, to slave labor, and the rapid depletion of the Indian population prompted the importation, begun in Pedrarias' time, of Negro slaves from Africa.

The period of free, though licensed, exploration gave way to one in which great royal control was exercised through appointed governors furnished with staffs designated by the king. All, for the first time, were to be paid out of crown revenues expected from the royal profits on the colony. The king's representative was responsible for seeing that such returns came in and kept track of all gold, pearls, and other income from trade and conquest and weighed out and safeguarded the king's share.

Governors had some summary powers of justice, but *audiencias,* or colonial courts, originally separate, were also established. The first *audiencia* in Santo Domingo, Hispaniola, had jurisdiction over the whole area of conquest. As settlement spread, others were set up, first in Mexico, then in Panama (1539), and later in Peru and New Granada. The position of the viceroy was revived for the rich empires of Mexico and Peru, and after 1567 Panama was attached to the Viceroyalty of Peru but retained its own *audiencia.*

Another title employed in the governmental system was that of *adelantado,* applied to those who had especially distinguished themselves in exploration. It combined the attributes of inheritable nobility and usually carried with it the title of captain or captain general. Balboa was the only *adelantado* in the history of Panama.

The royal prerogative of inspecting the state of affairs in the colonies was performed in two ways. Every official, at the end of his term of office, underwent a review and audit of his incumbency. For governors and other principal officials, it was usually conducted by a member of the *audiencia,* who also assessed penalties. The other form of inspection—performed by an agent who usually arrived without notice—was occasional and brought about by specific complaint or simply at the king's pleasure. Such agents reported either directly to the king or through the *audiencia* or viceroy.

The position of the Roman Catholic Church was of the greatest influence in the New World. Priests accompanied every expedition and were always counselors to the temporal leaders. The first bishop on the mainland came with Pedrarias, and his authority, received from the king, made him in effect a vice governor. He, rather than any civil official, governed when Pedrarias was absent or ill and participated in all deliberations. Later, bishops were often presidents of *audiencias,* and a number became viceroys.

The kings and the church, and particularly the Franciscan order, were concerned with the welfare of the Indians. The church was given the mission of Christian instruction and conversion and in general did its best to prevent Indian slavery. It also worked against the frequent abuses of the *encomienda* system, which in strict legality was neither slavery nor serfdom but a right—given to a Spanish official or private individual or to a church function —to the tribute of a group, village, or tribe of Indians, called an *encomienda*. In practice, the exaction of such tribute, even though the Indians were technically in free possession of their lives, labor, lands, and property, often produced a condition indistinguishable from slavery.

THE COLONIAL PERIOD

Pedrarias' successor arrived in the colony in 1526. By command of King Charles I of Spain he began a survey, the result of which was a strong recommendation to the emperor by Hernán Cortés (of Mexico) in 1529 that a canal be constructed in Panama. The king ordered a new study in 1534, but the acting governor reported convincingly on the difficulties and expenses of such a project. The idea nevertheless was considered for over thirty years, until finally discouraged by Philip II. Not the least of that monarch's reasons was a conviction that to join the oceans would run counter to Divine Will.

Stone surfacing and bridge construction on the Nombre de Dios trail from Panama started in 1529. Thus even before the conquest of Peru, the isthmus became an interoceanic route.

Interest in the discovery of Peru was generated in Panama, and the central figure in the exploration and conquest was Francisco Pizarro, who had served in the isthmian region since the Ojeda expedition of 1509. His expedition of conquest was launched in 1532, when he fortuitously arrived at a time of internal dynastic dissension in the Inca empire. The treasures of the Incas and the gold and silver from the mines of Peru could reach Spain only through Panama, since the voyage around Cape Horn was prohibitively dangerous.

By a decree of 1538 all Spanish territory from Nicaragua to Cape Horn was to be administered from Panama. The short duration (until 1543) of this *audiencia* can be laid to a belated recognition of the impossibility of its exercising jurisdiction over so vast an area. Panama was then placed under the *audiencia* of the Limits of Guatemala, and a separate *audiencia* was set up for Peru.

The New Laws of 1542, issued by the crown for the government of the colonies and containing many provisions ameliorating the conditions under which the Indians provided labor and tribute, had effects that emphasized Panama's relations with Peru. When the first viceroy of Peru arrived in 1544 with orders to enforce the New Laws, which were greatly resented by the colonists, Gonzalo Pizarro, Francisco's surviving brother, defeated him in battle and executed him.

Knowing the importance of the isthmus to an independent Peru, Gonzalo Pizarro in 1545 had a force under one of his lieutenants take Panama. The following year the newly appointed president of the *audiencia* to be formed in Peru arrived in Panama and adroitly won over Pizarro's man and with his help reconquered Peru and executed Pizarro in 1548.

In the same year in Panama a serious slave rebellion took place. For the thousands of African slaves brought to the Mainland (Tierra Firme), Panama was the distribution point and in fact absorbed many of them because of the depletion of the Indian labor force. Many Negroes escaped to the forests, from which they raided the Nombre de Dios trail and unprotected settlements. These *cimarrones* (bush dwellers; sing., *cimarrón*), as they were called, sometimes united under strong chiefs, as they did in 1548, under Bayano and Felipillo. Although the chiefs were captured, the Negroes were not entirely pacified until 1581. This pattern repeated itself at least once a generation until late in the eighteenth century.

Increasing prosperity in the region, owing principally to the Peru trade and transshipments, led to a new attempt to colonize Veragua. Bickering between rival expeditions resulted only in the settlement of Santa Fé. Nevertheless, the relinquishment of proprietary rights by the duke of Veragua enabled the reestablished Audiencia of Panama (1563) to receive jurisdiction on the Caribbean side from the still undefined western frontier of Veragua to the Atrato River and on the Pacific from the Gulf of Fonseca (Nicaragua) to Buenaventura, now in Colombia.

Prosperity Under Difficulties: 1563–1739

From early in the sixteenth century, Nombre de Dios, Veracruz, and Cartagena were the only three ports in Spanish America authorized by the Spanish crown to trade with the homeland, although supply ships for other ports might be specially licensed. By the mid-1560s the system became regularized, and two fleets sailed annually from Spain, one to Mexico and the other to the southern ports. They would then rendezvous at Havana and return together to Cádiz, in Spain. In principle, this rigid system remained in effect until the eighteenth century, but beginning in the middle of the seventeenth century, as the strength and pros-

14

perity of Spain declined, annual visits became the exception, and many years they were missed entirely.

On the Pacific side, shipments were made so that all the bullion and goods could reach Panama and be transported over the isthmus to be loaded for the fleet's return to Spain. For a short time after the conquest of the Philippines, Spanish ships returning from there came to Panama. By 1600 Acapulco (Mexico) was their sole port of transshipment. Panama's own contribution to the lading of the fleet was relatively small. Gold production was never great, and there was little exportable surplus of agriculture and forest products. Nothing was manufactured and, in fact, Spain discouraged the production of finished goods. The colony's prosperity, therefore, fluctuated with the volume of trade, made up largely of Peruvian shipments. When the gold of the Incas was exhausted, its place was taken for a century and a half by the great quantities of silver mined in Peru, supplemented eventually by sugar, cotton, wine, indigo, cinchona, vanilla, and cacao.

Except for traffic in African slaves, all foreign trade (unless the goods passed through Spain) was forbidden. Negroes were brought to the colonies on contract by Portuguese, English, Dutch, and French slavers, who were forbidden to trade in any other commodities. The efforts of the Spanish to retain their monopoly in the rich profits in trade with their colonies provided a challenge to the other rising maritime nations of Europe, which did not as yet have American colonies. The result was intermittent maritime warfare in the Caribbean and later in the Pacific. The first serious interference with trade came from the English.

For twenty-five years (1572–97) the name of Francis Drake was associated with most of the assaults on the Panama bottleneck. Drake's activities demonstrated the indefensibility of the open roadstead of Nombre de Dios, and in 1597 the northern terminus of the transisthmian route was moved to Portobelo, which, after Cartagena, was the best natural harbor anywhere on the Spanish Main.

Despite raids on shipments and ports, the registered legal import of precious metals increased steadily, decade by decade—nearly fourfold between 1550 and 1600—from almost 1.8 million pesos (1551–60) to just under 7 million pesos (1591–1600). The first part of the seventeenth century brought Panama's prosperity to its peak. This was the time of the famous fairs, or exchange markets, of Portobelo, where the merchandise of Europe to supply the commerce of the whole west coast south of Nicaragua and that of Argentina, Paraguay, and Uruguay was displayed. Accounts of the times speak of warehouses literally overflowing and bars of silver stacked in the streets unguarded. When the fair ended,

Portobelo reverted to the quiet existence of a small seaport and garrison town.

Panama City also flourished on the profits of trade. Following reconstruction after a serious fire in 1644, contemporary accounts credit Panama City with 1,400 residences "of all types" (probably including slave huts) ; most business and religious houses and the more substantial residences were built of stone. It was considered, after Mexico City and Lima, the most beautiful and opulent settlement in the Indies.

A canal project was revived early in the century by Philip III of Spain (1598–1621), but the king was dissuaded by his Council of the Indies on the grounds that, once constructed, it would draw attack from other European nations—an indication of the relative decline of Spanish seapower.

During the first quarter of the seventeenth century, trade with the isthmus remained undisturbed, while England, France, and the Netherlands, one or all almost constantly at war with Spain, began seizing colonies in the Caribbean. Such footholds in the West Indies encouraged the development of the buccaneer. English, French, Dutch, and Portuguese adventurers preyed on Spanish shipping and ports with the tacit or open support of their home governments. Because of their numbers and the closeness of their bases, they were more effective against Spanish trade than the English had been during the previous century. Their potential was greatly increased by the English capture of Jamaica in 1654.

The volume of registered precious metal arriving in Spain fell from its peak figure in 1600 until by 1660 it was less than the amount registered in 1560. Partial causes were the depletion of the Peruvian mines and an increase in smuggling, but the buccaneers had much to do with the decline, which accelerated after 1630.

Henry Morgan, who had held Portobelo for ransom in 1668, returned to Panama with a stronger force at the end of 1670 and, on January 29, 1671, appeared at Panama City with 1,400 men and defeated the garrison of 2,600 in pitched battle outside the city, which he then looted. The officials and citizens fled, some to the country and others to Peru, having loaded the most important church and government funds and treasure on their ships. The city was destroyed by fire, probably from the blowing up of the powder stores at the president's order, though the Spaniards blamed the looters. After four weeks Morgan left with 175 mule loads of loot and 600 prisoners. This city was never rebuilt, but in 1673 a new city was founded at the present-day location of the capital and was heavily fortified.

The buccaneer scourge rapidly declined after 1688, mainly because of changing European alliances. Spain by that time was chronically bankrupt; its population had fallen; and it was characterized by internal misgovernment and corruption, conditions that inevitably were reflected in colonial affairs.

Influenced by the reports from buccaneer sources about the ease of crossing the isthmus, which suggested to him the possibility of digging a canal, William Paterson, founder and ex-governor of the Bank of England, organized a Scottish company to colonize in the San Blas area. He landed near the site of Acla late in 1698 with 1,200 persons. Although well received by the Indians (as was anyone not Spanish), the colonists were ill-prepared for life in the tropics, with its attendant diseases. Their notion of trade goods—European clothing, wigs, and Bibles in English—was hardly calculated to attract the Indians. They gave up after six months, unknowingly passing at sea a second and a third reinforcement totaling 1,600. Spanish reaction began with news of these new arrivals, and the colony was blockaded from the sea. It capitulated and left in April 1700, having lost a total of 2,000 lives from the three parties, mostly from malnourishment and disease.

When the Hapsburgs were replaced by Bourbon kings in 1700, some reforms tending to increase trade by liberalization were attempted, but Spain's desperate efforts to maintain its colonial trade monopoly were self-defeating. The ability of England, France, and Holland to supply cheaper goods was welcomed by colonial officials and private traders alike, and dealing in contraband increased, to the detriment of "official" trade, still required by law to pass through Panama. Fewer merchants came to the Portobelo fair to pay Spain's inflated prices, when the foreign suppliers would furnish cheaper goods at any port at which they could slip by or bribe the coastal guards. The situation became so bad that only five of the once annual fleets were dispatched to America between 1715 and 1736, a circumstance that served only to increase the prevalence of contraband operations.

The temporary loss by Panama of its independent *audiencia* from 1718 to 1722 and its attachment to the Viceroyalty of Peru were probably brought about by the powerful Peruvian merchants' resentment of the venality of Panamanian officials and their ineffectiveness in suppressing the pirates (outlaws of no flag, as distinct from the buccaneers of the seventeenth century) who infested the coasts. Panama's weakness was further shown by its inability to protect itself against an invasion by the Mosquito Indians of Nicaragua, who penetrated from the Chiriquí Lagoon across the mountains to David, near the south coast. Also, another rising of the Indians in the Tuira Valley caused the virtual abandonment by the whites of the area that is now Darién Province.

The final blow to Panama's shrinking control of the transit trade between South America and Spain came before the middle of the eighteenth century. As one of the provisions of the Treaty of Utrecht at the end of the War of the Spanish Succession in 1713, Great Britain received the right to supply African slaves to the Spanish colonies (4,800 per year for thirty years) and also to send one ship a year of 500-ton capacity to Portobelo. The slave trade evidently worked out satisfactorily, but the trade in goods never did. Smuggling by British ships continued, and a highly organized contraband trade based in Jamaica was able—with the collusion of Panamanian merchants—to undersell the legal trade so as to cause it to almost vanish. By 1739 the importance of the isthmus had declined so far that Spain again suppressed Panama's autonomy by making the region a part of the Viceroyalty of New Grenada, which encompassed the northwest portion of South America.

In the same year, war broke out between England and Spain, and English Admiral Edward Vernon took Portobelo and later destroyed its four protecting forts, which were never rebuilt. Vernon's attack is usually blamed by Panamanian historians for the diversion of Spanish trade from the transisthmian route, but the Seville-Cádiz monopoly of colonial trade had been breached by royal decrees earlier in the century, and precedent was thus furnished for the merchants of the American colonies to agitate for direct trade with Spain and for intercolonial trade. Vernon's destruction of Portobelo furnished an additional argument. After 1740 the Pacific coast ports were permitted to trade directly through ships rounding Cape Horn, and the Portobelo fair was never held again.

The effect of the relaxation of the trading laws was beneficial to the rest of Spanish America and to Spain itself, but the economic decline of Panama was serious. Transit trade had for so long furnished the profits on which Panama had flourished that there had been no incentive toward development of any other economic base. The mines of Veragua had never produced great amounts of precious metal, and the richest gold mines at Cana in Darién had been abandoned because of Indian revolts.

After the suppression of its own *audiencia* in 1751, Panama became a quiet backwater and geographically isolated appendage of New Grenada, scarcely self-supporting even in food and producing little if anything for export. In its poverty the region had nothing to attract capable officials and was too weak even to suppress its own Indian rebellions.

Social and Cultural Aspects

In 1793, near the close of the colonial period, the first recorded attempt at a comprehensive census was made. Incomplete as it must have been, doubtless omitting most of the Indian and *cimarrón* population, and specifically excluding soldiers and priests, it recorded 71,888 inhabitants, 7,857 of whom lived in the city of Panama. Other principal towns had populations ranging from 2,000 to a little over 5,000 (see ch. 3, Physical Environment and Population).

Society throughout the colonial period was structured along rigid lines. At the top, the *peninsulares* (persons born in Spain) occupied all the best government posts, controlled commerce, and had all the other advantages of their jealously guarded positions. Next were the *criollos* (persons of pure Spanish ancestry born in the colonies), who occupied secondary and minor administrative posts in government and trade. Many of them were landowners, but socially and officially they could not aspire to equality of opportunity with the *peninsulares,* even though Spanish law made no distinctions. It is said that even among children of the same parents, a subtle distinction was made between those born in Spain and those born in America, at least by persons outside that family. Some *criollos* rose to fairly high positions in the church and government, but frequently policy demanded that they be transferred to posts outside their region or colony of origin.

In colonial times the term *mestizo* meant specifically the off-spring of Spanish and Indian unions. Originally, status depended to some extent on that of the white father and on the nature of the union, which ranged from the rare case of legitimate marriage through accepted, and often semipermanent, concubinage to the cases, probably a vast majority, of casual union. Through the three centuries before independence widespread racial mixture occurred, and some persons became accepted as *criollos,* but the vast majority were part of a social and economic group identified with farming, service occupations, and shopkeeping (see ch. 5, Social System).

The Indians were removed entirely from the body social and politic. Crown and church policies, from the beginning, were pointed toward the protection of the Indians, but the colonists, for economic reasons, took every means to evade the protective laws or get them changed, often with considerable success. The slaughter of the Indians by the thousands in the days of Pedrarias and their deaths from overwork as slaves and in the *encomiendas,* as well as from the white man's diseases, not only greatly reduced

19

the numbers of Indians in the settled regions but caused the survivors to retreat to the forests.

A special place in the society was held by the church. The first bishopric on the mainland was moved from Darién to Panama in 1521. The relationship between church and government was even closer than in Spain. Both the secular church and the orders gained great wealth, both through church tithes and the acquisition of land.

PANAMA AND COLOMBIA

Independence from Spain

Panama remained aloof from the early efforts of the Spanish colonies to separate from Spain. Lacking communication except by sea, which the Spanish generally controlled, it was out of the stream of events in Spanish America. Such hopes as Panamanians had for any improvement of their stagnant condition were lodged in Spain, which emerged from its Napoleonic domination in 1812 with a liberal constitution that permitted delegates from the colonies to the legislature. The isthmian delegate, with the support of the one from Cartagena, asked for the liberalization of trade and immigration, the reestablishment of the trade fairs, and support for education and other benefits but with little success. The king permitted foreign trade for a time, but pressure from the merchants of Cádiz caused him to withdraw the privilege, an act that served to awaken sentiment for separation.

Others, outside Panama, had no hesitation in using its strategic potential as a pawn in revolutionary maneuvers. General Miranda of Venezuela, who had been trying to attract support for revolutionary activities since as early as 1797, offered a canal concession to Great Britain in return for aid. Thomas Jefferson, while minister to France, also showed interest in a canal, but the isolationist policies of the new United States and the absorption of energies and capital in continental expansion prevented serious consideration.

An attempt by patriots from Cartagena to take Portobelo in 1814 was supported in Panama and, except for the persecution of known local sympathizers, the isthmus was not involved in Spain's reconquest of Colombia. The renewal of insurgent effort in 1819 brought another, and only temporarily successful, attack on Portobelo and a naval effort from liberated Chile that succeeded only in capturing Taboga Island in Panama Bay.

Panama's first act of separation from Spain came without violence. When Simón Bolívar's victory at Boyacá on August 7, 1819, in effect clinched the liberation of New Granada, the viceroy fled

Colombia for Panama, where he ruled harshly until his death in 1821. His replacement, a liberal constitutionalist, permitted a free press and the formation of patriotic associations. Raising troops locally, he soon sailed for Ecuador, leaving a native Panamanian, Colonel Fábrega, as acting governor.

Panama City immediately started plans to declare independence, but the city of Los Santos forced its hand by proclaiming freedom from Spain on November 10, 1821. This act precipitated a meeting in Panama on November 28, which is celebrated as the official date of independence. There was considerable discussion as to whether Panama should adhere to Colombia (then comprising both the present country and Venezuela) or to Peru. The bishop of Panama, a native Peruvian, who realized the commercial ties that might exist with his country, argued for the latter solution but was voted down. Accepting the situation, he lent the new government funds, since the Spanish governor's military expedition had emptied the treasury. A third course of action, a union with Mexico, proposed by emissaries of that country, was rejected.

Panama thus became part of Colombia, then governed under the Constitution of Cúcuta (of 1821) and was designated a department of two provinces, Panama and Veragua. With the addition of Ecuador to the liberated area, the whole country then became known as Gran Colombia. Panama sent a force of 700 men to join Bolívar in the south, where the war of liberation continued in Peru.

Termination of hostilities against the royalists (1824) failed to bring tranquillity to Gran Colombia. The constitution that Bolívar had drafted for Bolivia was put forward by him to be adopted in Gran Colombia as well. The country was divided principally over the proposal that there be a lifetime president, not responsible to the legislature and with power to nominate his vice president. Other provisions, generally centralist in their tendencies, were repugnant to some, and a few desired a monarchy. Panama escaped armed violence over the constitutional question but joined other regions in petitioning Bolívar to assume dictatorial powers until a convention could meet and announced its adherence to Gran Colombia as a "Hanseatic State" (an autonomous area with special trading privileges) until the matter was settled.

Panama considered it a great honor to be selected in 1826 by Bolívar as the site for a congress of the recently liberated colonies of Spain, called to discuss the formation of a league for common defense against possible attack inspired by the Holy Alliance, to which King Ferdinand of Spain adhered. Great Britain, Holland, and the United States were invited to send observers. Of the

North Americans, one died before reaching Panama, and the other arrived after the conclusion of the meeting. Their instructions from Secretary of State Henry Clay had, however, revealed the interest of the United States by including a directive to bring up the matter of a canal somewhere in Central America to be open to international commerce. Inconclusive though the conference was, it is celebrated in Panama as the inspiration and forerunner of the Pan-American Union.

At about the same time, a canal project was being considered by Bolívar, but lack of capital and the pressure of events caused it to be dropped.

Separatist Tendencies

In 1830 it was evident that the breakup of Gran Colombia was inevitable. The military commander and acting governor of Panama at the time opposed the policies of President Mosquera and was an ardent follower of Bolívar. When in the general chaos both Mosquera and his vice president resigned, the acting governor, with popular support, on September 26 declared the isthmus to be separated from the central government and sent a representative to Bolívar advising him of the act and requesting him to come to Panama to make preparations to reunite the country. Bolívar, already in his last illness, advised the acting governor to reincorporate the department. By act of a provisional junta, this was done on December 11, six days before the liberator's death.

Seven months later, when New Granada (the name then assumed by Colombia) was still in turmoil, a Venezuelan took advantage of the absence of his chief to seize power and exile his rival. He set up a dictatorship and on July 9, 1831, declared a second separation of the isthmus, but his rule was so arbitrary that he alienated all support. He attempted to resist the next appointive governor, a Panamanian, who defeated and executed him.

In 1840 civil war again broke out in New Granada over issues in which Panama was not involved. The isthmus, principally concerned with trade, could see no gain in permitting partisanship in its territory. Consequently, a third secession took place, declared by a popular assembly on November 18, 1840. The new government assumed the name of Estado de Istmo (Isthmian State), but reintegration with New Granada was decreed on December 31, 1841.

From Canal Possibilities to Railroad Reality

The death of Bolívar and the breakup of Gran Colombia did not long delay a resurgence of interest in a canal across Panama. In 1834 the president of New Granada sought and secured from his congress authority to enter a contract for the construction of a highway, railroad, or canal; and at the same time, the congress of the Central American Federation, which included all areas between Mexico and Panama, invited North American attention to canal possibilities. The United States Senate showed its interest by addressing a resolution to President Jackson requesting him to consider negotiating with both countries about protecting "such individuals or companies as might undertake" a canal and about assuring free and equal use of such a canal by all nations, upon the payment of reasonable tolls. In May the New Granadan congress authorized the use of Portobelo, Chagres, and Panama as duty-free ports for transit trade, effective for twenty years upon the opening of "interoceanic communication."

President Jackson's representative, Charles A. Biddle, was specifically directed to make full investigation of both the Nicaraguan and Panamanian routes before going to Bogotá. Instead, he went directly to Panama. Gaining strong impressions of separatist feelings, he advised the secretary of state to await events in the area before negotiating a concession. Upon arriving in Bogotá, he began to negotiate for a personal concession, which after some bargaining was granted him in association with Granadan capitalists. On his return to Washington, indignation at his effort to serve personal interests while on a national mission caused his repudiation.

The outcome of the Biddle affair and the lack of success in negotiating a trade treaty with New Granada, designed to lift certain discriminatory tariffs on United States goods, took North American attention away from Panama. Moreover, the rebellion in New Granada, which occasioned Panama's third separation, caused a diversion of interest on the part of the government. Financiers and commercial interests were, however, still anxious for some means of attaining a short route to the Pacific and, through pressure on the executive and congress in 1839, succeeded in having an agent sent to Nicaragua under government auspices to make a survey. The report indicated that such a canal was practicable, at a cost of US$25 million, but pointed to the continuing disturbances in Central America as a deterrent factor.

Once the New Granadan rebellion was suppressed, the new administration, aware of canal interests appearing in Europe and the United States and desiring to prevent Nicaragua from becoming the canal site, tried without result to get a consortium of powers, including the United States, Great Britain, France, Holland, and Spain, to guarantee the neutrality of a canal in the isthmus. In 1846 New Granada seemed to favor negotiation with the United States or at least, because of the existence of the Monroe Doctrine, feared the United States less than any of the powers interested in transisthmian transit. A treaty removed the existing restrictive tariffs and gave the United States and its citizens the right of free transit of persons and goods over any road or canal that might be constructed in the isthmus. In addition, the United States guaranteed the sovereignty of New Granada over, and the neutrality of, the isthmus with a view to assuring uninterrupted transit for the duration of the treaty, which was to be in effect for at least twenty years and thereafter as long as neither party gave a year's notice of desire to revise it. Called the Bidlack-Mallarino Treaty of 1846, it was actually ratified and became effective in 1848.

Another agreement relating to Panama was the Clayton-Bulwer Treaty of 1850, between Great Britain and the United States. Both had been involved in Nicaragua, where their interests appeared to clash. By the treaty both governments agreed specifically that neither would acquire rights to, or construct, a Nicaraguan canal without the participation of the other and extended the general principle to any canal or railroad across Central America, to include Tehuantepec and Panama. In effect, since neither government was at the time willing or able to begin a canal, the treaty was for the time an instrument of neutralization.

Even before the acquisition of California after the Mexican War (1846–48), the westward migration caused many to make use of the isthmian crossing in preference to the long and dangerous wagon route across the plains and mountains. The traffic was greatly increased by the discovery of gold in 1848. In 1847 a group of New York financiers organized the Panama Railroad Company and secured an exclusive concession from New Granada, allowing the company to construct a means of crossing, which at discretion might be by road, rail, river, or a combination. After surveys, a railroad was decided upon, and a new contract so specifying was obtained in 1850.

The railroad track followed generally the line of the present canal; construction followed the detailed survey as rapidly as possible, and the line was put into use, section by section, as rapidly as completed. The first through train from the Atlantic to the Pacific ran on January 28, 1855.

The gold rush traffic, even before the completion of the railroad, restored Panama's prosperity. Between 1848 and 1869, 375,000 persons crossed the isthmus from the Caribbean to the Pacific; and 225,000, in the opposite direction. Prices for food and services were greatly inflated, producing enormous profits for the meals and lodgings offered. On the other hand, the rate of US$0.80 a day plus board and lodging for common labor on the railroad was considered good pay anywhere during the mid-nineteenth century.

The railroad also created a new city and port at the northern terminus of the line. The town that immediately sprang up to accommodate the railroad offices, warehouses, docks, and shops and to lodge both railroad workers and passengers soon became, as it remains today, the second largest in the country. Originally named Aspinwall, for one of the founders of the railroad company, it was later rechristened Colón by the Panamanians in honor of the discoverer.

Another innovation for which the gold rush was responsible was the founding of a regular daily newspaper. The newspaper, printed in English, first appeared in 1849, founded by three men from the United States awaiting ship passage for California. It appeared as the *Panama Star* and soon amalgamated with the *Herald* to become the *Panama Star and Herald*. In 1853 a Spanish section, "La Estrella de Panamá," became a part of it. The newspapers have had continuous publication ever since (see ch. 7, Education, Culture, and Public Information).

The gold rush and the railroad also contributed to disorders in the country. A good proportion of the Forty-Niners—usually bored with an enforced wait for a ship to California, frequently drunk, and often armed—formed an unruly element. Many brought prejudice verging on contempt for the Latin Americans, Negroes, and others.

The completion in 1869 of the first transcontinental railroad in the United States resulted in the reduction in passenger and freight traffic across the isthmus and a considerable diminution in the amount of gold and silver shipped east. Even during the height of the gold rush, however, from 1855 to 1858, only one-tenth of the ordinary commercial freight was destined for, or originated in, California. The balance concerned trade of the North Americans with Europe and Asia. The railroad company, because of its exceptionally high rates on a capitalization that never exceeded US$7 million, paid a total of nearly US$38 million in dividends between 1853 and 1905. Panama received US$25,000 out of Colombia's annuity and benefited from the transient trade and some inflow of capital.

A Turbulent Period: 1850–86

The European revolutions of 1848, closely watched by many of the young elite of Latin America, had pronounced effects in New Granada, where there was a period of political turbulence to which violent solutions were sought almost habitually for the next thirty-five years or more. Liberal ideas, growing in strength through the 1840s, gradually produced a coalition that soon became known as the Liberal Party. This group elected presidents of New Granada in 1849 and 1853, as well as majorities in the congresses, and

25

Panamanian Liberals fared well. Laws passed by the Liberals provided for the abolition of slavery, the freedom of the press, the secularization of church affairs, and the expulsion of the Jesuits, who had been readmitted in 1844.

Under the administration established in 1853, a new constitution was approved, establishing universal free and direct suffrage and other liberties and, of particular interest to Panama, the local election of provincial governors. Although the last provision was hailed by all supporters of separatism, its first effect was to bring about bitter feuds and violence among the supporters of the principal families.

In 1855 an amendment to the constitution was passed permitting the isthmus to establish itself as a federal state, the Estado de Panamá. Under this arrangement the state had internal autonomy, but New Granada reserved the right to control foreign and military affairs and to levy federal taxes. It also reserved the public income from transisthmian traffic, to be applied to its foreign debt.

Regions other than Panama took advantage of the law permitting local autonomy, with the result that in 1858 the constitution was again changed to create the Grenadine Confederation. The states were so strong and the central government so weak that the confederation could not survive. By late 1859 uncoordinated rebellions were general, either of conservative minorities in liberal states or vice versa. Governor Obaldía of Panama resolved to keep the state removed from the quarrels in the main part of the country and was in general successful in keeping the peace within the isthmus. He publicly announced a threat of secession if the forces of legitimacy were overthrown, but his term expired before the end of these troubles.

The governor elected in 1860, Santiago de la Guardia, a conservative, continued the policy of aloofness from the war, which the liberals under General Mosquera were winning. In 1861 de la Guardia devised a document, called the Convention of Colón, setting forth the conditions under which Panama would continue its adherence to the federation. It reserved Panama's rights of neutrality and of accepting or rejecting the form of government the country might assume. In general, complete internal autonomy was declared, including the election and appointment of officials, complete independence of its judiciary, and the right to dispose of its own taxes except for an agreed sum contributed to the general government. It also undertook to guarantee free, unhampered transisthmian transit without the intervention of the central government.

The signing of the convention, regarded in Panama as a landmark, was followed by a revolution in 1862; by a new expulsion of the Jesuits; by the confiscation by the state of all church lands, property, and income except the churches themselves; and by the dissolution of the convents.

Internally, Panama fared no better under the formally approved Constitution of 1863 of the United States of Colombia. Between 1863 and 1886, when the next Colombian constitution was proclaimed, the isthmus had twenty-six presidents. Coups d'etat, rebellions, and violence were almost continuous, staged by troops of the central government, by the inhabitants against centrally imposed edicts, or by factions out of power. There were three interventions by United States troops under the Bidlack-Mallarino Treaty of 1846, all either requested by the Colombian government or undertaken in collaboration with it.

The chaotic conditions that had continued under the 1863 Constitution culminated in 1884 with the election of Rafael Núñez as president of Colombia by a coalition of moderate liberals and conservatives. Núñez called all factions to participate in a new constituent assembly, but his request was met by an armed revolt of the radical liberals.

Early in 1885 a revolt, headed by a radical general and centered in Panama City, developed into a three-way fight, one result of which was the virtual destruction of Colón. United States forces landed at the request of the Colombian government but too late to save Colón. Millions of dollars in claims were submitted by companies and citizens of the United States, France, and Great Britain, but Colombia successfully pleaded its lack of responsibility. Additional United States naval forces occupied both Colón and Panama City and guarded the railroad to assure uninterrupted transit. Subsequently, Colombian forces landed and assumed protection of the railroad. By July all United States ships except one had left.

When the new Constitution of 1886 established the Republic of Colombia as a unitary state, departments (former states) were distinctly subordinate to the central government; and Panama was singled out for special mention as subject to the direct authority of the government. Resentment of such treatment was high in Panama. The United States consul general reported that in his opinion three-quarters of the Panamanians wanted independence and would revolt, if they could get arms and be sure of freedom from United States intervention.

The French Canal

Between 1850 and 1880 the subject of a canal somewhere between Mexico and Colombia received attention in Great Britain,

France, and the United States. Both the United States and Great Britain made surveys, particularly in Nicaragua, and at different times concessions were obtained, but no definite action was ever taken. In the early 1870s the United States sent survey teams to explore all possible routes, with the result that the United States seemed definitely committed to a Nicaraguan route.

Colombia's attempt to attract canal interest finally brought French attention to bear on Panama. After several surveys a concession of exclusive rights was obtained from Colombia, and a company was formed in 1879 to construct a sea-level canal generally along the railroad route. Ferdinand de Lesseps, of Suez Canal fame, who headed the company, initially rejected the plan for a lock canal. The terms of the concession required completion in twelve years and the possibility of a six-year extension at Colombia's discretion. The lease was for ninety years and was transferable but not to any foreign government. The company also agreed to enter into an "arrangement" with the Panama Railroad Company, which it attained by purchasing most of the stock.

A ceremonious commencement of work was staged by de Lesseps on January 1, 1880, but serious earthmoving did not start until the next year. As work progressed it became evident to the engineers that a sea-level canal was impracticable. De Lesseps, a promoter but not an engineer, could not be convinced until work had gone on for six years. Actual work toward a lock canal did not start until late 1888, by which time the company was in serious financial difficulty. At the peak of its operations the company employed about 10,000 workers, largely Jamaican Negroes.

De Lesseps had to contend not only with enemies who hampered financing by spreading rumors of failure and by dumping stocks and bonds on the market but also with venal French politicians and government officials who demanded large bribes for approving the issue of securities. His efforts to get the French government to guarantee his bonds were blocked by the United States on the grounds that such action would lead to government control in violation of the Monroe Doctrine. The end result in January 1889 was the appointment of a receiver to liquidate the company, whereupon all work stopped.

Despite the French company's disastrous financial experience, an estimated two-fifths of the excavation necessary for the eventual Panama Canal had been completed. Many good headquarters and hospital buildings were finished, and some of the machinery left on the site was usable later; and the railroad had been kept in a fair state of maintenance. Another legacy of the French canal's bankruptcy was a large labor force, now without employment, most of which was made up of Jamaican Negroes. More than half were repatriated at British expense, but thousands remained, many of whom eventually worked on the United States canal.

Panama in the Centralized State

Despite the apprehensions of Panama about its new status as a department of the central government and its loss of the electoral power, the isthmus found in its first appointed governor, General Posada, a sympathetic character. The influx of money occasioned by the French canal project had not yet started to dwindle, and the metropolitan area of the capital felt culturally stimulated and cosmopolitan, as was indicated by the appearance of a French edition of the *Panama Star and Herald*.

Between 1893 and 1898 efforts were made to develop agriculture, crafts, and education. An attempt to bring a public water supply to Panama City failed for lack of funds. During this period occurred the thwarted Liberal revolt of 1895 in Colombia, which affected Panama only through an attack on Bocas del Toro from Nicaragua by Liberal sympathizers driven out by constitutional forces.

Panama was drawn into Colombia's 1899–1902 War of a Thousand Days by the same rebellious radical Liberals from Nicaragua. Like all Colombia, Panama itself was divided, and revolts in the southwest had hardly been suppressed when a Liberal invasion from Nicaragua through Costa Rica entered the country along the south coastal region and nearly succeeded in taking Panama City in mid-1900. The fortunes of war varied and, while a local armistice gave the legitimists temporary security in the Panama-Colón region, the rebels were in control nearly everywhere else in the isthmus. Meanwhile, by early 1902 the rebels had been defeated in most of Colombia proper. At this point the Colombian government asked the intercession of the United States to bring about an armistice in Panama, which was arranged aboard the U.S.S. *Wisconsin* in the Bay of Panama in November 1902.

The war had cost Colombia more than 100,000 lives, largely because it had degenerated into guerrilla actions, most of which, during the last year, had been fought in Panama. This served to inspire many Panamanian leaders, including even liberals, to join in attaining independence from Colombia. The economic prostration resulting from the war was exacerbated by the division, at the upper social levels, between the native Panamanians who had enjoyed the relative autonomy of "El Estado del Istmo" and the influx of Bogotá-appointed officials since 1886.

A Treaty Obtained and Rejected

United States canal interests, which had been actively promoted between 1869 and 1873 by the negotiation of an unconsummated treaty with the Colombian government during the presidency of Ulysses S. Grant, had since then pointed more in the direction of Nicaragua. Nevertheless, before 1898 many considerations, mainly political and diplomatic, postponed a decision in Congress. Nationwide interest became acute with victory in the Spanish-American War, in which the need for a canal was dramatically demonstrated by the ninety-day voyage of the U.S.S. *Oregon* around Cape Horn from the west coast to join the fleet off Cuba.

In 1899 a United States canal commission, under Admiral Walker, was appointed to investigate all possible routes. Quickly dismissing all except that of the French company, through Panama and the Nicaraguan route, it found the French unwilling to set a price for their rights. It also found itself under strong political pressure by the advocates of Nicaragua, and its preliminary report of November 1901, although indicating technical advantages in the Panama route, gave first priority to Nicaragua.

In the view of the United States, another necessary preliminary act to the building of a canal was a revision of the 1850 treaty with Great Britain. A new treaty, the Hay-Pauncefote Treaty, was ratified in December 1901, under which Great Britain withdrew from the provisions of 1850 and agreed to a canal constructed solely by, or under the auspices of, the United States, with guarantees of neutrality.

The Hay-Herrán Treaty with Colombia, signed in January 1903, granted the United States the concession to build, operate, control, and protect a canal, with a lease of 100 years, renewable on the sole option of the United States for like periods, within a zone 6.2 miles wide. The Colombian Senate, however, rejected this treaty on August 12, 1903, mainly because of a desire for a greater financial return and a reservation of the right to negotiate cancellation indemnities from the canal and railroad companies.

Subsequently, the Colombian Senate appointed a committee for restudy of possible treaty solutions. It then became clear that Colombia would wait until the date (1904) when the French concession as extended would lapse. At that time Colombia would have a free hand as sole owner and could hope to get better terms.

THE REPUBLIC OF PANAMA
The Revolution and Treaty

The stirrings of chronic Panamanian separatism were not diminished during the peace that followed the armistice of 1902, one of the provisions of which called for the release of all prisoners, military and political. The Colombian military commander court-martialed and shot "General" Lorenzo, an Indian who had led a Liberal force. He then closed and destroyed the plant of a Liberal newspaper that ventured to protest and, through his Bogotá connections, forced the dismissal of the nominally Conservative governor, who had also protested his actions. These events occurred in June and July 1903. The effect was to cause Liberal leaders, hitherto aloof, to join Conservatives who were already thinking of secession. Feeling was so strong that the new governor in his inaugural address made veiled references to the desirability of separation.

One of the most prominent initiators of revolt was José Agustín Arango, an attorney locally representing the railroad, the local administration of which had continuously been in the hands of United States citizens, even after the French purchased control of the stock. By July 1903, when the course of internal Colombian opposition to the treaty became obvious, a revolutionary junta was in existence. It was headed by Arango with at first only Manuel Amador Guerrero and Carlos C. Arosemena as members, but soon five others, all members of prominent Panamanian families, were added. Arango was considered the brains of the revolution, and Amador was the active leader put forward by the junta.

On October 15 the United States ordered certain naval ships in the Pacific south to Mexican and Nicaraguan ports; others in the Atlantic and Caribbean were alerted for movement.

Amador, who had been in the United States, left for Panama on October 20. Philippe Bunau-Varilla, a French citizen who held stock in the French canal company and had been campaigning to persuade the United States to build the canal in Panama rather than in Nicaragua, had promised Amador US$100,000 when independence was proclaimed. The revolution was, at Bunau-Varilla's insistence, to take place on November 3, barely a week after Amador's scheduled arrival at Colón.

In mid-October a rumor had started that a force of liberal exiles from Nicaragua had landed on the north coast of Panama. Governor Obaldía reported the incident to Bogotá, with the result that a battalion in Colombia under General Tobar was ordered to Panama by ship. The governor was also ordered to send the two gunboats to Buenaventura, on the west coast of Colombia, to pick up an additional force for Panama.

The U.S.S. *Nashville* arrived in the afternoon of November 2; and the Colombian ship, about midnight. There was no disturbance, and the next morning the *Nashville*'s commander, having no instructions, allowed the Colombian troops to land. This caused consternation in the junta at Panama, but the railroad superintendent persuaded General Tobar and his staff to go to Panama on the only transportation available and promised to send the troops when he had enough cars. Notified of Tobar's impending arrival, the junta arranged for the revolt to begin with a mass meeting in the plaza that afternoon.

Tobar's arrival was made an occasion of great and time-consuming ceremony. Becoming suspicious during the afternoon, Tobar made several unsuccessful attempts to hasten the arrival of his troops and, warned by several Colombian members of the government of approaching trouble, went to the barracks to assume command, whereupon he and his staff were arrested.

By this time the mass meeting was shouting for independence, and the municipal council of Panama issued a declaration affirming separation from Colombia under a freely elected government. This is taken as the first act of independence of Panama, and November 3 is celebrated accordingly. The only violent action in opposition was a desultory and ineffective shelling of Panama City by the *Bogotá*, whose commander was not part of the plot.

On the following day, at another mass meeting in Panama, a formal declaration of independence was issued, and a junta of provisional government was appointed, consisting of José Agustín Arango, Tomás Arias, and Federico Boyd. The junta announced a cabinet in which both the Conservative and Liberal parties were represented. Celebrations went on most of the day.

Meanwhile in Colón the Colombian battalion was still stranded. Its impatient commander made several threats of drastic action, particularly against United States citizens, but he was dissuaded by local and United States Navy officials. Upon the arrival on the evening of November 5 of the U.S.S. *Dixie* with a battalion of marines, the Colombians boarded ship and sailed.

The United States was informed on the evening of November 4 of the official declaration and the appointment of a government in Panama. This message was followed by another on November 6 that all municipalities had adhered to the new state and that its authority in the isthmus was uncontested. Later in the day, the United States granted de facto recognition to Panama, so notifying its consul there and its minister to Colombia. On November 14 de jure recognition was accorded by the United States, followed before the end of the year by seventeen other countries, including all the great powers.

The presence of United States naval vessels, with instructions to prevent any hostile landing, prevented any Colombian interference by sea. On November 17 a Colombian mission arrived at Colón by ship, headed by General Rafael Reyes, later president of Colombia, to try to negotiate a return of the isthmus to Colombian control. Despite offers of complete autonomy as a federal state with control of finances, and even a proposal to transfer the capital from Bogotá to Panama, the mission was unsuccessful.

Early in November Bunau-Varilla had been appointed Panamanian minister to the United States and started negotiations immediately after his presentation of letters of credence on November 13. The treaty thus prepared was to an extent based on the Hay-Herrán Treaty but with important differences. The most crucial was that, whereas the older treaty granted the United States a renewable lease while specifically reserving Colombian sovereignty in the area affected, the treaty with Panama granted in perpetuity "all the rights, powers and authority . . . which the United States would possess and exercise if it were the sovereign . . . to the entire exclusion of the exercise by the Republic of Panama of any such sovereign rights, power and authority." Further, and because of the grant of operative sovereignty, there was no provision for joint police power or joint courts within the zone. Because of such wording the question of sovereignty remained very much at issue in later years.

The United States was given specific authority to intervene in the cities of Panama and Colón in order to ensure the maintenance of public order and the enforcement of sanitary regulations, in case Panamanian officials showed inability to do so. The treaty also stated that the United States guaranteed, and would maintain, the independence of the Republic. The terms of payment were the same as those offered Colombia—US$10 million in cash and an annuity of US$250,000 after nine years—but Panama acquired no rights, reversionary or otherwise, in the existing railroad or French canal (see ch. 10, Foreign Relations).

In less than four days the treaty was drafted and signed on November 17, the day a Panamanian commission arrived in New York, thus removing any possibility of their considering or amending it. It next was sent to Panama, without change, where the government ratified the treaty on December 3. The United States Senate did not ratify it until February 23, 1904. Bunau-Varilla resigned on February 25, refusing any remuneration by Panama for his services. Although he was, more than any single man, responsible for their independence, Panamanians have never forgiven him the treaty.

In Washington arguments over the relative advantages of a sea-level route or locks continued for three years, but in 1907 Colonel George W. Goethals was placed in charge, and the digging of the canal began. A major contribution to the success of the operation was the eradication of malaria and yellow fever, an achievement credited to Dr. William Gorgas. After seven years, during which three locks were built at each end of the fifty-mile waterway and Gatún Lake was created eighty-five feet above sea level, the canal was opened in 1914.

The Young Republic: 1904–24

The next order of business in Panama was to enact a constitution, and a constituent assembly, which met in January, was elected. The drafting committee, under the presidency of Pablo Arosemena, presented a document for assembly debate, which was passed on February 13. The unitary character of the Republic was emphasized (and Spanish colonial tradition followed) by giving the municipalities more individual autonomy than the provinces, which were actually mere administrative dependencies of the central government. The representative character of government was founded on the principle of direct elections of the president and National Assembly through universal male suffrage. Presidents were elected for a four-year term; and deputies, for two. At each session the assembly elected three persons, each called a *designado* (vice president), one of whom would assume the presidency in case of death, disability, or absence of the president. This system remained until 1946, when direct election of vice presidents was provided for (see ch. 8, Governmental System).

An unusual feature, which in a sense made the constitution almost an enabling act to the canal treaty, was a specific provision (Article 136) for the intervention of the United States if necessary to reestablish public order and ensure the continuity of constitutional government. This provision remained part of the basic law until the Constitution of 1904 was supplanted by that of 1941, although the United States relinquished its right by a treaty signed in 1936.

Acquisition of the Canal Zone by the United States was accomplished on May 4, 1904. Almost immediately Panama became concerned over a United States ruling that appeared to threaten the entrance of Panamanian goods into the zone and sales to transients traveling through the zone when the canal was built. As a result, an agreement was negotiated to the general satisfaction of Panama; the agreement remained in force for twenty years. By 1906 (under the treaty clause making the United States responsible in the field of sanitation) construction of water and sewer systems and the paving of all streets in Colón and Panama were completed and served further to improve relations.

The first cabinet was bipartisan, but with liberals in the minority there was discontent within that party. After a demand that two of the Conservative cabinet members be removed, the minister

34

of war (one of those objected to) was replaced by another man, and the army was disbanded.

In December 1904 a national police force was created as the sole body under arms in the country (see ch. 14, National Security).

United States intervention in the elections to the assembly in 1906 was requested by the Liberal opposition, whose leaders traveled to Washington. It was refused by Secretary of State Elihu Root and Secretary of War William Howard Taft, who recommended that they accomplish their political reforms through the ballot box. In 1908, a presidential election year, Canal Zone representatives, by request, attended elections as members of a 'joint board to observe and to hear complaints. The election was peaceable, but the losers objected strenuously to the "intervention."

Tension in 1912 occasioned a request for more thorough United States intervention to supervise a presidential election. The administration candidate, representing the Conservatives and some dissident Liberals, was opposed by the main body of Liberals, who put forward Belisario Porras. Although Porras had been opposed to the revolution and had therefore been deprived of the rights of citizenship in 1906, his petition for reinstatement had been favorably acted upon by the assembly in 1907, and he became director of the Liberal Party. The parties accused each other of padding the voting lists, and the United States was requested to supervise both registration and polling. Army officers conducted the registration, and 200 troops and zone employees stood watch at the voting booths.

Porras won the election and served his full term (1912–16) in a period marked by the first transit of the canal (1914) and its opening the following year to commercial traffic. Great benefits accrued to Panama from the resulting trade, but more than ever the emphasis on national prosperity focused around the zone and took attention away from a wider distribution of economic development.

The first extraconstitutional effort at perpetuation in power occurred after the death of President Ramón M. Valdés, successor to President Porras, when the first *designado*, Ciro L. Urriola, in June 1918, suspended indefinitely assembly elections that would have resulted in the choosing of new *designados*. Again the United States intervened, for the first time on its own initiative, as permitted by the constitution. The elections were held under supervision (this at the request of Panama), and Porras became *designado* to fill out the Valdés term. United States intervention ceased after the elections except in Chiriquí Province, where troops were maintained for about two years to assist in the preservation of order and to protect the rights of United States citizens.

Porras remained acting president until January 1920, when he resigned to run successfully for the 1920–24 term. This term saw the only armed conflict with a neighbor in the history of the Republic. The Panama–Costa Rica boundary had long been in dispute, and in February 1921 Costa Rican troops attempted to seize the Coto region on the Pacific coast, long settled by Panamanians. A hastily raised Panamanian force defeated the Costa Ricans, but differences of opinion in Panama City brought about riots in which several were killed. The disturbed state of affairs caused new United States intervention in the form of a visit by two warships, which brought a return of quiet but caused public protest.

Porras had been president for nearly ten years of the 1912–24 period. Despite the several periods of disturbance, the telegraph system was modernized, the railroad in Chiriqui was built, and new buildings for the old Hospital of Santo Tomás and the private Panama Hospital were constructed with the assistance of the medical authorities of the zone. The revision and adaptation of Colombian law had been made, and Panamanian codes were established. The Public Register (of real estate) and the Civil Register (of all changes in civil status of persons) were instituted. The first faculty (Law and Political Science) of what would in 1935 become the national university was set up.

A Period of Revisions: 1924–49

By 1924 the division of the electorate into parties under the old Colombian labels of Conservative and Liberal no longer was valid. Consistent Liberal success since 1912 had almost destroyed the Conservative Party, of which in any case most of the old leaders had died. The Liberals, for want of coherent opposition, began to divide into factions, and parties became the personal preserves of political leaders, who formed shifting coalitions for the purpose of winning elections.

Rodolfo Chiari (father of the president elected in 1960) amassed a considerable personal following and won the 1924 election. His term was marked by rent riots in Panama and Colón that occasioned another intervention, on request, in 1925. The same year saw an uprising of the San Blas Indians, instigated by an adventurer from the United States, which was put down in about a month, after some loss of life. The Indians agreed to live in peace and, in turn, were given extensive autonomy in their own affairs and guaranteed protection from grasping officials.

A new canal treaty to replace that of 1903 and the Taft Convention (which expired in 1924) was proposed in 1926 but was rejected by the Panamanian National Assembly in 1927 as unsatisfactory to national aspirations.

Florencio H. Arosemena, elected in 1928, was the first president turned out of office by violence. A nationalist organization, Acción Communal (Community Action), which had come into being to oppose the 1926 treaty, armed itself and without great difficulty overcame the police and forced Arosemena's resignation. There was no intervention by the United States; Secretary of State Henry Stimson of President Herbert Hoover's cabinet had already initiated the nonintervention policy that came to full fruition in the next administration.

Arosemena's four-year term was finished out by Ricardo Alfaro, who endeavored to soften the effects of the 1931–32 worldwide depression, which seriously reduced canal traffic and trade. He was followed in the presidential chair by Harmodio Arias, who adopted a program of public works to ride out the depression.

A treaty negotiated in 1936 superseded important parts of that of 1903. The United States waived its right of intervention. The annuity, seriously affected by the United States departure from the gold standard (in effect a devaluation of currency), was raised to B/430,000, and a protocol made the balboa the equivalent of the dollar. A number of concessions were made by the United States favoring Panamanian trade in the zone and with ships in transit. By a separate convention the United States agreed to build a highway across the isthmus, later called the Boyd-Roosevelt Highway. Additional privileges were given the United States to take defense measures involving land in Panamanian jurisdiction —by previous consultation usually, but in emergency on its own initiative. Panama ratified the treaty in 1936, and the United States ratified in 1939.

Juan D. Arosemena, who was elected in 1936, died in 1939, and Arnulfo Arias was elected president in 1940 after a campaign in which the opposition made revolutionary threats. Within a little more than a month (in November 1940), he forced through the National Assembly a new constitution, which he called Panameñista—"a government of Panamanians for the benefit of the Panamanian people." Among other changes it extended the presidential term from four to six years. Under the old constitution, amendments could be made only through passage by two successive assemblies, but Arias, assuming power as the "supreme representative of the State," set aside the constitutional requirement and decreed a plebiscite for December 1940. The new constitution was ratified on January 2, 1941.

The press was strictly controlled. Political donations of up to 10 percent were exacted, even from women and day laborers among government employees. Hitherto illegal, gambling was made a source of revenue, and Arias established the bank of issue and started circulating paper money without sound backing.

One opposition movement worked toward a violent coup; another was led by cabinet ministers with the cooperation of the National Police. The situation solved itself in favor of the latter faction when Arias left the country on October 7, 1941, without the necessary legal notice to his government. The Supreme Court, appealed to by certain ministers, declared the first *designado* ineligible, and the second resigned on being appointed. Since the third was out of the country, the minister of government and justice, Ricardo de la Guardia, was made acting president.

De la Guardia promptly revoked all the unpopular decrees with the support of the assembly, declared war on the Axis powers immediately after the United States was attacked, and applied security measures that had not existed under Arias. In 1943, when the assembly should have elected new *designados*, it failed to do so, and de la Guardia continued as president until 1945. The presidential term legally ran until 1947, and de la Guardia tried to have the assembly extend his term again by the same method. The legislature refused and was dissolved by the acting president, who declared the constitution invalid and called a constituent assembly, ruling meanwhile through the cabinet. A new constitution was proclaimed on March 1, 1946, and the assembly named as provisional president Enrique A. Jiménez (see ch. 8, Governmental System).

After enactment of the 1946 Constitution, Acting President Jiménez served until the elections of 1948, in which, despite claims of fraud at the polls by Arnulfo Arias, Domingo Díaz was declared elected. He lived less than a year and was succeeded by First Vice President Daniel Chanis. The new president, anxious to consolidate his power, demanded the resignation of the commandant of police, José A. Remón, but Remón succeeded in compelling the president to resign. Having done so, Chanis appealed to the National Assembly on the grounds of duress, but Second Vice President Roberto Chiari was declared acting president. Chiari's appointment, however, was voided by the Supreme Court of Justice (also known as Supreme Court) within a few days. Remón's tactics had aroused popular indignation, and he threw his police strength behind Arias. Together, they induced the Board of Elections to reopen the case. In a matter of hours the board, claiming it had made a recount, declared Arnulfo Arias president on November 24, 1949.

The Period of National Patriotic Coalitions

Arias' return to power and his attempted reintroduction of a repressive program directed against the press and representative government created the circumstances for development of the National Patriotic Coalition (Coalición Patriótica Nacional—CPN), which was organized in 1951, won office in 1952, and remained in power until 1960. The CPN was largely the creation of Colonel Remón, commander of the National Guard and for some time an active political force behind the scenes. Remón had managed to acquire a crucial position in politics since his elevation to the chief security position in the country in 1947. Acquiring extensive wealth and many contacts among the elite, Remón had been relatively conservative in his use of the guard's power in politics during the years immediately after the war.

In 1949 his intervention became overt, and he was able to engineer the return of Arnulfo Arias to power. Two years later he replaced him with the first vice president, Alcibíades Arosemena, who served until the elections of 1952. This period enabled Remón to create the CPN from five existing parties: the Authentic Revolutionary Party, the Liberal Party, the Restoration Party, the Popular Union, and the National Revolutionary Party. These groups shared little more than a willingness to unite in a pro-Remón front.

In early January 1952 opposition forces began to coalesce. For a period a former ambassador to the United States, Rodolfo Herbruger, attempted to challenge Remón, using as his base the newly formed Panameñista Party. After considerable vacillation, Herbruger withdrew from the race in February, and the opposition gradually centered on the candidacy of Roberto Chiari, who had held office for five days during the unsettled period of 1949.

Chiari formed a rival coalition group, the Civil Alliance (Alianza Civilista—AC), an aggregation of four small parties: the National Liberal Party, the Patriotic Front, the Independent Revolutionary Party, and the Socialist Party. When Herbruger apparently shifted his support to Chiari, the latter assumed the role of principal opposition candidate. A three-man contest emerged when Morena Correa, a lawyer, qualified to run also.

The campaign was marked by extensive disorders and student strikes. Under the control of outgoing President Arosemena, the police were utilized extensively in curbing opposition activities. Finally on May 6, with the election five days away, the government brought all political demonstrations to an end. Strongly supported by the government as an official candidate, Remón acquired an early lead, enjoying the tacit support of both the police and the electoral supervisory board. Although the returns of 133,208 for Remón to 78,094 for Chiari were probably inflated, Remón had run a generally effective campaign, marked by his attack on Chiari as a captive candidate of the elite. After an unsuccessful appeal by Chiari to the election board, Remón was inaugurated as president in October 1952 and entered office with considerable popular support and a National Assembly thoroughly dominated by the CPN.

Remón's term was marked by notable progress both in dealing with economic problems and in the negotiation of a new treaty with the United States providing a Canal Zone arrangement much more favorable to Panama. Attempts to settle the internal debt were aided by advances from both the United Fruit Company and the Chase Bank of New York. Major tax revisions were introduced, and in 1953 the Institute for Economic Development was founded.

The Remón government was reportedly one of the most capable since the end of World War II. Fiscal matters were administered adroitly enough to reduce the national debt. A high standard of honesty was required throughout the administration, Remón providing a notable example at the top, a surprising occurrence since he had acquired great wealth while in his position as commander of the police force. By far the major accomplishment of his presidency, however, was the negotiation of a new treaty with the United States. Remón was effective in building strong domestic support for the canal negotiations, bringing to his assistance former opponents, such as Harmodio Arias and Ricardo Alfaro.

On January 2, 1955, Remón was assassinated; the background and motivation of the act have never become definitely known. Developments took a startling turn when José Guizado, who as vice president had succeeded to Remón's office, was arrested on suspicion of involvement with the murder. On his impeachment, Second Vice President Ricardo Arias, associated with the Restoration Party, took office and, with the support of Remón's widow, a political figure in her own right, promised a moderate constitutional regime based on the policies of his predecessor. His regime lasted through the rest of Remón's term until the 1956 elections and was marked by the continuation of the CPN front and the successful conclusion of the negotiations with the United States (see ch. 10, Foreign Relations).

The CPN dominated the elections of 1956 and the four years of political activity that followed it. Its leadership chose Ernesto de la Guardia, a successful businessman, as its candidate early in 1955, and the convention officially ratified the choice in July. A yearlong campaign was begun. Thoroughly discouraged by the

CPN's efficient organization—erected by Remón and maintained after his death by Arias—an opposition was slow to form. An additional barrier to opposition organization was the passage in 1953, under Remón's aegis, of legislation requiring parties appearing on the electoral ballot to have 45,000 registered members.

In the period preceding the campaign, strong demands were made for the relaxation of party-registration requirements, particularly by the Independent Revolutionary Party and the Youth Patriotic Front. When the Arias government held firm to the statutory requirements, the smaller factions were unable to unite to meet the minimal requirements in a coalition. As a result the only opposition party meeting the 1953 law's standards was the National Liberal Party, which nominated Victor F. Goytía as its presidential candidate. In the face of the government's support of the CPN ticket, the campaign was a perfunctory one.

The de la Guardia platform was relatively conservative, emphasizing programs aimed at improving economic conditions in the Republic and maintaining progress already achieved. He urged the establishment of an oil refinery in Colón and an accelerated program to provide new sources of electricity for industry and consumers. The electoral slogan was Pan y Libertad (Bread and Liberty).

Aided by the coalition's well-organized machinery, the CPN's campaign was marked by a noticeably diminished reliance on excessive promises of rewards for support of the government slate. This policy was in keeping with the general expectation that the CPN was assured of victory in any event. This expectation was borne out by the election results. Balloting on May 13, 1956, resulted in a final tally—approved by a government-dominated election board—of 177,633 for de la Guardia against 81,737 for Goytía. The National Liberals' protests of electoral dishonesty were rejected, and the election results were accepted; de la Guardia was inaugurated on October 1.

The election had produced an assembly overwhelmingly dominated by the CPN, composed of forty-seven deputies affiliated with the government coalition and only six representing the National Liberals, the sole opposition. With this type of political configuration, the CPN thoroughly controlled the Republic's political life for the following four years. The popular allure of the Remón name was effectively capitalized on by the appointment of Señora Remón to the position of minister of labor, social welfare, and public health. The appointment of Aquilino Boyd, one of the leading critics of the United States, as minister of foreign affairs was a harbinger of the prominence that would be given to conflict with the United States over the zone.

The principal events of de la Guardia's term of office did indeed occur in the realm of foreign affairs. These problems were so overwhelming that they markedly affected political affairs within the country. The first episode was rooted in the Egyptian seizure of the Suez Canal, which touched off conflict with the United States once more, less than two years after the conclusion of the new agreement.

The second major convulsion centered on the abortive invasion of the Republic in April 1959 by a force of eighty-seven men under the leadership of Roberto Arias, former ambassador to London; government forces effectively suppressed it. The highly unrealistic adventure was thought by some to have been partially sponsored by the Cuban government of Fidel Castro, though this was denied. As the general temper of political feeling rose, with considerable agitation by both Cuban and United Arab Republic (UAR) diplomats in Panama, the next crisis came quickly in the outbreak of violence over an attempt by young Panamanians to plant the Republic's flag in the zone as evidence of Panama's sovereignty (see ch. 10, Foreign Relations).

In domestic affairs two presidential programs of considerable scope—an expansion of social security and a more intensive education program—foundered on the resistance of elite interest groups to the heavier taxation involved. By the end of 1957 effective hopes for the realization of both had died.

Meanwhile, the CPN, undisturbed by an effective opposition in the National Assembly, began to suffer serious dissension within its own ranks. Disagreements over arrangements for the refinery facilities at Colón caused the cancellation of the plan. The formation of the National Liberal Movement, led by First Vice President Temistocles Díaz, created additional problems for the disintegrating CPN. The de la Guardia administration generally tended to be overwhelmed by its domestic problems and the rapid pace of events in foreign affairs. Nevertheless, de la Guardia enjoyed the considerable distinction of being the first postwar president to finish a full four-year term in office.

After the seizure of the Suez Canal in 1956 political leaders intensified their demands for resumption of "complete sovereignty" over the Canal Zone, and President de la Guardia was quoted as saying that the word *perpetuity* was purely academic. Among other things the Panamanian government demanded that all rights to minerals or oil discovered in the zone be conceded to Panama; that the United States again increase the annuity and share the total canal collections with Panama; and that Panamanian sovereignty be extended twelve miles off the coast. Panamanian authorities also demanded that the Panamanian flag be flown beside the United States flag in the zone, and **President Dwight D.** Eisenhower in 1959 agreed to fly the two flags in a central place in the zone—a decision that satisfied no one.

The Early 1960s

When Roberto Chiari, elected to the presidency in 1960, made a state visit to the United States in 1962, his meeting with President John Kennedy resulted in agreement that wages of Panamanians in the Canal Zone would be increased; that more Panamanians would be employed in the zone; and that United States authorities would withhold income taxes from non-United States workers in the zone and remit these funds to the Panamanian government. It was also agreed that the Panamanian and United States flags would be flown side by side at a number of points in the zone instead of the central place decreed by President Eisenhower.

The Panamanians, not satisfied with these concessions, increased their demands. Despite the fact that the United States was not making a profit from the canal and that the original cost had not been amortized, the Panamanians argued that they should share in the proceeds of tolls and that the United States could increase the total income by doubling or trebling the fees. They failed to take into account the fact that raising the fees would work a hardship on other nations, such as Peru, Chile, and Ecuador, the bulk of whose foreign trade moved through the canal.

In January 1964, when a group of American students raised the United States flag over their high school in the zone, Panamanians crossed into the zone to raise their own flag over the school. The resulting tussle between teenagers burgeoned into rioting, in the course of which mobs of Panamanians invaded the zone, United States soldiers were killed or wounded, a number of Panamanians died, and damage to property ran into millions of dollars.

President Chiari immediately broke off diplomatic relations with the United States but, after three months of talks, diplomatic relations were resumed. In December 1964, after the election to the presidency of Marco Aurelio Robles, the United States announced that it was prepared to negotiate a new treaty (see ch. 9, Political Dynamics and Values; ch. 10, Foreign Relations).

Thus, the canal has played a major role in forming politically conscious Panamanians' attitudes toward history. In a country that has existed as a sovereign state for less than seventy years, there are no national heroes, and political leaders cannot hope to gain popularity unless they advocate sovereignty over the territory occupied by the Canal Zone.

CHAPTER 3

PHYSICAL ENVIRONMENT AND POPULATION

Panama, with an area of 29,208 square miles located at the southeast extremity of Central America, forms the narrowest and lowest portion of the isthmus that links North and South America (see fig. 1). Near its midpoint the territory is divided by the Canal Zone, a strip of land 553 square miles in extent and 10 miles wide at most points. The airline distance between the Atlantic and Pacific terminals of the Panama Canal that bisects the Canal Zone is about 38 miles.

The name of the country is probably derived from an Indian term meaning a place where fish are abundant. The Spanish name —Panamá—applies both to the country and its capital city. In English, the name of the country is Panama (without the accent), and the capital is customarily referred to as Panama City—by Panamanians as well as by foreigners.

Shaped like a flattened letter S that extends west to east some 420 miles, the country has a width that varies between 31.5 and 113 miles. Because of the lateral nature of its extension and its curved contour, directions expressed in terms of the compass are often surprising. A transit of the canal from Pacific to Atlantic involves travel not to the east but to the northwest; in Panama City the sun is seen to rise out of the Pacific. In practice, compass points are not in general use as a means of describing directions. The two coastlines are referred to as the Atlantic and Pacific more often than as the north and south. (Atlantic, rather than Caribbean, is the terminology customarily used.) A resident of Panama City crossing the isthmus would think of himself as going over rather than up to Colón, the sister city at the Atlantic terminus of the canal. Similarly, in traveling southwest to Puerto Armuelles near the Costa Rican border, he would probably think of himself as going up rather than over or down to that town.

The dominant feature of the country's landform is the central spine of mountains and hills that forms the continental divide. It is highest at the Costa Rican frontier and becomes progressively lower as it extends eastward toward the canal, where it almost disappears before rising again to moderate heights as the Colombian frontier is neared. Rivers flowing to both oceans are numerous, but they do not play significant parts in the life of the country.

Situated close to the equator Panama has a deep tropical climate characterized by temperatures and humidity that are high the year round and by abundant rainfall interrupted by a dry season. Tropical and semitropical flora and fauna are plentiful and extremely varied, and most of the country is heavily forested.

Most of the better soils are found on the Pacific side of the continental divide, where the coastal lowlands are broader, savannas are more extensive, and rainfall and humidity are somewhat more moderate. Since the pre-Columbian era the population concentration has been heaviest between the present vicinity of Panama City and the Costa Rican border on the Pacific side. Toward Colombia and along the Atlantic, most of the territory is virgin forest or swampland, and the population is sparse.

Irregularly distributed by geographic region, the population in 1971 was fast becoming urbanized, particularly by migration from rural localities to Panama City and other densely populated places adjacent to it. The remaining urban places were growing only at approximately the rate of the population as a whole. As a consequence, the balance of population throughout the country's independent history had been becoming still more heavily weighted toward those provinces that consistently had the largest populations. There had been no significant shift in the settlement pattern of the rural population, which continued to make up slightly more than half of the total.

The outstanding features of the country's population dynamics during the years since World War II have been an increasingly high birth rate and rapidly decreasing rates of infant and general mortality. These dynamics have led to a progressive reduction in the median age of the population and an extension of life expectancy in all age brackets. In 1971 the country was still far from being overpopulated, but the rapid rate of growth in Panama City was creating problems of urban crowding. The increasing proportion of children in the population, resulting from rising birth rates and declining infant mortality, was placing a growing burden on the economically active sector of the population.

NATURAL FEATURES

The narrow land bridge that connects the continents of North and South America extends eastward from Lake Nicaragua and the San Juan Basin in Costa Rica to an abrupt termination at the beginning of the South American continent along what roughly corresponds to the frontier between Panama and Colombia. In

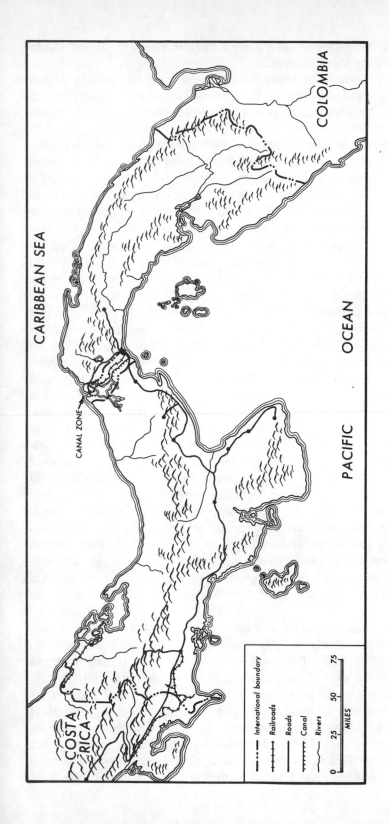

Figure 2. Topography of Panama

47

this sense, the Isthmus of Panama includes nearly all of Costa Rica as well as Panama itself.

The continental divide formed by the central spine of this land bridge does not form part of the great mountain chains of North America or Mexico, and only near the Colombian border are there highlands related to the Andean system of South America (see fig. 2). The spine that forms the continental divide is the highly eroded arch of an uplift from the sea bottom in which peaks were formed by volcanic intrusions.

The mountain range of the divide is called the Cordillera de Talamanca in Costa Rica. Across the Panama border it becomes the Serranía de Tabasará, and the portion of it closer to the low saddle of the isthmus that straddles the Canal Zone is often called the Sierra de Veraguas. As a whole, the continental divide between Costa Rica and the Canal Zone is usually referred to as the Cordillera Central by Panamanian geographers.

The loftiest part of the country is not, however, in the Cordillera Central. Between that range and the Pacific Ocean at the Costa Rican border, the Volcán de Chiriquí (also known as the Volcán de Barú) rises to nearly 11,000 feet and marks the eastern terminus of the volcanic axis of Nicaragua. The apex of a highland that includes the country's richest soils, the Volcán de Chiriquí is still referred to as a volcano but has been inactive for millennia.

From the Costa Rican border, the divide of the Cordillera Central continues eastward for about 110 miles, with maximum altitudes above 6,500 feet. The divide then descends to a little over 3,000 feet at a point very close to the Pacific coastline about 30 miles west of Panama City. At this point it subsides to follow low hills and ridges seldom exceeding 1,000 feet across the Canal Zone to a suburb of Panama City called Las Cumbres (the Summit). Here the divide rises toward the Cordillera de San Blas, a low but continuous range that crosses the isthmus at an angle to continue close to the Atlantic coastline, eventually reaching heights of more than 5,000 feet as it forms a portion of the Colombian frontier.

There are also several mountain systems that do not form part of the continental divide. Half of the territory has altitudes in excess of 1,000 feet. The most northern part of the country, in Colón Province east of the canal, is made up principally of mountain ridges with peaks of up to 3,000 feet. Near the Pacific coast at the Colombian border, a fan-shaped complex of highlands is connected with the Cordillera de Baudó of Colombia, a spur of the South American Andes. It consists of various highlands, with peaks of 5,000 feet or more, sometimes referred to collectively as the Darién Highlands (Altos de Darién). A portion of this complex has been drowned by the Gulf of San Miguel on the Pacific, but it rises again across the gulf to reach heights of up to 5,000 feet near the border between the provinces of Darién and Panama.

On the Pacific side of the isthmus between the Canal Zone and Costa Rica, the most important highland system is made up of the tumbled mountains and hills that blanket most of the Azuero Peninsula and is sometimes referred to as the Cordillera Occidental. Westward from it across the Gulf of Montijo, another range of hills follows the spine of the Las Palmas Peninsula near the border between the provinces of Chiriquí and Veraguas.

The more than 300 rivers emptying into the Pacific are longer and slower running than those of the Atlantic slopes, and their basins are more extensive. The largest of these is the Tuira, which empties into the Gulf of San Miguel and is the country's only major navigable stream. The second largest, the Bayano (also called the Chepo) in Panama Province, is to be the site of a major hydroelectric installation (see ch. 12, Agriculture and Industry). Drainage is generally poor on the Pacific side of the Cordillera de San Blas and is poor to good on the Pacific side of the Cordillera Central.

Despite their great number, the rivers of Panama have been of limited practical value, and only the name of the Chagres is well known, although in 1971 the development of their considerable hydroelectric potential was commencing. They are not used for transportation, and population clusters are found along their banks only in sparsely populated frontier regions where roads are non-existent; in most of the country the rainfall is sufficient to limit their utilization for irrigation.

The 490-mile stretch of Atlantic coastline is marked by several good natural harbors, but there are few towns on the Atlantic, and the only important port facilities are those of Cristóbal in the Canal Zone, located adjacent to the Panamanian city of Colón on Limón Bay at the Atlantic terminus of the canal. The numerous islands of the Bocas del Toro Archipelago near the Costa Rican border provide an extensive natural roadstead and shield the banana port of Almirante. The 366 islands of the San Blas Archipelago are strung out for more than 100 miles along the sheltered coastline of San Blas Territory.

The Pacific coastline, 870 miles in length, borders the Gulf of Chiriquí and the Gulf of Panama, separated by the Azuero Peninsula. The principal islands are those of the Las Perlas Archipelago in the middle of the Gulf of Panama, the prison island of Coiba in the Gulf of Chiriquí, and the decorative island of Taboga, a tourist attraction that can be seen from Panama City. In all, there are some 1,000 islands off the Pacific coast.

The principal Pacific-side port facilities are found in the Canal Zone town of Balboa at the terminus of the canal. Ships transiting the canal, however, ordinarily stop on the Atlantic side, where the facilities are more extensive. The only other harbors of any importance are at Puerto Armuelles in Chiriquí Province, from which bananas are shipped, and several small ports in remote Darién Province.

The Pacific coastal waters are extraordinarily shallow. Depths of 600 feet are reached only outside the perimeters of both the Gulf of Panama and the Gulf of Chiriquí, and wide mud flats extend up to forty-five miles seaward from the coastlines. As a consequence, the tidal range is extreme. A range of about 2 feet between high and low water on the Atlantic contrasts sharply with nearly 23 feet on the Pacific, and some eighty miles up the navigable Tuira River the range is 18 feet.

Geographic Regions

There is no generally recognized group of regions, and no single set of names is in common use. One system often used by Panamanian geographers, however, portrays the country as divided into five regions that reflect population concentration and economic development as well as geography.

Darién

The largest and most sparsely populated of the regions, Darién extends eastward from beyond the immediate hinterlands of Panama City and Colón to the Colombian border and comprises more than one-third of the national territory. In addition to the province of Darién, it includes San Blas Territory and the eastern part of Panama Province. Darién—a name that was once applied to the entire isthmus—is a land of virgin rain forest and swamp; roads are almost nonexistent, and less than 2 percent of the country's inhabitants live in the region. In 1971 the prospects were bright for development of its hydroelectric power potential and for completing the Pan-American Highway across the still-unbridged Darién Gap to Colombia. It was still, however, an empty land of only potential significance.

Central Isthmus

The Central Isthmus does not have precisely definable boundaries. Geographically, it is the low saddle of land that bisects the isthmus at the Canal Zone. Westward, it extends on the Pacific as far as the remnants of the Cordillera Central that rise a little beyond the town of La Chorrera, which is virtually a suburb of Panama City. Westward on the Atlantic side, it includes small villages and clustered farms around Gatún Lake. East of the Canal

Zone it terminates gradually as the population grows more sparse and the jungles and swamps of the Darién region begin. More concept than a region, the Central Isthmus, with a width of about sixty miles, is the densely populated historic transportation route between Atlantic and Pacific.

Central Panama

Central Panama lies to the southwest of the Canal Zone and is made up of all or most of the provinces of Veraguas, Coclé, Herrera, and Los Santos. It is located between the continental divide and the Pacific and is sometimes referred to as the Central Provinces. The sparsely populated Santa Fé District of Veraguas Province is located across the continental divide on the Atlantic side, however, and a frontier part of Coclé is also on the Atlantic side of the divide.

The hills and lowlands of Central Panama are dotted with farms and ranches and include most of the country's rural population. This is the traditional Panama that has seen relatively little change during the years of the Republic. Its heartland is a heavily populated rural arc that frames the Gulf of Parita and includes most of the country's largest market towns, including the provincial capitals of Penonomé, Santiago, Chitré, and Las Tablas. This is the agriculturally productive area with a relatively long dry season that is known as the dry zone of Panama.

Chiriquí

The remaining part on the Pacific side of the Cordillera Central is taken up by Chiriquí Province adjacent to the Costa Rican border. Some geographers regard it and Central Panama as a single region, but the lowlands of the two are separated by the hills of the Las Palmas Peninsula, and the big province of Chiriquí has enough individuality to warrant consideration as a separate region. The second largest and second most populous of the nine provinces it is still, to some extent, a frontier area as well as one of considerable economic importance. It is only in Chiriquí that the frontiers of settlement have pushed up well into the interior highlands, and the population has a particular sense of regional identity. A native of Chiriquí can be expected to identify himself, above all, as a Chiricano.

Atlantic Panama

Atlantic Panama is the part of Panama on the Atlantic side of the continental divide and west of the Central Isthmus. It includes all of Bocas del Toro Province, the Atlantic portions of Veraguas and Coclé, and the western districts of Colón. It is home to a scant 5 percent of the population, and its only important population concentrations are near the Costa Rican border where banana plantations are located.

Climate

Panama City is located at 9°N latitude, and the entire country lies deep in the humid torrid zone between the seventh and tenth parallels. Temperatures are uniformly high, and there is virtually no seasonal variation, although savannas are cooler than swamp or forest. Diurnal ranges are low; on a typical day during the dry season in the capital city the early morning minimum may be 76°F., and the afternoon maximum may be 85°F., with a mean range of from 72°F. to 85°F. Only seldom does the temperature exceed 90°F. for more than a short time.

Temperatures on the Pacific side of the isthmus are somewhat lower than on the Atlantic, and breezes tend to rise after dusk in most parts of the country. At El Valle, a two-hour drive southwest from Panama City, the cooler temperatures resulting from a 1,200-foot altitude make the locality a popular resort. Temperatures are cooler still in the higher parts of the Cordillera Central, and frosts occur in the mountains near the Costa Rican border. Except for a few localities in Chiriquí, however, the population at higher altitudes is exceedingly sparse.

Climatic regions are determined less on the basis of temperature than of rainfall, which varies regionally from less than 50 inches to more than 120 inches and falls almost entirely during the rainy season. This season occurs between the months of April and December and varies between seven and more than nine months in duration. The principal factors that determine the cycle of rainfall are moisture from the Caribbean, which is transported by northerly and northeasterly winds prevailing during most of the year, and the continental divide, which acts as a rain shield for the Pacific lowlands. A second influence that is present during the late autumn is the southwesterly wind off the Pacific, which brings some precipitation to Pacific lowlands. This wind is modified by the highlands of the Azuero Peninsula that form a partial rain shield for much of Central Panama. In general, rainfall is much heavier on the Atlantic than on the Pacific side of the continental divide; the annual average of less than 70 inches in Panama City is little more than half of that in Colón, less than forty miles distant across the isthmus.

The dry season in the portions of Central Panama shadowed by the highlands of the Azuero Peninsula lasts some five months, and the annual precipitation of about 50 inches is the country's lowest. It is only in parts of this so-called dry zone that vegetable growth halts entirely toward the end of the dry period. Elsewhere on the

Pacific side of the continental divide, the precipitation in most localities is from 70 to 100 inches, and there are three to four dry months. On the Atlantic side of the continental divide, precipitation is in excess of 100 inches, and the dry season is from two to three months in duration. At higher elevations of the interior, the precipitation is up to 100 inches. It usually falls in the form of drizzle or mist, and the dry season is not well defined. It is largely because of the better defined and longer dry season that the Pacific side of the continental divide is marked by seasonal forest and in places by woodland savanna.

Nowhere in the country is any month entirely free from rain. In March, the driest month in most regions, Panama City customarily records about one-half inch of precipitation, and Colón measures a little more than twice that amount. In November, the rainiest month, both places record precipitation fifteen to twenty times that of March. Although the dry season commences during the Northern Hemisphere's winter, Panamanians sometimes refer to the dry months as summer and to the rainy months as winter.

The relative humidity is notably high everywhere, with year-round averages of 80 percent or higher registered in most localities. In Panama City it varies from the high seventies at the height of the dry season to the mid-eighties during the rainy months. The area around the capital city, most of Central Panama, and a portion of the Chiriquí lowlands near David, however, are less humid than the other parts of the country. These are also the areas of lightest rainfall and the longest dry season and where the dry tropical forests are found.

The course of everyday life in Panama reflects a considerable accommodation to climatic conditions. The high humidity encourages mildew and rapid deterioration of clothing, leather goods, and veneer furniture. Combined with the salt air of the coastal localities where much of the population resides, it attacks metal articles. As a consequence, lights are left burning in closets or other techniques are used to counter the dampness and mildew, and certain kinds of personal and household furnishings and appliances are avoided.

When the rain comes, it falls in torrents, which make a raincoat almost useless; rainwater splashes or seeps inside it, or the garment itself combines with the humidity to drench the unhappy wearer in perspiration. The rain is almost always of limited duration, however, and, when clouds gather, people philosophically take cover and wait until the short storm has passed. In addition, the scheduling of outdoor events at the height of the rainy season is avoided. It is not coincidence that the professional baseball season opens at the beginning of the dry season and that the national open golf tournament is held during the dry month of February.

The tempo of business and social life in Panama City and Colón accelerates considerably at the beginning of the year with the cessation of rainfall and the small but perceptible decline in the humidity. The light showers that fall occasionally during the dry months, however, are insufficient to prevent an increasing dustiness that becomes so pervasive by April that people are ready to welcome the return of the rains.

Soils and Minerals

In the Chiriquí uplands there is a broad strip of rich volcanic earth where most of the country's coffee is produced. Elsewhere in the country, the soils are primarily lateritic and of far lower fertility. The topsoils, usually 6 feet or less in thickness, are moderately friable clays that are rich in organic material, high to moderate in acidity, and low in fertility. Above 800 feet, they are suitable principally for orchards, limited pasture, or forest. The best of the soils outside the Chiriquí uplands are found elsewhere in Chiriquí, in Central Panama, and in the Central Isthmus. Soils in Atlantic Panama and the Darién region are generally poor, and most of the limited amount of farming takes place on alluvial material around the courses of the streams.

Commercial mineral production during the late 1960s was limited to nonmetallics for the construction industry, pottery clays, and solar salt. Gold and silver had been mined extensively in Darién Province during the colonial period and intermittently during the twentieth century in the mountains of Central Panama.

The early hopes of riches in precious metals were never fully realized, and during succeeding periods the country's mines made progressively less significant contributions to the economy. Beginning in the late 1960s, however, a series of mineral discoveries and developments indicated that the riches might, after all, be considerable.

The most significant of these was the investigation concluded in 1969 by a United Nations team at Cerro Petaquilla in Colón Province. The ore, containing 0.2 percent to 4.4 percent copper in an extensive mineralized zone, occurs under a fifty-foot overburden. More recently, exploratory work was in progress at a reportedly large copper-molybdenum porphyry mass in Chiriquí, and a copper deposit in the Cordillera de San Blas was located by the United Nations team.

In mid-1971 magnetite iron ore and ilmenite titanium ore had been reported in beach sands forty miles southwest of Panama City, and manganese in commercially valuable quantities had been

54

found on the Boquerón River in Colón Province. Exploitation of an estimated 76 million tons of bauxite ore in Chiriquí was discouraged by its location under the city of David. Oil seeps in the provinces of Bocas del Toro, Los Santos, and Darién prompted unsuccessful exploratory drillings beginning in 1919. By 1971, however, interest had shifted to offshore possibilities.

Coal in commercially useful accumulations has never been discovered, but subbituminous and lignite deposits are known to exist in Bocas del Toro, in Central Panama, and submerged beneath the waters of Gatún Lake. Limestone is found in Colón Province and elsewhere, and other building materials are widely dispersed. Other minerals known or reported to exist include antimony, arsenic, asbestos, bismuth, cadmium, calcium, cinnabar, graphite, gypsum, hematite iron ore, kaolin, lead and zinc, nickel, platinum, rutile, sulfur, talc, and tin. Semiprecious stones found in limited quantities include agate, jasper, opal, and quartz. As of 1971 little more than 10 percent of the territory had been given thorough geological study, and recent intense prospecting activity indicated a growing belief that a great deal of mineral wealth might still be undiscovered.

Vegetation

About 95 percent of the country was originally forested and, even after centuries of land clearing for cultivation, as much as 85 percent remains either forested, swamp, or otherwise uncultivable land. The natural vegetation zones are the forested mountains, the forested hills and lowlands, the savannas of hills and lowlands, and the coastal mangrove swamps and tidal flats.

Most forests are broadleaf evergreen, occurring at altitudes below 6,500 feet where annual rainfall exceeds eighty inches annually. They cover most of Atlantic Panama, the Central Isthmus, and Darién, as well as parts of the Azuero and Las Palmas peninsulas and of Chiriquí near the Costa Rican border. More than 1,000 varieties of trees have been identified, but most are not well known on world markets and are therefore of limited commercial value. Among the major varieties are brazilwood, tropical cedars, ceiba (which yields pods from which kapok is taken), espavé (a reddish cabinetwood), jacaranda, laurel, lignum vitae, and rosewood. Mahogany is widely dispersed, with perhaps one tree growing in an acre of mixed forest. It is most valuable in Veraguas Province where the rainfall is relatively light.

The broadleaf trees of the humid tropical forest form a thick canopy some 100 feet above the ground, broken at intervals by giants extending to 160 feet or more. Beneath this canopy there is usually a lower tier. The great trees usually grow 20 to 50 feet apart and, because sunlight seldom penetrates to the ground except in the occasional glade, there is little undergrowth. Saplings and a tangle of lianas and vines makes passage through these woodlands extremely difficult, however, and orchids, lichens, and other parasitic growths are abundant on tree trunks.

The commercially useful large trees usually grow at altitudes below 2,000 feet in the humid tropical forest. At higher altitudes the forest is classified as humid-subtropical. Trees are smaller, undergrowth is denser, and many tree ferns grow. Above 6,500 feet in the Cordillera Central there is a deciduous rain forest with many oaks and alders.

Between the true tropical forests and the coastal swamps there is frequently a narrow belt of alluvial soil where many kinds of softwood trees, bamboos, palms, coarse grasses, and tangled vines are found. These lands are cleared more easily than those of the true forest, and small farms are numerous. At low altitudes near the Costa Rican border great banana plantations are located near both Atlantic and Pacific coasts.

In the dry-zone arc of land adjacent to the Gulf of Parita in Central Panama as well as in most of Chiriquí, the dominant type of vegetation is the tropical dry forest interspersed with savannas. Vegetation of this type is also found in a coastal strip that includes Panama City and extends from the vicinity of the town of La Chorrera on the west past the town of Chepo on the east.

This tropical dry forest is made up principally of semideciduous trees that tend to shed their leaves during the dry season, which is longest in this part of the country. Originally, it covered most of Central Panama and Chiriquí, with the exception of natural savannas west of the Gulf of Parita and small highland savannas at the base of the Volcán de Chiriquí. Much of the original cover, however, has been replaced by secondary and later growths resulting from the repeated clearing and burning of the land for shifting agricultural use. In addition, considerable areas have been converted to artificial pasture by the same means. In this region there are also areas where occasional trees are scattered among rough grasses and drought-resistant shrubs, and on alluvial terraces near rivers there are narrow forest galleries made up of trees of the humid-tropical forest.

Bananas and plantains grow along the coastlines, and there are palm trees of many kinds, except where mangrove swamps occur. Coastal mangroves are ubiquitous but most extensive in the provinces of Bocas del Toro and Darién. There are several varieties, and some reach heights up to eighty feet.

Most of the better known tropical fruits are cultivated or grow wild in the forests. Among the principle varieties are the citrus fruits, avocado, papaya, pineapple, mango, guava, banana, plantain, *chirimoya* (a custard apple), and the *nispero,* which resembles the crabapple. Common plants with medicinal qualities include arnica, camomile, lancepod, star apple, tamarind, and wormseed. In addition to indigenous food crops, such as yams and manioc, various introduced varieties grow semiwild in the forests as remnants of formerly cultivated tracts. Several plants yield vegetable dyes that are used locally. Species of flowers are limited in variety, but hibiscus, bougainvillea, and ginger grow in profusion; there are many flowering trees, and the countless kinds of orchid include the *espíritu santo,* the national flower.

Wildlife

The richness in the variety of wildlife species derives from the fact that through the ages the isthmus has been used by animals as a land bridge, and species indigenous to both American continents are found. As a consequence, the preserve maintained by the Smithsonian Institution on Barro Colorado Island in Gatún Lake serves as a unique laboratory for the study of tropical and subtropical American species.

The most frequently encountered predators are members of the cat family (pumas, jaguars, ocelots, and wildcats). Among the animals most often hunted for food are white-tailed deer like those of southern Florida, the peccary or *javalí* (a wild pig), the *conejo pintado* (a nocturnal rodent), the tapir, several varieties of monkey, and a rodent weighing up to eighty pounds called the capybara. The armadillo and various rabbits and squirrels are also native.

Among the amphibians are some highly venomous species and a Darién frog that can swallow prey larger than itself. Reptiles include two kinds of alligators, lizards, and various iguanas, some of which are eaten. Poisonous snakes belong to the viper, coral, and sea snake families. Vipers include the pit viper, fer-de-lance, bushmaster, and tropical rattlesnake. Mango snakes and boa constrictors common to forested areas are not poisonous but can inflict infectious bites. Yellow racer snakes are common but harmless.

Among the hundreds of varieties of tropical birds are macaws, toucans, parrots, hummingbirds, songbirds of various kinds, and numerous aquatic species. The Presidential Palace is known as the Palace of the Herons because of the white herons traditionally kept in its courtyard. Game and food birds include the curassow or wild turkey and migratory and tropical ducks, including the *guichiche,* a long-legged duck that is capable of domestication and is considered to be a delicacy.

Fish are plentiful in streams and in both oceans. The best fishing grounds are in the Gulf of Panama near the Las Perlas Archipelago and in Piña Bay in Darién Province, which boasts some of the world's best game fishing. Salt water species include corvina, grouper, red snapper, and gamefish, such as sailfish, tarpon, and marlin. Trout are stocked in the streams of Chiriquí, and *tucunaré* (tropical game fish), in the streams of Central Panama. Shrimp, spiny lobsters, various kinds of shellfish, and edible sea turtles are also plentiful. Anchovy and herring are taken for the production of fishmeal.

BOUNDARIES AND POLITICAL SUBDIVISIONS

The two international boundaries have been demarcated, and there are no outstanding disputes. The 143-mile boundary with Costa Rica was demarcated in 1944, and the 124-mile boundary with Colombia was demarcated in 1938. The principal features of both frontiers are highland crests, but courses of streams and straight surveyed lines also make up parts of both.

At the midpoint of the Central Isthmus, the country is divided by the Canal Zone. The zone is ten miles in width at most but not all points. It is wider than ten miles on the Atlantic and much narrower on the Pacific where Panama City extends to within a mile of the canal. Its borders extend substantially beyond the regular ten miles to follow a 100-foot contour above the waterlines of Gatún Lake and Madden Reservoir. Except in the vicinities of these artificial bodies of water, the zone's border follows surveyed lines rather than natural features. Because of the special status of the Canal Zone, these lines are not considered international borders.

By the Constitution of 1946 the country claims the sea bottom of the continental shelf, which has been defined by law to extend to the 500-meter submarine contour. In addition, a law of 1958 asserted jurisdiction over a 12-mile limit from the coasts, and since 1967 a 200-mile perimeter has been claimed.

Internally, the country is divided into nine provinces, plus the San Blas Territory (Comarca), which, in most of the country's official documents, is treated for statistical purposes as a part of Colón Province. The provincial borders, which have been unchanged since the country's birth, are defined from east to west principally by the continental divide and from north to south principally by the courses of streams.

The provinces are divided into districts that, in turn, are divided into sections called *corregimientos*. Configurations of these subdivisions are changed frequently to accommodate changes in population concentration. The population census of 1970 reflects several changes in both districts and *corregimientos* made since the 1960 census.

POPULATION STRUCTURE AND DYNAMICS

The country in 1970 had a population of 1,425,343, as reported provisionally from the population census conducted during that year. Earlier censuses had shown the population to have been 622,576 in 1940, 805,285 in 1950, and 1,075,541 in 1960 (see table 1). The average annual rate of growth increased from 2.54 percent between 1940 and 1950 to 2.94 percent between 1950 and 1960 and to 3.04 percent between 1960 and 1970. For the year 1970 it was estimated at about 3.4 percent, and the population for 1971 was estimated at almost 1.5 million.

Throughout the country's independent history males have outnumbered females by an ever-decreasing margin; males were recorded at 51 percent of the population in the 1960 census. The provisional 1970 census data did not include information on population distribution by sex. According to a United Nations estimate, however, the proportion of males had declined to 50.3 percent by 1969. Both the male preponderance and its decline result principally from the once considerable but progressively declining flow of predominately male immigrants. A second influence has been the decline in the incidence of deaths from childbirth as a factor in female mortality.

The reported birth rate dropped irregularly from 37.4 per 1,000 in 1941 to 33.8 in 1950 before rising sharply to 41 in 1960. Thereafter, it declined to 37.9 per 1,000 in 1969.

Birth rates are higher in rural than in urban localities, a worldwide phenomenon that reflects an inverse ratio between birth rates and the universally higher urban levels of education and income. In 1969 the reported urban and rural birth rates were 34.3 and 41.2 per 1,000 of the population, respectively. The higher rural birth rate can also be measured by the 1960 child-woman ratio of 927 in rural and 554 in urban localities. The child-woman ratio is defined by the United Nations as the number of children under the age of five per 1,000 women in the child-bearing age group from fifteen to forty-nine years. The significance of the higher rural rates as a factor in population distribution can, however, be easily overemphasized—many women migrate from country to town after having given birth to their children, but there is no evidence of any offsetting reverse migration.

The reported general death rate declined sharply from more than 13 per 1,000 in 1941 to 8.4 in 1952, a function largely of the

Table 1. Population of Panama by Provinces, Censuses for Selected Years, 1911–70

Province	Actual Population						
	1911	1920	1930	1940	1950	1960	1970 [1]
Bocas del Toro	22,732	27,239	15,851	16,523	22,392	32,600	40,776
Coclé	35,011	45,151	48,244	55,737	73,103	93,156	117,949
Colón [2]	32,092	58,250	57,161	78,119	90,144	105,416	134,311
Chiriquí	63,364	76,470	76,918	111,206	138,136	188,350	236,256
Darién	8,992	10,728	13,391	14,930	14,660	19,715	22,627
Herrera	23,007	28,984	31,030	38,118	50,095	61,672	72,492
Los Santos	30,075	34,638	41,218	49,621	61,422	70,554	72,212
Panama	61,855	98,035	114,103	173,328	248,335	372,393	576,866
Veraguas	59,614	66,603	69,543	84,994	106,998	131,685	151,854
TOTAL	336,742	446,098	467,459	622,576	805,285	1,075,541	1,425,343

Province	Actual Increase (rate per thousand inhabitants)					
	1911 to 1920	1920 to 1930	1930 to 1940	1940 to 1950	1950 to 1960	1960 to 1970
Bocas del Toro	20.3	55.6	4.0	30.1	38.3	24.1
Coclé	28.7	6.6	13.9	26.8	24.5	25.4
Colón [2]	68.5	-1.9	30.3	14.1	15.8	26.1
Chiriquí	21.1	0.6	35.8	21.4	31.5	24.3
Darién	19.8	22.4	10.4	-1.8	30.1	14.8
Herrera	26.0	6.8	19.8	27.0	21.0	17.3
Los Santos	15.8	17.5	17.9	21.0	14.0	2.4
Panama	52.5	15.3	40.7	35.7	41.3	47.6
Veraguas	12.4	4.3	19.3	22.7	21.0	15.2
TOTAL	31.7	4.7	27.7	25.4	29.4	30.4

[1] Preliminary data.
[2] Including San Blas Territory.
Source: Adapted from Republic of Panama, Contraloría General de la República, Dirección de Estadística y Censo, *Panamá en cifras* (*Compendio Estadístico, años 1965 a 1969*). Panama City, 1970, p.10.

increased use of antibiotics during World War II and the immediate postwar years. It was at somewhat higher levels during the remaining years of the 1950s before declining irregularly to 7.3 per 1,000 in 1969.

In 1952 the country's vital statistics system was revised to improve the collection and refinement of data. The apparently sharp increase in the birth rate and the interruption in the decline of the death rate that was reported during the early 1950s are probably a reflection more of the success of this program than of an actual change in trends concerning vital statistics. Reporting in 1965, a group of Panamanian authorities stated that birth data assembled during the early 1960s were substantially complete but that mortality figures should still be regarded as deficient. Concurring in both of these judgments, demographers for the United Nations accepted as accurate the data on births included in that organization's *Demographic Yearbook, 1969* but estimated that mortality figures for that period were as much as one-third below the real level.

The median age of the population declined from 19.3 years in 1950 to 18.3 in 1960 and was estimated at less than 17.2 years at the beginning of 1970. In 1960 the median ages of the urban and rural sectors were 20.6 and 16.4 years, respectively, a reflection of the higher rural birth rate coupled with a heavy country-to-town migration of young adults. Between 1961 and 1970 the proportion of the population under the age of 15 was estimated to have increased from 43.4 percent to 44.3 percent of the total, although in all other age brackets the proportion decreased. Although the continued reduction in the mortality rate during the period resulted in a substantial gain in the actual number of elderly people, it was insufficient to offset the increasing number of births coupled with the decline in infant and child mortality. As a consequence, the proportion aged 65 and over moved downward from 3.6 to 3.3 percent of the total.

As of 1970 the most recent data available concerning life expectancy at time of birth were United Nations estimates for 1960 and 1961 that showed the expectancy to be 57.6 years for males and 60.8 years for females. For members of both sexes who survived early infancy, expectancies at the age of 1 year were about 4 years higher. At more advanced ages, expectancies were progressively lower.

MIGRATION AND SETTLEMENT PATTERNS

Between 1958 and 1965 an average of about 750 persons per year entered the country documented as immigrants. In 1966 the number entering in this category dropped sharply to 194, and by 1969 a further drop to 97 was recorded. The decline after 1965, however, reflected not an actual falling off in immigration but the enactment of legislation permitting persons who had entered with temporary documentation to acquire immigrant status while in Panama.

Specific data on numbers of emigrants are not available, but a consistent and substantial excess in reported departures from the country over reported arrivals during recent years suggests a considerable net emigration. From 1965 through 1969 all departures exceeded all arrivals by margins ranging from 5,000 to 47,100 annually and totaled more than 125,000 during the five-year period.

A flood of immigration during the first years after independence was made up primarily of Jamaicans and other West Indians arriving for work connected with the construction of the Panama Canal. Immigration later declined somewhat but remained substantial until the beginning of World War II and, immediately after the war, a limited effort was made to attract displaced farmers from Europe. No special legislation for the promotion of immigration was enacted, however, and a scanty immigrant flow gravitated to urban centers rather than to the countryside.

In 1971 the most recently available data concerning the composition of the foreign-born sector of the population were based on the census of 1960, when 4.4 percent of the population had been born abroad. The proportion had shown an unbroken decline from a high of 11.6 percent registered in 1911. The relatively advanced age of the foreign-born sector in 1960 also bore witness to a progressive decline in immigration. Some 30.6 percent of the foreign-born and only 5.6 percent of the population as a whole were sixty years of age or older. Conversely, 25 percent of the population as a whole and only 12.5 percent of the foreign-born were between the ages of fifteen and twenty-nine years.

In 1960 a large majority of the people who had come to the country as immigrants resided in urban areas. They made up 12.9 and 6.5 percent, respectively, of the heavily urbanized provinces of Colón and Panama. In Chiriquí Province they made up 1.5 percent, and in the four predominately rural provinces of Central Panama they made up a fraction of 1 percent. They did, however, represent more than 15 percent in the scantily settled frontier provinces of Bocas del Toro and Darién.

Since World War II the settlement pattern of Panama, like that of other Latin American countries, has been changed radically by a massive migration of people from rural to urban localities. Preliminary 1970 census data show 48 percent of the population to

have been urban, slightly more than the 47.3 that had been pre-
dicted for the year 1975 by an international population studies
organization only two years earlier. Earlier censuses had shown
the urban sector to have included 36 percent of the population in
1950 and 41.5 percent in 1960.

The urban proportion in 1970 might be reported as higher still
were it not for the strictness of the Panamanian definition of an
urban locality. In order to qualify as urban, the locality must have
a population of at least 1,500 together with urban characteristics,
such as electric lights, public water and sewerage service, commercial and communications facilities, sidewalks, and a secondary
school. In 1970 some thirty-three places were determined to have
met these requirements. In 1960 the most heavily urbanized provinces had been Panama, with 77.7 percent, and Colón, with 56.5
percent. In Veraguas two urban localities had represented 9 percent of the population, and in Darién Province there had been no
urban localities.

Country-to-town migration has flowed primarily toward the
urban localities of the Central Isthmus. So important is the urban
portion of this region that for official statistical purposes it has
been designated as the Metropolitan Area, and the remainder of
Panama is known as the "rest of the country" (resto del país).
The Metropolitan Area consists of the cities and districts of
Panama and Colón, together with seven largely urban adjacent
districts including the towns of La Chorrera and Arraiján in
Panama Province. Between 1960 and 1970 its population increased
from 40 percent to 46 percent of the country's total.

By far the most important focus of urban concentration is
Panama City itself. Between 1950 and 1960 the city's population
increased from 127,874 to 294,359. By 1970 it had grown to
418,013, or almost two-thirds of the entire urban population. The
phenomenal growth between 1950 and 1960 had been accomplished
in large measure by annexation of nine adjacent suburbs that had
already been rated as urban localities. The rapid additional growth
between 1960 and 1970, however, was accomplished without further territorial annexations, and the collective growth rate of the
corregimientos of Panama District remaining outside the city
limits exceeded that of the city.

With a 1970 population of 67,641, Colón remained the country's
second largest city, but its growth from 52,204 in 1950 and 59,598
in 1960 had been of a rate less than that of the country as a whole
and substantially less than that of the urban sector. The city's
ability to grow, however, is physically restricted by its location
in the middle of the Canal Zone on an island connected with the
mainland of the zone by a causeway. The corregimientos of Colón

District located outside the city grew much faster than that of the city itself.

Even the largest of the urban centers outside the Metropolitan Area retain the characteristics of market towns. The most important of these is David in Chiriquí, with a population that increased from 22,924 in 1960 to 35,538 in 1970. Of the remaining urban centers, nearly all located in Chiriquí and Central Panama, only Puerto Armuelles in Chiriquí, Chitré in Herrera, and Santiago in Veraguas had 1970 populations in excess of 10,000.

Continuing urbanization has had the effect of making the more heavily populated provinces grow faster than the lightly populated ones. There has been no important shift in the relative densities of rural settlement patterns, however, and the relative sizes of populations of the provinces have undergone little alteration during the years since independence.

A small proportion of the rural population is settled in nuclear villages of some density or in relatively compact aggregates of houses strung along roads. Most of it, however, is scattered about the countryside, and there are no clearly defined areas where village living is exclusively the custom and where no isolated one-family farms are found. Settlement along the coast and on streams is common principally in the Atlantic Panama and Darién regions where roads are virtually nonexistent.

The settlement pattern of Panama differs sharply from that of other Central American countries and from most of Latin America in general, to the extent that the highlands of its interior have remained almost uninhabited. In all parts of the country the more heavily populated areas are found at altitudes below 1,500 feet. Some settlement at higher altitudes has taken place since about 1920 in intermont depressions in the vicinity of the Volcán de Chiriquí, but the mountain slopes of the Atlantic Panama and Darién regions remain empty, and in eastern Chiriquí and Central Panama the frontier of settlement remains well below the heights of the continental divide.

The reluctance to take advantage of the pleasanter mountain climate has been attributed to the heavy forest cover of the highlands and the fact that the Spanish settlers who set a pattern for the future were attracted to the savannas of the Pacific lowlands where the countryside resembled that of their homeland. More important has been the continuing significance of the narrow waist of the isthmus. It was first the site of Indian trails, second of the Gold Road of the conquistadores, third of the railroad, and finally of the canal and the transisthmian highway. In other countries the population moved naturally into the high interior, where agricultural lands were better and there was freedom from sea marauders. Uninviting climate, the incursions of Sir Henry Morgan and Sir Francis Drake, and the lack of agricultural promise of what was to become the Central Isthmus were insufficient to prevent the development of that critically important focus of trade as the political and economic center. There was no chance for a political and economic center to develop in the highlands and, without such a center, the agricultural hinterland of Panama developed in lowland areas with relatively ready access to the Central Isthmus (see ch. 2, Historical Setting).

The dynamics of settlement in Panama have also been different from those in other Central American countries to the extent that the years since World War II have not been marked by a settlement of the lowlands of the Atlantic coast. In 1970 Atlantic Panama's 5 percent of the country's population represented a proportion slightly lower than that of 1950. Climate and soils of this region are generally uninviting, existing urban localities to serve as staging points for settlement movements are few, and roads are nonexistent.

Elsewhere in Central America similarly natural conditions prevailed, yet surplus population has spilled out of heavily populated highland regions down to the Atlantic plain. In Panama the mountains were themselves almost uninhabited, and the highlands of the continental divide represented a barrier rather than a starting point for migration toward the Atlantic coast.

In 1971 it appeared unlikely that the long-established pattern of rural population distribution was likely to shift. There was no discernible reverse-migration from town to country and, although there was considerable inter-rural migration from one place to another, none of it seemed likely to disturb the rural pattern of settlement.

Since World War II succeeding political administrations have attempted to provide land for farmers, but this resettling has not involved a change in the overall pattern of settlement. A government land reform program begun in 1963 had resulted in the distribution of lands to about 1,800 families by the end of 1968, and fragmentary data indicated an acceleration of the program after that date. The thrust of the program, however, was directed principally toward making land available to squatters or renters, who in 1960 had made up six out of seven of the farm operators. The farms distributed were generally in parts of the country already extensively farmed, and there was no particular aspect of the program directed toward the opening of frontier regions of Atlantic Panama and Darién.

A relatively small part of the migration that takes place between rural areas is by itinerant farm workers. A much larger part involves the sporadic migration of squatters who clear small plots of land, farm them for several years until the soil is exhausted, and then move on to other places. Very little information is available concerning this inter-rural migration, except to the extent that it involves a transfer of residence from one province to another. The 1960 census showed that 19.7-percent of the rural people, as compared with 34.5 percent of the urban people, were not natives of the province in which they were residing.

In general, it appears that a large part of the migrant population relocating from one rural locality to another is often a semi-transient one but that those who move from country to town usually remain as permanent residents. Among the people counted in the 1960 census who had migrated from another locality, 53.4 percent of the urban population, as compared with 34.6 percent of the rural inhabitants, had been residents of the locality for ten years or more. Conversely, 10 percent of the urban population and 14.6 percent of the rural people had been residents for one year or less.

Migration from country to town, however, comes in stages. Only 51.5 percent of the migrant urban population in 1960 had come from rural localities. Some 30.6 percent had come from another urban place; and the remainder, from the Canal Zone, from abroad, or from an unidentified place of origin. Details concerning this intra-urban movement are not available, but it apparently consisted of a movement from the smaller urban places of the interior to Panama City or elsewhere in the Metropolitan Area.

The migrant population tends to be young. The 1960 census showed the median age of persons who had migrated from another locality was twenty-nine years, substantially higher than the median for the country as a whole. Small children seldom engage in migration, however, and most of those counted in 1960 had already resided in their place of residence for several years. The census summary carried the notation that, during the previous fifty years, most of the internal migrants had been between the ages of fifteen and thirty.

Of the several factors causing people to migrate, the search for employment is undoubtedly the most important and, because of the relatively small number of female employment opportunities in rural localities, most of the urban migrants are young women. In the 1960 census female migrants were found to outnumber males by a proportion of 100 to 89 in the country as a whole, but the ratio was 100 to 82 in heavily urbanized Panama Province, where increasing numbers of jobs were becoming available for women in industry, commerce, and domestic service. Most of the migrants to rural localities, however, were male. In the predominantly rural frontier provinces of Bocas del Toro and Darién, the ratio of male to female migrants was greater than 100 to 70.

POPULATION PROBLEMS

An announced aim of the government's land reform program has been a slowing of the country-to-town migration that has been proceeding at a pace too fast to permit effective development of the country's agricultural potential. In addition, this migration has had the effect of heightening the intensity of such urban problems as those involving increased demand for housing and public and social services. Panama in 1971, however, was less densely populated than many countries of Latin America and, although the geographical distribution of the population was a cause for some concern, nationwide population pressure was still distant.

A much more immediate problem involved the extreme youth of the people. Between 1961 and 1970 the population dependency ratio climbed from 88.7 to 90.9 and, with constant fertility as of 1970, would rise to 96.2 by the year 2000. The dependency ratio is defined as the number of persons in the dependent age groups (under the age of fourteen, and sixty-five years and over) per 100 persons in the economically productive age bracket of fourteen through sixty-four years.

A rise in the dependency ratio results in an added burden for the economically active age sector. In Panama the effect of this rise is being accentuated by the removal of large numbers of persons over sixty-five from the labor force through retirement under the expanding social security program and, more important, the deferral of the entry into the labor force of a rapidly increasing proportion of young people over fourteen who are staying in school for additional years (see ch. 4, Living Conditions; ch. 7, Education, Culture, and Public Information).

Organized family planning that might lead to a lowering of the dependency ratio in Panama commenced early in 1966 with establishment of the Panamanian Family Planning Association—a private organization that by 1969 had established six family planning clinics. During 1968 its modest record of services rendered included 4,730 first-visit contraceptive services and 9,114 follow-up consultations. The organization, which receives assistance from the International Planned Parenthood Federation, in late 1969 transferred three of its clinics to the Ministry of Public Health. The ministry, at this time, announced plans for opening twelve additional clinics.

CHAPTER 4

LIVING CONDITIONS

In Panama City and Colón, and to a lesser degree in the other urban localities, the conditions under which people lived during 1971 differed sharply from those prevailing on the farms and in villages, where traditional values and practices persisted. In rural areas transportation, markets, and recreational facilities were few; housing was primitive; and public services were almost non-existent. In urban places a generally prosperous people purchased a wide variety of goods and services; in the countryside a majority derived their livelihood from farming at, or close to, the subsistence level.

For most of the urban half of the population, the quality of life was profoundly influenced by the existence of the great interoceanic canal. The visits of countless businessmen and travelers of all nationalities brought to the isthmus by the canal and the nearby presence of the prosperous North American population of the Canal Zone combined to give life in urban Panama a cosmopolitan flavor.

DIET AND NUTRITION

Composition and adequacy of the diet vary substantially by locality and by level of income, but Panamanians are generally well fed. The per capita daily availability of food for consumption increased from 2,330 calories in 1960 to 2,484 in 1967. Protein availability rose from 58.5 to 64.7 grams daily, and fats rose from 49.7 to 54.4 grams. The series quoted did not include direct consumption figures. Data from another source showed per capita caloric intake to have risen further to 2,564 units in 1969. The figure was well above the 2,000 calories considered by many nutritionists to represent minimum requirements. In the mid-1960s, however, a low average intake of calcium, vitamin A, and riboflavin was reported, and nearly one-fourth of all children under the age of fifteen were said to be suffering from varying degrees of malnutrition.

It was estimated in 1967 that Panama produced between 85 and 90 percent of her food requirements by value. This proportion gave the country a degree of self-sufficiency in food approximately the same as that of Brazil, Ecuador, Peru, and Uruguay.

Cereals in 1967 provided over half of the calories and nearly half of the protein content in the diet. Rice, by a wide margin the most important cereal staple, was followed by corn and by wheat, the principal food import item. The consumption of tubers and root crops was negligible. White potatoes appear only on tables of the urban well to do, and the sweet potatoes and manioc that are important food items elsewhere in Latin America are seldom seen.

Green vegetables are of importance only in the terminal cities (Panama City and Colón). In the country as a whole, tomatoes are the most popular and are followed in order by onions and garlic, lettuce, cabbage, carrots, and red peppers. The wide variety of tropical fruits grown locally are less prized than imported temperate zone species, but consumption of fruits far outmatches that of green vegetables. They appear most frequently as desserts at meals. Bananas and plantains, eaten extensively by lower income groups, represent about half of all fruit consumption. Citrus fruit, pineapples, and avocados are also popular, but there is a traditional prejudice against papayas, which are regarded as unsuitable food for well-bred persons.

Meat consumption varies by locality and income group. It is generally moderate and represents only about one-fifth of the protein intake. Most Panamanians are able to afford some meat, however, and the per capita consumption of beef, the most popular variety, rose sharply from twenty-eight pounds annually in 1950 to forty-five pounds in 1970. Pork is second among meats in popularity, and most rural families keep poultry. Most of the small chicken and egg consumption, however, is urban. Pasteurized milk represents a little less than half of the entire milk production. Its use is limited except among prosperous urban families. A high proportion of the milk produced is used in cooking or conversion into cheese. Butter is available at moderate price, but its consumption is negligible in rural localities.

Fish provides about 8 percent of the protein in the diet, but consumption is concentrated in the terminal cities. About two-thirds of the catch—consisting almost entirely of salt water species—is consumed fresh; the balance is divided about equally between shellfish and fish products. Corvina is first in popularity.

Some *chicha* is fermented from corn, and palm wine is occasionally drunk, but beer is the national beverage. The National Brewery Company is the country's largest private employer, and the 1967 production of beer available for domestic consumption was about equal to the availability of all nonalcoholic bottled beverages combined.

In the polyglot cities of Panama and Colón a cosmopolitan cuisine is found, and a wide variety of foods generally comparable with that in urban centers of North America is available. Meat is customarily not aged and is of only fair quality, but cuts can be obtained in far greater variety than in most parts of Latin America, and the variety and quality of the seafood available are excellent.

In the countryside the variety of food available is limited—particularly in the households of the many subsistence farmers. Except in the areas with direct access to fish, game, and cattle, most of the protein must come from vegetable sources, frequently from kidney beans, which are an almost daily feature of the diet. They appear most frequently cooked with rice as *guacho*, a national dish. Rice in some form appears at least once a day on the tables of the urban well to do as well as of the rural poor. For many lower income people in town as well as in country, rice may be the only item on the luncheon menu.

National dishes are few in number and generally similar to those found elsewhere in Central America. Among the most nearly universal is a meat and vegetable stew called *sancocho*. *Ropa vieja* (literally, old clothes) is shredded beef that is boiled and mixed with onions, garlic, tomatoes, and peppers and served with rice or manioc. *Guacamole* is a spread made from avocados, and *ceviche* is made by marinating raw fish in lemon juice. For many rural people the thin corn pancakes called *tortillas* take the place of bread. *Empanadas* are pastries filled with meat. A colorfully named dessert, *sopa borracha* (drunken soup), is sponge cake soaked in rum.

DRESS

Urban men who can afford to do so customarily dress in wash-and-wear suits of lightweight materials, usually in dark colors. These have largely replaced the white cotton suits that in an earlier day were worn with four-in-hand ties during the day and with black bow ties for more formal evening wear. Well-to-do women wear lightweight fabrics in styles not discernibly different from those of North America. Slacks are accepted, but shorts are seldom worn on the street.

Status is an important factor in determination of urban dress, and elegance and formality are of compelling importance to the emerging middle class. Anxious to make evident a distinction between his appearance and that of manual workers, the white-collar worker does not often discard his coat and tie. Men of the working class dress more comfortably in inexpensive open-necked shirts and cotton trousers. These costumes, and the washable cotton frocks worn by their wives, are readily within the means of most working class people.

Rural clothing patterns do not differ materially from the urban, except that coats and ties are less frequently worn even by the upper class rural persons. Working garments are often put together at home, but the traditional home weaving of clothing materials has been almost entirely discontinued. Farmers tend to wear wide-brimmed strawhats and to go barefoot in the fields, but in 1971 these customs of dress could no longer be cited as invariable habits of rural people. Similarly, the San Blas Indian women still wear colorful indigenous costumes, but their number was relatively so small that in 1971 the significance of their costumes was of real importance principally to students of their culture and to the tourist trade.

The national costume is the *pollera* for women and *montuno* for men; a simpler form of the woman's dress is the *montuna* (see ch. 7, Education, Culture, and Public Information). These decorative garments are worn for fancy dress only, but a great many men have *montunos*, and the *pollera* is considered an essential part of the female wardrobe.

HOUSING

Preliminary data from the 1970 census show that there were 287,571 housing units occupied in the country as compared with 219,420 in 1960, an increase of 31 percent. Between 1960 and 1970 the population increased by 32.5 percent. During the intercensal period the rate of housing construction was higher in rural than in urban localities.

The average occupancy rate in 1970 was about five persons per unit, but the units themselves were small and crowded. Official data for 1961 found that one-room units constituted 47 percent of the total in the country and less than 5 percent consisted of five or more rooms. There were three or more occupants per room in 38 percent of the urban, and 50 percent of the rural, dwellings.

The country's housing shortage is both quantitative and qualitative. The 1960 census found that by the country's own standards 61 percent of all housing units were deficient to some extent, a majority of these because of lacking or inadequate sanitary facilities. In addition, at the end of 1966 the Union of Industrialists of Panama—a management association—estimated the overall housing shortage at 154,000 units.

In 1961, as reported by a government agency, some 86.4 percent of the rural housing units were owner occupied, but 68.3 percent of the urban units were rented. In both rural and urban sectors, a small proportion of the units were occupied on some basis other than ownership or tenancy. The proportion of rental units is highest in the terminal cities. In 1960 it represented some 75 percent of the total in Panama City and more than 94 percent in Colón, where the lack of available space for new construction prevented newcomers from the countryside from solving the rental problem by erecting the squatter shanties that were proliferating around Panama City during the 1960s. Many of the squatter units may not have been included in the available statistical series.

In 1961 some 64.5 percent of the housing units in the country as a whole were individual dwellings, 9 percent were apartments, and 26.4 percent were rooms in other dwellings of collective establishments called *casas de vecindad* (literally, neighborhood houses). Units of this kind differ from apartment units in that they do not have individual sanitary facilities. Equipped only with communal water supplies and toilets, these slum tenements are almost entirely urban phenomena.

Casas de vecindad are concentrated in the center of Colón and in downtown neighborhoods of Panama City, such as Chorillo, Calidonia, and Santa Ana. Their replacement is a major target of the government's housing program, and during the 1960s only a small number were constructed despite their relatively low cost. In 1967 it was estimated that the average cost of building a unit in a *casa de vecindad* in Panama District was B/1,312 (B/1 equals US$1) as compared with B/6,636 for an apartment unit and B/9,004 for a separate dwelling.

These tenements are usually flimsily constructed of wood with two or three stories and common balconies running the length of each floor. The household units, seldom more than a single room in size, are frequently so crowded that cooking and other activities are accomplished in makeshift kitchens on the balconies, shielded from rain and wind by a sheet of galvanized iron or some other material. The communal showers and toilets are housed in dark corners of the tenements. The *casas de vecindad* constitute fire hazards, and the fact that more of them have not burned testifies to the great efficiency of the corps of firemen.

The centrally located tenements are occupied by persons with downtown employment and by those with occupations nearby in the Canal Zone. New arrivals from the countryside and others who cannot afford housing in even these marginal rental properties frequently erect makeshift squatter dwellings of scrap materials. Often erected overnight, these dwellings are called *casa brujas* (witch houses), and the shantytowns in which they are clustered are called *barrios de emergencia* (emergency settlements).

Confined largely to Panama City, they are located in the fast-growing outlying sections of the city and strung out along the route of the transisthmian highway. It was estimated in 1970 that some 7,800 families lived in these squatter settlements that have been the products of rapid urban growth during the years since World War II.

Middle-class housing construction is usually of masonry or other fireproof material with tiled roofs and floors. Most units are small chalets and units in small apartment houses. Some high-rise apartment buildings were constructed in close-in areas during the 1950s and 1960s, but the bulk of the considerable amount of construction was in the suburbs of Panama City. Most middle class families rent their houses unfurnished, and a substantial portion of their income is spent on prestige appliances, such as refrigerators, washing machines, radios, and television sets. The possession of a full bathroom is a hallmark of middle-class status in housing, but in even the most expensive dwellings showers are used rather than tubs.

Owner occupancy is customary principally among the very well to do in the terminal cities. There are a few mansions, but in general even the largest homes are not ornate, and seldom do they exceed two stories in height. Materials used in construction are similar to those used in the better middle class homes.

Casas de vecindad and *casas brujas* are rarely found in the towns of the interior, but simple mud dwellings with dirt floors are common. The newer and more substantial homes are customarily of masonry or other fireproof material, with tile floors and roofing. The average cost of construction during the 1960s was considerably below that prevailing for single-family units in the cities of Panama and Colón.

The rural home serves not only as a residential unit but also as a workshop and storage point. Aside from variations in construction that reflect economic status, the domestic establishment is more or less uniform in its design. In dense roadside and village settlements the house is placed at the front of the yard and is connected with neighboring houses, hiding from the passer-by the rear where latrines, kitchens, and other outbuildings and work areas are aligned along the rear boundaries of the yard. In the dispersed farmstead, the residence is usually in the center of the clearing, with outbuildings and work areas distributed more or less at random. Depending upon the amount of livestock and on variations in regional style and individual taste, the yard may or may not be enclosed by a fence.

74

The typical rural dwelling is either a *rancho,* an impermanent structure with cane walls and thatched roof with packed dirt floors, or a house made of *quincha* (wattle and daub). The more solidly built *quincha* home may have tile roofing and floors and is found closer to roads in more prosperous neighborhoods. It is also sometimes found in towns. The *rancho* is the typical residence of the seminomadic subsistence farmer.

The two types of dwelling are characteristic of rural localities on the Pacific side of the continental divide. On the Atlantic, in Bocas del Toro Province, wooden construction predominates in rural areas, and in Colón Province houses are of wooden or fireproof materials.

The *quincha* and *rancho* houses are identical in their basic plans, which include a rectangular floor and a framework of hard, termite-resistant posts, with twigs and cane stalks interwoven to form a curtainlike wall. Frequently the roof is extended to form a porch. In *quincha* houses, the walls are finished with a coating of clay. In villages and more compact settlements, the house is often divided by a partition separating the interior into a bedroom and a parlor. To provide additional floorspace, a cane ceiling may be constructed to form an attic that serves as a granary or an additional bedroom. Yards are usually kept free of most vegetation to avoid insects, snakes, and other common pests, but many have a hibiscus bush or some other decorative plant.

The countryman's home furnishings are customarily either obtainable from local sources or are a product of his own labor and ingenuity. Seating is provided by a variety of benches and stools made of crude planking or logs. Leather-seated chairs are also made. The bed is usually either a canvas cot or a platform of poles supported on short legs and frequently covered with a woven straw mat or a piece of hide. Many homes have hammocks used by children for sleeping and used by others as resting places during lulls in the daytime routine.

In more prosperous homes the parlor may contain a piece or two of commercially made furniture, and it usually is decorated with lithographs of the Sacred Heart or calendars obtained from merchants.

The kitchen is usually a separate hut without walls but with loft space for storage. Equipment kept in the kitchen includes pottery jugs, cooking pots, gourds, plates and knives, kerosine tins in various stages of readaptation, and a large pottery jug in which drinking water is kept. There is also a grinding stone and wooden mortar for the preparation of cornmeal. Cooking is done over an open wood fire, in pots supported on tripods of stone. Above the fire is a shelf on which the salt is kept to protect it from the humidity. Storerooms, workshops, and outhouses are also separate from the main dwelling. Less than half of the rural houses, however, have toilet facilities of any kind.

Lighting is almost invariably provided by kerosine lamps. Domestic electricity is usually available only in urban localities; its availability is, in fact, one of the census requirements that a locality must meet in order to be defined as urban (see ch. 3, Physical Environment and Population). In 1960 some 90 percent of the rural, as compared with 17 percent of the urban, housing units were without electric lighting.

During the late 1960s the private sector accounted for 75 percent or more of all new housing construction. Public sector residential construction is primarily the responsibility of the Institute for Housing and Urbanization (Instituto de Vivienda y Urbanismo—IVU), which was established as an autonomous agency in 1958 and reorganized in 1960. According to IVU reports, some 5,657 units for low and moderate income families were constructed from 1967 through 1970. Total investment in the program at the end of 1969 was B/12.3 million, including B/7.3 million from external sources.

IVU activities are concentrated in urban localities, particularly in Panama City where the housing shortage is the most acute. During the late 1960s the IVU programs were aimed at low income groups earning less than B/80 monthly and moderate income groups earning between B/80 and B/200. Programs include financing of low-cost individual units, high-rise buildings, mortgage and loan guarantees, and initiation of housing cooperatives. Supplementing the activities of the IVU, the Insured Mortgage Development Institute, founded in 1963, encourages lending by the savings and loan associations.

In rural localities the Panamanian Cooperative Housing Foundation, a private nonprofit entity, works to promote and organize housing cooperatives. At the end of 1969 it had made possible the construction of 155 units, and fifty-five were under consruction in 1970. The homes are of the shell type and cost less than B/500 per unit.

PATTERNS OF LIVING AND LEISURE

Holidays and Business Hours

Sundays are days of rest. The national holidays are New Year's Day (January 1), Constitution Day (March 1), Labor Day (May 1), Columbus Day (October 12), Day of Independence from Colombia (November 3), Day of Independence from Spain (November 28), and Christmas (December 25). November 3, regarded as the true independence day, is celebrated with a verve not matched on November 28.

Work virtually ceases during Carnival—the four days that precede Ash Wednesday—and in the terminal cities those official United States holidays not observed in the Republic are marked by a slowing in the tempo of business activity. Local religious holidays are celebrated in various parts of the interior; the festivals of Candelaria in February and San José in March are the most generally observed. In addition, there are secular festival days, such as the opening of the professional baseball season in December and of the bullfight season in January.

Business hours vary. Formerly, public and some private offices observed the *jornado único* (single day) in which the working day was uninterrupted and concluded in time for a late luncheon. Afternoon business hours have become general, but a long *siesta* luncheon break is sometimes observed. The business day starts as early as 7:00 A.M. and concludes between 4:30 P.M. and 6:00 P.M. Except in the cases of government offices and banks, Saturdays are considered regular days of work.

In 1971 the question of exactly at what time business houses were required to close was a matter of lively debate. Legislation dating from 1963 prescribed a mandatory closing hour of not later than 6:00 P.M. in Panama City. Restaurants and places furnishing entertainment were excepted from the requirement, but there appeared to be general dissatisfaction with it, and the law's constitutionality with respect to such establishments as pharmacies and shops in hotels was under sharp question.

Consumption Patterns

Times were generally prosperous during the 1960s, and people had progressively greater amounts of money to spend for consumption. Between 1962 and 1967 the per capita national income increased from B/357 to B/477, a gain of better than 33 percent. During the same period the consumer cost of living index rose by no more than 5 percent.

Private consumption expenditures during 1967 for the traditionally essential expense categories of food and drink, housing and housing-related costs, and clothing included nearly three-quarters of all consumption expenses (see table 2).

Data on consumption patterns by income group are scattered and available only for the urban sector. Figures collected for 1962 but still used in 1970 in publications of international organizations show food and beverage consumption expenditures of low income families to have represented proportions of income twice those of high income families. Clothing and housing-related costs, however, were highest for the middle class; it was in this category that display expenditure demonstrating middle class status was most significant.

In general, the available data reflect a pattern characteristic of a prosperous population in which food and drink expenditure is relatively low and clothing and housing-related expenditure is relatively high. In addition, the data show a proportion of Panamanian income available for entertainment or for miscellaneous expenses substantially higher than the average for countries of Latin America.

Table 2. Composition of Private Consumption Expenditures in Panama, 1967

(in millions of balboas) [1]

	Amount	Percent
Food	202.7	35.44
Beverages	33.4	5.84
Tobacco	12.1	2.11
Clothing	44.2	7.72
Rent, water, fuel, and light	65.9	11.52
Furnishings and household operation	69.4	12.13
Health and hygiene	29.0	5.07
Transport and communications	53.3	9.32
Entertainment	47.7	8.34
Miscellaneous services	14.1	2.46
TOTAL	571.8	99.95 [2]

[1] 1 balboa equals US$1.
[2] Does not add to 100 percent because of rounding.

Source: Adapted from Economic Intelligence Unit, *Quarterly Economic Review: Central America, Annual Supplement, 1970*, London, 1970, p. 44.

Recreation

The wide difference between living conditions in urban and in rural localities may be the most evident in the availability of recreational outlets. In cities and towns they are abundant and in large measure are commercialized; in the countryside they are relatively few and are largely informal byproducts of work or of family or communal gatherings.

In urban localities team sports that attract large crowds of spectators are immensely popular. North American influence is strong, for baseball is far ahead of any other sport in popularity, and basketball is easily second. A professional baseball league plays during the dry season between December and April, and outdoor basketball courts are planned as standard facilities in the designing of new schools in towns of the interior. Soccer, generally thought of as the number one Latin American sport, attracts relatively scanty attention.

Weekend horseraces are offered year round at the Hipódromo Presidente Remón in Panama City, and cockfights can be seen at the Club Gallístico in the capital and in arenas in many of the interior towns. Bullfights are staged in the Plaza de Macorena during the dry season, but they have become popular only since the opening of the first real tourist hotel—the El Panamá in 1950 —and then its introduction appeared to have been in large measure an effort to entertain tourists rather than in response to a compelling domestic demand.

Some of the world's best sailfish and marlin fishing is available in the oceans, and the mountain streams are well stocked for sport fishing; large and small game is available in many parts of the country; modern bowling lanes are found on the transisthmian highway just outside Panama City; and an annual international golf tournament in February attracts some of the world's leading professional players. Although the country's warm climate and long and picturesque coastline encourage tourist folders to emphasize the lure of swimming and sunbathing, the lack of good beaches within easy reach of the centers of population limits the significance of these recreational outlets.

Lottery tickets are available in all parts of the country. Tickets for the National Lottery are settled by weekly drawings in Panama City's Plaza Arango and can bring B/90,000 as the grand prize for a complete ticket or a bare recovery of the ticket's cost for the *terminales* (the last two digits) of the four-digit third prize. The full ticket of ninety pieces costs B/49.50, and a single fraction sells for B/0.55. Participation in the lottery is a part of the national way of life, and profits from it subsidize much of the country's welfare program. In 1968, on the basis of some B/69 million realized from ticket sales, the net income to the national treasury after prizes and operating expenses were deducted was about B/12.3 million, or approximately 10 percent of the government's ordinary revenues.

The *bolito*, an extralegal private lottery, operates daily with about the same odds as those offered in the national undertaking. A public bingo game is offered periodically in the city of Colón, and bingo may be enjoyed as an adjunct to dinner at one of the popular restaurants in Panama City. Parimutuel betting is available at the racetrack, and there are gambling casinos in Panama City hotels and on the island of Taboga.

In the more remote rural parts of the interior commercial recreational outlets are very few, but the homogeneity of the population makes for an easy, informal social interchange among neighbors in small towns and villages where there is much playing of cards and dominoes. The wide dispersal of the farm population makes frequent social congregation difficult, but on holidays the small stores scattered along the roads serve as rural gathering places. Few country people are abroad after dark, however, and extended congregational drinking bouts do not play significant parts in the rural scene.

In both rural and urban Panama the communal fiesta has a recreational importance of the first order. In rural localities occupied only by scattered farms, it customarily takes the form of some kind of *junta,* a communal gathering assembled to accomplish a particular task, but in which recreation has an important part. When the working party has completed its assignment it is expected that the person or group on whose behalf the task was undertaken will play host at a party.

In towns and villages the equivalent of *junta* festivity is the communal fiesta in which the day of the community's patron saint or the occasions of Holy Week are celebrated, and most of the cost is defrayed by the more affluent local residents. In addition, several towns have periodic commercially inspired fairs. Country people flock to the towns for fiestas, and all social classes congregate for athletic contests, parades, cockfights, races, and gambling. Later, the wealthier townsmen may go to private gatherings in clubs and homes, while the remainder engage in public dances or patronize the local cafés and bars.

A phenomenal growth of the tourist industry during the 1950s and 1960s has been reflected in a corresponding mushroom growth of urban hotels, restaurants, nightclubs, and discotheques for those able to afford them. Previously, night life had been confined largely to noisy cabarets clustered on Colón's Front Street and Panama City's Central Avenue and catering principally to United States servicemen and to passengers and crewmen of vessels visiting Colón or traveling the canal.

The cosmopolitan and affluent people in Panama City and Colón, however, entertain extensively in their homes. Panama is an exception to the customary Latin American pattern that tends to confine entertainment in the home to certain defined and very formal occasions. For people with scantier incomes, housing is frequently so crowded and inadequate that even the simplest entertainment in the home is inadequate, and leisure time is sometimes referred to colloquially as time spent in the street. Open-air beer gardens and restaurants are of particular importance to those whose homes are inadequate for entertainment but whose incomes make possible the spending of some money for recreational purposes.

HEALTH

Administration of Public Health Program

The Ministry of Public Health is in general charge of the country's public health program. In addition, a medical program is maintained by the Social Security Fund on behalf of its members; the National Water Supply and Sewerage Institute (Instituto de Acuaductos y Alcantrillados Nacionales—IDAAN) has primary responsibility for environmental sanitation; the National Lottery proceeds are in large measure earmarked for support of the public health program; and the National Commission for Health Planning is a high-level advisory board with overall concern for matters related to the national health. In order to preserve coordination among these several entities, the minister of public health serves as president of their directive boards. Coordination with the health-related faculties of the University of Panama is maintained through the membership of the dean of its medical faculty on the National Commission for Health Planning.

Administratively the country is divided into three public health regions: the eastern consists roughly of the Darién region and the Metropolitan Area, the central is made up of Central Panama and adjacent portions of Atlantic Panama, and the western includes the provinces of Chiriquí and Bocas del Toro. Most of the participating doctors and dentists are employed on a part-time basis. The program of the Social Security Fund is supported by contributions from insured workers and their employers. Between 1960 and 1968 the current and capital expenditures for public health and water and sewerage increased on a per capita basis from B/15.41 to B/35.32. In 1970 some 11.7 percent of the national budget was expended on public health, the most costly undertaking after education.

Health Hazards and Preventive Medicine

Preliminary data for 1969 showed heart disease to have been the principal cause of death, followed in order by pneumonia and bronchitis, cancer, and accidental and violent deaths. Refined data for the year 1966, including only medically certified deaths (during the 1960s about half of all deaths recorded were medically certified), listed heart disease as first with 14.2 percent of the total. It was followed by cancer, 9.7 percent; accidents, homicides, and suicides, 8.3 percent; dysentery, enteritis, and colitis, 7 percent; and pneumonia and bronchitis, 5.5 percent. The other major causes of death listed, excluding the diseases of the newly born, were tuberculosis, congenital malformations, and tetanus.

By age group, the principal causes of death among persons sixty-five years of age and older were heart disease and cancer. Tuberculosis and the several causes of violent death had their highest incidence among those between fifteen and forty-four years of age, and the other cited major causes were associated principally with infant mortality.

Among the medical complaints calling for recorded consultations at public facilities the most numerous during 1966 were those involving respiratory difficulties, and the next in number were those involving intestinal parasites. Third were those where no discernible ailment could be found. The fourth involved prenatal consultations by expectant mothers.

In the listing of releases from public hospitals during 1966 the discharges after treatment for accidents were the second most numerous and the only major category not directly or indirectly related to maternity. First in order among releases was discharge after uncomplicated childbirth. The other major listings were for intestinal disorders affecting the very young, for miscarriages, and for complications related to pregnancy.

On the basis of a quantitative tally, it appears that people seeking public medical assistance solicit it for problems relating to respiratory ailments, ranging upward in severity from the common cold, and for the repair of damage resulting from accidents or acts of violence. People also readily seek assistance including bed care for maternity cases.

Tuberculosis is the most serious of the endemic diseases; in the late 1960s its fatality rate was about twenty-eight per 100,000 of the population. Malaria was also serious in most of the country, and between 500 and 1,000 cases of vitamin deficiency and of goiter were reported annually. Intestinal diseases and worm infections were common only in rural areas. Chagas disease, common throughout much of Latin America, was occasionally found from the western rim of the Canal Zone through Coclé Province.

Venereal disease is found most frequently in the terminal cities; gonorrhea is its most common form. Leprosy is endemic but has become more rare. Yellow fever is no longer a problem in urban Panama, although it continues occasionally to be introduced by travelers and, from South America, by howler monkeys. Dengue fever was last reported in 1941.

Infectious hepatitis is endemic but rarely is reported. Among the more significant of the respiratory ailments are diphtheria, streptococcal disease, and meningococcal meningitis. The last reported cases of smallpox were in 1958; there were 126 cases of diphtheria reported in 1963.

The Ministry of Public Health carries on nationwide campaigns against malaria, tuberculosis, typhoid and paratyphoid, dysentery and related ailments, leprosy and related ailments, and mental illness. It also supports local programs including immunizations against more than twenty diseases. In addition, during the late 1960s the IDAAN environmental sanitation program directed preventive measures against typhoid and paratyphoid, dysentery and related diseases, and infections from various parasites.

The key element of the Ministry of Public Health's nationwide preventive medicine program is the Central Command (Comando Central). It includes the National Campaign Against Tuberculosis (Campaña Nacional Antituberculosa—CNAT), the National Service for the Eradication of Malaria (Servicio Nacional de Erradicación de la Malaria—SNEM), the Program for Control of Ambulatory Leprosy (Control Ambulatoria de Lepra), and the Mental Health Program (Programa de la Salud Mental).

Between the mid-1950s and the mid-1960s the relative rate of mortality from tuberculosis so declined that the disease dropped from third to tenth place among the country's causes of mortality. Institutional care for patients was provided in a public health hospital in Panama City, but the relative incidence was greatest among lower income rural people in Veraguas, Darién, and Colón. In particular, the Cuna Indians in San Blas were affected.

Organized efforts at malaria control began in about 1931 and were directly aimed at elimination of the larvae of the mosquito vector. After World War II the massive use of DDT spraying began, and intensive use of antimalarial medication was introduced in areas of particular hazard. The SNEM was established in 1956, and in 1957 the program began a move to what is called —in phraseology employed by the World Health Organization—the attack stage. In the late 1960s the areas where the disease remained most prevalent were Darién Province, the Barú District of Chiriquí (where it was brought in by migratory farm labor), portions of Atlantic Panama, the littoral of the Gulf of Montijo, an area in the Central Isthmus between Gatún Lake and Madden Reservoir, and Chepo District to the east of Panama City.

Malaria is a weakening rather than a mortal disease, and many people suffering from it undoubtedly did not report their ailment. Between 1957 and 1966 its reported incidence declined from 760 to 297 per 100,000 of the population, and the proportion of positive reactions on blood smears of persons tested (between 7 and 8 percent of the population) declined irregularly from 10.8 to 3.8 percent.

The program for control of leprosy was initiated in 1961 with support from the United Nations Children's Fund (UNICEF) and the World Health Organization. The one leprosarium on the isthmus is at Palo Seco in the Canal Zone; it is maintained by the zone, and Panamanian patients are lodged in it on a reimbursable basis. Slightly less than half of the Palo Seco patients are Panamanians, and most are elderly. As reported in 1970, no new patient had been admitted since 1962. In December 1968 there were 168 known cases; ninety-five of these were under ambulatory supervision, and the remainder were hospitalized.

Until 1933 the country's mental health patients were cared for in the psychiatric hospital at Corozal in the Canal Zone. Mental cases were then moved to a psychiatric section of Santo Tomás Hospital and, later, to the psychiatric hospital in Panama City. Since 1966 the Infant Guidance Clinic in Panama City has provided mental care for the young. Periodic psychiatric outpatient care is also provided in Panama City, Colón, Aguadulce, Chitré, Santiago, and David. Preventive care is emphasized. Statistics for 1966 showed that 66 percent of the hospitalized psychiatric patients resided in the eastern health zone; 22 percent, in the central; and 10 percent, in the western.

There is a moderately active immunization program. The number of live polio vaccinations (two-treatment course) increased from 5,761 in 1965 to 14,010 in 1968. Smallpox vaccinations declined slightly from 55,701 in 1966 to 44,935 in 1968; Bacillus Calmette-Guérin (BCG) tuberculosis treatments rose from 29,300 in 1966 to 34,073 in 1968; yellow fever courses of treatment dropped from 6,832 in 1966 to 6,370 in 1968.

Medical Personnel

In 1969 the proportions of physicians, dentists, and graduate nurses per 10,000 of the population were 5.8, 1.16, and 8 percent, respectively. These proportions represented substantial relative as well as absolute gains in each of the professions during the 1960s. In 1969, however, some 71 percent of the physicians, 64 percent of the dentists, and 70 percent of the graduate nurses were located in Panama City.

A disproportionately heavy concentration of medical and paramedical personnel in the capital city is characteristic of Latin American countries. The concentration in Panama City is particularly pronounced because the capital is also the center of the Metropolitan Area and because the second city in size, Colón, is so close to the capital that it has no compelling need for separate corps of personnel. In 1969 the proportion available in Colón was scarcely above the national average.

Medical students are prepared in a seven-year course of study at the University of Panama followed by a two-year internship and a residency in which the period of duration may vary. Few of the country's doctors, however, have been prepared at home. In 1968 there were 150 students enrolled in the University of Panama Faculty of Medicine, while 543 were reported in a government-sponsored survey as engaged in medical studies abroad. Most were in schools in Spain, Brazil, and Mexico; only a scattering were in United States institutions.

In 1969 some 635 of the country's 782 practicing physicians were on the staffs of the country's hospitals and medical centers, and about 500 of these were attached to government-operated institutions. Most of those with public connections, however, devoted part or most of their time to private practice. Medicine is an elite profession of the highest order, and the proportion of doctors among those holding high political office is far higher than is customarily the case in North America.

The level of professional competence of Panamanian doctors is such that it is not uncommon for residents of the Republic employed by the United States government and eligible for Canal Zone medical care to make use of the services of Panamanian doctors.

Because the Faculty of Dentistry at the University of Panama was not established until 1968, all of the country's dentists in 1971 had obtained their education abroad, a majority of them in the United States and secondarily in other countries of Latin America. Like medical doctors, dentists practice almost entirely in the larger urban centers—in 1969 there was one dentist listed as practicing regularly in the entire province of Bocas del Toro.

People in the countryside are served occasionally by dentists in mobile units, but the rural population as well as people of lower income in urban localities have little awareness of the importance of preventive dental hygiene, and a large portion of the work of dentists consists of extractions. During 1969 the number of dental appointments by public health dentists engaged in making extractions outnumbered those concerned with fillings by more than ten to one.

Graduate nurses were formerly trained in the school of nursing located in the Santo Tomás Hospital. That program was terminated in 1969, however, and nurses have since been trained at the University of Panama, which offers the bachelor degree in nursing science.

In 1969 the 1,075 members of the graduate nursing corps were supplemented by 1,700 nursing auxiliaries. More than 70 percent of both nurses and auxiliaries are formally attached to some kind of medical facility. The graduate personnel are concentrated in the hospitals and other places offering bed care, but a large proportion of the auxiliaries staff the subcenters and other outpatient facilities of the interior towns.

In cosmopolitan Panama the career of nursing is held in higher esteem than in many of the other countries of Latin America, and a few daughters of the aristocracy have found nursing a suitable occupation. It is one of the few countries in which graduate nursing personnel outnumber physicians. In 1968 the proportion between graduate nurses and the population as a whole was double the average for Latin America, and the proportion of auxiliary personnel was well above the average.

This abundance of trained nursing personnel probably relates to the closeness of the Canal Zone and its example with respect to the proportions of nurses required to treat illnesses. Despite the relatively large number of nurses available in the Republic, in 1971 there was a shortage; the Social Security Fund found it necessary to bring in some twenty-five Salvadorean nurses to serve under a year's contract in Panamanian hospitals.

Medical Facilities

Like medical personnel, medical facilities are heavily concentrated in the capital city where nearly all of the laboratory and special care services are located. The Ministry of Public Health operates the Central Medical Center, consisting of three Panama City hospitals; these are the Santo Tomás general hospital facility, a psychiatric hospital, and an antituberculosis hospital. It also operates regional health centers in Panama City, Aguadulce, and David. In addition, the Social Security Fund operates a general hospital in Panama City, the Amador Guerrero Hospital in Colón, and clinics in various localities. Aside from the large facilities maintained by the Chiriquí Land Company in the provinces of Bocas del Toro and Chiriquí, most of the installations in the interior that are equipped with beds for inpatient care are small. In 1968 there were in all some thirty-two public and eleven private hospital units.

In 1969 there was a total availability of 4,455 beds including 2,539 in public general hospitals, 596 in private general hospitals, and 1,320 in public special-care hospitals. There were no private special institutions. By province, the availability of beds ranged from eleven per 10,000 of the population in Veraguas to sixty per 10,000 in Bocas del Toro, where a substantial Chiriquí Land Company hospital was located. About half of all beds available were located in Panama City, where the ratio of availability was sixty-one per 10,000. The number of beds available did not change appreciably during the 1960s; the principal thrust of the public health program was directed toward reapportionment and conversion of existing facilities and toward the opening of health subcenters in areas of the interior that did not have hospital beds.

The rate of occupancy of beds in units of all kinds dropped sharply from 91.5 percent in 1965 to 83.2 percent in 1969. The decline registered was from 71.8 percent to 66.6 percent in public general hospitals and from 43.1 percent to 37.9 percent in private general institutions. In the badly overcrowded public special hospitals, it was from 140.4 percent to 136.7 percent.

The relatively low rate of occupancy in the private hospitals reflected their high cost. The crowding of the public special facilities occurred principally at the 749-bed psychiatric hospital in Panama City, which has suffered chronically from heavy over-occupancy and has been able to furnish little more than custodial care.

Outpatient clinics are much more evenly distributed about the countryside than are the hospitals and health centers. In 1969 there were 181 public health clinics of all kinds, or an average of 1.3 per 10,000 population. The ratio varied from 1.9 per 10,000 in portions of Herrera Province to 0.4 per 10,000 in portions of Chiriquí. In addition, there were four mobile health units.

It was estimated in 1966 that about 83 percent of the country's population lived in localities accessible to places where medical attention was regularly available. The proportion varied between 96 percent in Panama Province to 65 percent in Veraguas. Accessibility was defined as residence in a locality not more than two hours in round trip distance from a medical station by the means of transportation most commonly used in the locality.

Folk Medicine

Although many rural households are located within a short bus ride of some kind of public health unit, there is evidence that many do not make use of accessible medical services. Attitudes toward scientific medicine vary from total acceptance and willing use, through occasional use of modern facilities as an acceptable alternative to folk medicine, to total rejection of medical doctors and hospitals.

Culturally expressed interest in the body and its ailments is high. Theories of causation, pathology, and cure are varied and detailed, and most rural localities have several persons specialized in the treatment of disease by various techniques. Disease is generally seen as the result of complex causative factors, some natural and some supernatural. The folk pathology shares many of the common disease concepts of the more urbanized segment of the population: indigestion, dysentery, and a vague complex of symptoms known throughout Latin America as liver condition. Other combinations of symptoms appear that are not usually accorded medical recognition as diseases.

Dysenteric symptoms are generally known as *pujo*, which can be either simple or complicated with colonic bleeding. A common theory is that the condition results from excessive drinking. A vague complex of dyspeptic symptoms, known as *empacho*, is usually ascribed to a person's becoming overheated and is treated by herbal remedies of purgative effect.

Other ailments—*pasmo, aire*, and *viento*, which are overlapping concepts describing various complexes of symptoms—are believed to be caused by sudden changes in environmental and body temperature. Treatment of such ills can be either by physical and herbal means or by techniques that are frankly supernatural.

There is a belief that supernatural forces, either impersonal or purposefully directed, can cause serious ailments. A common source of illness for children, in folk conception, is the evil eye, which is cast either voluntarily or involuntarily by pregnant women and by persons whose disposition is upset, usually as a result of insomnia. Witchcraft, either directed out of a witch's own malice or at the behest of one's enemies, can cause a variety of ailments, most of which result from the belief that frogs and other small animals have been placed, by magical means, in body cavities.

To treat these and a large number of other ailments, a mixture of physical and supernatural techniques is employed. Rural Panama has a rich tradition of herbal cures and pain relievers, some of which are administered only by specialized curers, others are in general use by all. Physical curing techniques include considerable use of massage as a means of relieving pain and removing from the body evil influences that are conceived as root causes of certain diseases.

Many supernatural cures are used as specific antidotes to witchcraft; others are directed at conditions resulting from the evil eye; and certain techniques are used in the treatment of all serious complaints. The most frequently applied technique is called *santiguar* (roughly, to bless) and involves continued prayer and signing with the cross, usually by a specialized curer.

There are several classes of persons specialized in curing. Some (called *curanderos*) are specialized in most phases of folk medicine and are particularly skilled in making diagnoses, usually by examining the patient's urine. Many rural neighborhoods have one or more midwives (*comadronas*), who have specialized techniques. Other curers, usually women, use massage as their main therapeutic technique. Each of these specialists has a field of action in which his techniques are considered to be particularly useful.

A certain fatalism with regard to illness and death, along with the chronicity and subclinical grade of ailments, makes it difficult to introduce modern hygiene and medicine. The faith that continues to be exhibited with respect to the practitioners of folk medicine also retards the development of rational programs of medical care and disease prevention.

Health problems in the terminal cities, for the most part, do not result from lack of medical facilities or from disinclination on the part of people to use them. There are few, if any, folk practitioners, although there is widespread use of folk preparations, particularly in the treatment of impotence. The health problems of lower class urbanites are not cast in terms of cultural traditions that tend to restrict regular use of modern treatment facilities, but result rather from conditions of housing, diet, and environmental sanitation, over which they have only very limited physical control. Probably the main attitudinal component of the health problem among the urban poor lies in dietary habits that result in dependence upon a narrow range of foodstuff, mostly carbohydrates.

Environmental Sanitation

Substantial progress in the extension of water and sanitary facilities was made during the 1960s, but in 1967 more than one-third of the population was without direct access to water other than that gathered at random from streams and ponds, and nearly one-fourth did not have access to any means of waste disposal.

By 1967 the entire urban population was reported to have access to some kind of water supply (although the 1970 census was to find that 2 percent of the homes in Panama City had none) and that a little more than one-third of the rural people had a regular means of securing water, most of it from wells. All of the urban water was piped, and most of it came from household connections. A large proportion of the dwelling places, however, were the *casas de vecindad* in which the individual units did not have private connections and the *casas brujas* and some other homes that drew water from public taps.

Nearly all of the urban population also had access to some means of waste disposal by 1967, although the 1970 census also showed 2 percent of the dwellings in Panama City to have access to none.

Some two-thirds of the rural people used some system, but the latrine or outhouse was the commonly used facility. In 1960 about 28 percent of the population as a whole had used private facilities, and 36 percent used communal facilities.

In the mid-1960s Panama City and Colón were supplied with water from the Canal Zone and distributed by government facilities. Most of the systems in towns of the interior were nationally owned. There were also eight municipal and five privately owned systems. The towns of Chitré and David had filtration plants, and in most of the remaining parts of the interior the water was drawn from deep wells. Water supplies in Panama City, Colón, David, Santiago, Las Tablas, Chitré, Penonomé, and Bocas del Toro were said to be satisfactory. National sewerage systems were in operation in Panama City, Colón, La Chorrera, San Carlos, Antón, Penonomé, Aguadulce, Chitré, Los Santos, Las Tablas, Santiago, and David. Puerto Armuelles had a municipal system, and there were private systems in Las Cumbres and Almirante. Sewage from Panama City, Colón and Puerto Armuelles was flushed into the sea without treatment. Most of the other systems had primary treatment plants usually consisting of septic tanks from which the effluent was dumped into streams.

In 1969 the Panamanian government signed a B/17 million contract with a United States firm for the construction of a new water supply system for Panama City that would take water from the Madden Reservoir and be independent from the Canal Zone source of supply. Construction was expected to take four years.

Municipal governments in the cities of Panama City and Colón provide regular service for street cleaning and removal and disposal of trash. Since human waste is not used as a fertilizer, a majority of the fruits and vegetables are regarded as satisfactory at their source. Pasteurized milk is readily available, but refrigeration facilities are limited, and meat and other products deteriorate rapidly. In addition, methods of processing and handling foods in the open-air markets are not always sanitary.

WELFARE

The principal public welfare instrument is the Social Security Fund, an autonomous government agency established by law in 1941 and modeled on systems then in existence in Mexico and Chile. Inaugurated as a retirement program that included burial benefits for wage and salary earners in the districts of Colón and Panama only, it also was given responsibility for government employees in all parts of the country who were already covered by 1935 legislation. In 1943 it expanded its activities to include the provision of certain medical services to insured personnel. In

1954 its geographical area of coverage was widened to include various districts in the interior of the country, and in 1962 its schedule of benefits was broadened to include survivor pensions and some medical services for dependents.

The social security program was initiated with the aim of ultimately making participation in its benefits available on a voluntary basis to the self-employed. It was also to be obligatory for all wage earners other than those in certain categories, such as elderly persons working for the first time, some family members, some foreigners, and seasonal and occasional workers. Voluntary subscription has been minimal, and by 1966 the program had been placed in effect in only fifteen of the sixty-four districts into which the country was then divided. These, however, included Panama City, Colón, David, and all of the other heaviest populated districts in the country. By 1969 the coverage had been extended to some 142,000 workers, or about 33.2 percent of the labor force as compared with 26.3 percent in 1965. There were also about 94,700 dependents of workers enrolled.

The proportion of self-employed persons choosing to participate under the program increased slightly during the 1960s, but in 1969, remained negligible at less than 1 percent of the total. Employees of private enterprises represented 60.8 percent, and central government employees represented 28.1 percent of the total. The balance was made up of municipal employees, employees of autonomous and semiautonomous agencies, and workers for enterprises receiving government assistance.

Between 1965 and 1969 the number of cash benefits under the program increased from under 14,000 to about 24,000, and the amount paid ascended from about B/7.5 million to B/14.7 million. The most numerous beneficiaries—and those receiving most of the payments—were old-age retirees. Other benefits paid involved disability, survivor pensions, maternity costs, and layettes for infants (see table 3).

The Social Security Fund also maintains its own hospital and outpatient system for the benefit of insured persons and dependents. Overall, the cost of inpatient and outpatient services rendered rose from B/8.6 million to B/15.1 million. The program is financed by contributions of 5 percent of the base pay contributed by workers, 7 percent of the payroll contributed by employers, and 8 percent of total covered earnings contributed by the government.

Men who have reached the age of sixty and women who have reached the age of fifty-five are eligible for retirement after having made contributions to the fund for 180 months. The benefit paid consists of 50 percent of the monthly wage plus the equivalent

Table 3. *Number and Amount of Social Security Benefits Paid in Panama, 1965 and 1969*

Benefit	1965		1969	
	Number	Amount [1]	Number	Amount [1]
Retirement and Pensions:				
Old age	5,682	5,230,724.61	9,226	10,409,214.40
Disability	917	715,373.60	1,119	1,069,647.54
Reduced	14	9,664.57	40	23,905.62
Survivors	1,149	297,735.31	2,675	865,773.57
Total Retirement and Pensions	7,762	6,253,498.09	13,060	12,368,541.13
Other Benefits:				
Funeral	392	39,100.00	469	49,508.00
Maternity (insured)	2,710	959,466.45	3,790	1,722,058.43
Maternity (beneficiary)	1,962	78,480.00	2,693	107,720.00
Temporary disability	1,800	210,876.10	3,163	413,166.71
Infant layettes [2]	0	0	847	17,087.79
Total Other Benefits	6,864	1,287,922.55	10,962	2,309,540.93

[1] 1 balboa equals US$1.
[2] Payments commenced in 1966.

Source: Adapted from Republic of Panama, Contraloría General de la República, Dirección de Estadística y Censo, *Panamá en cifras (Compendio Estadístico, años 1965 a 1969)*, Panama City, 1970, p. 46.

of 1 percent additional for every twelve months' contribution during the first 120 months. The monthly stipend is also increased slightly when a male pensioner is married or when a female pensioner has an incapacitated husband and increased by a smaller amount for each child under fourteen (or under eighteen if a student, and at any age if incapacitated). In no case, however, may the stipend be less than B/50 or more than B/500 monthly. The minimum and maximum apply also to disability and survivors' pensions.

Pensions for disability are awarded insured persons who as a result of injury or accident are determined unable to earn a wage equal to one-third of the average wage of persons of similar ability and training. They are payable to persons who have made payments to the fund for at least thirty-six months. The amount, the same as that payable for old-age retirement, is awarded provisionally for a period not exceeding five years and is discontinued if the insured person regains more than 50 percent of his former earning capacity.

Funeral expenses, amounting to B/100 in 1969, are payable on behalf of the insured person. Survivor benefits are payable to widows, to children under the age of fourteen who are disabled, and to students under the age of eighteen. The payment is in the amount of 50 percent of the insured person's salary or pension to widows and 20 percent to children. When there is no eligible widow or orphan, under specified circumstances a pension may be paid to parents, brothers, or sisters. The widow's pension is paid initially for a period of three years; it continues if she is disabled or has reached fifty-five years of age. In all cases, however, it ceases on her remarriage.

A maternity subsidy usually equal to 50 percent of her wages is paid for a period of six weeks preceding and eight weeks following childbirth to an insured woman whose wages are not continued by the employer during that period. Illness benefits are granted to any insured person who has contributed for six or more of the preceding twelve months. They include provision of or payment for medical, surgical, or dental care, pharmaceutical attention, and hospitalization. Benefits are for a maximum period of fourteen weeks but may occasionally be extended; they include a subsidy for temporary disability if the illness results in an inability to work. Wives of insured persons and their children under the age of sixteen are entitled to the same medical and surgical services, but they are not entitled to hospitalization. In addition, persons pensioned for old age and disability have the 5 percent quota deducted from their pensions and are entitled to receive the sickness benefits.

Illness benefits are not granted if the sickness and incapacity are the result of industrial accident or occupational disease, for which the employer is responsible under law. A cabinet decree of March 1970 ordered incorporation of insurance against industrial hazards into the general social security framework, thus implementing provisions of the Labor Code. The program was to cover all persons insured by the Social Security Fund and was to be made mandatory for workers in domestic service, for self-employed persons, and for workers in nonmechanized undertakings after the preparation and issuance of regulations establishing the form that such insurance might take.

By terms of the decree, there is no length-of-service requirement for establishing eligibility, and the nature of the benefits prescribed differ somewhat from those for illness under the regular social security program. The new program is to be financed solely by employers through a schedule of contributions to the Social Security Fund to be determined by the degree of risk assigned to the undertaking. In the meantime, however, employers were to continue to carry insurance with private insurance companies against occupational hazards. These companies would ultimately suffer considerable loss of business and were quick to protest the issuance of the decree.

A few private firms, most of them foreign, furnish the additional benefit of a group life insurance program under which the employer pays an initial death benefit amount of between B/2,000 and B/4,000 for the worker, and the remainder is financed by deduction from his pay. The policy provides double indemnity as well as straight life insurance and is applicable whether or not the death is work connected. In addition, the Chiriquí Land Company maintains its own coverage of hospital, loan, and retirement benefits in districts where the social security program is not in effect.

Kinship and neighborhood organization provide a degree of protection from the hardships of life, supplementing or even replacing formal welfare systems. The typical family, among both rural and urban dwellers, is nuclear in organization, containing at most one set of parents and their children, but there are variations. Orphaned children are distributed among more distant kin without serious disruption of the adopting household. When a male household head is missing, the lack is frequently made up by reorganization into a so-called grandmother family, consisting of a woman, her mother, and her children. This type of unit, quite common in the terminal cities, provides security and supervision for children who would otherwise suffer considerable neglect because of the necessary absence of the mother, on whom sole responsibility for support of the family has fallen.

In general, although kin and locality groups are not highly structured, there is a strong obligation to offer mutual aid and support, which are of importance to the geographically and economically isolated rural population. A person in economic difficulty can seek refuge with kinsmen or turn his children over to their care, temporarily or permanently. Neighbors living within convenient distance of one another commonly engage in various cooperative activities, particularly in the sharing of agricultural labor and housebuilding, which provide economic benefit and recreation to many rural Panamanians.

Most informal, neighborhood-based cooperation in the rural areas involves sharing of labor. In some parts of the interior there are formally organized burial cooperatives, which minimize individual expense through sharing of funeral costs. Such cooperatives also exist among the West Indians of the terminal cities.

CHAPTER 5

SOCIAL SYSTEM

Panama is customarily regarded as a country with a racially mixed population in which no one element predominates, but ethnic considerations continue to be a significant factor in determining the status of members of the society. The basic amalgam consists of three major components—the indigenous Indians, the invading Spaniards, and the Negro slaves brought in from Africa soon after settlement began. To these have been added several immigrant groups attracted by opportunities for employment, the foremost of which are the West Indian Negroes who entered the country in recurrent waves after 1850 and who are still a clearly recognizable segment of the population.

Though now including any ethnic fusion, in colonial times the term mestizo meant specifically the offspring of Spanish and Indian unions. During the three centuries before independence, however, all possible degrees of racial mixture occurred, involving corresponding nuances of social status. A few of the more enterprising, usually light-skinned and relatively prosperous, became accepted as *criollos* (in principle, persons of pure Spanish ancestry born in the colonies), but the great majority, in many cases with a further admixture of Negro blood, constituted the predominant element of the population, mostly identified with agricultural labor and service occupations. All mestizos were entitled before the law to equal treatment with the white minority; they could, in theory, and some did, in fact, qualify for minor positions in the government or the clergy.

Elements of each of the several ethnic strains have been preserved in remote parts of the country in relatively unmixed states. The Indians—such as the Cuna or Guaymí—who lived in, or retreated to, inaccessible areas were able to resist both cultural and biological encroachment. The Antillean Negro ethnic component (relatively recent immigrants in contrast to the older slave component) remains largely unmixed; it has not become assimilated into the prevailing Spanish-speaking culture and therefore has been treated as an alien group.

These islands of ethnic purity are, nevertheless, exceptions, as the vast majority of the population is the product of racial mixing. The term mestizo in popular usage includes all varieties and proportions of amalgamation, irrespective of the measure in which any element appears to dominate an individual's ancestry. The correlation of ethnic factors with status can be generalized only to the extent that white elements are more apparent at the top of the social pyramid, and recognizably negroid features tend to cluster near the bottom. Members of the Spanish ruling class placed a high value on unmixed blood and tended to marry within their own group. Although it would be impossible to estimate their degree of success in maintaining racial purity, members of the upper class continue to accept it as a criterion of status, even though it has been steadily eroded in the face of new standards based on wealth and achievement.

The Panamanian's view of his own society identifies three separate groups: the Spanish-speaking majority, called Panameños, the tribal Indians, and the Antillean Negroes. This set of categories is based primarily on cultural rather than racial factors. Hostility or resentment between members of these groups is based on failure to become assimilated into the predominant Hispanic culture.

Smaller alien groups—Jews, Chinese, Lebanese, and others—are found mainly in the cities. Although numerically insignificant, they are noticeable primarily because of their concentration in retail trade. Most United States citizens live under separate jurisdiction in the Canal Zone and have little impact on Panama's ethnic structure. Their presence, however, does have a significant effect on the country's social, economic, and political attitudes.

For the most part, cultural discrimination has not been incorporated into laws or regulations to such an extent that it cannot be readily avoided by assimilation into the cultural mainstream of the society. National policy is to treat all groups equally, if somewhat paternalistically in the case of the Indians.

Spanish is the country's official language and is spoken by almost all Panamanians. English is a popular and prevalent second tongue, used extensively by the Antillean Negroes and abetted by the presence of the North Americans in the Canal Zone. A number of indigenous languages are in common use among the tribal Indians, but the total number of users of these dialects is small. Spanish is replacing these dialects as increasing numbers of Indians are incorporated into the mainstream of national life.

The class structure of the national society is marked by a sharp difference in character between its rural and urban elements and, second, by a distinction between native born and immigrant that is particularly noticeable in the urban centers. Some 52 percent of the population is reported as rural, consisting mainly of poor, native-born farmers. Some own the land they work, but most are squatters and tenants, and there are wage-earning agricultural workers in certain areas.

Scattered over thousands of villages, hamlets, and isolated farmsteads, the rural dwellers have little communication with one another or with urban society. In each community a man's social status is determined largely by his economic situation, but there is little internal differentiation. Except for the plantation workers, the peasants have not come into serious conflict with the landholding elite, largely because there is so much state land available and because the large landowners generally do not practice the kind of plantation agriculture that would involve the peasants in a closely dependent relationship.

For the most part the rural scene remains culturally isolated and marked by local traditional folk expression. Urban ideas, fashions, and living patterns rarely penetrate the interior, as the usual channels of communication have limited effect because of high rural illiteracy and the general remoteness of large numbers of peasants. Increased radio usage in recent years, however, has been gradually bridging the communications gap and steadily bringing to the interior the modernizing effect of the urban mode of life.

Urban life and its complexity of social organization is confined almost exclusively to the two largest cities, Panama City and Colón, which contain one-third of the country's population. Urban social patterns involve more elaborate stratification and more closely defined groupings than their rural counterparts. The old families of Panama, traditional holders of political power and economic privilege, constitute the backbone of the upper class. Most of the old families are thoroughly urbanized, although many retain ties with the interior in the form of landholdings. They guard their political preeminence and their white, Hispanic heritage carefully. Although wealth may serve as a claim to higher status, only birth or marriage provides entry into the more restricted inner circle of the elite.

There is a steadily growing middle class, a development of the twentieth century and found almost entirely in the cities. The bulk of the urban population, however, belongs to one level or another of the lower class, which is distinguished from the rural peasantry chiefly by the greater economic vulnerability of the wage worker.

Despite the impact of alien cultural influences, family and kinship behavior continues to be founded predominantly on traditional Hispanic social patterns. The Panamanian family is basically mother oriented, with the mother taking the main responsibility for activities within the home; her focal point of interest is the household, along with a narrow circle of relatives and friends. The father is usually preoccupied with the affairs of the outside world and, though his interests may be primarily outside the home, he still considers himself the undisputed head of the household and the final authority and arbiter on matters affecting the family as a whole.

ETHNIC GROUPS

Panameños

The term *Panameños* refers in its inclusive sense to all citizens of the republic, but used restrictively it denotes the Spanish-speaking, mainly Roman Catholic, and predominantly mestizo majority of the population. It includes whites and native Spanish-speaking Negroes and others who adhere to the prevalent Hispanic tradition but excludes West Indian Negroes, tribal Indians, and other minorities. Preliminary figures from the 1970 census give an indication, though not a precise count, of the country's ethnic composition. These show approximately 70 percent regarded as mestizo, 10 percent of white European ancestry, 13 percent Negro (of which 8 percent are Antillean Negro), 6 percent Indian, and 1 percent Oriental or Levantine.

The mestizo element, which is concentrated largely in Coclé, Herrera, and Veraguas provinces, is numerically dominant at all but the highest social levels. The white element accounts for more than 10 percent of the population in Panama, Colón, Chiriquí, and Los Santos provinces, all of which are among the more urbanized areas of the country.

Although mestizo is often used to refer to white-Indian mixture, it is used in Panama for any combinations found in the population. The mestizo component has been increasing steadily, reportedly some 10 percent since 1950, and has reflected commensurate declines in the proportions of the other components. The process is difficult to evaluate, but it must be presumed to be a continuing one, particularly in Darién, where the amalgamation of Indians and Negroes is readily observable.

An undetermined number of Panameños are full-blooded Negroes, descendants of slaves brought into the country or more recent immigrants from across the Colombian border. Although counted as Negroes in the census, along with the Antilleans, they are completely Hispanicized and are fully accepted as culturally Panamanian. They usually resent any confusion with the West Indians. These Spanish-speaking Negroes are found in greatest concentration in Darién and Bocas del Toro provinces; many are agricultural laborers, and for the most part they do not show the preference for urban settlement so prevalent among the Antilleans.

The cultural animosities that have marred intergroup relations focus attention on the Spanish language as the distinguishing mark of the Panameño, but there is no strong sentiment attached to linguistic purity. Some advocates of fundamental purity decry the Anglicisms that have entered the language, but in general the Panameños show little eagerness to safeguard Spanish against alien intrusions. There are, nevertheless, official efforts to assist the Indians in learning Spanish, and the introduction of Spanish instruction in Canal Zone schools was received favorably in the republic.

Antillean Negroes

The term *Antillean* refers only to the Negro group that has immigrated to Panama from the Caribbean islands formerly under British control. Unlike the native Panamanian Negro population, the West Indian Negroes speak English and are mostly Protestants. Antilleans began to arrive on a large scale to work on construction of the transisthmian railroad around the middle of the nineteenth century. Canal building and subsequent canal operations attracted increased numbers, and some also became agricultural plantation workers.

In 1971 the distribution of West Indians in the country still reflected the circumstances of their arrival. Most resided either in the two principal cities or in the Canal Zone. There was another concentration around Puerto Armuelles, in Chiriquí Province, one of the few instances of sizable Antillean employment outside the major urban areas. There has been relatively little new West Indian immigration since World War II, and the number of recognizable Antilleans has been gradually declining. The 1970 census indicated that they represented some 8 percent of the population. This compared with 9.5 percent in 1960 and 11 percent in 1950.

The Antilleans originally came from various parts of the West Indies and were united at first by persistent loyalty to the British crown, to which they had owed allegiance in their home islands. Many migrated to Panama only to earn enough money to enable them to return home and retire. This apparent transient status, along with their language and religion, further separated them from the local population. Another factor was the hostility of the Panamanians, which increased as the Antilleans prolonged their stay and became entrenched as workers on the canal. That hostility welded them into a minority group united by the cultural antagonisms around them.

Nevertheless, there is some evidence of a slight trend toward assimilation into the predominant Hispanic culture, although longstanding separation has made the process difficult. Race is not a problem, and the Antillean does not find his color a handicap. Given the possibility of choosing between a hereditary way of life and that of the national society, the young man or woman is faced with a hard decision. Although increasing numbers of young West Indians are becoming bilingual and joining the mainstream of society, major assimilation still appears to be some time off.

An Antillean may be drawn to the legacy of his ancestors or urged in that direction by older members of his family; if he works in the Canal Zone he may choose to identify himself with his principal employer and the special conditions and interests of the zone, or he can opt for complete assimilation into Panamanian society. Each choice presents both gains and sacrifices, but he must choose one course or the other.

Indians

In 1971 it was estimated that there were between 60,000 and 70,000 Indians living under tribal organization in the country. According to preliminary census figures, this number represented some 5 percent of the population—an increase over the 1960 estimate of nearly 10,000 in the absolute total but a drop of approximately 1 percent in the proportion of the overall population. There were three major groups—the Guaymí, the Cuna, and the Chocó. They were concentrated in three distinct and widely separated localities, where they were thinly distributed and exposed to varying degrees of contact with the rural Panamanians in the same territories.

The Guaymí occupy generally the northwestern part of the country; the Cuna, the northeast and along the Atlantic coast; and the Chocó, inland from the coast in the southeast. The Indians have elected to remain in their own semiautonomous communities, subject to tribal government, and live according to their own traditions.

The tribes are assisted in certain respects by the central or the provincial governments, particularly in matters of public health and welfare, and are regulated by the Ministry of Government and Justice when circumstances warrant. They are considered apart from the civil population and have a separate and largely autonomous political status. This does not, however, deprive them of the rights of citizenship, and they exercise full voting privileges. They are not restricted to their tribal areas, but most remain there by choice, reflecting their longstanding resistance to assimilation and their acceptance of a marginal role in society.

The preponderance of the mestizo on the isthmus is evidence that, historically, there was considerable intermingling of the local Indians with the invading Spaniards. Large numbers, however, resisted the encroachment of Spanish culture and withdrew into inaccessible areas in order to preserve their traditional way of life. Although there was some intercultural exchange and adaptation, neither element completely dominated the other, the Indian moving aside to make way for the superior force and preserving, in relatively static form, the ways to which he was accustomed.

The present-day Indians live in villages and build their thatched houses along well-defined streets. Hammocks and simple wooden furniture continue to be used as they were before the conquest. The most conspicuous change has been the introduction of European-style dress, principally trousers or skirts and straw hats. Traditional ornamentation, such as nose rings and necklaces, is gradually disappearing, and featherwork is rarely seen except on ceremonial occasions. Determined efforts have been made by the Catholic missions, and more recently by Protestants, to convert the tribal Indians to Christianity, but most of them still hold to their ancient beliefs, even though they have modified their practices extensively.

The Indians are primarily engaged in slash-and-burn agriculture, using the digging stick. Hunting and fishing remain important, and native techniques still survive: such tools as nets, spears, bows and arrows, and harpoons are widely used. For river travel the narrow dugout canoe is still in use and, on land, goods are carried in large baskets supported by tumplines or yokes.

In the sphere of social relations there have been significant changes in the role of the sexes and in the marriage relationship. The performance of agricultural duties has shifted from women to men. There is also a growing distinction in the clothing of boys and girls. Although polygamy is still permitted, the prevalent form of marriage is monogamous. The couple, however, continues to take up residence with the bride's family, and households are usually made up of several families related along maternal lines. Authority is patriarchal, the senior male heading the household with authority passed on to the eldest son-in-law.

The Guaymí

The Guaymí are the largest Indian group, making up about 50 percent of the indigenous population, and are located in the provinces of Bocas del Toro, Chiriquí, and Veraguas. The Guaymí are descended from various preconquest groups whose migrations brought them to their present location only after the arrival of the Spanish. Closely related Indian groups are found across the border in Costa Rica.

The Guaymí are generally classified into separate groups on the basis of language and the use of Spanish as a second tongue. Three principal categories are recognized: those who speak an Indian dialect exclusively in the home; those who speak Spanish as a second language; and those who speak Spanish at home. Indians and Panameños live side by side in some areas and are often nearly indistinguishable in their mode of life. The degree of contact and the use of Spanish decrease, however, from the southeastern perimeter of Guaymí settlement to the coastal area of Bocas del Toro near the Costa Rican border.

Government statistics on linguistic habits indicate that in Bocas del Toro and Chiriquí approximately 97 percent speak an Indian dialect at home; 55 percent also speak Spanish; and 3 percent use Spanish exclusively. This compares with Veraguas Province, where 69 percent speak an Indian dialect; 21 percent know Spanish as a second language; and 31 percent use Spanish in the home.

The degree of Hispanic cultural influence generally is closely associated with the use of the Spanish language and, as the use of the language decreases, traits and customs not shared with the Panameños become more apparent. The Guaymí engage mainly in hunting and fishing as their means of subsistence, but most, including the women, also engage in small-scale cultivation of such crops as tobacco, fruits, corn, and rice. In the summer the men often work as herdsmen or as agricultural laborers on nearby farms and estates.

The Cuna

The Cuna are the most highly organized and economically active Indians in the country and preserve their native customs with relative ease in their isolated habitat. Most of them live on the islands of the archipelago of San Blas, off the northeastern coast, where they fled originally to escape the Spaniards; several mainland groups have even less contact with Panameños because of their inaccessibility.

The Cuna constitute about 42 percent of the Indian population and are considered the group with the best chance of retaining their cultural individuality. They engage in considerable trade with surrounding Panamanians and, as a result of these contacts, speak Spanish extensively. Local surveys indicate that almost 37 percent are bilingual, and some 20 percent speak Spanish in the home. They maintain, nevertheless, a close-knit internal organization that tends to shield them from the eroding effects of over-exposure to alien influences. Even during periods of sizable migration to work in the Canal Zone, as occurred during World War II, they demonstrated little cultural accommodation. Although little of the art of the preconquest era is practiced, Cuna women have preserved many native handcrafts.

The Chocó

The Chocó, constituting 8 percent of the Indian population, occupy a region of Darién Province in the southeast that approaches the border with Colombia and impinges on mainland Cuna territory to the north. Because of their geographic remoteness, there is relatively little information available on the Chocó. Indications are that they are not as strongly opposed to assimilation as other tribes but retain their individuality more from inaccessibility than from conviction. It is known that they do not have a strong internal tribal organization, and most of them speak Spanish as well as their own indigenous tongue. Since the beginning of the 1950s, there has been a continuing infusion into the area of Spanish-speaking Negroes from Colombia fleeing disturbances in their own country. These have intermarried freely with the Chocó, but the cultural consequences of the mixtures are not known.

Minor Groups

The more prominent groups among the small minorities are the Chinese, Hindus, Jews, Middle Easterners, and North Americans. Except for a handful of United States citizens engaged in business in the cities, the only significant cluster outside the Canal Zone consists of a number of retired zone officials residing in Chiriquí. Those living and working in the zone, however, cannot be considered a part of the national society of the republic.

Most members of the other groups live in the cities and are engaged in commerce, and they are identified almost entirely with a single branch of trade, as in the case of the Chinese, for example, who hold a virtual monopoly of the retail grocery business. Although Spanish speaking for the most part, all of these groups tend to maintain their separate communities. Most adhere to their native social and religious practices, but none of the groups is large enough or so pointedly alien as to arouse hostility, as has been the case with the Antilleans.

There are no published statistics on minority totals, and there are estimates only on the Jewish population, which is reportedly between 2,500 and 3,000. They comprise three major areas of ancestry: Spanish and Portuguese Jews, Central and Eastern European Jews, and immigrants from the Middle East. The first group includes many families that have resided in Panama for more than a century; the second represents the refugee wave of the 1930s; and the third, which includes about half the Jewish population, consists of arrivals in the decade of the 1960s.

SOCIAL STRUCTURE

In the society of the early colonial period the Spaniards provided the management, and the conquered Indians supplied the labor in an economy based on the extraction of gold and on commerce and trade. Within a short time Indian labor was largely replaced by imported Negro slave labor, and traffic in slaves accounted for a significant part of the trading activities of the Spaniards. In 1610 the population of Panama City consisted of 4,801 persons—3,500 African slaves, 148 free Negroes, and 1,153 Spaniards, some of whom were of mixed parentage.

Two centuries later, toward the end of the colonial period, the general makeup was about the same, except that the white element was divided into *peninsulares* (those born in Spain) and *criollos* (those born in the New World), and most of the population was increasingly mixed in character. The upper levels of administration and private enterprise were occupied by *peninsulares*, and secondary positions, by *criollos*. Manual labor and menial services were provided by Negroes, most of whom were still in bondage, and Indians.

After independence the *criollos* moved into the dominant positions in the society, and slavery was abolished. Construction of the transisthmian railroad and later the canal introduced large-scale immigration into the sparsely populated country, and many foreigners, mostly West Indian Negro laborers, crowded into the major cities of Panama City and Colón. The accompanying expansion of the economy, which provided new opportunities for employment and the acquisition of wealth, contributed to the development of a middle class. Mestizos were able to assume many of the attributes of social position that had been monopolized by the white *penisulares* and *criollos* during the colonial period, and status and class, except at the topmost level, became an achievable goal for any individual with the energy, ability, and drive.

The process of change, however, did not entirely eliminate the association of high social status with white skin color. Peasants still tend to refer to highly placed townspeople as "the whites" (*los blancos*), and the old aristocratic families still voice disapproval of the Negro immigrants, whom they claim turned the country's urban areas into "black cities." The upper class is, with some exceptions, relatively unmixed racially; the lower class elements, however, take scant notice of skin color, except as it is associated with alien cultural habits and loyalties.

Urban Society

Urban society is restricted almost exclusively to the major cities of Panama City and Colón; the other larger towns of the interior, though classed as urban by the census and having some urban attributes, are in fact predominantly rural in their economy and outlook. Although the great majority of townspeople are agricultural workers of the lower class, there is a small element of well-to-do inhabitants that have more in common with the city dwellers than with their peasant neighbors. The towns do not have the social complexity of the major cities, but they provide a social link between urban and rural extremes.

Urban society contains elements of all social ranks, and there are distinguishable upper, middle, and lower classes. Though partly derived from a rural environment and still connected to it by the extensive landholdings of the few wealthy elite families, urban society bears the cosmopolitan imprint of the country's commercial legacy. There is considerable social mobility, primarily from the lower to the middle class and generally on an individual, rather than a group, basis. Wealth, occupation, education, and family affiliation are the principal factors affecting such mobility. In addition, there is considerable movement from rural areas to the cities, which may also involve a change in social status.

Urbanization, particularly the movement of rural dwellers to Panama City and Colón in search of employment, has led some Panamanian scholars to claim that it has depopulated the countryside. Urbanization has not, as a matter of fact, been of great magnitude, especially when compared to its extent in other Latin American countries. Nevertheless, the extension of education and the expansion of employment in the governmental and commercial sectors of the urban economy have given some individuals an opportunity to move upward in economic and social status more than they could possibly have done in the rural areas.

In contrast to the relative homogeneity of the rural population, urban society is diverse and complex, characterized by a wide range of factors that include power, wealth, occupation, education, culture, religion, national origin, and social standing. It is built upon a mixed economy that is primarily commercial and secondarily industrial and agricultural. Because the country is one of the major gateways of world commerce, it was natural that commerce should predominate. It was, indeed, the isthmus and the commerce it attracted that built the republic's two principal cities and determined the structure and character of its urban population.

The country has been steadily growing industrially, and since 1965 there have been significant increases in manufacturing, electrical output, mining, food processing, and other economic enterprises (see ch. 12, Agriculture and Industry). Although teachers and government workers make up a significant proportion of the middle class, white-collar workers in industry have served to increase the economic basis for the development and growth of the urban middle class. As a group they are demarcated from those above and below by relative economic status and by a positive set of social aspirations that are modeled largely on upper class standards and values.

The Upper Class

Urban society includes virtually all members of the upper class. Centered mainly in the capital, this class is composed of the old Panamanian families of Spanish descent, augmented to a slight degree by newer immigrant elements. Both components are substantially wealthy, but the old families have the stronger legacy of tradition and generally dominate the political scene. The newer elements are fully accepted, however, moving with ease in the society.

The upper class comprises mainly large landowning families and those who have acquired wealth through commerce or industry. It also includes leaders in government or diplomacy and some who have achieved success in the professions. It is a small, close-knit group that has developed strong ties of association and kinship over the years, and the same names recur frequently in reports and news of activities affecting the nation. Prominent among these are such families as the Arias, Arosemena, Alemán, Chiari, Goytía, and de la Guardia. People of lower classes who attain economic success can, nevertheless, move into the upper class and gain complete social acceptance. Intermarriage has been a primary factor in this process, and the joining of an old aristocratic name with a recently acquired fortune has often unified formerly disparate elements.

An important aspect of traditional upper class ideology is the view held regarding employment. The fields of endeavor considered appropriate for a member of the landowning elite are strictly circumscribed and are generally limited to government or the professions. A gentleman is expected to have ample leisure, and any form of manual effort is considered demeaning. For newer members of the elite, social status and power derive more from wealth than from ancestry and, with less preoccupation with background, most take pride in their achievements in business or commerce.

Since colonial times education has been recognized as a mark of status, and virtually all men of the upper class receive a university education. Most have attended private schools either at home or abroad, and many study a profession, generally favoring a degree in law or medicine. The practice of a profession is not necessarily a means of livelihood but rather a symbol of elite status and an aid in furthering a career in the political field. The upper class has always maintained a dual cultural allegiance, and elite families have generally sent their sons to Europe or North America for advanced schooling. Increasing numbers of women are also attending universities, but this training is not yet regarded as essential.

Upon completion of their education young men may go into government, law, medicine, journalism, or business. It is politics, however, that particularly attracts young men of the upper class, and most of the prominent old families are well represented in this sphere, usually providing the presidents of the republic, the cabinet ministers, and many members of the National Assembly. Young women are increasingly finding employment and are liberally represented in government administrative positions and commercial business offices. Young women of the upper class, however, rarely enter the professions customarily associated with women, such as teaching and nursing.

Many upper class families are closely interrelated and have been careful to avoid racial mixture. Negro blood is usually an obstacle to entry into the elite, though it is not an insurmountable barrier if accompanied by other factors, such as sufficient wealth or accomplishment. There is a greater degree of admixture with mestizo elements, and many mestizo families have entered the upper class and intermarried with members of the traditional elite.

The proximity of North Americans in the Canal Zone has resulted in a noticeable influence on the life style of the upper class. This is evident in dress, consumer goods, automobiles, and leisure-time activities. It is an inadvertent absorption rather than a conscious emulation, but United States products, styles, and fads are readily adopted not only because they are desired and appreciated but also because they are readily available. This is the case to a considerably lesser degree with the middle and lower classes, who cannot afford most such products.

The Middle Class

The middle class is predominantly mestizo, but it does include some whites and Negroes. It also has immigrant elements that include Jews, Chinese, and Levantines, as well as Christian Europeans. The middle class, like the upper class, is almost entirely an urban phenomenon. It consists of small businessmen, professionals, managerial and technical personnel, and administrative functionaries. Its membership is drawn from those who, by economic or social status, are not identifiably upper class but who, because of education, occupation, and income, have moved up from the lower class. It is steadily developing a social awareness as an entity but still looks largely to the upper class for its model of behavior and outlook.

Members of the middle class who have had such status for any length of time are rarely satisfied to remain fixed in the social scale. Emulating upper class norms and attitudes, they exert great pressure to continue their upward mobility. They are aware of the importance of occupation in determining status and recognize the role of education in helping to achieve their goals. Middle-class parents often make great sacrifices to send their children to the best schools possible, preferably to private schools where they will receive the same education available to the upper class. Further sacrifices are made to send their offspring to a university, with every effort to send them abroad to study. The young men are pressed to acquire professions, and young women are urged to take office jobs in business or government; in contrast to the upper class, young women are encouraged to enter the teaching field.

The middle class shares with the upper class the distaste for manual labor, and census occupational statistics reflect a relatively high percentage in administrative positions. Although there are no figures on the numbers constituting the middle class, it can be assumed that they comprise most of the economically active population in white-collar occupations. Government statistics indicate that some 25 percent of the urban labor force works in administrative fields. In 1969 their distribution showed approximately 10 percent in clerical positions, 9 percent in the professions (mainly law, teaching, and medicine), and 6 percent in managerial posts (as business executives and government officials).

Political observers have noted within the middle class a sharp distinction in political consciousness between the Spanish-speaking native element and the unassimilated immigrant groups. The latter tend to be preoccupied with their commercial pursuits and are conservative and largely passive in their approach to politics. The Panameños, however, are among the most militantly active and nationalistic persons in the field of politics. This is particularly noticeable among university students, the majority of whom are from middle-class families. Students are among the most nationalistic elements in the country, and they are generally in the forefront of most political struggles (see ch. 9, Political Dynamics and Values). Whereas the smaller number of students from the social elite tend, as they grow older, to accept society as they find it, middle-class students retain much of their political radicalism as they reach adulthood.

The Lower Class

The lower class constitutes the bulk of the urban population, accounting for over two-thirds of the country's city dwellers. It is made up mostly of unskilled and semiskilled workers and includes artisans, vendors, manual laborers, servants, and those engaged in personal service occupations. Incomes are relatively low in relation to middle-class earnings but are fairly adequate by general Latin American standards. Minimum-wage scales of B/0.40 (1 balboa equals US$1) an hour are observed for the most part, though the law is often circumvented by furnishing some compensation in kind, such as housing and meals. Even low-paid work is not always available, however, and most cities and towns have a high rate of unemployment.

Unemployment, which ran close to 10 percent in the cities in 1969, affects primarily the lower class and is most acute in unskilled labor and service occupations. Many of the unemployed are found among women who have come to the city from rural areas in search of employment as domestics. These constitute a sizable group and contribute significantly to the numerical excess of women over men in the country's urban areas. Government welfare and assistance programs attempt to improve the lot of the most needy, but the rate of urbanization, modest as it is, continues to outstrip the limited resources available for aid.

Ethnically the lower class has two principal components—the Panameño, which is mostly mestizo, and the immigrant, composed mainly of West Indian Negroes. Although there is some social mixing and intermarriage, religious and other cultural differences have largely kept the two elements apart. Later-generation Antilleans are gradually becoming Hispanicized, but the first generation usually remained oriented toward its British West Indian origins, and the second generation came under United States influence through exposure in the Canal Zone where most of them were employed. Although the middle class has some West Indians in its ranks, the great majority is concentrated in the lower class.

Increasing numbers of lower class parents are sending their children to school and often make considerable sacrifices to ensure that their offspring receive the best and most extensive education available. A secondary school diploma, in particular, serves as a permit to compete for white-collar employment and elevation to the middle class. This type of mobility has been on the increase throughout the twentieth century and has been accelerating slightly since World War II. Elevation from lower to middle class has been mostly among the mestizo element but has included some West Indians, who, in addition to meeting educational standards, must conform to the predominant Hispanic cultural norms.

The wide range of occupations and the diversity of interests represented in the lower class have worked to prevent the development of a group consciousness embracing all its varied elements. There is little cohesion or organization as an entity and, as a result, there has been little group exploitation. The country's organized labor force is extremely small, reportedly under 10 percent of the total labor force, and as such is hardly worth courting as a potential political factor. Conversely, it is not in a position to exert pressure. On the whole, members of the lower class give little indication of unity, except possibly sharing common hopes and aspirations to improve their lot. Although there are some signs of a dawning consciousness of improved standards and economic horizons, for the most part the lower economic sector has been placid and tractable, showing few signs of dissatisfaction or militancy.

Rural Society

A subsistence-level agriculture and a concentration of landownership in the hands of the state and the ruling elite are the two main factors that have molded the structure of rural society. It is a simple system made up almost exclusively of persons who work the land and differ in economic status only in the matter of degree. Most are poor by urban economic standards, but few are indigent. The few middle class or upper class individuals who might be found in rural areas would almost invariably have urban roots or connections of residence, employment, or interests that would, in effect, place them more in the urban than in the rural segment of society.

The two-thirds of the population residing in rural areas are almost entirely *campesinos*—persons who engage in agricultural labor either on their own or on someone else's land. Most are mestizos; there are a few Indians and Negroes and a sprinkling of whites. Nearly all were born in the country, are Catholics, and have little or no formal education.

Although the social distinctions that characterize the urban areas are not found as such in rural society, there are, nevertheless, gradations within the rural population. The *campesino* recognizes a distinction based on income that separates those who are "poorer" from those who are "better off." An individual may move from one status to the other, but this is not a formal classification or designation, and all are considered members of the lower class, itself an indication of some degree of poverty.

The rural population is mostly self-employed; because of the subsistence nature of the agricultural economy there are relatively few wage workers. It is made up mostly of tenant farmers, squatters, sharecroppers, and some small farmowners and wage laborers. Of those engaged in agriculture in 1970, some 85 percent worked for themselves or as unpaid family workers, 14 percent worked for wages, and 1 percent were employers. The land provided an adequate subsistence but little monetary return.

Despite the existence of agrarian reform laws designed to facilitate title to occupied farms and the availability of ample cultivable land, most rural Panamanians still do not own the land they work. An agricultural survey taken in 1966 indicated that 66 percent of the country's agricultural workers were squatters, with the remaining 34 percent divided between tenants and owners. In 1970 it was estimated that, at most, 15 percent owned their land, most of it in small parcels that provided a minimum subsistence.

Throughout the country's history there has generally been available land. In colonial times all land was the property of the Spanish crown, but large tracts were granted to favored subjects who had served the government through military service or civil administration. These grants formed the basis of the holdings of the present-day elite. Some land was sold to villages in the form of estates to be owned collectively by the inhabitants. These were either worked on a communal basis or assigned to individual families for their own use but did not become their individual property.

After independence crown lands became state lands. The government of the republic has made continuing efforts to increase landownership among the *campesinos* but has met with limited success. Plans have been made to break up communal landholdings and government-owned tracts and make them available to individual peasant families. The *campesinos*, however, illiterate and uninformed, have mostly failed to apply for title or taken steps to acquire the property they may have lived on and worked for generations.

Squatter occupancy is the most prevalent form of tenure, with landless families moving into vacant land, constructing their houses, and establishing homesteads. Usually state land is involved, but sometimes squatter occupancy is extended to private property. Aside from the difficulty of ousting them once they have become established, there is actually little desire to displace the interlopers, as in most cases the land would not otherwise be utilized. The squatters, in turn, are satisfied for the most part, and few do anything to alter their status. Although many could easily acquire their own land through agrarian reform grant or purchase, they prefer the familiarity of their established arrangement; it gives them freedom for mobility and relieves them from having to take on ownership problems of taxation, supplies, crop rotation, and other landowner responsibilities.

The general pattern of rural settlement is that of scattered individual farms interspersed with clustered villages, and most communities are relatively isolated both geographically and culturally. Poor communication with other areas acts as a barrier to social change, and the traditional immobility of the rural dweller, along with a lack of political consciousness, has left the rural population somewhat remote from national influences. Events in the capital, except for a major nationwide upheaval, generally have little impact on life in the countryside.

Most peasants own their own houses, but these are generally small and primitive, with dirt floors, and of cane, straw, or palm leaf construction. The *campesinos* live mainly on goods that they produce and have few commercial products in the home. The more prosperous or "better off" element, which is less than a third of the rural population, has larger houses of more permanent construction and sells some of its produce to get cash for consumer goods. Some acquire a modest degree of relative wealth and own their properties, which may include orchards, wells, or a few head of cattle. Their houses are most often grouped in villages, and the uppermost economic layer of the group is considered the basis of an incipient rural middle class.

Among the less prosperous members of rural society, the agricultural wage workers have generally low annual earnings and the least security. Usually paid on a piecework or daily basis, they are subject to changing conditions and demands and are frequently faced with unemployment. With no means of subsistence other than their wages, loss of work often results in serious hardship. The wage workers are concentrated primarily in the large sugar and banana plantations and the extensive cattle ranches. Geographically, most are in Bocas del Toro, Chiriquí and Coclé provinces. At the other end of the scale, a few of the elite landholders may live in the towns of the interior, although most reside in the capital. They constitute less than 1 percent of the landowners, but they control more than 50 percent of the country's privately owned land—still a small total compared with the extensive holdings of the state.

FAMILY

As in other Latin American countries, the family is the basic unit of the society. The role varies somewhat with social class, but at all levels it serves to integrate the individual into the culture.

The nuclear family—typically consisting of a couple and its children—and the wider kin group remain the focus of social stability within the structure, but the deep-rooted Hispanic legacy of patriarchal family life is gradually giving way before the changing tempo of modern life.

As a result of social and economic pressures and, to an extent, improved communications, a gradual decrease in the importance of the larger kin group is evident. In the past it defined the scope of an individual's orbit in society and generally restricted his activities to the extended family. Although some elements of this tradition are still retained, especially in outlying rural areas, its functions are increasingly being taken over by the nuclear family and by outside institutions.

Expanding commerce, with its greater economic opportunities and changes in the tempo of daily life, has tended to undermine the centrality of the family and kin group. The focus of economic power has shifted from the hereditary control of lands and from family-run enterprises to the political field and to industrial activities dependent primarily on impersonal organizations. Increased economic opportunity has brought to the ranks of wealth and prominence numbers of men with no family ties to the traditional upper class; in the society based on political power and prosperity, wealth has largely replaced pedigree in determining social status.

Despite changes, traditional Hispanic concepts and attitudes with respect to the family still largely apply, even in households of common-law unions. These attitudes place great emphasis on family loyalty and accord them a moral priority over virtually all other social obligations. In this view, families see their greatest hope of security and well-being in close blood ties and kin-based mutual support.

Wealth has historically been largely concentrated in the hands of a few families and acquired or transmitted by inheritance. The combination of family-controlled wealth, power, and privilege has traditionally been reflected in strong tendencies toward dynastic organization in upper class society. Groups of relatives, aware of their community of interest and collective social status, forged bonds of intimate and unquestioned loyalty that have persisted over generations and included the most distant kinsmen. In addition to affection and trust, a prominent feature was the collective supervision over the behavior of the individuals of the group. For the small elite, class consciousness has, in effect, been kinship consciousness.

In the traditional ideal of family life, the husband and father, in addition to being protector and provided for the household, is also its undisputed head. As such, he retains ultimate control over all aspects of family life, although much of this authority is commonly delegated to the mother in routine matters. A man also enjoys the freedom to come and go as he pleases and to spend his leisure time as he sees fit—including extramarital liaisons, provided that they are carried on with discretion. By contrast, the ideal for wives, held in various degrees at all social levels, emphasizes dependence and submission. In this view, women are seen as properly limited in their activities and concerns to the household and family circle (see ch. 6, Social Values).

For upper and most middle class families, kinship solidarity rests upon stable marriage. Formal church and civil weddings result in permanent parental responsibilities that can be neglected only at the risk of social disapproval. Further, the complex of paternal and maternal responsibilities is generally considered to outweigh the personal relationships between husband and wife. The emphasis of responsibility is on a man's legal wife and legitimate children, and public opinion views rather casually his obligation in the case of an informal union. In the urban lower class and among the peasants, common-law marriage is as prevalent as formal matrimony. Attitudes toward such unions vary widely. In many rural communities a majority of common-law unions are fully as durable as legal marriage and are seen as entailing the same degree of responsibility. In the cities and many parts of the countryside, however, casual arrangements are frequently less permanent, and paternal desertion is quite common.

The patriarchal pattern of family life has been subjected to some degree of challenge, both by changing social conditions and by the emergence of a nascent feminist sentiment among the relatively small number of educated women. The law provides for equality between the sexes in political and economic matters, and increasing opportunities are being made available to women to participate in national life. A number of women have come to reject their subordinate and dependent status in marriage, but these still constitute a very small minority. Despite evidence of change, in 1971 probably a majority of all Panamanians continued to accept the old ideal, and prevailing family patterns still bore the imprint of masculine supremacy. Civil law continued to recognize paternal dominance within the household and provided that the ultimate right of decision in matters affecting the welfare of the family rested with the husband.

For most couples parenthood is a welcome role. Men see fatherhood as a fulfillment and as evidence of masculinity, and women are conditioned from childhood to look upon maternity as their most exalted role. The birth of a child is therefore usually an occasion for rejoicing. The typical domestic unit consists of a father and mother living in permanent, though not necessarily formal, union, along with their unmarried and minor children. It is estimated that some 20 percent of all nuclear family groups contain other relatives as regular family members. A few upper class families conform to the old tradition and tend to be larger, including grandparents and more distant relatives, but few middle or lower class households have the space or resources to support an extended family.

Youth

Under the prevailing social view of family life, children are seen as "belonging" to the mother, who bears ultimate responsibility for their welfare. Mother-child relationships are close, and strong sentimental values are attached to the concept of maternity. Birth control, though increasing, is still relatively rare and is limited largely to the cosmopolitan and educated upper and middle classes of the cities. Mean family size nationwide in 1971 was reported as 5.1 members, with averages of 4.7 and 5.4, respectively, for urban and rural districts. In the same year 42.3 percent of all rural families had more than 3 children under the age of fifteen as compared to 29.2 percent for urban households.

Small children are pampered for the most part, and discipline and training are casual. Corporal punishment is rare, and there are few restrictions until children enter school. Children of the urban upper class are usually in the care of indulgent nurses up to, or even beyond, school age, but boys and girls of *campesino* families are introduced early to family responsibilities. This is usually done, however, through a combination of work and play, the children becoming familiar with their future adult roles by imitating and assisting their parents.

As they grow older, urban boys of the middle and upper classes become accustomed to an unrestricted life of freedom that foreshadows the adult masculine pattern. They receive little supervision outside of school and have no domestic responsibilities. Girls, however, receive some training in running a household, but in most upper and many middle class families there are servants to perform the more burdensome tasks. The girls are carefully supervised; while their brothers can range freely in search of adventure, girls are kept close to home, and their friends and playmates are subject to selective scrutiny by their parents.

Children of the urban lower class spend much of their time in the streets. Housing is usually marginal and uncomfortable and often precarious. Poverty, with its attendant conditions of disease and malnutrition, takes its toll in childhood life and health. Many boys augment the family income by working as bootblacks or newsboys, but others join delinquent gangs that frequently get into trouble with the authorities. The girls are somewhat more sheltered but must usually help with the work around the house or take early employment as domestics or in other occupations. Some inevitably drift into prostitution.

Young *campesinos* slip easily into adult life, as the necessary apprenticeship to their rural adult roles, like their formal schooling, is of short duration. Adolescence is merely a brief period of transition from the status of child to that of adult. Establishment of a new household for the large percentage of subsistence farmers who are squatters on state lands is simply a matter of selecting an accessible piece of unoccupied land and erecting a house, usually with the help of kinsmen. When he moves into his newly constructed hut with a woman bound to him by either formal or informal union, the young countryman has attained full adulthood.

Both boys and girls of the upper and middle classes of the large cities usually continue their education until they have completed their secondary schooling, and many, including increasing numbers of young women, go on to college. For most upper and middle class boys adolescence is a carefree period of few cares and little responsibility. With only the most perfunctory supervision, the young university or secondary school student is free to seek adventure and self-expression, traditionally through enthusiastic pursuit of girls or wholehearted dedication to politics. When his student days are over, the young man enters upon his career or profession as determined by his education and social status. At this point, he is ready to consider serious courtship of a suitable mate and ultimately marry and establish his homestead as an adult.

Girls of the upper and middle classes are usually presented formally to society at the time of their fifteenth birthday. After baptism, this debut constitutes the most important ritual connected with childhood and youth and is as elaborate as the family's finances permit. Dating is not ordinarily permitted for at least two years thereafter, but a girl may receive in the home young men whom her parents have approved. Panamanian girls enjoy relatively greater freedom than is customary in most Latin American countries, but supervision is still strict, and chaperonage among the upper strata continues to be quite prevalent.

Most young unmarried women of the middle class and some from the upper class seek employment in business or government, and the working woman has become the norm rather than the exception. Many middle-class women continue to work even after marriage in order to maintain a higher standard of living in their newly created households.

116

Ritual Kinship

Panama shares with all of Latin America the institution of *compadrazgo,* the complex of relationships between a child and his godparents. The selection of godparents (*padrinos*) is an important step usually taken at the time of a child's baptism; it is one that can have a pronounced influence on the child's welfare and on his future. It results in a quasi-kinship relationship that carries with it moral, ceremonial, and religious significance and broadens family ties of trust, loyalty, and support.

Parents ordinarily choose for their children godparents whom they respect and trust and who are as high in the social scale as possible. A certain degree of formality and ceremony is expected of godfathers (*compadres*) or godmothers (*comadres*) in social interaction, but the bonds involve primarily protective responsibility and a willingness to render assistance in adversity.

The duties of godparents include assumption of all expenses involved in the baptism, such as parish fees and christening robes, and often a substantial contribution to the celebration of the occasion. In the event of the child's death, the godfather is responsible for providing his funeral. In the accepted view, godparents are seen as interested participants in the child's spiritual and moral education and welfare. In fact, godparents are often so far removed from the child, either in social status or abode, that close contact is infrequent.

Campesinos establish ties of *compadrazgo* along two distinct lines. In many cases the godparent sought is a relative or friend, particularly one who lives in the same general area. Such relationships tend to reinforce those already existing on other bases and to cement local loyalties. In other cases a man will seek a person of wealth, power, or prestige. Thus he not only gains in personal stature by reflection but also establishes a claim on the potential support and protection of the more powerful man. Such a contact can give the parent confidence to launch his offspring into an alien outside world in which he may have little personal status.

Influential political and commercial leaders are usually not averse to establishing ties of ritual kinship with *campesino* families, as the network of mutual respect and obligation can result in strengthening the patron-client relationship to mutual advantage. *Compadrazgo* is not quite as important in the cities as in the countryside, but the institution still carries considerable weight and is generally observed and respected. As a general rule, it is frowned upon as bad form for a person of position to refuse a bid to serve as a godparent.

CHAPTER 6

SOCIAL VALUES

Although in many respects the country's social values derive from the Hispanic cultural tradition found in most of Latin America, in many instances the Panamanians have deviated from the customary expression of these traditions and have molded and tempered them to fit a constantly developing national temperament. Moreover, throughout its history Panama has been exposed to a wide variety of outside cultural and social influences.

Because of its strategic location as a link between two oceans, it has had continuing contact with waves of transient and immigrant foreigners who have brought with them an alien, and often disparate, set of social values. Nevertheless, the basic Hispanic-derived views regarding the individual and his relations with society persist and have left their distinctive imprint on the nation's culture. If, in fact, Panamanian views and values change, they do so deliberately and slowly.

There is, nevertheless, a fundamental set of central values that is generally uniform throughout the national territory and is found at all social levels. These include the concepts applicable to the worth of the individual and his role in society, a strong sense of family loyalty, and a general acceptance of the principle of male predominance. There is also a strong sense of hierarchy that permeates virtually all social relationships. Stemming from an age-old Hispanic heritage, it stresses the importance of authority in all walks of life and sharply defines status. The tradition of rigid stratification is one that has been consistently reinforced by the church, which, while asserting the ultimate equality of all men before divine justice, has usually tended to support the temporal status quo.

There are relatively minor, but still perceptible, differences in urban and rural values. Among the urban population, particularly the middle class, there is a stronger sense of nationalism, which leads to a rejection of foreign ideological influences and a desire to revert to bucolic standards that may or may not have ever actually existed. The city dweller, who is subjected to persistent social and economic pressures, is less likely to be as fatalistic as

119

the more isolated *campesino* (peasant) and will be more prone to take action to affect his destiny. The countryman is not faced with the competition, bustle, and social mobility that confront the urbanite, and the struggle for advancement typical of the middle class has little meaning for a subsistence farmer living in the relatively unchanging interior. His hopes and aspirations are modest, and if he meets with reverses he accepts them as a result of forces beyond his control, placing a high value on patience and endurance in the face of adversity.

The Roman Catholic Church has exerted a pervasive, though moderate, influence on the country since colonial times. It has, for the most part, avoided involvement in politics and restricted its activities to spiritual matters, thus securing a firmly established position of esteem and respect. Panama has largely averted the surge of anticlericalism that pervaded the political life of many other Latin American countries in the late eighteenth and nineteenth centuries.

Under Spanish rule the church had had a special place in the society, and the relationship between church and government was even closer than in Spain. Prelates often sat as members, or even presidents, of *audiencias* (colonial courts) and held civil as well as canonical authority. Both the secular church and the religious orders acquired considerable wealth—the orders in particular profiting from banking activities in the absence of organized commercial facilities. The church built schools and hospitals in addition to elaborate churches, and such education as was available was in the charge of priests, friars, and nuns. The first Panamanian university, the short-lived San Xavier, was established in 1749 by the Jesuit order.

By the start of the twentieth century the position of the church had changed significantly. The expulsion of the Jesuits in 1767 was followed by a long period of religious apathy, during which the church lost much of its power and wealth. During the nineteenth century in particular, liberal thought and the belated effects of the European "enlightenment" resulted in widespread lack of interest and support, although there was little of the actual hostility that was prevalent in many other Latin American countries.

Though not constitutionally the country's state religion, the Catholic faith is recognized as the religion of the majority. The present-day church holds a respected position in the society and devotes its energies to the nation's spiritual welfare, as well as assuming an increasing concern with matters of social improvement. At the same time, although religion is accepted as an integral part of the social fabric, neither religious zeal nor manifest piety have become significant elements of the nation's social values.

BASIC ATTITUDES AND VALUES

Personalismo

One of the principal themes of the Hispanic-derived social view is the primacy accorded individuality. There is a strongly held conviction regarding the uniqueness of the individual and the existence in every person of an inner dignity and personal integrity. These qualities are apart from social status and are both inalienable and worthy of respect.

The emphasis on individuality is reflected in a complex of beliefs and assumptions that have become subsumed under the concept of *personalismo* (personalism), which stresses personal qualities and interpersonal trust over abstract ideology or institutionalism. It involves a strong sense of personal honor and sensitivity to praise, insult, or slight. Events are conceived to be more the product of individual men than of impersonal social forces or the application of intangible ideas. In general, it is considered that a man's well-being lies in his relationships of trust with other men more than in the functioning of institutions or in adherence to specific doctrines.

Personalismo, with its emphasis on uniqueness, conceives personal status to be wholly independent of social status, and, in this view, an individual can fulfill his potential at any social level, no matter how humble. Some stratification, as in the armed forces or in matters of employment, is, of necessity, inevitable; but in relations between persons of different rank, the superior is expected to treat a subordinate with due recognition of his worth as a person. Thus relations between employers and employees, leaders and followers, and patrons and retainers should ideally reflect a friendly and active concern of the former for the latter. The one may treat the other as a subordinate but not as a nonentity.

There are clear distinctions between the respect accorded social status and that accorded personal dignity. There are fixed formalities for expressing the respect of followers to leaders and that of the humble to those of higher social status, but the behavior of one person toward another is also prescribed. Cordiality between social equals is emphasized but, in modified form, is also stressed between persons of unequal rank. Although the individual of superior rank is not expected to behave toward his inferior as an equal, he is expected to treat him with the dignity due an individual.

Interpersonal relations tend to be warm and punctilious. Hospitality is highly valued, and the exchange of gifts is popular and prevalent. A greeting between friends is usually effusive, demonstrative, and voluble, and it would be considered discourteous not to display outward human warmth even in a casual relationship. Within the family, normal courtesies and amenities are equally cordial but less formal than between more distant acquaintances.

The emphasis on personal individuality at times discourages involvement with large numbers of people. Although recognizing his rather impersonal relationship as a member of the nation, the average citizen is somewhat reluctant to form close associations with persons other than his kin and his close friends. Within this framework he considers that his uniqueness is understood and fully appreciated, and he need not maintain the defenses he feels he would need in social interactions with larger groups. For the most part, he is not a joiner, and social circles tend to be small and relatively exclusive.

Relationships based on interplay of personality and personal acquaintance usually inspire more confidence than those resulting from purely formal contacts. The term *hombre de confianza* (man of confidence) is used to denote a person to whom one's relationship is on an intimate and well-defined basis, such as kinship or *compadrazgo*, the relationship between a child and his godparents (see ch. 5, Social System). *Personalismo* also enters into politics, with an equal emphasis on the personal, as opposed to the abstract or institutional. Thus in the political field contenders are supported or attacked and, in turn, back or assail others on an intensely personal basis. Whereas political candidates do make speeches concerned with issues, the outcome of the voting, particularly in rural areas, is likely to depend on the personal influence that has been brought to bear by the candidate or by local political bosses.

Notwithstanding the respect for individuality and the high value placed on personal uniqueness, the social view also entails a generally accepted range of ideal personal qualities, and an individual derives much of his status from the degree to which he fits these molds. This is particularly the case with the traditions of masculine dominance and the sharply differentiated social roles of men and women, which are reflected in widely contrasting male and female personality ideals.

Masculine Personality Ideals

As in virtually all of Latin America there is a deep-rooted tendency to emphasize the masculine role and exalt a concept of masculinity as an essential personality characteristic. The complex of beliefs and attitudes defining this image is called *machismo* (literally, maleness—see Glossary), and includes such qualities as forcefulness, daring, and virility. Leaders in particular are expected to exemplify the male value and must project inherent courage and self-confidence.

The *macho* (see Glossary), the accepted model of ideal masculinity, was basically a man of dramatic action, with a personality that radiates evident heroism, histrionic flourish, and self-confidence bordering on the daring. These qualities not only represent the abstract model of male personality but also serve as primary, though not the sole, criteria in forming personal judgments. They are particularly applicable in politics or intellectual life, where forcefulness and daring of expression are major factors in attracting a following or acquiring personal prestige.

It has traditionally been the domineering politician of imposing personality and impassioned oratory, rather than the able, but plodding administrator, who has enjoyed the greater success. In intellectual life the brilliant and aggressive polemicist, rather than the quietly intelligent but retiring contributor to substantive knowledge has usually had the greater appeal. Appreciation of the true *macho* is characteristic of all social classes, but the opportunity to gain the limelight before a large audience, whether in politics, oratorical flourish, or other situations permitting the heroic gesture, has been limited largely to the small, educated upper social strata. The average citizen of lesser stature can only testify to his *machismo* locally in his daily life, possibly achieving prominence for his forcefulness among his fellows. This he may do through physical or vocal effort, by demonstrating qualities of leadership, or by gaining a reputation for prowess with the opposite sex.

Although the majority of Panamanians are baptized Catholics, religious ardor is not usually included as a basic aspect of the male personality ideal. Church precept, particularly its restrictive morality and emphasis on humility and abnegation, are at direct variance with the salient features of *machismo*. Hence, while subscribing to Catholicism and recognizing it as part of their national and cultural heritage, most men look on manifest piety and strict observance of church rites as more properly the concern of women and children.

There are still traces of an earlier traditional value associated with the *caballero,* or upper class gentleman. Paralleling the precepts of *machismo,* the model of the *caballero,* though including many of the *macho* qualities, also implies wealth, leisure, refinement, and disdain for any form of manual labor. The social and economic developments of the twentieth century, however, with their broader educational opportunities, have largely eliminated an aesthetic leisure class, and it would be difficult to find a true *caballero* in the traditional sense of the word. Most members of the country's small traditional elite are engaged in some enterprise or occupation, but they restrict their activities to socially acceptable fields of endeavor, such as politics, law, medicine, or journalism. Newer members of the upper class are often engaged in commerce or industry.

The term *machismo,* along with its basic concepts, has had longstanding currency in Hispanic America. Although it presents a highly stereotyped prototype of ideal manhood, it is one that is generally accepted throughout the nation. Nevertheless, although *machismo* continues to be an important theme in social relations, some of its precepts and values are beginning to be suspect, and there is growing evidence of some questioning of its total validity among more informed and sophisticated men of all classes. Possibly the best indication of this is the fact that it is becoming the butt of satirical ridicule. In 1970 it was attacked editorially in a number of leading Latin American newspapers, and in the summer of 1971 it was the topic of a Mexican-published comic book entitled "Tragic Machismo," which characterized it as a ridiculous, false, and exaggerated sense of male superiority and manliness.

Feminine Personality Ideals

The traditional image of ideal womanhood is in many respects the antithesis of that of the ideal man and is no less stereotyped. In contrast to male aggressiveness and zest for competition, the proper female is seen as exhibiting gentleness, passivity, and acceptance of a status derived from her husband and family. She is also expected to accept with resignation and dignity any failings and shortcomings on the part of her spouse. If in actuality women show initiative in domestic affairs and, as occurs in many cases, work in support of the household, their husbands still expect to maintain their position as the sole and final arbiter of family welfare.

The ideal woman in the cultural view is acquiescent, passive, understanding, and, in general, self-denying. She is the gentle mother who, accepting her frequently unrewarding lot, nevertheless has the strength to undertake, if necessary, the support of her children. In all classes the ideal, if not always the actual, adjustment of women is passive acceptance and faith in divine justice.

Although women have traditionally had a significant place in society only within the family and household, in these areas their role is a demanding one. Both motherhood and filial affection are imbued with an aura of devotion and tenderness that is a recurring theme in daily life, as well as in literature and song. In the social ideal a woman dedicates her entire life to the welfare of her children, with virtually sole responsibility for their early rearing and training and, if necessary, their economic support. She is, in fact, often faced with the need to assume full charge in view of the high incidence of paternal desertion, particularly in the lower classes.

A traditional view of femininity shared by all classes is that in relations between the sexes the woman is a submissive and passive follower. Although economic conditions result in a high incidence of informal unions, common law marriages are in many cases fully as stable as more officially sanctioned contracts and in most cases receive the same degree of social acceptance. Premarital chastity and marital fidelity are vital to the ideal image of womanhood, particularly among the middle and upper classes, and this tradition is reflected in the closer supervision over unmarried girls in higher status families. Although chaperonage in its strictest form has all but disappeared from the modern scene, there is still a good deal of restraint in social relations between young men and women and a minimum of unaccompanied dating, despite the relative ease with which a common law household can be established.

Women have traditionally borne most of the responsibility for the rituals and duties of kinship, and to them have fallen most of the routines for observance of family functions, whether celebrations or mourning. The cohesiveness of kin groups is largely reinforced by the visiting and socializing on the part of female relatives, who generally maintain contact with even the most remote relations. Outside of purely domestic affairs and those of the kin groups, other activities customarily considered as a proper realm for women are in religious observance and in charitable affairs. The mother usually has sole charge of ensuring her children's religious education, and in general she is looked on as the family's representative before the church. In the organization and operation of charities women have always played the prominent role, particularly in the urban areas. Although generally limited to women of the upper class, such activity forms an important aspect of the ideal feminine image.

As in other aspects of daily life, social and economic changes are slowly modifying traditional feminine roles. There has been a noticeable growth of feminist sentiment, particularly among women of the middle class, and expanded educational and employment opportunities have provided new fields of activity. Nevertheless, no clear-cut value criteria that define these new roles and the more aggressive stance of women have as yet emerged. Although the image of womanhood projected in the traditional ideals grows increasingly remote from reality, the old established values continue to persist.

Interpersonal Relationships

Interpersonal relationships and social responsibilities are strongly influenced by the high value attached to family and personal loyalty. The highest confidence is placed in persons rather than ideas or institutions and, the more relatives and friends a man has, the more secure he is and the better able he is to cope with his social and economic environment. The man who has personal connections with an individual of lofty position or power is considered particularly fortunate.

Loyalty to one's kinsmen is a strong and traditionally ingrained value, and family ties are considered to be one's first line of defense against a hostile world. This loyalty often outweighs that which is attached to a spouse, and a man will frequently give priority to his responsibility to his parents or brothers and sisters over that extended to his wife. In politics, business, or other social activities, it is commonplace for a person to use his position in the interest, or to the advantage of, his kinsmen, and there is little or no stigma attached to such practice.

Family loyalty is strongest in the upper class, where the wealth and power are traditionally concentrated in the hands of a few families and are handed on along bloodlines. It is here that the dynastic organization of the group of blood kin is most evident, and the extended family, with its control over the behavior of even its most distant members, is most prevalent. These old ideals of intimate kinship are shared to an extent at all social levels, but in the lower class, where many households do not include a father, it is more difficult to foster any degree of kinship consciousness (see ch. 5, Social System).

Response to social relationships, whether with respect to ties of family or friendship, vary slightly with social status, but at all levels they are recognized as a strong bond affecting mutual interdependence. A man's kinsmen and friends are an extension of his self, and they are expected to defend his honor, plead his cause, share his fortunes, and safeguard his confidence. Solid friendships usually take long to develop, and acquaintances usually become really intimate only after confidence is firmly established and the two persons know each other's families at least by name. The prelude to almost any social contact is usually a detailed conversation showing interest and concern for the health and welfare of each other's kin.

Although kinship and friendship provide the means of cementing loyalties among men of equal social status, there are also well-defined bases upon which those of different levels can establish relations of intimacy and trust. In general, a powerful or wealthy man who maintains bonds of personal loyalty with those of more modest position is known as a *patrón* (sponsor or protector; pl., *patrones*). Men seek aid and protection of *patrones* by attaching themselves to the wealthy and powerful as loyal retainers. Typically, the *patrón* is an employer, a political leader, a landowner or, sometimes in rural areas, a merchant. The relationship with his retainers is a special one—marked by mutual affection, loyalty, trust, and willingness to render mutual assistance. Like friendship, *patrón*-retainer ties can develop through long-term association and are often as strong; but conversely, the association carries no implication of equality. The *patrón* offers a paternalistic interest, protection, and security through economic favors or use of his influence on behalf of his retainers who, in turn, return not only affection but also deference and obedience.

Hierarchy

The inner dignity ascribed to each individual by *personalismo* is not based on convictions of egalitarianism. It does not imply the equality of men but rather their individuality and uniqueness. A stress on hierarchy and rank has been a dominant theme in the country's social history, and most interpersonal relations are defined in terms of dominance and subordination. A father ideally exercises firm authority over all members of his family and, in politics and the social and economic fields, most direct relationships are between superior and subordinate.

The Hispanic social and political traditions emphasized strict stratification of power and privilege and a pyramidal structure of authority that allowed little leeway for local initiative or collective decisionmaking. Communications barriers made for frequent violations of the edicts and practices of the colonial system, but the maintenance of a rigid hierarchy and centralization was no less important as an ideal. Initiative and rule were seen as properly vested in officials from Spain, and administrators in the colony were considered little more than the executors of imposed policy. Little or no intercommunication was permitted officials at the same level, and most official communication consisted of orders and directives passed down from the home government to colonial administrators.

The establishment of the Republic brought little change in concepts of hierarchy, although social mobility permitted changes in individual positions within the structure. The country's leaders have always professed adherence to democratic principles and decentralized power, but for the most part they have continued to conform to the traditional Hispanic patterns. The people's sense of hierarchy is evident in the general acceptance of the leadership of the old families in national politics and in the deference to the authority of recognized *patrones* in the countryside, men who are generally the wealthiest and most prominent members of their community.

The popularly accepted concept of leadership is somewhat different from that generally envisioned in democratic theory and doctrine, and the leader is usually seen less as a moderator and executive for a group of equals than as the spokesman of his group and the unquestioned arbiter of its policies. He can act in the group's interests with little or no consultation with other members. As long as such a leader remains in command of the situation, largely by the projection of a forceful and persuasive personality, and as long as he inspires group confidence in his ability to further the collective interest, there is seldom any strong opposition to his decisions or acts. Such a leader imposes his will by force of personality and by virtue of his position, inspiring confidence in those associated with him that he can attain their goals. It is not considered at all unreasonable in the logic of the social tradition that such a man be the best spokesman for group interests; both out of admiration for his qualities and gratitude for his forceful representation, his followers accord him deference and loyal obedience.

A corollary to the concept of strongman leadership is that any man in power must expect to be constantly challenged, as men are seen as being in continual competition. If followers recognize in a challenger a man better fitted to represent their interests, they will readily shift their allegiance. The successful leader must embody the ideals of *machismo*, and the aspirant who does not successfully project himself becomes a retainer. It is recognized that not everyone can occupy the top position, and the status of retainer, while lower in the hierarchy, is still invested with a degree of validity of its own. The forceful loser can still continue to contend, and in the meantime he is rewarded for his support with material benefits and a sense of identity with the leader.

In addition to the assurance that their leader is capable of furthering their interests, men expect him to be wise and honest in dealing with them. The traditional image of the *patrón* assumes importance in the quality of leadership, and the *patrón* maintains a bond that is one of trust and obligation. He keeps on a footing of intimacy with his retainers and takes pains to communicate his interest in their well-being. In politics in particular, the popular political figures mingle freely and often with their retainers. Personal appearances symbolize the man-to-man bond between the leader and his followers and at the same time affirm their respective places in the hierarchical structure.

The notable feature about the country's social values, including the views on hierarchy and authority, is that they have survived for over 400 years with little change. Bringing to the New World an ethic long entrenched in Hispanic society, the basic code of guiding principles largely resisted the pressures and vicissitudes of changing conditions in a new and alien environment. For the most part, the values that guided the society in Spain have remained valid throughout the history of the nation and have managed to persist in the face of the turbulence of the nineteenth century and the increased tempo of the twentieth. Despite alteration and adaptation to new conditions, they have demonstrated that their firm roots in the culture would probably ensure their continued acceptance and resist rejection for some time to come.

RELIGION

The Constitution of 1946 prescribes that there shall be no prejudice with respect to religious freedom, and the practice of all forms of worship is authorized. It is recognized that the Roman Catholic faith is the country's predominant religion, and there is a provision that it be taught in the public schools. Such instruction or other religious activity is not, however, compulsory if so requested by a child's parents or guardians.

The 1946 Constitution does not specifically provide for the separation of church and state, but it implies the independent functioning of each. Church relations with the government are generally harmonious, and religion is accepted as a significant element of the social fabric. Members of the clergy may not hold civil or military public office, except such posts as may be concerned with social welfare or public instruction.

Preliminary census figures for 1970 indicate that approximately 93 percent of the population is Roman Catholic; and 6 percent (roughly 90,000 persons), Protestant. The remainder is composed of the small number of Jews, Chinese, Hindus, and Muslims of Middle Eastern origin. Government statistics do not include the country's tribal Indians, the majority of whom do not profess Christianity. Although efforts to convert the Indians have met with limited success, traditional indigenous religions have virtually disappeared from the national scene. A few isolated beliefs and practices have survived but only as superficial reminders of a once pervasive cult. There have been some limited attempts at proselytizing by various Protestant sects, but these have met with little success, particularly in the more strongly Catholic hinterland. For the most part, Protestantism remains of minor importance in the nation's religious life, and the few other minority sects have no impact whatsoever.

Therefore, when one speaks of the church, it is the Roman Catholic Church. The devout regard church attendance and the observance of religious duties as a normal feature of everyday life, and even the most casual or nominal Catholics adjust the orientation of their daily lives to the prevailing norms of the religious calendar. Though some sacraments are observed more scrupulously than others, baptism is almost universal, and the last rites of the church are administered to many who during their lives were most indifferent to the precepts of the faith or its religious rituals.

The small minority groups who practice their own faiths do so without public disapproval or interference. Protestantism is the only other religion that is represented in any significant numbers. It is strongest among the Antillean Negroes, most of whom were emigrants, or descendants of emigrants, from the predominantly Protestant British West Indies (see ch. 5, Social System). There has not been any concerted effort to convert them, but a few do adopt Catholicism, largely as part of the process of Hispanization. The Protestant churches themselves have established some missions, mostly in the vicinity of the zone and in Chiriquí Province. They have not been notably successful, however, in reaching the strongly Catholic population, and in some areas there has been popular resistance to the establishment of such missions.

The Roman Catholic Church has been conducting a concerted drive in recent years to revive active interest in religious affairs, raise church attendance, and increase the incidence of church marriage. This has been a continuing effort since 1958, when a lay mission group, the Santa Misión Católica, arrived from Rome to stimulate and support the local clergy. Focusing first on the lower social strata in the capital, the campaign spread throughout the country. Before the departure of the delegation it helped introduce church-sponsored social welfare projects and served to rouse the clergy from the lethargy that had been traditional with the church in Panama.

Although the drive did not spur a widespread religious revival, it did, initially at least, almost double the percentage of church weddings and increase attendance at services to new levels. It has been difficult to maintain the momentum of the drive, however, and the church has continued to be confronted with obstacles, such as a shortage of priests, the general indifference of the young in religious matters, and the prevailing secular attitudes of the urban population.

Development of the Modern Church

Members of the clergy accompanied the Spanish conquistadores from the earliest days of New World exploration and conquest, and a close association of crown and church was maintained during the entire colonial era. Papal authority granted the crown extensive powers over religious affairs, such as regulation of church government, clerical appointments, and disposition of ecclesiastical tithes, and the church in effect became an instrument of the crown. The government relied heavily on church support, and churchmen worked closely with civic leaders and strongly influenced colonial policy. In practice, the two were mutually supporting and both clerics and civil officials often combined religious and temporal duties and responsibilities.

The first church established in the country was Santa María la Antigua del Darién, built in 1510. Four years later it became the seat of the first diocese to be established on the mainland of the Western Hemisphere. The Diocese of Castilla del Oro, as Panama was then known, was transferred in 1521 from Darién to the city of Panama. The relationship with Seville continued until 1548, at which time the episcopate in Panama was moved to the jurisdiction of the Archdiocese of Lima, Peru, which had been newly created by Pope Paul III.

Nearly three centuries later the Diocese of Panama became part of the Archdiocese of Santa Fé de Bogotá, Colombia, where it remained until 1901, when it passed to the control of the Archdiocese of Cartagena. In 1925 the autonomous Archdiocese of Panama was established by papal decree, and the following year the Apostolic Vicarage of Darién was formed. A suffragan of David was named in 1955.

After independence from Spain, but before Panama separated from Colombia, the close association between church and state continued for a number of years. As the nineteenth century progressed, however, the country underwent a period of marked decline in religious interest and a widespread apathy toward church affairs. The church steadily became less important in secular matters and lost much of its temporal power. The religious and the civil authorities continued to be mutually supporting, but their respective functions and authority were more clearly defined and more distinctly separated.

131

The position of the church was specifically outlined in 1887 in a concordat signed that year between the Catholic hierarchy and the government of Colombia. This provided for the independence of the church from civil authority and its right to establish religious orders and recognized the sovereignty of the Holy See in the appointment of bishops. It also recognized Catholic matrimony as fully binding and provided that religious instruction be compulsory at all levels of education.

The Concordat of 1887 governed church-state relations until Panama seceded from Colombia. The Constitution of 1904, the first constitution of the newly independent Panama, provided for complete religious freedom, claimed no government jurisdiction in the appointment of church officials, and specified no restrictions on church management of internal religious or economic affairs. No religious criteria were required for holding public office, and religious instruction in the public school system was provided only for those who wanted it. Except for a few scholarships at the Catholic Seminary, the government did not contribute funds for support of church activities. The Roman Catholic Church was recognized as the religion of the majority, and the state assumed the responsibility for encouraging the conversion of the tribal Indians. An envoy to the Vatican was accredited for the first time in 1929.

The country's current charter, the Constitution of 1946, did not alter the basic principles governing the church's activities or its relations with the government. Since the early years of independence the church has continued to emphasize its spiritual role and has generally avoided involvement in secular affairs. It has, for the most part, received a moderate degree of public support, bolstered at times by militant Catholic action groups, such as federations of Catholic doctors and lawyers, that have periodically campaigned for a more dynamic role for the church and for religion.

The Contemporary Church and Religious Practice

In 1971 the Roman Catholic Church held a respected, though not powerful, position in the society and was a familiar facet of daily life. Since World War II it has gone far in overcoming traditional passivity and has been taking a more active part in social welfare activities. Church relations with the government were amicable for the most part, and its ubiquitous presence had made it a moderately influential factor in the cultural stream of the nation.

Virtually every town has its Roman Catholic Church, although many do not have a priest in residence. Many rural inhabitants in the more remote areas receive only an occasional visit from a busy priest who must travel periodically among a number of isolated villages. In 1971 there were 257 priests in the country, including some 176 members of religious orders. These included Jesuits, Carmelites, Paulists, and La Salle Christian Brothers. Women's orders included Franciscans, Salesians, Bethlehemite Sisters, and Servants of Mary. The Visitandinas were the only order of cloistered nuns represented.

In the church hierarchy, in addition to the archbishop and the five resident bishops, there is an Apostolic Vicar (of Darién), a Papal Nuncio, and a Nullius Prelate (of Bocas del Toro). The head of the Roman Catholic Church is Monsignor Marcos Gregorio McGrath, the Archbishop of Panama, who is a United States citizen. The country is organized into 101 parishes, and there is also a seminary (with thirty-two seminarians in 1970), a Catholic university, and forty-two Catholic schools.

Catholicism permeates the environment of most citizens, but its impact is not as pronounced as it is in many other Catholic countries. This is owing in part to the small number of clergy, with only one priest for each 6,000 of the population, one of the lowest ratios found in Latin America. These priests, however, make an effort to provide much of the population with rites and services.

Religious attitudes and customs differ somewhat between urban and rural areas, but the presence of the Catholic faith is felt in most routine social activities. Birth, marriage, or death are marked by religious rites, and many of the national holidays are religious celebrations. The church is usually a central and imposing building in both urban and rural communities, and in many homes religious symbols are prominently displayed.

One of the first social functions in which a newly born member of the family participates is the sacrament of baptism, which symbolizes his entry into the society and brings him into the church community. In the cities, facilities are readily available, but in rural areas families must often travel some distance to the nearest parish center for the ceremony. The trip is considered of great importance and is a task willingly undertaken. Baptism is, in fact, generally considered the most significant religious rite, more important even than marriage, and is one in which virtually every Panamanian participates.

Children are exposed early to the teachings of the church, and are usually taken to mass regularly by their mothers. As they grow older they take an increasing part in church liturgy and by the age of ten are usually full participants in such activities as catechism classes, communion, and confession. Boys, in most cases, as they approach manhood tend to drift from the church and from conscientious observation of church ritual. Few young men attend services regularly, and even fewer take an active part in the religious life of the community, although they continue to consider themselves Catholics. Their lack of participation is reflected in the small number of Panamanian youths who enter the priesthood.

Girls are encouraged to continue their religious devotions and observe the moral tenets of their faith. It is a generally accepted belief that women are more involved than men, and clerics accept this as a basic axiom. The community exerts a degree of social pressure on a woman to become involved in church affairs, and most women, particularly in urban areas, respond. As a rule they attend mass regularly and take an active part in church and church-sponsored activities. Religious gatherings and observances are among the principal forms of diversion for women outside the home, and to a great extent these activities are social as much as they are devotional.

The Sunday service is a high point of the week in the community, and religious fetes are among the most popular holidays of the year. For the isolated farm family these events are usually the major diversions of their daily life, and they look forward to the weekly trip to the nearest community center to attend both the Sunday mass and the local market.

In some respects religion is somewhat stronger in rural areas than in the cities. The people are more ingenuous, and there is a simpler ingrained basic faith. On the other hand, many precepts and proscriptions of the faith are ignored or violated, and it is rare that this draws any public censure. Qualities considered important in leaders seldom include religious zeal or devotion, and many men, including prominent community figures, attend church infrequently or not at all. Village leaders as well as ordinary citizens often live in common law unions that are frowned on by the church, but this is accepted without reproach as most of the neighbors have similar unsanctified arrangements.

In the cities, religious practice is also an integral part of community life, but again, more from the social aspect than from the spiritual. Although Sunday mass is a welcome occasion, its primary attraction is that it leads to extensive socializing—making calls, going for a drive, or promenading in the town square. The women of the upper and middle classes tend to be the most active in church affairs for most men feel that religious matters are more properly within the realm of feminine interests.

Secularism is more prevalent in the cities than in the towns and villages. In the smaller communities the tradition of patronage and dutiful observance tends to keep the people more actively involved than is the case with their counterparts in the more anonymous climate of the large urban centers.

In some respects, such as direct personal contact and appeal, a church in an urban working-class parish bears greater resemblance to a rural church than to an upper-class urban one. It is not, however, so much a center of social activity, as working-class women have little spare time after fulfilling the demands of their household duties and, often, their jobs.

Attitudes toward the church vary with education and social class, but it is generally viewed as a traditional institution more involved in the externals of ritual and form than in daily life. It is also commonly considered that the church is more concerned with individual salvation than with the social environment. The emerging social consciousness of the church and its growing concern with social justice have, however, increased its prestige in many circles, and there is evidence that more men, traditionally indifferent, are giving it greater heed.

Many Antillean Protestants live and work in the Canal Zone, and some of their religious practices are conditioned by the norms of the zone authorities. The administration, for example, rents housing in the zone only to legally married couples and restricts school and hospital facilities to wives and their legitimate children. As in any other community, however, the Protestants span a wide range of religious observance and zeal. Many, especially among the older residents, are ardent church-going and dedicated Christians; whereas others, particularly among the young, maintain a casual and purely nominal church affiliation, with few practicing members of a religious congregation.

CHAPTER 7

EDUCATION, CULTURE, AND
PUBLIC INFORMATION

In 1971 secondary and higher education were available only in urban localities, where about half of the population lived, but schools offering at least partial primary schooling were available to nearly all of the rural population. Considerably more than 80 percent of the population over ten years of age was literate. Advances in education in general, particularly literacy, during the 1950s and 1960s served as an important stimulus to artistic and intellectual expression as well as to journalism and other aspects of communications. The average educational level of the population rose from 3.6 years of schooling in 1950 to 4.4 years in 1960.

During the 1960s and early 1970s the government attached importance of the first order to improving and expanding the educational system, and budgets of the Ministry of Education were far larger than those of any other ministry. Enrollments, particularly at the secondary and university levels, increased at rates much faster than that of the population as a whole.

By the late 1960s female and male enrollments were approximately equal at all levels of schooling, and nearly all schools were coeducational. Private schools, most of them urban, educated only a small proportion of the student population, but considerable prestige attached to these schools, and their retention rates were generally higher than those of public schools. Until the establishment of a small private university in 1965, only the University of Panama offered higher education. Many of the children of the well to do, however, continued to go abroad for their university training.

Vocational schooling was far less popular than the academic; although there had been considerable progress during the 1960s, the teaching personnel and facilities remained inadequate. Special funds were earmarked for improvement of the vocational and technical school system in 1971, however, and development of this program appeared to represent the principal challenge to education during the 1970s.

The Hispanic legacy has formed the foundation of the country's cultural development, but French and North American influences have also been strong. Historical and nationalistic themes have been prominent in the country's literature. The avant-garde trend in poetry led originally to the adoption of exotic themes, but since the early 1960s the subject matter treated in this genre has been drawn primarily from the national experience. Considerable enthusiasm was generated in 1971 for a new trend in drama known as "popular theater," in which the performers took their art to the people in the city slums and isolated rural areas.

Contemporary painting includes abstract works as well as the more traditional landscapes and portraits. The country's best expression of modern architectural trends is the complex of buildings that make up the University of Panama. Brazilian influence is apparent in the emphasis on natural light and shadow and the use of open space as an element of composition. Musical creativity and appreciation are promoted by the National Institute of Music and the National Symphony Orchestra. Panama has long been noted for the vitality of its folk art, especially the traditional dances performed in colorful costume throughout the country at fiesta time.

In addition to formal education and formal and informal artistic expression, a strong influence on the minds and emotions of the people is radio broadcasting, which is steadily increasing in importance as a channel of public information. The transistor receiver, which enables people in isolated rural areas to hear the same news, entertainment, and political broadcasts as listeners in urban areas, is a major factor in unifying the people in the cities and in the countryside. Another means of mass communication—television—reaches about 1.5 viewers, most of them in the principal population centers.

Although freedom of the press is guaranteed by the Constitution, Panamanian radio, television, and publications in 1971 operated under a system of self-censorship established when the National Guard assumed power in 1968. Two leading daily newspapers were under government influence or supervision. The total circulation of seven dailies and one weekly was estimated at less than 150,000.

EDUCATION

Administration and Finance

Education and cultural affairs are primarily the responsibility of the Ministry of Education. Its principal components are the directorates of primary education, secondary education, private education and planning and the departments of vocational education, physical education and sports, literacy and adult education, teacher selection, and fine arts. The Department of Fine Arts administers the School of the Dance, the National Museum, the Institute of Musical Education, the National Symphony Orchestra, and the National Theater. The National Printing Office and the public library system are also under the ministry, and the minister of education sits on the Directive Council of the University of Panama. The National School of Agriculture is administered by the Ministry of Agriculture and Livestock.

Under the Directorate of Primary Education, a provincial inspector supervises the activities of primary schools in each province. Public secondary and vocational schools are supervised individually by the Directorate of Secondary Education and the Department of Vocational Education.

Inspectors are responsible for ensuring that official curricula are followed, assisting teachers in improving the methods of instruction, evaluating teacher performance, and overseeing the maintenance of facilities and equipment. Primary school inspectors must have seven years of teaching experience, and secondary school inspectors must have university degrees, including a specified number of credits in school direction and supervision. Geographical isolation makes regular inspection of many of the rural schools difficult or impossible, and there has been some criticism that inspectors spend too much time at their desks. It was found in 1965 that inspectors in Panama Province found it necessary to devote 45 percent of their working hours to administrative matters.

Private school curricula, teaching programs, and school organization are subject to supervision by the Ministry of Education through the corps of inspectors. Schools that do not accept this supervision are referred to as free (*libre*) institutions, and diplomas and other certificates awarded by them are not recognized. Private schools are not eligible for public financial aid, but they have occasionally received building sites without cost.

The school year runs from early April through December—corresponding generally with the dry season—except for some rural localities where the schedule is adjusted to harvesttimes and planting times. The University of Panama commences its academic year in June.

School days are customarily five hours in duration, with the session broken at midday, although separate morning and afternoon schools are held in some crowded urban institutions. A large proportion of the university classes take place during the evening hours.

The public education program was expanded substantially in

1965 by establishment of the Institute for Training and Utilization of Human Resources (Instituto para la Formación y Aprovechamiento de Recursos Humanos—IFARHU). IFARHU maintains registers of trained manpower, conducts vocational training courses in various localities, and administers the country's scholarship and loan programs. During the 1965–68 period it administered 280 university scholarships for study abroad and 216 for study in Panama.

Public education is free at all levels except at the University of Panama, where a small tuition is charged. Successive governments have placed great emphasis on education, and budget expenditures of the Ministry of Education have consistently far exceeded those of any other ministry. Its current budget expenditures plus those of the University of Panama increased from B/27.4 million (1 balboa equals US$1) in 1966 to B/43.1 million in 1970. The total for the period was about 28 percent of the entire current expenses budget. In addition, capital investments executed increased from B/1.8 million in 1966 to B/4.5 million in 1970. According to Ministry of Education data, between 1965 and 1969 the cost per student in public primary schools rose from B/62.81 to B/79.77, and the cost per secondary student rose from B/176.12 to B/190.80.

During the 1960s a large part of the financing for the educational system was provided by loans from the Inter-American Development Bank and by the International Development Association (a member of the World Bank Group). The Ministry of Education also regularly makes use of funds deposited under the social security program; these funds are also used to make loans at moderate interest rates to schools in the private system. In addition, a special education tax of 1.25 percent payable by employers and 0.75 percent payable by workers for the development of technical and vocational education was to become effective on September 1, 1971.

The Canal Zone government maintains a separate system of free primary and secondary schools and a junior college for the children of Canal Zone employees, both American and Panamanian, and of military personnel. Their organization and curricula correspond to those of schools in the United States, although since the 1940s special emphasis has been placed on Spanish and other subjects that stimulate interest in the local environment.

Canal Zone schools receive many applications from Panamanians not employed in the zone who are eager to secure for their children the benefits of better academic standards, modern teaching methods, and sound training in the English language.

The children are admitted as tuition students on a space-available basis.

Primary Schools

School attendance is compulsory between the ages of seven and fifteen or until the six grades of primary school have been completed; under the age of fifteen, young people may legally be employed only after they have completed their primary schooling. Preprimary school is not a required part of the system, but in 1969 about 7,500 children were enrolled in public and private preprimary units, a majority of them in Panama City.

Primary attendance increased from 203,429 in 1965 to 238,027 in 1969 (see table 4). Private enrollments, almost exclusively in urban localities, accounted for a scant 5 percent of the total in 1965 and 6 percent in 1969. The proportion remained at 6 percent in 1970.

The 1960s were marked by a sharp shift in population away from the countryside and toward the cities and towns; between 1965 and 1969 the rural sector declined from about 55 to 53 percent of the total. During this period of general population decline in the countryside, the rural primary school enrollment increased from 124,023 to 154,667, climbing from a proportion of 61 to 65 percent of all students at the primary level (see table 5).

This apparent anomaly is partially explainable in terms of the anatomy of the rural-urban population shift that was taking place. The migrants were predominantly unmarried young adults and older persons with grown children. During a period in which the relative number of rural adults was decreasing sharply, the number of school-age children was left virtually undiminished. In addition, the average number of children per family was substantially greater in rural localities.

The relative increase in rural enrollments was also a consequence of a continuing expansion of school facilities available to farm children. A considerable proportion of the rural units are located in remote places where a single teacher conducts classes in a school offering a few grades or, in some instances, a single grade. Only a minority of the frontier units offer children the full curriculum of six primary grades. In 1965, however, the Ministry of Education embarked on a policy aimed at expanding the curricula of incomplete schools by one grade each year, in most instances providing further training to enable incumbent teachers to conduct the additional grades. Between 1965 and 1969 the proportion of all schools offering the full schedule of six years increased from approximately 50 to 70 percent of the total; during

Table 4. *Number of Primary and Secondary Schools, Teachers, and Students in Panama, 1965 and 1969*

	1965	1969*
Primary:		
Public:		
Schools	1,520	1,613
Teachers	6,047	7,505
Students	192,497	223,645
Students per teacher	32	30
Private:		
Schools	60	75
Teachers	344	440
Students	10,932	14,382
Students per teacher	30	33
Total:		
Schools	1,580	1,688
Teachers	6,391	7,945
Students	203,429	238,027
Students per teacher	32	30
Secondary:		
Public:		
Schools	40	48
Teachers	1,470	2,096
Students	31,648	45,118
Students per teacher	22	22
Private:		
Schools	150	115
Teachers	1,168	1,108
Students	23,258	24,786
Students per teacher	20	22
Total:		
Schools	190	163
Teachers	2,638	3,204
Students	54,906	69,904
Students per teacher	22	22

* Preliminary data.

Source: Adapted from Republic of Panama, Contraloría General de la República, Dirección de Estadística y Censo, *Panamá en cifras (Compendio Estadístico, años 1965 a 1969)*, Panama City, 1970, pp. 53–55.

the same period the corresponding increase for urban schools was from 87 to 90 percent. It is customary, however, for urban as well as rural units to open as incomplete schools and subsequently to expand the number of grades offered; in 1969 a scattering in urban as well as in rural localities still offered only a single grade.

The Ministry of Education considers primary school dropouts a serious problem, but the incidence reported during the 1960s was well below the average for the countries of Latin America.

Table 5. *Primary School Enrollment in Panama, by*
Geographic Area, 1965 and 1969

	1965	1969*
Urban:		
Public	69,542	70,000
Private	9,864	13,360
Total	79,406	83,360
Rural:		
Public	123,495	153,645
Private	528	1,022
Total	124,023	154,667
Total:		
Public	193,037	223,645
Private	10,392	14,382
Total	203,429	238,027

* Preliminary data.

Source: Adapted from Republic of Panama, Contraloría General de la República, Dirección de Estadística y Censo, *Panamá en cifras (Compendio Estadístico, años 1965 a 1969)*, Panama City, 1970, p. 57.

Of the 47,918 students who had enrolled in primary school in 1964, 25,488 had reached the sixth and final grade in 1969 (see table 6). This retention rate of 53.1 percent was a considerable gain over the 43.4-percent retention rate registered for the 1960–65 period. Of those reaching the sixth grade in 1969, about 96 percent graduated, as compared with 85 percent in 1965. In both periods the retention and graduation rates for girls were slightly higher than those for boys.

Table 6. *Primary School Enrollment in Panama, by Grade, 1964 and 1969*

Grade	1964	1969*
First	47,918	61,131
Second	38,239	46,879
Third	36,988	40,466
Fourth	29,832	34,552
Fifth	24,129	29,511
Sixth	19,306	25,488
TOTAL	196,412	238,027

* Preliminary data.

Source: Adapted from Republic of Panama, Contraloría General de la República, Dirección de Estadística y Censo, *Panamá en cifras (Compendio Estadístico, años 1965 a 1969)*, 1970, p. 57; Pan American Union, *América en cifras, 1967: situación cultural: educación y otros aspectos culturales*, Washington, 1969, p. 85.

During the 1964–69 period the retention rate to the sixth grade was about 77 percent in urban and 45 percent in rural establishments, in great part a reflection of the larger proportion of urban schools offering the full six grades. The contrast was even greater between the private schools, with a retention rate of 80 percent, and the public schools, with a 50-percent rate.

Although enrollment is very small, the private school system has considerable social significance. Some charity schooling is offered by religious orders, but most of the students are children of the well to do. Nearly all complete the primary cycle, and many go on to secondary education in schools directly associated with the primary unit. In many instances their higher education is obtained in prestige universities abroad.

The school enrollment data available do not show enrollment by sex. In both 1960 and 1967, however, girls represented about 48 percent of the total student body and were in a slight majority in the private sector. The average age of girl students was nearly a year less than that of boys. All but a small proportion of the enrollment was between the mandatory-attendance age limits of seven and fifteen years. Rural children frequently do not commence school until the age of nine or older, but these are among the children who most frequently do not complete the primary cycle.

The standard primary curriculum includes some practical study in such fields as agriculture, hygiene, manual arts, and home economics as well as general studies in Spanish, science, mathematics, social studies, and religion. English-language studies are added in the upper years.

Secondary Schools

Between 1965 and 1969 the enrollment in the regular secondary school system rose from 54,906 to 69,904 (see table 4). During the late 1960s about 70 percent of all primary graduates matriculated in secondary schools—one of the highest proportions in Latin America. Unlike the primary, the secondary school enrollment was largely urban; a high proportion of the rural children failed to finish the primary grades because of economic reasons or because of the absence of a nearby school offering the full six-year curriculum, and almost all of the secondary units were in urban localities.

Between 1965 and 1969 the proportion of students in private institutions declined from approximately 42 to 35 percent of the total. Between 1961 and 1967 the proportion of girls in all secondary schools increased from 51 to 53 percent of the total.

The six years of secondary school are divided into two cycles of three years each. The lower cycle is of a general or exploratory nature with a standard curriculum that includes Spanish, social studies, religion, and art or music. The upper cycle consists of studies in arts and sciences pointing toward university entrance or of terminal vocational or technical schooling pointing toward immediate employment.

Both Panamanian and international organization statistical series with respect to the size, composition, and retention rates in the several kinds of lower and upper cycle secondary schools invite erroneous conclusions regarding the structure and dynamics of their enrollments. This results principally from the statistical inclusion of almost all students in the lower cycle under the heading of general studies. In the upper cycle only those engaged in college-preparatory work are included under the same general-studies heading. This mixing frustrates the effort to determine the relative retention rates in specialized academic and vocational courses that, for the most part, are offered only in the upper cycle.

In the smaller urban centers of the interior, the secondary school offers only the lower cycle, and its completion represents the fulfillment of educational goals. A majority of those going on to the upper cycle enter vocational and technical schools with curricula of varying lengths. In 1969 less than one-third of the 6,634 students graduating from some kind of secondary school were in the general or academic cycle (see table 7).

Admission to university traditionally requires only the graduation certificate or *bachillerato* (baccalaureate) awarded on completion of the upper cycle academic course (although a 1969 decree empowers the University of Panama to determine standards for admission). The *bachillerato* is generally regarded as an essential ingredient for maintenance of, or aspiration to, middle-class status.

The public secondary schools with *bachillerato* upper cycles are complete high schools that also offer the lower cycles. They are located in provincial capital cities. The oldest, largest, and most highly regarded of these is the National Institute in Panama City. The University of Panama grew out of it, and the school has produced so many public figures that it is known as the Nest of Eagles (Nido de Aguilas). It tends to draw its student body from upward-moving rather than established elements in the society, and its students are perennially active in political causes.

The larger private *bachillerato* secondary schools enjoy considerable social prestige; their academic records are good; and their graduates usually go on to a university in Panama or abroad. The majority are located in Panama City and have attached primary

Table 7. Number of Students Graduated from Schools
in Panama, 1965 and 1969

	1965	1969
Primary	17,670	24,521
Secondary	5,985	6,634
General	1,705	2,053
Vocational and Technical		
Commercial	2,249	2,539
Industrial	810	685
Home Economics	688	807
Pilot (nautical)	55	43
Radio Broadcasting	0	n.a.
Agricultural	38	80
Subtotal	3,840	4,154
Normal	440	427
Nursing (including postgraduate)	58	59
University	386	498
Public Administration and Commerce	27	94
Agronomy	11	6
Architecture	6	19
Natural Sciences and Pharmacy	66	125
Law and Political Science	18	2
Philosophy, Letters and Education	216	227
Engineering	19	8
Medicine	23	17
TOTAL	24,099	31,712

n.a.—not available.

Source: Adapted from Republic of Panama, Contraloría General de la República, Dirección de Estadística y Censo, *Panamá en cifras* (*Compendio Estadístico, años 1965 a 1969*), Panama City, 1970, p. 59.

school units. One of the most highly regarded, the Colegio La Salle (La Salle College), operated by the Christian Brothers, for a time shortly after independence acted as government administrator of the primary public schools in most of the country.

Reported vocational and technical secondary enrollments often differ radically by virtue of inclusion or exclusion of private schools and on the basis of whether or not enrollments in short-term private business institutions are included. A comprehensive Organization of American States report showed enrollment increasing from 10,781 in 1960 to 19,552 in 1966; this total did not include enrollment in the normal schools, where teachers for the primary system are trained. Girls consistently outnumbered boys by a small majority, and about three-fourths of the entire enrollment was in the private sector. In all, the number of graduates rose from 3,840 in 1965 to 4,154 in 1969.

The heaviest enrollment occurred in the commercial schools, which represented nearly half of the 1966 vocational and technical enrollment and more than half of the graduates. Only three of the forty-six schools offering commercial courses were in the public sector, and girls outnumbered boys by a margin of nearly three to one. The courses of study ranged up to three years. The great popularity of commercial studies for women reflects a very sharply increased rate of female participation in commercial activities during the 1950s and 1960s. It reflects also the pronounced preference of all people with some education for the white-collar employment that is found with relatively greater frequency in the commercial than in the industrial sector (see ch. 12, Agriculture and Industry).

Next in popularity in the technical-vocational sector are the industrial secondary schools, which in 1966 had an enrollment making up about one-fourth of its total. Almost all of the students were male, and only four of the seventy-three schools were public.

The largest and most important of the public industrial schools is the Melchior Lasso de la Vega School of Manual Arts and Trades, located near Panama City. It is an upper cycle school offering three years of specialization in various industrial fields to students who have completed a lower secondary cycle. The Institute of Mechanical Arts in Divisa offers to primary school graduates the equivalent of a lower cycle program with specialization in any of several trades. Other public industrial schools are located in David and in the city of Colón. Of particular prestige and importance among the many small private industrial units is the Don Bosco Technical Institute in Panama City; it is the secondary section of an orphanage school operated by the Salesian Fathers.

Enrollment in the agricultural schools edged upward during the 1960s, and in 1966 there were 395 students, all of them male. The principal public entity, the National School of Agriculture, is a part of the National Institute of Agriculture, which also maintains administrative services and an experiment station. The three-year course is open to persons sixteen years of age or older who have completed the lower secondary cycle. In addition, the Felix Olivares industrial school in David offers three years of agricultural vocational schooling to primary school graduates.

Other vocational and technical secondary establishments are the schools of home economics (including dressmaking and tailoring), a school of radio broadcasting, and a school for nautical pilots (*educación náutico*). The collective enrollment in these schools was 3,965 in 1966. Most of the numbers were girls and young women enrolled in the home economics courses, which consistently produced more graduates during the period between

1965 and 1969 than did the industrial schools at the secondary level.

Primary school teachers are prepared in normal school courses at the upper secondary level. The course is open to those who have completed the lower cycle and includes practice teaching in the second and third of the three years. Although programs for prospective teachers are offered by several public and private schools, most of the teachers receive their training at the Juan D. Arosemena Normal School, which was established in 1938 in Santiago. During the late 1960s more than three-fourths of the normal school enrollment was female; the retention rate was far higher than in any other part of the secondary system; and well over 400 students were graduated annually.

Higher Education

A university established by Jesuits in 1749 was closed after the expulsion of that order from the New World in 1767. Early in the nineteenth century postsecondary schooling was offered by the Colegio del Istmo (College of the Isthmus), but that institution did not prosper; Panamanian children in search of higher education were required to go to Colombia or abroad until 1935, when the public University of Panama was founded as an outgrowth of the National Institute. The secondary schools provided classroom space for the new institution until 1950, when the university moved to its new campus on the outskirts of Panama City. In 1965 a second institution of higher learning, the private University of Santa María la Antigua, was established in Panama City with temporary quarters in what had been the archbishop's palace.

The University of Panama's enrollment increased steadily from 1,700 in 1950 to nearly 12,000 in 1969—including some 2,000 in five regional centers located in Chiriquí Province and Central Panama. Serious student riots at the end of 1968, however, resulted in the closing of the institution for five months. After a complete reorganization that involved the naming of new deans, the dismissal of many faculty members, and the expulsion of students who had not maintained C averages for the previous three semesters, the university was reopened in June 1969 with a substantially reduced enrollment. At the beginning of the 1971/72 school year, the already modest tuition fee was reduced to B/20 a semester, and a lively response to this reduction raised the enrollment to 12,568 students, not including 1,618 in the regional centers. The University of Santa María la Antigua had an enrollment of 232 during its opening year and a 1970 enrollment of 1,057 (see table 8).

Table 8. *University Enrollment in Panama, by Faculties, Selected Years, 1965–71*

Faculties	1965	1968	1969	1971[1]
University of Panama:				
Faculties:				
Public Administration and Commerce	1,658	2,866	2,118	5,583
Agronomy	156	130	103	322
Architecture	313	360	293	440
Natural Sciences and Pharmacy	1,574	2,241	1,224	2,153
Law and Political Science	339	434	359	638
Philosophy, Letters and Education	2,340	3,029	1,956	2,672
Engineering	352	360	272	537
Medicine	127	150	155	118
Dentistry	0	9	47	105
Total Faculties	6,859	9,579	6,527	12,568
Regional Centers	1,792	1,969	651	1,618
TOTAL	8,651	11,548	7,178	14,186
University of Santa María la Antigua:				
Law and Administration	154	276	410	n.a.
Sciences	36	116	249	n.a.
Philosophy and Administration	42	52	66	n.a.
TOTAL	232	444	725	1,057[2]
GRAND TOTAL	8,883	11,992	7,903	....

n.a.—not available.
[1] Preliminary data.
[2] 1970 enrollment.

Source: Adapted from Republic of Panama, Contraloría General de la República, Dirección de Estadística y Censo, *Panamá en cifras (Compendio Estadístico, años 1965 a 1969)*, Panama City, 1970, p. 58; and *La Estrella de Panama* (Panama City), June 14, 1971.

Between 1960 and 1966 the enrollment of women at the University of Panama increased from 41 to 46 percent of the total, and in 1965 and 1966 women were in the majority at the University of Santa María la Antigua. In 1967 women made up 48 percent of the combined student bodies of the two universities.

Panamanian university students are, on the average, perhaps the youngest in Latin America. In 1966 almost two students out of three were under the age of twenty, and much less than one in ten was over the age of thirty. Most of the remainder were between the ages of twenty and twenty-four. Women were relatively a little more numerous in the older age groups.

This age distribution contrasts sharply with that found in most other Latin American countries, where most of the university population is over the age of twenty, a large proportion is over thirty, and the average age of men is greater than that of women. In the past, however, it was possible for students at the University of Panama to fail courses and to enroll in new programs of study the following year. This process could continue indefinitely, but many perennial students were among those expelled in early 1969, and the decree reorganizing the university's administration severely restricted the possibility of successive enrollments by older students.

As reorganized in 1969, the University of Panama is an autonomous public institution with its own budget. The supreme agency is the Directive Council, made up of the minister of education, the rector, the senior dean, a student with high academic standing, and three public members. Through its authority to appoint the public members and the de facto membership of the minister of education in this council, the government plays a role in the administration of the university.

In 1971 the university was made up of nine faculties (in turn, composed of thirty-two schools). Under the 1969 reorganization, each faculty is presided over by a dean assisted by faculty boards on which students have minority representation. These boards, which determine much of the administrative policy within the faculty and make selections for teaching positions within it, replaced the single Administrative Junta, on which student representation had been equal to that of the teaching staff. The change had the immediate effect of reducing student power and increasing the already considerable autonomy exercised by the faculties.

In Panama, as in other Latin American countries, the term *faculty* (*facultad*) applies not to the teaching staff but to the basic teaching unit of the university, which is comparable to, but has greater individual identity than, the academic departments in North American institutions of higher education. The university is a place for specialized education, and the student matriculates directly to the faculty offering schooling in the field of specialization that he has selected; the general schooling customarily provided during the lower class years in North American colleges and universities is provided during the upper cycle years of secondary school. Transfer from one faculty to another is not common, and all or most courses are taken in the faculty in which the student is enrolled.

The most common university degree is the *licenciado*, roughly comparable to a master's degree in a United States university. Depending on the field of studies, it is obtained in from four to seven years. Four years of study are required for the degree in biology, chemistry, and philosophy; five years, for public administration, economics, social work, mathematics, physics, and pharmacy; six years, for law, political science, and architecture; and seven years, for engineering. A degree in philosophy and letters and additional courses in education are required for a professional degree (*profesorado*) in secondary education. Only the Medical School confers the degree of doctor (*doctorado*). Candidates for the medical degree attend the Medical School for four years after completing the premedical course in the Faculty of Natural Sciences and Pharmacy. A proposal was initiated in 1969 for shortening the premedical course from three to two years.

During the 1960s by far the most popular of the faculties were those in public administration and commerce; natural sciences and pharmacy; and philosophy, letters, and education. The fastest gains in enrollment were registered by the faculty of public administration and commerce, which in 1971 had a student body making up almost half the enrollment on the Panama City campus. Enrollments in faculties devoted to the learned professions were far lower, and in them the dropout rate was higher. Public administration and commercial studies gave promise of office jobs, to which young people seeking to solidify middle-class status could aspire. A large proportion of children of the well to do preparing for such careers as law and medicine went abroad for their higher studies, as their fathers had done before them. Higher education during the late 1960s continued to be handicapped by its newness, to the extent that there was as yet no tradition encouraging the younger generation to obtain its higher education in Panama.

A survey conducted in 1968 found that 29 percent of university graduates in the country had received their degrees abroad and that about 2,000 were studying in other countries; many of these people were in professional fields. The survey listed 543 medical and 377 engineering students abroad. For all university students abroad, the most popular countries in order of preference were the United States, Mexico, Spain, and Brazil.

On the basis of an average curriculum of five years, the nearly 3,000 matriculants in 1964 set off against the 500 graduates in 1969 indicates an average retention rate through graduation of well under 20 percent. Most of the dropouts occur early in the course of study; in 1966 the size of the enrollment during the second year was only a little more than half of that in the first. Retention rates for women were somewhat superior to those of males in all years through the fourth; the fourth year marked the end of the courses in humanities and education in which a high proportion of the female students were enrolled.

Literacy and Adult Education

Literacy is defined in Panama as the ability to read and write a simple paragraph in any language. The literate proportion of the population is determined on the basis of the number of persons over the age of ten, not including the Indian population (numbering about 60,000 in 1970). The standard international cutoff age is fifteen years, but Panamanian statisticians employ ten years as the age at which the child who commenced his primary education at the regular age of seven years had completed three years of schooling, the number generally recognized as necessary in order to achieve functional literacy.

On the basis of these criteria, the rate of literacy among children between the ages of ten and fifteen has been generally above the national average since World War II; literacy above the age of ten is slightly higher than that above the standard minimum age of fifteen years. The Organization of American States estimates that between 1960 and 1967 the literacy rate of those over the age of fifteen averaged about 77 percent.

Census data show that between 1950 and 1960 the female literacy rate moved past that of males—the rates in 1960 were 78.4 and 78.1 percent for females and males, respectively. By age, the proportion of the population considered literate in 1960 ranged downward from 87 percent among those under the age of nineteen to 50 percent for those aged seventy and over.

In 1960 some 93.8 percent of the urban and 64.6 percent of the rural population were literate. By size of locality, the proportion ranged upward from less than 50 percent in rural sections with populations numbering fewer than fifty people to over 80 percent in all urban localities. In both Panama City and Colón the proportion was 94.2 percent.

Within the Ministry of Education, the regular adult training program is the responsibility of the Department of Literacy and Adult Education. In 1970 it was estimated by the Ministry of Education that 105,000 persons had received instruction, of varying kind and duration, since 1960. The incomplete statistical data available indicate that achievement of literacy and completion of the equivalent of a primary education were the principal objectives of this program. In 1970 some 3,200 adults were reported qualifying as literate through its classes, and 4,300 were able to complete their primary educations. An additional 4,300 were awarded certificates for completion of vocational courses, and 154 learned light industry (artisanry) skills. Night secondary school courses were also offered to adults in Panama City.

Another significant element in the adult education program is the Institute for Training and Utilization of Human Resources (Instituto para la Formación y Aprovechamiento de Recursos Humanos—IFARHU), which was founded in 1965 as an entity to supplement the activities of the Ministry of Education. The adult education phase of its activities is aimed principally at young working-class adults between the ages of eighteen and twenty-six and at unemployed heads of families. It offers training programs in needed skills for the various economic sectors in selected localities, endeavors to establish comprehensive apprenticeship programs, and serves as a major instrument in the government's attempt to stimulate the interest of young people in skilled blue-collar vocations.

Teachers

Teaching in primary and secondary schools is a respected profession, and teachers represent a large and articulate part of the country's growing middle class. In addition, it is not considered inappropriate as a vocation for the children of the wealthy. The security and status of the profession gained significantly from the 1946 Organic Law of Education, which formally barred political influence in the appointments, transfers, and dismissals of personnel. Salaries paid are moderate on the basis of urban middle-class pay schedules, but in the interior of the country teachers made up most of the corps of civil servants and, as such, ranked after the employees of banks and financial institutions as generally the best paid in the white-collar category.

More than 80 percent of the 8,000 persons engaged in teaching in the primary system during 1969 were women, and nearly all were certified graduates of the secondary-level normal schools that prepare primary teaching personnel; less than 4 percent of the total remained uncertified. During the late 1960s an average of more than 400 teaching diplomas were awarded annually, and uncertified personnel were not permitted to teach in the schools of Panama City and Colón. Finding qualified personnel to conduct practical courses was not easy, however, and personnel in all teaching specialties were reluctant to accept assignments in the more remote rural posts. At the beginning of the 1969 school year a considerable number of qualified persons were not able to find posts in the more desirable localities, but a number of persons without teaching certificates who had completed some other kind of secondary school were given temporary appointments to teach in the more remote places.

Teachers for the secondary schools are trained in the Faculty of Philosophy, Letters and Education of the University of Panama. In 1969 a little over half of the corps of 3,200 were women. The male proportion was highest in the vocational and technical secondary schools and in the private system, where many of the classes were taught by members of religious orders.

The number available for academic secondary teaching during the late 1960s was sufficient to ensure a generally satisfactory student-teacher ratio, but continuing shortages prevailed in the fields of mathematics and science, for qualified personnel were reported easily able to command a better income in private industry. To meet these shortages the Ministry of Education in mid-1971 announced acceptance of applications for a twenty-two-month accelerated course for graduates of general secondary and normal schools in these fields as well as in English, education, and physics. In addition, however, during the late 1960s there was a much more serious chronic shortage of qualified personnel of all kinds to conduct the specialized courses in the vocational and technical secondary sector.

Between 1965 and 1969 the number of teachers increased from 284 to 343 at the University of Panama and from eighteen to seventy at the University of Santa María la Antigua. About one-fourth of the combined total were women. In 1969 the student-teacher ratios were nineteen to one at the University of Panama and ten to one at the University of Santa María la Antigua, but at least half were professional people devoting a few hours weekly to teaching assignments undertaken as much for social or for political reasons as for the modest salaries received. With the exception of a few instructors at the School of Nursing of the University of Panama, all teachers held at least undergraduate degrees. A large majority of the university teaching corps hold degrees from foreign institutions. Doctorates are often earned from European or other Latin American universities; master's and bachelor's degrees are received more frequently from the universities of North America.

Salary scales compare favorably with those in private industry, but many derive their principal income from other occupations. Under the 1969 reorganization of the University of Panama, teaching personnel are eligible for pensions under terms generally more generous than those available under the regular social security program. Regular professors acquire tenure after a probationary period of five years and thereafter may be removed only for misconduct, incompetence, or failure to fulfill their obligations.

Many of the professors, as well as the students, are intensely preoccupied with the discussion of politics. In the past, reunions, conferences, and commemorative programs often interrupted the academic programs, and teachers sometimes took active parts in social disturbances. After the riots and the closing of the University of Panama in 1969, however, the dismissal of about forty teachers appeared to herald the beginning of a period of relative quiet for the teaching staff.

ARTISTIC AND INTELLECTUAL EXPRESSION

Scholarship

Panama's educational progress has permitted a vigorous intellectual development within the middle class, which began to produce the poetry, essays, short stories, novels, and scholarly works that form a national literature. Authentic Panamanian themes have become characteristic of this literature.

The dominant trend in philosophy shifted toward the end of the eighteenth century from scholasticism and Aristotelian logic to the rationalist philosophy of the Enlightenment. German romanticism gained popularity during the first half of the nineteenth century, but by the beginning of the twentieth century positivism, as exemplified in the works of Justo Arosemena, had eclipsed all other systems of thought. The positivistic approach, rejecting metaphysics in favor of empiricism, is now taken for granted in most disciplines, and the attention of philosophers has been drawn to other issues, such as nationalism and internationalism.

During the colonial era Panama had several historians who recorded the early events of the isthmus, but the nineteenth century was comparatively barren of historical scholarship. Mariano Arosemena is regarded as the precursor of national historical writing. He began in 1868 to publish a history of his country, *Apuntamientos Históricos, 1801–1840* (Historical Summary, 1801–1840). Although Arosemena was able to publish only four of the projected eight volumes, his son, Justo Arosemena, reedited and published most of the other volumes. The complete work was published in 1949 in an addition prepared by a leading contemporary scholar, Ernesto Castillero.

Immediately after the founding of the Republic, the writing of history flourished as never before. Less than a year after the revolution, Ramón Valdés published *La Independencia del Istmo de Panamá* (The Independence of the Isthmus of Panama), a general outline of historic events of the isthmus. In 1911 Juan Sosa published *Historia de Panamá* (History of Panama), a text for secondary schools and colleges of the Republic on which most later general histories of the country have been based.

In 1921, in order to stimulate the study of the national history, the government established the Academy of Panamanian History. The academy was directed by some of the Republic's best scholars, including Ricardo Alfaro, Enrique J. Arce, and Octavio Méndez Pereira. In 1933 the academy began publishing a bulletin that for the next decade set the tone for national history emerging from the academy.

In 1953 the Republic celebrated its first half century of independence. As a contribution to the commemoration, a series of historical studies were completed under the auspices of the University of Panama. Ernesto Castillero wrote the most important of the series, *Panamá y los Estados Unidos* (Panama and the United States). Under the direction of the academy, which in 1935 became a part of the University of Panama, numerous other histories have been published. One of the more recent ones is Alfredo Castillero's *Episodios de la Independencia de Panamá* (Episodes of Panamanian Independence), published in 1957. *Universidades*, established in 1936 by the faculty of the university, is Panama's most scholarly journal and carries articles on history as well as other academic subjects.

Scientific work in some form has been underway in Panama since 1581, when the astronomer Alfonso Palomeras de Vargas observed an eclipse of the moon and determined the exact geographical position of the isthmus. Scientific efforts have been largely concentrated, however, in the field of medicine, particularly in the control of contagious diseases. The first notable scientist to address himself to this problem was Isidrio Arroyo, who worked at the San Juan de Dios Hospital during the last years of the eighteenth century and sought to control an epidemic of smallpox in 1800. He also wrote a paper on the history of yellow fever on the isthmus.

The government of the Republic took over many of the techniques and some of the medical equipment used by the North Americans in combating yellow fever in the early twentieth century. In 1914 the Panamanian government, with the assistance of the Rockefeller Foundation, began a program to eliminate hookworm. Within fifteen years hookworm had been effectively eliminated. The government has also launched programs against malaria, tuberculosis, intestinal parasites, cholera, and other health menaces and has established some of the best equipped hospitals and laboratories in Latin America (see ch. 4, Living Conditions).

An important contribution to natural history is the book *Los principales mamiferos silvestres de Panamá* (The Principal Wild Mammals of Panama) by Eustorgio Méndez, a member of the zoology department of the Gorgas Commemorative Laboratory. It was published in 1971.

The National Museum of Panama, founded in 1925, has become an important scientific institution for the study of natural science, archaeology, ethnology, and the history of Central America and an object of nationalistic pride. The archaeological section is scientifically the most valuable collection in the museum. The exhibits, consisting mainly of pottery and objects of wrought gold, show the various stages in the culture of the ancient inhabitants of the isthmus. Most of the gold work was discovered in Chiriquí, Veraguas, and Coclé; it is fashioned in imitation of the jaguar, the alligator, and other wild species. The objects were symbols or totems, used in place of writing.

The collection also includes some stone sculptures, mostly idols, uncovered in Coclé Province. Other stones were sculptured in the shape of jaguars and other simple forms. It is believed that some of these were stones for grinding corn and other foods. One curious object that has puzzled the archaeologists is a monolith representing, in its upper part, the figure of an elephant, suggesting a connection between the cultures of the Orient and those of Central America. The museum also has a section devoted to the exhibition of contemporary Indian artistic skill. Exhibits include a wide assortment of carpets and blankets patterned in rare and fanciful designs, necklaces of beads, shells, bones, and teeth of animals, musical instruments, idols of wood and children's toys.

A new archaeological museum was inaugurated in 1971 in the city of Penonomé in Coclé Province. Its exhibits include pottery and sculpture in gold and silver from Coclé, Veraguas, and Chiriquí.

Literature

During the colonial era Panama produced little of the noteworthy literature that might have been expected from a region with such a colorful and variegated history. Panamanian historians attribute this dearth to two circumstances; the isthmian preoccupation with commercial activity and the comparatively long absence of stimulus to intellectual activity that, in other Spanish colonies, was provided by the early establishment of universities (see ch. 2, Historical Setting).

Only three men are remembered for major literary accomplishments during the eighteenth century. Manuel José de Ayala (1726–1805), a member of the Spanish Council of the Indies and the outstanding jurist of his day, recorded contemporary events in Panama. Sebastián López Ruíz (1741–1823), a physician and naturalist, wrote commentaries on the societies of Panama and Granada (Colombia). Victor de la Guardia y Ayala (1772–1824) wrote a tragedy in verse, *La Política del Mundo* (The Politics of the World), which was the first dramatic work composed and performed in Panama—in 1809. The play was about Napoleon's invasion of Spain in 1808 and showed in its style the French influence that had by then reached Panama.

The printing press was introduced into Panama in the first quarter of the nineteenth century, and thereafter nationalistic political literature poured from the press. The most influential writer of this period was Justo Arosemena (1817–96), philosopher, statesman, and ardent Colombian nationalist.

During the nineteenth century Panamanians believed that their literary talents were held in check by a political and cultural dependency that permitted only modest achievements in poetry and journalism. Panamanian writers lived under the formal literary traditions prevailing throughout Latin America, and neither poets nor prose writers found their themes within the isthmus. The best-known prose writer, Darío Herrera (1870–1914), for example, laid his narrative scenes in Buenos Aires and in the Chilean Andes.

After the creation of the Republic in 1903, a new era in literature began, assisted by greater official encouragement and recognition. Although hampered by illiteracy and the economic aftereffects of the civil war of 1899–1902, the new nation nevertheless developed, by means of comparatively rapid advance in public education, an audience for a generation of national writers. The voice of nationalist sentiment, until recently directed against Colombia, was now aimed at the United States, from which so much had been expected.

Among the first to express disapproval of the presence of foreigners was a poetess, Amelia Denis de Icaza (1836–1910). Her poem "Al Cerro Ancón (Ancón Hill) spoke with regret of the loss of the strip of land through which the canal was dug. The poet Demetrio Korsi added his verse to the oratory against North American influence.

The theme of injury to the Republic by foreigners recurred years later in the works of Ricardo Miró, a nephew of Amelia Denis de Icaza; Miró became the national poet. Many of his poems achieved renown throughout the Spanish-speaking world. A notable example is "Patria" (Homeland), in which he speaks with particular affection of his country and its scenery. Known to all schoolchildren, Miró's poem has served, as has no other literary work, to unify national feelings.

A book of stories entitled *De la Ciudad y del Campo* (From the City and the Countryside), by Ignacio Valdés, illustrated this emphasis by its realistic portrayal of life in the cities and villages of Panama. After Valdés came other writers who have reaffirmed the local flavor of Panamanian literature. Although the initial simplicity of form has given way to a search for metaphors and symbols, there has been a continuing tendency to look for inspiration to the country's own history and social themes.

The total output of novels has been small, and the works have seldom enjoyed international acclaim. One exception was *El*

Tesoro del Dabaibe (The Treasure of Dabaibe), by Octavio Méndez Pereira, which was later reissued under the title *Vasco Núñez de Balboa* in Argentina, where it sold more than 100,000 copies. Inspired by the life of the discoverer of the Pacific Ocean, it is considered to be one of the most readable historical novels of Spanish America. Among the novels popular in the 1960s were *El Cabecilla* (The Ringleader), by Cajar Escala, a novel based on the extortion practiced by the politicians on the *campesinos* (peasants) ; *San Cristóbal,* by Ramón Jurado, which describes the low status of the laborer on a sugar plantation in Panama; and *Plenilunio* (Full Moon), a surrealistic novel by the poet Rogelio Sinóu.

Yolanda Camarano de Sucre has received widespread acclaim for two of her novels published in the late 1960s. *La dona de la paz* (The Gift of Peace) treats sympathetically the efforts of a United States Peace Corps volunteer to improve the health conditions in a small mountain village; and *Los Capelli* (The Capellis) traces the history of Panama from 1851 through the experiences of four generations of an Italian immigrant's family. In *Los Capelli* the importance of the canal in the country's political evolution is stressed. Cesar A. Candanedo's *La otra frontera* (The Other Frontier), published in 1966, treats the importance of the canal from a different perspective, that of several generations of peasants who lost their land as a result of it.

Contemporary poetry is dominated by the avant-garde trend, which was transplanted from Europe in the early 1930s. It was initially characterized by surrealistic and futuristic elements, but it later evolved a formal style rich in metaphysical subjects and touched with nostalgia and melancholy.

One of the first poets to popularize this trend in Panama was Carlos Francisco Chan-Marín. His best known volume, *Poemas Corporales* (Corporeal Poems), published in 1955, has been described by another noted Panamanian poet, Aristides Martínez Ortega, as "a resolute song of hope in the struggle for social justice." Younger avant-garde poets include José de Jesús Martínez, whose metaphysical contemplations are reminiscent of the Spaniard Miguel de Unamuno, and Guillermo Ross Zanet, whose work is filled with humor and irony. Many of Jesús Martínez' best poems are found in *Poemas a ella* (Poems to Her), published in 1963. Zanet's most outstanding volume, *Sin el Color del Cielo* (Without the Color of the Sky), was published in 1964.

Despite the country's relatively high literacy rate, it does not have a large reading public. Editions are rarely printed beyond a thousand copies, and writers are unable to support themselves from their sales. In 1971 the Lotería Nacional (National Lottery) initiated a program of financing the publication of works by Panamanian authors. The first of its publications is to be an anthology of the short stories of the late Darío Herrera entitled *Horas Lejanas y Otros Cuentos* (Far Away Hours and Other Stories).

One of the factors aiding and encouraging literary output has been the existence of several literary magazines. At least three such journals existed before Panama gained its independence from Colombia. Shortly after independence patriots of literary inclination became conscious of the need for intellectual stimulation as well as for an outlet for their literary endeavors. To meet these needs *El Heraldo del Istmo* (The Herald of the Isthmus) came into existence in January 1904. This first literary review was a monthly illustrated magazine of sixteen pages, which continued to appear fairly regularly until September 1906. It was dominated by a small group of intellectuals who were largely influenced by the French literary school. Its goal was to stimulate these intellectuals into producing first-class literary work to the end that a national literature might be established. Magazines such as *Nuevos Ritos, Variedades,* and *Lotería* later carried on the tradition. The most popular contemporary literary journal in 1971 was *Lotería.*

Theater

One of the national aspirations has been a desire for a flourishing theater. The National Theatre, built in 1907 in Panama City, is owned by the government and depends for support on the Ministry of Finance and Treasury. In design it belongs to the eighteenth century, with its rococo ornamentation and tiers of pink and gold boxes in semicircle. Panamanians are proud of the National Theatre as a symbol of their Hispanic heritage and use it to perpetuate Spanish drama as part of their culture. It is available to traveling or local opera companies and to orchestras and dramatic groups. Few touring dramatic companies of professional caliber ever perform on its stage, however, and there are no professional companies resident in Panama. Hence, semiprofessional and amateur actors have been responsible for keeping the legitimate theater alive, and the audience for theater remains small.

Europeans who migrated to Panama have contributed to the demand for dramatic activity. Immigrants from Spain in particular have helped to revitalize the Spanish classics and introduce modern Iberian plays. Although the Panamanian stage reflects a combination of Spanish, French, and North American influences, the Spanish legacy remains dominant, both as to content and acting style.

160

In 1956 the minister of education established the Academy of Dramatic Arts and appointed as its director a Catholic priest, the Reverend Ramón María Condominis, born in Barcelona and trained in the Spanish classic theater. The academy, through its producing organization, the Experimental Theatre of Panama, has dedicated itself to the task of reminding the audience of the country's rich heritage. Ventura de la Vega's *The Death of Caesar* and Jacinto Benavente's *The Buffoon of Hamlet* have been two of the organization's greatest successes.

The Panamanian Company of Modern Theatre, a group of semi-professionals under the direction of the Spanish playwright and director Manuel de Heredia, stresses dramatic techniques learned from the United States and has performed plays by North American authors. The acting, direction, and scenic design have been imitative of North American trends. The actors have freed themselves of the nineteenth-century Spanish declamatory style typical of most Latin American theatrical performances.

In 1959 the University of Panama established a university theater and produced its first play, Thornton Wilder's *The Matchmaker*, translated into Spanish as *La Casamentera*. The play attracted much public attention, and the university drama group was immediately accepted as a part of the cultural scene of Panama.

Among the more successful playwrights are Mario Riera Rivilla, Mario Augusto Rodríguez, and Maria Olimpia de Obaldía. The country's best known theatrical director is José Quintero. He has achieved international recognition for his directing in New York and Paris and has been decorated by his government with its highest honor, the Order of Vasco Núñez de Balboa.

In 1971 the director of the university theater, Roberto McKay, organized a new "popular" theater group known as Los Trashumantes (The Nomads). Its objective was to take the entertainment and inspiration of drama to the people throughout the country, especially to the rural villages and urban slums. Its first presentation, *Una flor para mascar* (A Flower to Chew), included skits, music, and dancing and called for audience participation.

Architecture

The country's geographic position exposed it to the influence of a great variety of peoples and cultures, but this very fact long impeded the development of a characteristic Panamanian architecture. Because of the importance of the isthmus, the Spanish crown built the city of Panama, but it fell prey to the pirates who sought Spanish treasures. The city was later reconstructed on a

161

different site and, in order to protect it from the pirates, it was built as a fortress city surrounded by high walls. Thus most of the architectural monuments that have survived from the colonial era are the ruins of castles and other remains of a military architecture, along with some religious structures.

During the nineteenth century Panamanian architecture was stimulated by the French example in buildings associated with the French canal project. The balcony, gothic arch, and grillwork thus became part of the country's architecture. In 1903 the government began constructing administration buildings and schools. The Presidential Palace, the National Theatre, and the National Institute were completed in the early years of the Republic. In the same period the United States began building the canal and introduced North American architectural ideas as well as the most modern concepts of sanitation. Architectural accomplishments in the urban areas were not matched by any building program in the interior for the government continued to focus its attention on the center, ignoring the politically and economically less significant interior.

In 1915, a year after the opening of the canal, public buildings, such as schools and hospitals, were built for an international exposition. This brief surge of governmental building stimulated construction by private enterprise in the urban areas of Panama. Architectural developments, however, presented a confused and varied pattern. In the years between World War I and World War II cities expanded gradually but without plan or architectural pattern. Most government buildings were neoclassical in design, and residential building tended to imitate colonial architecture.

It was not until the late 1940s that the government became concerned about city planning and organized agencies to assist in the planning of housing. The government also entered into the building of low-income housing to take care of the laborers who had entered the country during the war years.

After World War II architecture began to take a new direction, at least in the urban centers. A new generation of architects turned away from European models and attempted to design buildings according to the needs of the land and climate. The new trend broke with architectural tradition by emphasizing the importance of construction materials and the concepts of harmony and function. Such modern architectural landmarks as Tocumén Airport and the luxurious Hotel Panamá were built.

The best example of Panama's contribution to contemporary architecture is the University of Panama. The architects, including Guillermo de Roux, René Brenes, and Ricardo Bermúdez, had a special opportunity between 1949 and 1952 to create a new campus with financial assistance from the government. Topographical problems were resolved in such a way as to take advantage of the contours of the land. The complex, furthermore, is well integrated into its urban setting. Brazilian influence is apparent in the use of tiles, the brise-soleil (sun screen), and the plastic interruption of planes. The School of Architecture at the university continues to be the country's primary source of innovation in the field.

Painting and Sculpture

During the colonial era painting was devoted mainly to the Roman Catholic Church. The few works of art done on the isthmus during the 300 years of Spanish rule adorned church altars and walls. They depicted scenes of sacred history and were usually copies of the works of South American painters of the Quito school of religious painting.

In 1870 Epifanio Garay (1849–1903), a Colombian who had studied in Europe, moved to Panama and began painting portraits. For more than thirty years he exerted a profound influence on the development of painting in Panama. Panamanian art turned toward secular subjects as he encouraged his students to paint still life and to concentrate on painting what they actually saw. William LeBlanc, a well-known Parisian artist, was another who spent many years in Panama and influenced the native artists. He left the majority of his paintings to the government, but a fire in Panama City destroyed most of them.

Roberto Lewis (1874–1949) helped to establish a school of art and served as director of the National School of Painting for several decades. Under his direction, a distinctive kind of painting emerged on the isthmus, stressing landscapes, portraits of public figures, and murals. From 1904 to the late 1930s Panamanian artists generally followed Roberto Lewis' approach to painting. During that same period the government aided in the development of painting by awarding scholarships for study in Europe as well as at the National School of Painting.

Under the influence of Humberto Ivaldi (1909–44), who had been a student of Lewis, a new generation of artists emerged during and after World War II. Some of the artists were devoted to the lush isthmian landscape; others turned their backs on the local scene and tried through abstraction to fall in line with international trends. Guillermo Trujillo, a contemporary abstract painter, graduate of the University of Panama, and student of painting at the Institute of Hispanic Culture in Madrid, returned to Panama to win numerous awards for his work. He adapted the aboriginal art of Central America to the modern abstractionist spirit. Artists such as Trujillo have, for the first time, given Panama representation abroad. His pictures and those of other Panamanian artists have been exhibited since 1951 in the biennials in São Paulo and, in 1961, Trujillo had a one-man show in the United States.

Early sculpture in Panama included the work of the Indians and the unsigned contributions of a few amateurs of the colonial era. Roberto Lewis, the painter, occasionally sculpted busts of outstanding political leaders during the first two decades of the twentieth century, but with this exception Panama produced no sculptor of note in these years. In the late 1950s Carlos Arboleda returned to Panama after twelve years of study in Florence and Barcelona.

The slow and halting development of the graphic arts is largely because of the local market. The commerce-oriented Panamanian elite has never developed the habit of patronizing the arts.

Music

Gonzalo Brenes, historian of the music of Panama, finds development in musical expression confined, for the most part, to the period since independence. Before that time, salon and concert music was mainly the work of European artists who crossed the isthmus or settled there. Since 1903 the development of music has been almost exclusively the work of the national government. Only through official action has the dissemination of musical knowledge and appreciation been attempted. In 1904 the government founded the National Conservatory of Music and appointed as director Narciso Garay (1876–1953), who had just returned from a long stay in Paris where he had studied music.

Despite governmental support, the conservatory was forced to close in 1921 because of lack of popular interest. For twenty years there was no official institution for the teaching of music in the country. In 1941 the government reestablished the National Conservatory of Music under the direction of the violinist Alfredo de Saint-Malo. In the same year the National Symphony Orchestra was established under the direction of Herbert de Castro. It has given many concerts in the capital and in various cities and towns of the interior. It has been under the direction of Eduardo Charpentier, Jr., since 1966.

The government also contributed to the musical culture by establishing the National Theatre. It opened in 1908 with a performance of *Aida*. Although only a few professional artists have performed at the theater, Panamanians have been able, from time to time, to hear concerts and operas performed by some of the outstanding artists of the Americas and Europe.

Contemporary composers of note include Roque Cordero, who became director of the conservatory after it was reorganized in 1953 as the National Institute of Music (Instituto Nacional de Música). He was recognized by the Latin American Festival of Music in Caracas in 1954 as one of the prominent composers of the hemisphere. Narciso Garay was an able composer in the folk idiom. Gonzalo Brenes wrote the music for the popular musical *La Cucaracha Mandinga* (The Devil Cockroach). The best known Panamanian composer of popular music is Ricardo Fábrega.

Alberto Galimany, former director of the national band; Luis Azcarrage; and Avelino Muñoz are also well known among contemporary composers. Among the country's most noted performers in 1971 was pianist Jaime Ingram, who occasionally accompanied the National Symphony Orchestra and had performed in Europe and several Western Hemisphere countries.

A musical group that was enjoying strong governmental backing in 1971 was the Orquesta 11 de Octubre (Eleventh of October Orchestra), named after the date of the coup d'etat through which the National Guard assumed power. Its conductor, Captain Victor M. Paz, and its musicians were active members of the guard. The group had performed in several Latin American countries and had won prizes in both national and international competition.

Folk Art

Although classical music has had a very limited audience, Panamanians of all classes have patronized the country's folk music. Musical elements from Spain, Central America, the West Indies, the coastal regions of northern South America, and the United States have all contributed to Panamanian music, placing it among the most varied and colorful in the Americas. The style of Panamanian song is seldom melancholy but conveys rather a sense of optimism and happiness. The singer slides effortlessly through tonal intervals of great distance with the carefree intonation of one who sings for sheer pleasure.

The most important types of song are the *mejorana* and the *punto*. The *mejorana* was probably brought from Spain during the eighteenth century. Both can be either vocal or instrumental; they are played or sung by men exclusively and are never danced. The national dances are the *tamborito* and *cumbia*. The *cumbia* is performed to the rhythm of *maracas* (pebble-filled gourds) and drums, with dancers in couples, men and women dancing around each other, in a moving circle.

The *tamborito* is an old dance that was popular in the seventeenth century in Spain as well as in Panama; it is considered to be of African origin. The most popular native dance of Panama, at carnival time it is performed in the fashionable nightclubs of the city as well as in the rural areas. The dancers stand in a circle, but not in couples, as the music begins, and all clap their hands in rhythm. A man steps to the center of the ring, salutes the ladies, and bows to one of them, who then steps forward to meet him. He dances to her and around her, as the others join in until everyone is in motion. The dance combines the quality of stateliness with its vigorous movement (see ch. 4, Living Conditions).

At fiesta time Panamanians also enjoy a tradition of elaborate dress. The *pollera,* a dress made of white fabric, is worn by almost every Panamanian woman who can afford one. Members of the Panama Academy of Spanish Language have said that the *pollera* came originally from Andalusia and was taken over by the slave women of Panama. It was once exclusively a folk dress, but in recent decades, as upper class Panamanians became conscious of its beauty, it became a national and often very costly costume. It is a two-piece dress with a full skirt worn over several white petticoats trimmed in lace. The sleeveless blouse has a round neck edged in lace with a drawstring so that it can be worn high or low on the shoulders. Both blouse and skirt are elaborately embroidered in colored flower, leaf, and bird designs.

As a result of the increased cost of the *pollera,* the country women took up the *montuna* as a festive costume. It has a blouse like that of the *pollera,* but the long gathered skirt is fashioned of bright cotton print. A black-and-white hat is worn over braided hair, and a fiber bag hangs from the waist. The rural male costume is the *montuno,* a straight hip-length shirt of homespun cotton embroidered or painted with colorful figures. Knee-length trousers, a hat, and sandals complete the costume. The *montuno* is believed to be either a modification of the ceremonial tunic worn by pre-Columbian Indians or an extreme adaptation of Spanish armor (see ch. 4, Living Conditions).

For the rural Panamanian the religious festivals, principally the extended one associated with Holy Week, embody elements of religious observance, folklore, and entertainment. Religious processions, folk music, dancing, and popular sports are mingled during this week of festivity to form the best single expression of the various folk arts (see ch. 6, Social Values). Urban and rural dwellers alike enjoy another major celebration, the carnival season ending on Ash Wednesday, which brings together some of the elements of folk art—notably music, dance, and costume—but without the same religious connotations.

With the assistance of the Ministry of Education, Manuel F.

Zarate and Doria P. de Zarate have published books and articles dealing with the themes, the instruments, and the historical and cultural implications of the country's folklore.

PUBLIC INFORMATION

Provisions for freedom of expression were contained in early constitutions and reiterated in the Constitution of 1946, under which the country was governed in 1971. Article 38 states that every person can freely express his thoughts without being subjected to previous censorship but that he is "legally responsible when . . . the reputation or the honor of persons, or the security of society or the public order, are attacked."

Decrees providing for censorship of newspapers issued between 1940 and 1951 were repealed, but a decree promulgated in 1952 provided that radio commentators, before going on the air, must submit texts to the legal representative of the network or station. This decree was subsequently applied to newspapers, and during periods of political tension prior censorship of dailies was exercised. When Brigadier General Omar Torrijos assumed power in 1968 a number of newspapers were closed, and a decree providing for close supervision of the mass media was issued. In 1971 the minister of government and justice announced the appointment of a three-man censorship board with power to ban presentation by any means of material that "would be offensive to the national dignity," would take the form of propaganda for "exotic theories or totalitarian systems," or would seek "destruction of the country's democratic and republican system of government or would be contrary to public order."

Informal dissemination of information and ideas plays an important role—particularly in rural areas, where rumors travel rapidly by word of mouth. Much gossip is retailed by bus drivers on country roads or retailed at village fiestas and after church services. Other centers for the exchange of news and views are cafés, bars, country stores, markets, and the homes of schoolteachers in country towns.

Newspapers, Periodicals, and Books

The history of newspapers in Panama dates back to the first quarter of the nineteenth century. The first newspapers were published shortly after José María Goytía opened the country's first printing establishment in 1821. Between that year and 1849 more than thirty newspapers were published, including the *Gaceta del Istmo de Panamá, El Fiscal y La Ley,* and *La Miscelanea.* Most of the early newspapers were legal gazettes or journals of opinion championing independence from Spain. United States citizens were the founders of some newspapers published during the second half of the nineteenth century. One of them, A. B. Boyd, was the publisher in 1852 of the *Panama Star and Herald*, predecessor of *La Estrella de Panamá*, which was still being published in 1971.

In 1971 there were seven daily newspapers and one bilingual weekly with an estimated circulation of about 140,000. *Matutino*, which describes itself as independent, was one of several dailies organized into a group (Editorial Renovación) closely supervised by the government. The others were the *Panama American*, *Crítica, La Hora,* and *El Panamá América,* all of which had previously been opposition newspapers.

El Panamá América, with morning and evening editions and a broad coverage of news, appealed to a general readership and had a reputation for being highly influential. It also published an English edition, the *Panama American,* which was popular with Canal Zone residents. *La Estrella de Panamá,* the leading morning newspaper, had a reputation for effective coverage and impartial reporting. Its English-language version, the *Star and Herald,* was intended primarily for Canal Zone readers.

La Hora was a tabloid popular among lower income groups. Before coming under government control it had been known for its gossipy approach to national politics and its emphasis on scandal and crime, but in 1971 no newspapers were permitted to carry stories in these categories. *Crítica,* another tabloid, was aimed at a general readership and was reputed to exercise moderate influence. The *Panama Tribune,* a weekly tabloid published in English and Spanish, appealed to blacks—notably Jamaicans— and featured local names and news.

In 1971 the leading metropolitan dailies, all published in Panama City, carried extensive foreign news coverage—usually on the front page. News regarding Panama's international position, particularly in its relations with the United States, is usually featured. The metropolitan newspapers carry society news, fashion plates, and other items of interest to women. Notices of births, birthdays, anniversaries, travel, and other activities of prominent persons fill the society newspapers and sports sections are extensive— devoted mainly to horseracing and baseball. Major dailies and tabloids publish lottery results and horoscopes and carry comic strips—many of North American origin. Leading newspapers have large classified advertising sections and depend heavily on advertising patronage, lack of which in the past has forced many to discontinue publication.

Domestic periodicals play a minor role as information media.

The best known in 1971 was *Lotería,* published by the government department that operated the lottery. It was a monthly publication featuring articles on literature, history, and art read mainly by intellectuals. Foreign periodicals were popular mainly among the educated upper class, who read the *Economist* (London), *Paris Match, Life* and *Time* magazines, and *Visión.*

The country has no domestic press news agency. In 1971 most newspapers relied on West European wire services such as Agence France Presse (AFP), Reuters of Great Britain, EFE of Spain, and the United States agencies Associated Press (AP) and United Press International (UPI). A number of Panamanian newspapermen employed by Panamanian newspapers also served as correspondents for foreign news agencies.

In 1971 students interested in the profession could attend the school of journalism at the University of Panama. Sons or other relatives of prominent newspaper owners often attended schools of journalism in the United States.

Books played a minor role as sources of information and recreation. There were a number of bookstores, publishers, and printers in Panama City, including the National Printing Office (Imprenta Nacional), but few books were published. The National Printing Office published some works in the field of humanities and official publications on history and international relations, but the principal output consisted of the *Official Gazette* and documents of the various ministries.

Radio, Television, and Motion Pictures

Although the press continued in 1971 to hold a position of primary importance in influencing public opinion in the cities, radio was rapidly increasing its impact on the society as a whole. The technical facilities of radio stations were well developed, and their broadcasts reached many rural communities along secondary roads where newspapers were not readily available. The emotional appeal that verbal exhortations have to many Panamanians enhanced the importance of the radio stations as mass media; and burgeoning use of portable transistor sets brought broadcasts to an ever-increasing number of listeners.

In 1971 the country's privately owned radio transmitters were licensed by the Directorate General of Posts and Telegraphs (Dirección General de Correos y Telégrafos), and radio broadcasters belonged to the Panamanian Broadcasting Association (Asociación Panameña de Radiodifusión). A significant development was the opening by the government of a powerful station— Radio Liberty (Radio Libertad), broadcasting on ten kilowatts—

and the establishment of Panama's first domestic radio service. With its repeater stations, Radio Libertad was designed to reach the most remote parts of the country with news and educational and cultural programs. Repeater stations were being equipped to originate broadcasts that could be disseminated throughout the network. Governmental liaison with press, radio, and television was maintained by the Office of Public Relations of the President, which compiled news bulletins dealing with presidential or top-echelon governmental activities.

In 1971 there were more than eighty privately owned broadcast stations in the country—about thirty-five of these in Panama City. The number of receivers was estimated at 430,000, including sets in more than 80 percent of the homes. The mainstays of radio programs were popular music, soap operas, and news commentaries. Some stations carried cultural and religious programs and broadcasts of local interest. The Voice of Barú (Voz del Barú) in David, for example, features programs of interest to farmers. Commercials, which represent the principal source of revenue, are interspersed through the programs, and some stations have disc service and transcription contracts with foreign broadcasting companies—mainly in the United States and Mexico. Major networks relay the United States Voice of America and broadcasts of private United States networks. A satellite ground station relays programs from North America and Europe.

Two powerful stations—each ten kilowatts—were Radio Republic (Radio República) [HOB50] in Chitré and RPC Network (Circuito RPC) [HOHM] in Panama City. A few stations used power of approximately five kilowatts, and all others utilized one kilowatt or less.

In 1971 Panamanian television stations numbered two, with repeater stations in major population centers. All telecasts used 525 lines. Most programs had commercial sponsors, and stations were buying an increasing number of packaged programs from United States producers, including situation comedies. There were an estimated 122,000 television receivers in the Republic, of which some 80,000 were in Panama City; 15,000 in Colón; 12,000 in Chiriquí; and 15,000 in the Central Provinces.

Both Panamanian stations used programs transmitted via the United States satellite, and plans were underway to inaugurate daily Eurovision newscasts on both local channels.

Motion pictures are a popular form of recreation for city dwellers, but few rural dwellers see them regularly. All commercial films are subject to censorship. Of the approximately sixty theaters showing thirty-five millimeter films, most are in Panama City and Colón. There is also a considerable number of small theaters equipped for screening sixteen-millimeter films, including a few in the interior. In the absence of a domestic film industry, all films are imported—the majority from the United States. European and Mexican productions are also exhibited.

Although the government did not maintain diplomatic relations with the Soviet Union and the communist party was illegal, the Soviet Union, as it had in the past, participated in the 1970 Panamanian International Film Festival. For the first time, the festival was sponsored by a Panamanian government agency.

Foreign Government Activity

In connection with his presence at the film festival in 1970, the Soviet cultural affairs officer in Bogotá met with Panamanian officials in the cultural field to offer programs of educational exchange and Soviet scholarships (see ch. 10, Foreign Relations). In addition to arranging concerts for high school students and an art exhibit, he negotiated for the placement of a master ballet instructor either in the University of Panama or in the School of the Dance and submitted a Spanish translation of a Soviet textbook on the social sciences to be considered for publication in Panama.

The French government operates a cultural center that is noted for its encouragement of the plastic arts and for its language program. Other European countries and a number of Latin American countries sponsor binational cultural associations and offer scholarships (see ch. 10, Foreign Relations). The French have placed professors at the University of Panama, and the Spanish have maintained a traditionally strong influence at the University of Panama and the University of Santa María la Antigua through the placement of Spanish clergy. In September 1970 they participated in the University of Panama's book exhibit and were working with the Ministry of Education.

The United States Information Service has provided materials to newspapers, radio stations, television stations, and commercial theaters and has maintained an exhibit program that includes multimedia participation in rural fairs and exhibits at the national university, at the national library, and in secondary schools. A number of Panamanians have participated in a variety of exchange programs with the United States, and the American Field Service has also arranged student exchanges.

CHAPTER 8

GOVERNMENTAL SYSTEM

According to the Constitution of 1946 Panama is a republic with a unitary form of government. The Latin American tradition of personalistic leadership is reflected in a strong executive branch, with the presidency as a symbol of nationhood. The constitutional checks on presidential authority were not in evidence in 1971, but during more than half a century of independence a balance usually has been found between the need for a strong president and the danger of a wholly unrestrained executive.

In 1971 the country was governed by a provisional junta established by the National Guard after that body had forcibly ousted the president, Arnulfo Arias, on October 11, 1968, and seized control. Arias had been elected president of the Republic for the third time in May 1968 and had assumed office on October 1. One of his first acts was to make appointments to the National Assembly without regard for the constitutional requirement for the free election of these individuals. On October 8, at the president's request, the Ministry of Government and Justice, which administered the National Guard, issued orders for the transfer to less important posts of about fifteen senior officers of the guard. These orders were to be effective October 11, but on that day the president was deposed (see ch. 14, National Security).

Two National Guard colonels were appointed members of a governing provisional junta—one of them serving as president. The National Assembly was dissolved, and eleven articles of the Constitution were suspended. These articles concerned fundamental guarantees of individual and social rights, including freedom from arrest, freedom of speech, freedom of assembly, freedom of travel, and the inviolability of the domicile. In December 1969 the National Guard colonels resigned from the junta and were replaced by two civilians—Demetrio Basilio Lakas and Arturo Sucre—but the real power was vested in the person of the commander of the National Guard, Brigadier General Omar Torrijos. In July 1971 some of the suspended constitutional rights had been restored but, as of August 1971, the National Assembly had not been reconvened and the government ruled by decree.

The legislature has not played an important role in the political system. The multiparty system, which prevents any single party from obtaining a legislative majority, tends to blunt the power of the legislative branch. Yet in the past the legislature has performed necessary functions and has been a crucial force in the preservation or amendment of the constitution. The judiciary is important in the same sense, but it too is subordinated to executive initiative.

There is little difference between the first constitution, that of 1904, and the most recent, that of 1946. All three constitutions, including the second (1941), have provided detailed outlines for the organization of society. The amended Constitution of 1946, in force in 1971, emphasized individual rights and liberties, the welfare of labor, and assistance to social institutions, such as the family. This emphasis reflects the great value placed on human welfare, both as social ideals and as juridical concepts (see ch. 6, Social Values).

Many provisions of the Constitution and basic laws serve more as a set of goals to be achieved than as a blueprint for actual practice. To a great extent, the realities of political power and freedom have been determined more by custom than by the formal and explicit political structure. Most political power in the past has been shared by a small group of old, established families (see ch. 9, Political Dynamics and Values).

EARLY DEVELOPMENT

The history of Panama as a sovereign nation dates from 1903, but the form of its political institutions has been heavily influenced by the preceding periods of Spanish and Colombian rule (see ch. 2, Historical Setting). Panamanian government therefore reflects values stressed by Latin and Hispanic societies—the family, the individual, and Western Christian ethical precepts in general—as guiding tenets for social organization. In addition, the libertarian political concepts developed in Western Europe and North America in the eighteenth and nineteenth centuries have also influenced Panamanian institutions and thought. Elaborate guarantees are provided in the Constitution to protect the legal status of the family, social and political freedom of the individual citizen, and the integrity of political instruments designed to secure these goals. Nevertheless, the realities of political life have always been conditioned more by the habitually dominant role of the few old families making up the social elite than by constitutional provision. Their privileges have been protected throughout by their effective monopoly of key posts (see ch. 6, Social Values).

One of the dominant aspects of the period since 1903 is an ambivalent and complex attitude of envy, respect, fear, and hatred of the country that intervened to help Panama separate from Colombia in 1903. Article 136 of the 1904 Constitution provided that the United States would be able to intervene in Panamanian affairs "to re-establish public peace and constitutional order" in the event that that nation guaranteed Panama's independence. This obligation had been undertaken by the United States in the Treaty of 1903 with Panama, and the legal right of intervention in the country's internal affairs was thereby validated. The Republic remained a de facto protectorate of the United States until 1936, when the latter renounced both the guarantee of independence and the concomitant right of intervention. Since that time, however, the vast interests of the United States in the isthmian region have continued to exercise an extremely strong influence on Panamanian affairs (see ch. 10, Foreign Relations).

Constitution of 1904

After Panama's declaration of independence, thirty-two delegates were elected to a constituent assembly that was to draft a constitution. The draft was completed in only three weeks and was adoped on February 13, 1904. It was based largely on Colombia's 1886 fundamental law.

The first article provided for an "independent and sovereign nation regulated by a republican and democratic form of government." Citizenship was extended to all persons born on Panamanian territory, and suffrage was granted to all male citizens over twenty-one. Foreigners were granted equality before the law with Panamanians. Freedom of religion was also specified, but Roman Catholicism was recognized as the majority faith. Education was acknowledged as a function of government, and primary education was to be both free and compulsory. Individual rights were guaranteed but could be suspended in emergencies by the National Assembly or by the president when the legislature was not in session. In the latter case the president was to have all his ministers sign the suspension decree and to recall the assembly to ratify the action taken.

The constitution provided for a unitary centralized government composed of the executive, legislative, and judicial branches. Executive power was vested in the president and ministers of his selection who together formed the Cabinet Council. Presidents were to be chosen in a direct popular election on the same day as the National Assembly members. A four-year term was stipulated, and immediate reelection was forbidden. The three vice presidents (*designados*) were to be selected by the assembly every two years. In the event they were absent or unavailable, the cabinet would elect a cabinet minister as the successor to the presidency.

Legislative powers were entrusted to a unicameral National Assembly that was to be popularly elected every four years. Formally, the National Assembly was coordinate with the other branches; in practice, it tended to be dominated by the executive. Among its principal duties and responsibilities were the enactment of legislation; election of the three vice presidents; selection of an election court, the procurator general, and the manager of the National Bank; approval of the comptroller; and ratification of public treaties. It had the power to impeach the president, vice presidents, ministers, and justices of the Supreme Court of Justice and the powers to declare war and to levy taxes.

Judicial power was vested in a court structure headed by the Supreme Court of Justice (also known as the Supreme Court), with five members appointed by the president for ten-year terms under a system of staggered tenure by which one justice was replaced every two years. In this way, each president usually appointed two justices during his four-year incumbency. The Supreme Court justices, in turn, selected a superior tribunal for each of the two separate judicial districts. These tribunals then chose circuit judges, who in turn named the municipal justices. Certain judicial powers were also exercised by mayors, police judges, and other local officials.

The 1904 Constitution limited the national territory according to the terms of existing and future treaties with the United States, thus incorporating two basic concessions made by Panama in the Hay-Bunau-Varilla Treaty of 1903:

> 1. Panama granted to the United States "in perpetuity" the use, occupation and control of a ten mile strip of land and water—the Canal Zone. The United States also received rights of perpetual use, occupation and control of other areas outside the Zone—certain islands in the Bay of Panama as well as islands in the Zone, that might be "necessary and convenient for construction, conservation, service, sanitation and protection" of the Canal.
>
> 2. Panama conceded "all rights, powers and authority" in the Canal Zone to the United States "that the United States can exercise as if she were sovereign" in that territory "with the complete exclusion of the Republic of Panama in the exercise of such rights, powers and authority."

The implementation of these provisions has continued ever since to be the subject of dispute (see ch. 10, Foreign Relations).

Even more crucial than the concessions concerning the Canal Zone were the provisions that made the country a virtual protectorate of the United States. It was stipulated that the "government of the United States will be able to intervene in any part of the Republic of Panama to reestablish public order and constitutional order" if it also assumed the obligation of guaranteeing Panama's independence and sovereignty. This provision, along with the Canal Zone arrangements, was thought by Panamanians to have impaired the Republic's sovereignty and led to increasing discontent until its abrogation in 1936. Even thereafter the issue of sovereignty in the Canal Zone has remained a sensitive constitutional and legal question.

The sole method of amending the constitution was through legislative act. Amendments could be proposed to the National Assembly by the government, and the approval of two-thirds of the assembly was necessary for ratification. The difficulty of obtaining the two-thirds necessary for amendment, in a National Assembly divided into personal factions, led to increasing deviation of practice from constitutional prescription.

By the 1930s the need for changes to restore harmony between constitutional theory and political practice, combined with a lapse in the traditional United States policy of suppressing revolution, enabled Harmodio Arias to stage the country's first coup de'etat. Assuming office as provisional president in 1931, he was subsequently elected president from 1932 to 1936. At the end of his term he was responsible for the second major departure from the status quo by negotiating a crucial revision of the 1903 treaty with the United States. Under this new treaty arrangement—not ratified by the United States Senate until 1939—the United States gave up its right of intervention in Panamanian affairs, and the country emerged from its protectorate status (see ch. 2, Historical Setting; ch. 10, Foreign Relations). These changes formed the prelude to more basic developments in the 1940s.

Constitution of 1941

The national elections of June 2, 1940, marked a break in the Republic's conservative constitutional development. Arnulfo Arias —an anti-United States, Harvard-trained physician and brother of Harmodio Arias—was the official government-sponsored candidate. His party, the National Revolutionary Party, in coalition with four others, secured an electoral victory with the aid of the government (see ch. 2, Historical Setting).

Shortly after his inauguration President Arias presented to the National Assembly a draft of a revised and pointedly nationalistic constitution. In urging its adoption, Arias stressed the critical international situation of that period and the need for modernizing Panama's political institutions. Its adoption by the National Assembly was denounced as illegal by the opposition since the deputies had not followed the method of amendment stipulated in the 1904 Constitution. Legislative amendments were supposed to have been debated and voted on a second time by a different assembly. Arias, however, impatient of delay, issued a decree in late November 1940 that suspended this requirement. On the cabinet's approval of this measure, the president then assumed "supreme representation of the state" and called for a plebiscite on the new constitution. An overwhelmingly favorable vote in mid-December 1940 led to the promulgation of the constitution in early January 1941 at a mass rally in the National Stadium.

The new constitution extended the terms of the president and the National Assembly members from four to six years, providing retroactively for President Arias's retention of power until 1946. Coupled with the enlargement of executive powers and increased centralization, this provision cast doubt on the future of representative institutions in the country.

Another radical departure from previous constitutional tradition was found in certain citizenship provisions that discriminated against non-Spanish-speaking Antillean Negroes. This development reflected political tensions as well as cultural conflict. Arias attacked the "corrupting" inroads made into Panama's Hispanic heritage by the Antilleans from the British West Indies. Politically, the upper class Panamanian of pure Spanish background feared the growing numbers of non-Spanish-speaking Negroes, employed mostly in the Canal Zone, who were gaining in political consciousness. Many of these Negroes identified their economic interests and future with the Canal Zone and United States interests rather than with Panamanian society. Large numbers frequently returned to their home islands for vacations or retirement. This indifference to the Republic and its culture further embittered the Spanish-speaking Panamanians, who already resented the Antillean linguistic advantage in competing for desirable positions in the Canal Zone. A favorable climate therefore existed for the discriminatory provisions of the new constitution.

A brief nine months after the promulgation of the 1941 Constitution, President Arnulfo Arias was deposed in a bloodless coup d'etat. He had become repressive and autocratic since the adoption of the new constitution and had quickly alienated significant elements in the elite. In addition to silencing press opposition, he had insisted on deducting 10 percent from the salaries of all government employees in order to pay for his election campaign. He had also allowed gambling to become so rampant that the economy's stability was threatened. In foreign affairs he had pursued a pro-Axis foreign policy that had alarmed much of the population.

As a result, members of his own cabinet, with the support of the police force, seized the opportunity presented when the president left for a short visit to Cuba without securing the necessary legal authorization. His deposition was accomplished on October 9, 1941, and Ricardo Adolfo de la Guardia, Arias's minister of government and justice, assumed control of the executive. He received the support of all political factions and set about to undo many of Arias's innovations.

It was generally believed at the time that de la Guardia would remain in the presidency until the National Assembly chose the new vice presidents on February 15, 1943, but in January of that year the assembly decided not to select vice presidents for the 1943–45 period. As a result, de la Guardia continued in the presidency. By 1944 the political atmosphere had changed, however, and in December of that year the National Assembly declared itself in opposition to the incumbent administration.

President de la Guardia retaliated by dissolving the legislature, as well as the 1941 Constitution, and called for the election of a constituent assembly to meet in June 1945. The cabinet responded to this action by resigning in protest. A government was then formed that theoretically distributed power equally among the various cabinet members, the president of the Cabinet Council performing the executive functions. Elections were then held for a new constituent convention, which saw its task as the overthrow of the Arias Constitution's innovations and the reestablishment of traditional constitutional forms.

On June 15 Panama's second constituent assembly met and elected a provisional president, Enrique A. Jiménez, and two vice presidents. The members worked through the remainder of that year, and on March 1, 1946, the president promulgated a new constitution.

THE CONSTITUTION OF 1946

The amended Constitution of 1946 (in effect in 1971) has fourteen sections containing twenty-two chapters with 256 detailed articles. The structure of government is defined as "a unitary and independent state" with a "republican, democratic and representative government"; the country is pledged to respect the rules of international law. Power emanates from the people and is divided among the three traditional branches of government. The Republic's territorial limits follow the previously existing boundaries as defined by treaties with Colombia and Costa Rica, and jurisdictional limitations accepted before the Constitution took effect (a reference to the Canal Zone) are recognized. The recognition of the Canal Zone in the country's Constitution was displeasing to the Panamanians and was one of the principal reasons for their insistence upon a new canal treaty with the United States. The country is divided into "autonomous municipalities grouped into nine provinces." Spanish continues to be recognized as the national language.

Citizenship may be acquired by birth or naturalization. Those born within the Republic of a Panamanian father or mother or those born abroad of Panamanian parents legally domiciled within the Republic are automatically citizens. Conventional procedures regarding naturalization are provided, although overtones of the 1941 Constitution appear in the requirement that persons naturalized before adoption of the 1946 Constitution must learn Spanish and be integrated into Panamanian culture. The stated purpose of civil institutions is to protect the "life, honor, and property" of all citizens and foreign nationals within the country's jurisdiction and "to assure the effectiveness of individual and social rights and duties."

All residents—Panamanians and foreign nationals alike—are equal before the law, and discrimination on the basis of sex, social class, religion, race, birth, or political persuasion is forbidden. Special regulation of the activities of foreigners as a general group is permitted if necessary or advisable for reasons of "health, morality, public security, and national economy."

More specific safeguards of personal rights reflect traditional principles of civil liberty derived from both Anglo-Saxon and Roman legal systems. Unauthorized deprivation of liberty is proscribed; imprisonment for debt is forbidden. The concept of habeas corpus was included in the Constitution, as was protection against self-incrimination and incrimination of blood relatives to the fourth degree of relationship and relatives-in-law to the second degree of relationship.

The inviolability of the home is declared, and entry without consent of the home dweller is permitted only on proper authorization or in cases of obvious and pressing need. The privacy of correspondence and other private written communications is guaranteed. Humane conditions within penal institutions are required, and the death penalty is outlawed. There is a general prohibition of ex post facto criminal punishment. An exception to the requirement of due process is made for those who insult or act disrespectfully toward public officials in the performance of their duties; arbitrary fines or arrest may be imposed in such cases.

Religious freedom is provided for as long as "respect for Christian morality and public order" is observed. Provision is made for religious instruction in the public schools, though the children of dissenting parents may be exempted. The rights of free expression and of peaceable assembly are upheld. The rights of petition and of the free, untaxed practice of the professions and crafts are guaranteed.

Private property is recognized as inviolable except as expropriation—court-sanctioned and with prior indemnification—might be applied to serve "public utility or social interest." The executive may decree the "expropriation or seizure of private property" whenever "war, grave disturbance of the public order, or urgent social interest" requires prompt action. In such a case indemnification, though obligatory, need not precede the act of expropriation, and early return of the sequestered property is required.

In the event of internal or external crisis, the whole national territory or any part of it may be declared by a decree of the National Assembly to be in a "state of siege," and guarantees of personal freedom are then subject to partial or total temporary suspension. If the crisis occurs when the National Assembly is not in session, the president, the cabinet members, and the members of the Permanent Legislative Commission—a body representing the National Assembly during adjournment—may sign such a decree, though this step would necessitate recalling the legislature to vote confirmation of the "state of siege" within five days. In such a case, the National Assembly would act to terminate the state of siege and restore any suspended rights at the end of the crisis. If the legislature were again not in session, the cabinet, acting with the approval of the Permanent Legislative Commission, would restore all constitutional guarantees at the conclusion of the crisis.

The section on individual and social rights and duties, the most extensive of any in the Constitution and consisting of seventy-seven articles, also covers the status of labor. It describes work as "a right and duty of the individual." The goal of total employment of the available labor force is stated in the Constitution, and activities by the state in furtherance of this goal are sanctioned. Economic conditions adequate to assure every worker "a decent existence" are to be sought by public institutions.

On October 12, 1968, the day after the National Guard coup that deposed President Arnulfo Arias, several constitutional guarantees were suspended. These concerned deprivation of liberty, habeas corpus, inviolability of the domicile, freedom of travel, inviolability of correspondence, confiscation of property, freedom of expression, the right of assembly, and redress against false arrest. One year later some of these rights—individual liberty, habeas corpus, and inviolability of private homes—had been restored. In November 1969 a new decree announced by the provisional gov-

ernmental junta listed seven kinds of acts considered subversi,
and set penalties for these at from one month to fifteen years in
prison (see ch. 14, National Security).

According to Article 252 of the Constitution of 1946, the Constitution may be amended only by a legislative act enacted by the
National Assembly in regular session, and the act must then be
published and transmitted by the executive to the National Assembly during the first session after the new elections for deputies so
that it may be debated and approved by an absolute majority of
its members. The president may take exception to the proposed
amendment only after it has been debated for the second time by
the National Assembly.

The National Assembly was dissolved in October 1968, and, as
of November 1971, it had not been reconvened. In October of that
year, however, Cabinet Decree No. 280 was published, creating a
commission for amendments to the national Constitution. It was
to be made up of twenty-five members and their respective alternates. In order to be a member of the commission an individual
was required to be a Panamanian by birth; over twenty-five years
of age; in full enjoyment of civil rights; and must not have been
convicted of crimes against the nation, persons, or property.

The sessions of the commission could be attended, with a right
to vote, by the members of the provisional government junta, the
president of the Supreme Court of Justice, the commander in
chief of the National Guard, the cabinet ministers, the attorney
general, and the directors of the autonomous institutions. After
all the members of the commission have been appointed, the commission would have a period of six months in which to draw up a
draft for dissemination throughout the nation.

In its deliberations the commission may be advised by elements
representing labor, farmers, and religious, teaching, student,
civic, and welfare activities. If it is deemed necessary public officials may be asked for oral or written reports or may be asked
to attend the sessions of the commission.

OPERATION OF GOVERNMENT

In 1971 the functions of the executive branch were carried out
by a two-man provisional junta appointed by the National Guard.
The president was Demetrio Basilio Lakas, an engineer, and the
additional member was Arturo Sucre, a lawyer. The Constitution
was in effect, although not all the constitutional guarantees that
had been suspended in October 1968 had been restored. The president's cabinet continued to function, as did the judiciary, but the
National Assembly had been dissolved in October 1968 and by
1971 had not been reconvened.

Executive

According to the Constitution of 1946 the president of the Republic is elected by direct popular vote for a term of four years. The two vice presidents (formerly three under the Constitution of 1904) were termed *designados* and elected every two years by the National Assembly. After 1946 they were to be elected by popular vote and were also to serve four-year terms, concurrent with that of the president.

Article 140 of the Constitution states that the president must be thirty-five years old and a native-born Panamanian. An incumbent is ineligible for reelection for the following two terms. The president may not leave the country while performing his duties; to do so entails loss of the office. In 1941 President Arias flew to Havana ostensibly to consult an oculist, and his cabinet declared the office vacated.

The president has the power to appoint as executive department heads ministers of state who hold office at his pleasure, to conduct foreign relations, to appoint and dismiss provincial governors, to sign or veto bills, and to serve as commander in chief of the nation's "public forces" (see ch. 14, National Security). He also must present the National Assembly with a proposed budget within the first ten days of each regular session. He is granted emergency power of decree-legislation, subject to authorization by the National Assembly. The countersignature of the minister of the department concerned is required, but the effect of this limitation is nominal because of the ministers' thorough subordination to the president.

The ministers of state under the chairmanship of the president constitute the Cabinet Council. Under the Constitution of 1946, ministers may not be closely related by family to the president or to one another, but this article (158 of the Constitution) has not been closely adhered to. The Cabinet Council serves as a general advisory body to the president. It also participates with the president in the choice of members of the Supreme Court.

In 1971 there were nine ministries: the Ministry of Government and Justice, the Ministry of Foreign Affairs, the Ministry of Agriculture and Livestock, the Ministry of Commerce and Industry, the Ministry of Education, the Ministry of Finance and Treasury, the Ministry of Labor and Social Welfare, the Ministry of Public Health, and the Ministry of Public Works. The president is assisted by an additional agency called the Office of the Presidency, which coordinates the functions of the other ministries, the Cabinet Council, and the autonomous agencies. It is presided over by a minister who serves as the secretary general of the presidency and secretary of the Cabinet Council.

The Ministry of Government and Justice is perhaps the most important of the nine ministries and is the only one whose functions are not made evident by its title. The minister and vice minister are charged with overall responsibility for administration and are assisted by several housekeeping bodies. The ministry administers several public services—the National Guard, which is a police force rather than a militia; the fire departments of twenty-six cities; the Department of Correction, including supervision of the penal colony on the island of Coiba and the Panama City and Colón jails; the telegraph and radio systems; and the Department of Civil Aviation. Other offices that fall under the authority of the Ministry of Government and Justice are the National Archives, the Public Registry, the Office of Forensic Medicine, and the ceremonial Republican Band.

The importance of the ministry derives from the fact that provincial and local governments are organized under its supervision. The governments of the nine provinces—Bocas del Toro, Chiriquí, Coclé, Colón, Darién, Herrera, Los Santos, Panama, and Veraguas—and administration of the special Indian reservations fall directly within its jurisdiction. It is through this means that the executive structures the administration of the provinces and municipalities.

In 1952 the National Assembly created an Indian affairs department within the structure of the Ministry of Government and Justice that was to supervise the proper discharge of its special constitutional and statutory mandates concerning the Indian population. A policy was adopted over the years for dealing with the indigenous inhabitants of the country by creating *comarcas* (territories) for them, the most prominent of which is the *comarca* of San Blas, which occupies most of the northeastern coastal region. There are, however, other *comarcas* in Veraguas, Chiriquí, and Bocas del Toro provinces that have been created by law and are generally under the supervisory jurisdiction of the ministry's Indian affairs department.

Effective domination of this ministry by the executive enables that branch to control both the subordinate levels of government and the National Guard, the only armed force in the Republic.

Legislative

The Constitution calls for a unicameral National Assembly composed of members elected from districts set up on the basic ratio of 1 deputy for every 25,000 inhabitants and 1 additional

184

deputy for a remainder of not less than 15,000. Two alternates are also elected for each deputy and may serve in his absence. The deputies and alternates serve for four-year terms.

The regular term of the National Assembly is four years, and the annual sessions begin on October 1. The deputies are required to appoint ten of their members to serve as principal members and alternates on the Permanent Legislative Commission that functions between sessions. The commission's most important function is to review suspensions of constitutional guarantees, the issuance of decree-laws by the executive, and the issuance of supplementary budget items.

In the legislative process itself, a differentiation is made between laws dealing with the most important areas of public policy —designated organic laws—and enactments of lesser importance. Organic laws require the approval of an absolute majority of the chamber; others require only a majority of members present. All bills are subjected to three readings—which take place on separate days—and must receive the president's approval to be enacted into law.

The Constitution also provides for standing commitees (*comisiones permanentes*), which function within the National Assembly to study proposed legislation and report their views to the body's membership as a whole. The first reading takes place within the appropriate committee. After the tentative approval of a bill by the assembly but before its third reading, the president must consider it within a limited period of time, during which he may exercise a whole or item veto. Bills held by the executive over the maximum period of time must then be promulgated by him as passed. A veto of an entire bill can be overridden by the assembly in a two-thirds vote after its third reading. Bills to which the president raises the objection of unconstitutionality may be sent, at the assembly's request, to the Supreme Court of Justice for a decision. A favorable opinion obligates the president to give his approval and order its speedy promulgation. An official gazette is published, and laws come into force from the date of their promulgation unless otherwise specified.

In 1971 the legislative body of the Panamanian government was not functioning. It had not been reconvened since its dissolution in 1968. Legislation was achieved by decree-laws carried out by a two-man provisional junta. When the National Assembly was dissolved, forty-two seats were distributed as follows: Panama, fourteen; Chiriquí, seven; Veraguas, five; Coclé, Colón, and Los Santos, four each; Herrera, two; Bocas del Toro and Darién, one each.

When functioning, the National Assembly had organized its own legislative committees and elected from among its own members the Permanent Legislative Commission, composed of seven deputies and the same number of alternates. This group served as a surrogate for the assembly when it was not in session.

The Constitution provides the National Assembly with important functions in the area of appointments. It names the procurator general, the deputy procurator general, and the comptroller general (whose office is responsible for supervision, regulation, and control of the public funds). It approves the naming of the magistrates of the Supreme Court of Justice, and it may also pass votes of censure against cabinet ministers and functions in a juridical capacity when considering charges of misconduct against government officials.

In 1969, one year after the National Guard coup, Brigadier General Torrijos was asked at a press conference when the people could expect a democratic government based on a freely elected National Assembly. His attention was invited to a broadcast by a member of the National Guard on October 12, 1968, that stated "as soon as the country has returned to normal, national elections will be called for president, vice-president, deputies and councilmen throughout the Republic." General Torrijos replied that (at that time) he saw no reason why general elections could not be held during 1970. He later stated that certain reforms for the betterment of the Panamanian people had greater priorities than the reconvening of the National Assembly.

The year 1970 passed with no more discussion about a general election, but on October 11, 1971, Cabinet Decree No. 280 was published, calling for the election of an assembly of representatives of the municipalities to take place in August 1972. This assembly was to be composed of citizens to be elected at the rate of one principal and one alternate for each municipality, of which there were 475. The electoral tribunal was responsible for outlining the procedures for holding the elections. In order to be nominated, a candidate had to be a Panamanian by birth, over twenty-one years of age, in full enjoyment of his civil rights, and a resident of his municipality at least twelve months prior to the election; he also must not have been convicted of certain crimes.

The Judiciary

The Constitution establishes a judiciary consisting of the Supreme Court of Justice and a hierarcy of other courts that function under its supervision. The Supreme Court consists of nine magistrates, one of whom is appointed every two years for a term of eighteen years. Each has an alternate, appointed for the same term, who replaces the principal during absences. A permanent vacancy is filled by a new appointment for the remainder of the respective unexpired term.

In its functioning the Supreme Court is divided into three chambers, one each for civil, penal, and administrative cases. After 1946 an additional chamber was added to handle cases of a general nature. Magistrates must be Panamanian by birth or by naturalization with more than fifteen years of residence in the country, at least thirty-five years old, in full enjoyment of civil rights, and law graduates and must have completed at least ten years of professional legal practice.

The power of judicial review is explicitly delegated to the Supreme Court, which decides the constitutionality of any bill passed by the National Assembly and questioned by the executive; it also passes on the validity of any law, resolution, executive decree, or order challenged by a private citizen. In all instances involving an issue of constitutionality, the decision of the Supreme Court is final. The actions of autonomous and semiautonomous public agencies are also subject to its review.

Article 177 of the Constitution provides for the Public Ministry, headed by the procurator general. This organization embraces all district attorneys, solicitors, and others engaged in legal representation of the state. In addition to the usual duties of prosecuting offenders, overseeing the conduct of public officials, and defending the province or district that they represent, such officials also serve as counselors for public officials in their jurisdiction.

The term of the procurator general is fixed at ten years, and candidates must have the same qualifications as members of the Supreme Court of Justice. The procurator general is elected by the National Assembly, and other officials in the Public Ministry are appointed by the official immediately superior to them.

Constitutional provisions for the court structure are fairly general; authorization for a supreme court of justice is the only reference in the basic law to a specific court. There is, however, a general provision for the creation of lower courts, which leaves the levels, designations, number, and characteristics of these courts to the Judicial Code and subsequent enactments.

The judiciary is constitutionally independent, however, and is responsible only to "the constitution and the law." Recourse to the courts is free for all citizens and is practiced. More specific rules of procedure and principles of Panamanian law are detailed in the judicial, civil, and criminal codes. The legal system was not affected by the coup that deposed President Arias in 1968, and the courts continued to function as before.

The Supreme Court of Justice

The Supreme Court of Justice is the most authoritative body in the judiciary and is responsible for the supervision of the functioning of the lower courts. In its civil chamber it takes cognizance of appeals for cassation and review from decisions of lower courts. Its criminal chamber has exclusive jurisdiction over offenses committed by judicial personnel, cabinet officers, diplomatic representatives, and other high-level functionaries. The third chamber handles administrative litigation and takes cognizance of cases involving illegal administrative decrees, decisions, and orders. The fourth or "general matters" chamber is responsible for the correctness of civil status and property registrations, disciplinary action against lawyers for violations of professional ethics, and the drafting of items of interest to the administration of justice.

Lower Courts

Under the Supreme Court of Justice are superior tribunals, circuit courts, and municipal courts. The country is divided into three judicial districts. The first of these has the first and second superior tribunals and is responsible for the administration of justice in the provinces of Panama, Colón, and Darién. Each of these tribunals has five circuit courts, those of the first for civil and those of the second for criminal cases. The second judicial district has the third superior tribunal and includes the provinces of Veraguas, Los Santos, Herrera, and Coclé. This tribunal has two circuit courts for each province, one for civil and one for criminal cases. The fourth superior tribunal is in the third judicial district and handles the administration of justice in the western provinces of Bocas del Toro and Chiriquí. In each of these provinces there are two circuit courts, one each for civil and criminal cases.

Each of the superior tribunals has either three or five judges, elected by the Supreme Court of Justice for six-year terms. Requirements for election to a superior tribunal include: Panamanian nationality by birth or naturalization with ten years' continuous residence in the country; being thirty-five years of age and in full exercise of civil and political rights; and having a law degree and five years' practice in law.

Circuit courts have both civil and criminal jurisdiction in all nine provinces. They may be either exclusively set up for criminal or civil cases, but in locations with small populations the judges may take cognizance of both types. Judges sitting on the circuit courts are designated circuit judges rather than being given the title of magistrate, which is reserved for the members of the superior tribunals and the Supreme Court of Justice. Appointment to circuit court is for a fixed term of four years and is the responsibility of the members of the superior tribunals. In order to be eligible for appointment to this office, a candidate must have some form of legal experience, either an advocate's diploma or five years of experience as secretary to a judge or public attorney at least on the circuit level.

Municipal judges have two alternates with concurrent terms of office. The term of office is three years. In order to be appointed a municipal judge in one of the larger cities, it is necessary to have a law degree or to be able to certify one's capacity to practice law. Municipal judges in the outlying areas, in addition to these qualifications, must have either practiced law for a period of two years or served in some capacity in the judiciary for the same period. The reason for more rigorous qualification requirements for judges in the rural areas stems from the fact that outside the larger cities there are fewer opportunities for appeal, and it is therefore more important to ensure high standards on the bench,

The Protective Tribunal for Minors is under the Supreme Court of Justice. The judge is appointed for a six-year term and is responsible for the supervision of proceedings involving minors and the protection of their interests.

In addition, there are administrative courts, customs courts, tax courts, labor courts, traffic courts, and an electoral court composed of three magistrates that has national jurisdiction over cases of offenses violating the rights of suffrage and free election.

The Public Ministry

Responsibility for the administration of justice is vested in the Public Ministry. The senior official is the procurator general, who has an assistant, and below them are district attorneys and municipal attorneys on the local level. These officials have the functions of directing state prosecutions, enforcing laws and regulations, and serving as legal counsel to government officials.

The same qualifications are required to be procurator general as to be a magistrate of the Supreme Court of Justice, and his term of office is ten years. The special functions of the procurator general are: to arraign before the Supreme Court of Justice those officials whose trials pertain to that body; to ensure that all other officials of the Public Ministry faithfully discharge their duties; and to appoint and remove employees in the Public Ministry subordinate to him.

The procurator general is elected by the National Assembly. He appoints an auxiliary attorney (*fiscal auxiliar*) who is responsible for the supervision of the country's investigative functions.

The subordinate levels of the Public Ministry correspond to the organization of the judiciary. There are four superior attorneys of the judicial districts appointed by the procurator general. Two are designated for the first and second districts and are responsible for justice in the provinces of Panama, Colón, and Darién; one is assigned to the third district covering Veraguas, Los Santos, Herrera, and Coclé; and one is assigned to the fourth district with the responsibility for Bocas del Toro and Chiriquí.

Provincial and Local Government

For administrative purposes the country is divided into nine provinces, each having a governor and a deputy governor appointed by the president. The provinces are in turn divided into sixty-five districts. The districts are governed by a mayor appointed by the president and by a popularly elected municipal council that serves for a four-year term. The number of councilmen is proportional to the district's population. The councils range in size from a minimum of 5 for a district with less than 5,000 population to 15 for a population of over 50,000. Each councilman has two alternates elected at the same time. In 1968 there were 469 councilmen.

The districts must cooperate with the national government in the realization of social welfare and in complying with and enforcing the Constitution, the laws of the Republic, and the decisions of the courts of justice. They must also contribute their share toward the promotion of education. The state may intervene in the management of a municipality in case of crises, such as an epidemic or serious disturbances of public order.

Local officials, including mayors, have primarily administrative duties; they enforce the Constitution, laws, executive decrees and orders, and the rulings of judicial bodies. Additional functions of local government are mainly concerned with housekeeping duties. The mayor supervises the municipal employees in their work and ensures that expenditures are consonant with the budget and proper methods of accounting.

Some degree of independence is allowed local government in that acts of the councils, commissions, or mayors may be revoked only by competent judicial authority. This stipulation is not always observed, however, and the national government frequently plays a direct role in decisionmaking.

Municipal councils may create and appoint permanent or temporary commissions from among their membership. The principal powers of a municipal council include the construction, conservation, and improvement of public parks and thoroughfares;

construction of markets, slaughterhouses, and cemeteries; establishment of schools and other educational centers; approval of contracts covering municipal services; provision of water supply, lighting, telephone, gas, sewers, and drainage; disposition of municipal property; levying of taxes to meet expense of administration; and regulation of the use, leasing, and sale of municipal property.

Independent Agencies

Several independent agencies have been developed out of the need or desire to administer certain areas of public activity outside the three branches of government. These agencies embrace a wide range of activities, and some of the more important are: the National Bank of Panama, the Savings Bank, the Social Security Fund, the Institute for Economic Development, the Institute for Housing and Urbanization, the Office of Price Control, the University of Panama, and the Colón Free Zone. Officials are appointed to these agencies by the executive, the National Assembly, and private groups (see ch. 11, Character and Structure of the Economy).

The origin of the independent agencies was perhaps more circumstantial than planned. Nonetheless, several of them afford an instrument of cooperation between the different branches of government that might otherwise be lacking.

CIVIL SERVICE

In 1970 there were about 7,200 persons in the Civil Service, or about 18 percent of the total employed by the national government and the autonomous and semiautonomous agencies. Two characteristic aspects of the service are that it covers few of the 39,800 government employees in the government and autonomous and semiautonomous agencies and that it does not guarantee immunity from political pressures. Decree No. 7, dated July 1962, provides that, when a person is nominated for a Civil Service position, the director of personnel of the ministry involved and the director of the budget must concur in the individual's nomination and acceptance. The executive office of the presidency then considers, and rules on, the recommendation. Despite this concession to political appointment, in many instances civil servants have been apolitical.

Decree No. 7 establishes two sections: the Technical Classification of Posts, which requires the director of personnel of the ministry involved to study duties, functions, and responsibilities; and the System of Classification of Positions, Wage Scales, and Compensation (commonly known as the SCP), which decides on incomes, increases, promotions, transfers, exchanges, and all movements of personnel and which also groups occupations in careers and services. Pay scales for Civil Service personnel are set up in twenty-five grades, with a base, five intermediate steps, and a top grade for each.

Despite the absence of built-in guarantees of job permanence and pay increases, government employment confers status and provides security and the possibility for advancement. In 1966 pay standards of government employees were higher than comparable pay in private industry.

CHAPTER 9

POLITICAL DYNAMICS AND VALUES

Until the coup d'etat of 1968, which resulted in a moratorium on organized civilian political activity, power had been wielded almost exclusively by a small number of wealthy, educated families. The middle class, generally aspiring to upper class status, had not developed a distinctive set of values or goals. Individuals of middle-class background had occasionally gained political prominence, but as a whole the middle class, most of whose members depended upon government jobs, was constrained from an active role in politics, and the slow pace of industrialization had limited the political participation of the urban labor force.

The lower class in general had lacked organization and leadership and had been distracted from a recognition of common problems by the ethnic antagonisms between those of Spanish or mestizo background and the more recent immigrants from the West Indies. Students, both university and secondary, have attempted to fill the vacuum by serving as spokesmen of lower class interests and frustrations.

The multiparty system that existed before the coup d'etat served as a means of regulating competition for political power among the leading families. Individual parties characteristically served as the personal machines of leaders and clients, who anticipated jobs or other advantages if their candidate were successful. The country was generally governed through shifting coalitions of several such parties.

Of the major parties that competed in 1968, only the highly factionalized National Liberal Party had a history of more than two decades. The only parties that had developed clearly identifiable programs were the small Socialist and Christian Democratic parties. The largest party, the Panameñista Party, was the electoral vehicle of former President Arnulfo Arias.

The National Guard, the country's combined police and armed forces, had begun to expand its domestic political role in the 1930s, and since the late 1940s it had served as the final arbiter of political controversies. Since deposing elected President Arnulfo Arias and seizing control of the government in October

1968, it has consolidated its authoritative position through strict control over the press and educational institutions and through large-scale arrests and banishments of actual or potential political leaders.

In 1971 effective executive authority was exercised by Brigadier General Omar Torrijos, commander of the National Guard, although the country was nominally governed by a junta composed of two civilians, Provisional President Demetrio Basilio Lakas and his deputy, Arturo Sucre. No formalized legislative body had replaced the National Assembly, half the membership of which accompanied Arnulfo Arias into exile in 1968, and political parties were officially declared "extinct" in March 1969. General Torrijos declared in November 1970, "The principal goal of the Panamanian experiment is to eliminate the politician and implant the revolution as an irreversible fact."

Traditionally, the political values and attitudes of the population at large have been those that have filtered down from the oligarchy, with little reciprocal flow in the other direction. These have involved deference to authority and acceptance of the political dominance of the upper class. The widespread lower class support attracted by Arnulfo Arias in 1968 through his attacks on the oligarchy, however, suggested that the traditional value system was being undermined. The military government, with predominantly middle-class leadership, has also indicated awareness of the increasing political consciousness among the lower classes. In November 1970 General Torrijos declared, "Having finished with the oligarchy, the Panamanian has his own worth with no importance to his origin, his cradle or where he was born."

The focal point of consensus in political life, cutting across both social and partisan cleavages, has been nationalism. Nationalistic sentiments, directed primarily against United States operations in the Canal Zone, have been catered to in varying degrees by all who held positions of leadership or who sought popular support. Attitudes toward the political system itself before the coup d'etat appeared to be ambivalent. Although skepticism toward the validity of elections was expressed in the popular saying, "The one who counts the votes, elects," voter turnout was customarily high. As there had been no election since 1968 and freedom of expression had been curtailed, there was no means of determining to what extent the acquiescence that has been the rule since 1969 has been a reflection of intimidation, apathy, or support. It was apparent in 1971, however, that General Torrijos was attempting to build a popular base for his government among peasants and workers. He had traveled by helicopter to villages throughout the interior to explain the agrarian reform and other new programs. He had also championed the nationalist issue of sovereignty over the Canal Zone (see ch. 10, Foreign Relations).

POLITICAL VALUES AND ATTITUDES

Social Determinants

Rural-Urban and Ethnic Cleavages

Attitudes toward social and political institutions, toward other Panamanians, and toward the society at large are strongly affected by the Hispanic antecedents of most of the population, which have encouraged an acceptance of the elite's general pre-eminence and its specific dominance of politics. Voters have traditionally been faced with the necessity of aligning themselves with one or another of the shifting factions of the elite in order to give expression to their political views.

The chasm that separates the rural sector from the urban population of Colón and Panama City has great influence in differentiating attitudes. In general, the rural population is little aware of the world outside its immediate vicinity, much less of life in the cities or outside the Republic. Thus, only the attitudes of the urban population that is clustered around the two major cities have been readily observable. Exceptions to this rule have existed, mainly among the rural wage workers who have often been highly expressive and critical of social institutions. In the 1960s, for example, the strongest support for the nationalistic and populistic Panameñista movement of Arnulfo Arias derived from the highly urbanized provinces of Panama and Colón and the western provinces of Bocas del Toro and Chiriquí, where rural wage workers are concentrated.

The educated elite's preference for oligarchical social order has radiated through most of the society and has been accepted by most of the Hispanic part of the population. Large segments of the population, however, do not function wholly within this Hispanic culture—principally the Antillean Negroes, but also several other immigrant groups. Political tension has often arisen from strained relations among the ethnic subdivisions. The Spanish-speaking part of the population at all class levels has generally been antagonistic to the non-Hispanic groups; attitudes toward them are directed at the refusal or inability of the group in question to assimilate the dominant culture. Though popular attitudes toward the English-speaking Antilleans are quite antagonistic, there is no corresponding antagonism to the Spanish-speaking Negroes who are integrated into the culture. The term *chombo* is applied to Antilleans but not to Spanish-speaking Negroes, who are highly conscious of the difference between themselves and the Antilleans and are insistent on recognition of their different status in the society. Organizational activity in the 1960s indicated a growing political consciousness among Antilleans and an increased disposition to take collective action to advance their interests.

Attitudes of the Hispanic majority toward other groups vary, depending usually on the economic status and vulnerability of the group in question. The small Jewish community appears to be accepted. The willingness of Jews to learn Spanish and accept Panamanian citizenship, along with the lack of religious intensity in Panamanian society, probably accounts for this degree of assimilation. Chinese and Hindus are more obviously disparate and suffer the disadvantages of being more closely identified with a special kind of economic activity.

The Chinese enjoyed a near monopoly on grocery stores in the cities until 1941, when Arnulfo Arias attempted to expropriate and transfer their businesses to Panamanians. Ultimately, the Chinese managed to reacquire them and have since been relatively unmolested. Hindus, too, are shopkeepers and are thus visible candidates for the ire of Panamanians.

The tribal Indians, geographically remote and especially protected by law, are little involved with other inhabitants of the country and do not figure prominently in the attitudes or hierarchy of status important to most of the population, except as they leave their own areas to enter into the national society. Some, such as the Cuna Indians of the San Blas Islands, have their own highly sophisticated political cultures (see ch. 5, Social System).

The Social Hierarchy

The oligarchy consists of a group of notable families drawn together by blood and marital relationships, shared political prominence, the possession of wealth, common social values and history, and theoretical "racial purity." This core of the upper class is supposed to conform to a model of white, *criollo* (a person of pure Spanish ancestry born in the colonies) antecedents but, in fact, the upper class is of much more diverse ethnic background. The Panamanian elite is generally considered one of the more ethnically heterogeneous elites in Latin America. The appearance of non-Spanish families reflects the extensive contacts of isthmian society with a wide variety of national and racial groups. This heterogeneity is reflected in a selection of names of some of the notable families: Boyd, Duque, and Arias. Historically, a cosmopolitan and extroverted upper class in Panama has been willing to integrate new arrivals upon their acquisition of the membership qualifications of wealth and education (see ch. 6, Social Values).

Almost all great holders of property and capital have been integrated into the elite and thus share or inherit its intense interest in politics. Most members of the elite who are active on the higher levels of politics are identified with the economic life of the country, often with one particular area of economic activity. Arnulfo Arias is closely identified with the coffee industry; Harmodio Arias and the Duque family, with publishing; and the Chiari family, with the sugar industry, in which it holds a dominant interest.

The economic interests of the oligarchy, which often determine its political activity and attitudes, made some members intensely, if covertly, opposed to reform programs instituted by the government in 1961. For example, the attempt of the Institute for Housing and Urbanization (Instituto de Vivienda y Urbanismo—IVU) to provide low-cost housing for slumdwellers in the vicinity of Panama City was combated by an anonymous letterwriting campaign organized by wealthy owners of slum housing.

The economic interests of political figures are often penalized by hostile governments; penalties have ranged from cancellation of government contracts to confiscation of property. Harassment and imprisonment are vicissitudes that, in the past, have had to be accepted philosophically if an out-of-office politician remained in the country. One politician out of favor with the National Patriotic Coalition was imprisoned twelve times during the eight-year rule of that group. This type of imprisonment involves no loss of social or political prestige, however, and can be useful in imparting an aura of the martyr, which is redeemable in the political arena. Before the 1968 coup d'etat, imprisoned politicians were treated with respect and housed in special quarters. This special treatment was probably derived from the customary deference shown oligarchs and the realization on the part of those in power that the fortunes of politics can quickly change.

The harsher actions of the Torrijos government against the oligarchy appear to represent more than a difference of degree. The government has directed its attacks not only against individual opponents, but also against the ruling class as a whole.

The middle class, active in professional, clerical, and lesser commercial roles, tends to absorb the political outlook of the upper class, although it has furnished a more nationalistic milieu than any other single group in the country. It is less dependent on commercial activity than is the rule in Latin America; entrepreneurial business is largely the domain of the elite or of non-Panamanians.

A disproportionately large number of Panamanians of middle-class status are drawn from two groups: teachers and government workers. Teachers compose the largest single group in the middle class, and the government working force is notoriously inflated. Much of the intense nationalism of the middle class is probably attributable to the influence of teachers, who play a key role in the transfer of political attitudes to their students. The leadership of the National Guard has been increasingly drawn from the middle class. General Torrijos, for example, is the son of a school-teacher.

In general, the middle class has not aligned itself strongly with any of the political parties. The Hispanic segment of the middle class is nevertheless the major source of pressure for moderate reform; the elite are fearful that reform might threaten their economic interests, and the lower classes are either out of touch with national problems in the interior or tend in the cities to favor radical political programs.

Action by the urban lower classes was traditionally channeled into support of the various upper class parties and coalitions. The historic weakness of trade unionism vitiated that avenue of possible political organization, and ethnic antagonisms have distracted attention from the common problems of poverty. Lacking organization and spokesmen of their own, the volatile lower classes in the two major cities have swung their support in various directions with little partiality for any particular orientation, other than a tendency to support anti-United States positions and leaders with charismatic appeal, such as Arnulfo Arias and José Antonio Remón.

The West Indians apparently represent a potential one-third of the voting population. Evidence of their increasing political consciousness was manifested in the formation in 1960 of the Independent Afro-Panamanian Association, which drew its support mainly from second-generation West Indians. Because of the natural linguistic advantage they have in competing for employment in the Canal Zone, many of the Antilleans have achieved improved economic status through clerical positions and have been absorbed into the middle class.

In the rural areas political consciousness and activity have always been limited. Some peasants have followed the lead of their landowner patrons in voting. Others, especially wage workers on foreign-owned plantations, have been attracted to appeals to nationalism. Although some peasants have seized land, most have remained passive and politically inarticulate. Tribal Indians have voted and, in several instances, served in the National Assembly, principally as alternate members, but they have not developed organizations of their own at the national level.

Attitudes Toward the Nation and the Political System

Attitudes of most Panamanians toward their own country have usually been heavily involved with their attitudes toward other countries. Historically, they have felt that first the Colombians and then the North Americans have interfered with their achievement of a national destiny. They have also been disturbed by the presence in the Republic of many persons who have not assimilated the national culture—mainly, Antilleans. Thus, much of Panamanian nationalism has appeared, at least superficially, as a ,response to negative stimuli. Basically, most Spanish-speaking Panamanians see the Republic as an independent nation built on Hispanic culture and institutions.

Nationalism is reflected in a general lack of interest in submerging national identity in a close association with the country's immediate neighbors and in an extreme sensitivity to any United States activity or policy that appears to compromise the Panamanian belief in sovereign independence. Nationalist sentiment is the surest foundation for any attempt to mobilize people of all classes in support of government policies.

In the absence of a clear, institutionalized pattern for the organization of political power, attitudes tend to focus on the personalities and factions that emerge from the oligarchy to contend with each other in the political arena. This tendency, which has become known as *personalismo* (personalism), involves a sense of reciprocal obligation. A political leader assumes an obligation to provide his followers with certain benefits. These may range from high political honors and important contacts for oligarchs closely associated with him to adjustments of small personal difficulties for less eminent supporters.

Reactions to any given leader or group may be vehemently favorable or unfavorable, but the population has tended to be quiescent about the maintenance of elite control. Some members of the middle class have emerged since World War II as nationalist leaders, and a few Antilleans in the 1960s were included prominently in this development—for instance, Mrs. Thelma King, a deputy in the assembly, and George Westerman, a journalist and civic leader. More traditional patterns remained paramount, however, until the 1968 coup d'etat. This was particularly true in the rural areas, where a few individuals were relegated most of the decisionmaking. Estate owners or other persons of high social status who emerged as political bosses played a central role in influencing the attitudes of their neighbors toward the government and its policies were generally expected to deliver the vote for their respective areas.

Because party alignments as well as the avowed policies of public figures often fluctuated widely from one election to the next, firm attachments and party loyalties were infrequent. A politician could count on certain reservoirs of fairly constant popular feeling, notably that which favored national self-assertion, but his ability to tap these to his own advantage depended on his personal magnetism as well as on his success in satisfying the relatively permanent economic interests of a sufficient number of social and occupational groups. The highly manipulative character of the system made for popular disregard for political promises and a ready acceptance of practices that did not necessarily serve the interests of the whole society.

Governments have often manipulated elections and electoral campaigns in order to assure their own or a chosen successor's election to office. Methods have included: securing the nomination of the desired candidate; utilizing the legal requirements of party registration to the detriment of the opposition; disqualifying opposition voters; purchasing votes; voting by deceased, absent, or nonexistent individuals; and, perhaps the most effective technique, simply miscounting votes. The election of 1960 was the first in the country's history in which an opposition candidate was elected to the presidency.

The coup d'etat of 1968 precipitated riots in a few urban slum areas, demonstrations by students, and an insurgent movement among peasants in Chiriquí Province that persisted for several months. After early 1970, however, there was little evidence of concerted opposition, and a sharp upturn in investments indicated that the initial discomfiture of the business community had been overcome (see ch. 13, Trade and Transportation).

POLITICAL PARTIES AND ELECTORAL PRACTICES

Panama inherited the traditional political parties of Colombia—Liberal and Conservative—which continued to vie as competitors in the isthmus until the 1920s. This was a relatively unnatural party system for Panama, as political interests in the Republic had never been so neatly polarized along the lines of institutionalized parties as had been the case in Colombia. After the government of Rodolfo Chiari, the Conservatives, who had always suffered from lack of identification with the movement for separation, were no longer a serious factor in politics.

Since the 1920s political parties have been much more representative of elite factions clustered around specific personal leaders, though the Liberals did continue to enjoy the traditional support of peasants in the countryside, who tended to follow the lead of estate owners in identifying with this party. The 1932 presidential election—contested by the National Liberals, the Reform Liberals, and the Doctrinal Liberals—typified this process of fragmentation. All these groups claimed ideological descent from the original Liberal Party, although each was in fact merely the representative of an elite faction. Party names, in general, have been meaningless. The Agrarian Labor Party, for example, formed in 1960, had neither an agrarian base nor organized labor support.

The inability of any single party to attain anything approaching majority support in the recent past has necessitated the formation of coalitions as vehicles for both elections and the governments that followed them. This tendency to form coalitions was further reinforced by the official membership qualifications for parties to achieve recognition and rights. In 1953 the Remón government drastically raised the requirement to 45,000 members, but this was subsequently relaxed to 5,000. The former requirement had been so stringent that all opposition parties except the National Liberal Party (Partido Liberal Nacional—PLN), led by Roberto Chiari, were excluded from the 1956 elections.

The official government party, from its formation in 1952 until 1960, was the National Patriotic Coalition (Coalición Patriótica Nacional—CPN). It was the product of the merging of several factions under the guidance of Remón. The PLN was the central element in the National Opposition Union (Unión Nacional de Oposición—UNO), which retrieved former liberal factions from the CPN after Remón's assassination. It became the official government coalition after the 1960 elections.

In the 1964 elections there were nineteen national and seventeen municipal parties. Several smaller parties joined the PLN in the UNO coalition, and five joined the CPN in the National Opposition Alliance (Alianza Nacional de Oposición). The new Panameñista Party of Arnulfo Arias stood alone. The four remaining parties each entered a candidate, but only the Christian Democratic Party received enough votes to retain legal status. The UNO placed its candidate in the presidency, but the Panameñistas took control of the National Assembly, capturing thirty of the forty-two seats. The CPN ceased to be a major political contender after its coalition finished a poor third.

The PLN fielded a candidate and organized a coalition for the 1968 elections, but the important faction headed by Roberto Chiari had spun off to support the Panameñistas. The Panameñista Party was formed by the followers of Arnulfo Arias after he was deposed from the presidency in 1951. It became a **registered party** in 1960 after an understanding was reached with Chiari concerning the restoration of Arias' political rights in return for Panameñista participation in the PLN-dominated coalition. It grew into the largest single party primarily because of the charismatic appeal of its leader. He had earlier drawn generalized support through his vehement nationalism and in the 1960s had attracted the urban poor through his attacks on the oligarchy. Like most of the other parties, however, the Panameñista Party had no clearly recognizable ideology or program.

The only programmatic parties of any significance in the 1960s were the Christian Democratic Party and the Socialist Party, both of which called for substantial social reforms and expanded participation in democratic processes. The Socialist Party was founded as a splinter of the Liberal Party in 1937; it was strong until 1940 but dwindled thereafter. The Christian Democratic Party was registered for the first time in 1964. Both parties won one assembly seat in the 1964 elections.

A communist party was organized in the late 1920s but never attracted a large following. It has been illegal since 1953. Some of the party's dissenting members were reported to have joined a guerrilla group known as the National Liberation Movement of November 29th, but the government in 1971 had imprisoned, exiled, or coopted most of its leaders.

All of the parties were declared illegal after the National Guard seized control of the government in 1968. In late 1969 Juan Materno Vázquez, a close associate of General Torrijos and at that time minister of the presidency, announced the formation of the New Panama Movement. It was originally intended to incorporate peasants, workers, and other social groups into an organization patterned after that of Mexico's Institutional Revolutionary Party. No organizational structure had been established by mid-1971, however, and it appeared that the idea had been abandoned.

Until the 1968 coup d'etat the formal basis for electoral practices was found in the Constitution of 1946 and the Electoral Code, which provided for universal suffrage and the secret ballot. As with many other areas of Panamanian political behavior, however, actual practice was determined more by social custom than by formal prescription.

The number of deputies each province sent to the assembly was determined on a ratio fixed in proportion to the population, most recently one for every 25,000 citizens (see ch. 8, Governmental System). Parties met in conventions to select their candidates and frame their programs, the site often being smaller provincial centers selected to maximize support from certain areas. Often, the directorate of a party preselected the slate, as occurred in 1956 with Ernesto de la Guardia, and the convention process was merely one of ratification. In 1953, under the leadership of Remón, the requirements for a party's participation in elections was raised to 45,000, a move designed to do away with the many splinter parties that had always necessitated coalition governments; this requirement was adopted over heated protests. After the Remón period the requirement was dropped to 5,000 registered supporters, enabling a multiplicity of parties to function in both national and local politics.

Frequently, a government proscribed further political demonstrations or rallies several days before the elections. There were two election days in May, balloting for municipal offices being held on one Sunday throughout the country and voting for national offices taking place on the following Sunday. Actual election procedures were monitored by a complex system of supervisory bodies (see ch. 8, Governmental System). Parties were responsible for the preparation of their own ballots, which were inserted into envelopes furnished by the government and deposited in the polling boxes.

Presidential, vice-presidential, and National Assembly candidates appeared on the same ballot under the symbol of their parties. A perforation between the section of the ballot for president and vice presidents and the section containing candidates for the assembly enabled the voter to separate the two parts of the ballot and thus split his vote. A voter was further permitted to mark off undesired assembly candidates from the slate on the ballot. This was done either by drawing a line through individual names or by placing a large inclusive X across a whole group of names not favored by the voter. Lethargy inclined the average voter to prefer the large X method to canceling meticulously each name one by one. Examiners' decisions on such personally marked ballots were often extremely technical, the general practice being that if a single letter of a candidate's name was marked, he must be excluded. Since the first and last names on the ballot were least likely to be touched by voters using the X technique, these were the most coveted places on the ballot, and they were usually allotted to the party's leaders.

Several methods were adopted to frustrate multiple voting. One was to shave the hair off the arm of a voter. Another was to mark a voter's fingers with indelible ink as he left the polling place.

A major party campaign was an expensive undertaking. It was customary for the presidential candidate to subscribe at least 50 percent of the campaign costs. There were no statutory limits on campaign expenditures.

Though many sources described the electoral system as involving proportional representation, election methods prevented the exact correspondence between votes cast and party representation in the assembly that is usually associated with proportional systems. No mathematical factor was utilized in determining a party's representation; simple pluralities for individual candidates were the determining factor in election. Runoffs were not held. The system came closest to proportional representations in that multimember voting units were used and the size of a province's delegation was determined by its population.

After the National Guard assumed control of the government in October 1968, a committee, composed largely of "nonpartisan" lawyers, was appointed to draw up a new electoral code. In mid-1971 the committee was still deliberating. No new law had been promulgated, and no date had been set for general elections.

The only election that had taken place under the new government was that of mayor, treasurer, and municipal council in San Miguelito upon its incorporation as the country's sixty-fourth municipal district in April 1970. The election was considered a test of some of the new formulas under discussion by the committee. Candidates nominated by trade groups and other nonpartisan bodies were elected indirectly by a council of electors, which had, in turn, been elected by neighborhood councils. The government expressed satisfaction with the degree of positive civic response to this procedure.

POLITICAL DEVELOPMENTS SINCE WORLD WAR II

The immediate postwar period saw a temporary shift in the locus of power from the civilian aristocracy to the National Guard under Commander José Antonio Remón. Colonel Remón acted as a behind-the-scenes manipulator in the late 1940s. He installed Arnulfo Arias in the presidency, for example, in 1949 and engineered his removal in 1951. Meanwhile, he had organized the CPN, which facilitated his own election to the presidency in 1952.

Remón's vigorous attempts at social reform and economic development ended abruptly with his assassination in 1955. Though the first vice president, José Ramón Guizado, was impeached and jailed, he was never tried, and the origin of the crime remained unclear. The second vice president served out the remainder of the term, and in 1956 another CPN candidate, Ernesto de la Guardia, was elected as president.

The administration of de la Guardia, a conservative businessman, tended to be overwhelmed by a combination of domestic and external problems, and the CPN, lacking effective opposition in the National Assembly, began to disintegrate. Most of its dissenting factions joined the PLN in the UNO, which in 1960 succeeded in electing its candidate, Roberto Chiari, to the presidency. De la Guardia became the first postwar president to finish a full four-year term in office, and Chiari had the distinction of being the first opposition candidate ever elected to the presidency.

Chiari attempted to convince his fellow oligarchs that change was inevitable and that, if they refused to accept moderate reform, they would be vulnerable to sweeping change imposed by radical forces over which they had no control. The tradition-oriented deputies who constituted a majority in the National Assembly did not heed his warning. His proposed reform program was not vigorously opposed; it was, for the most part, simply ignored.

In foreign affairs Chiari's message to the assembly on October 1, 1961, called for a new revision of the Canal Zone arrangement. Pressure for such a revision and nationalist resentment of United States recalcitrance mounted to such a point that a flag-raising incident in January 1964 set off a major riot in which Panamanian mobs attempted to invade the Canal Zone. After three days of shooting, looting, and burning that resulted in more than twenty deaths, the National Guard was called in, and order was restored. After a three-month period in which relations with the United States were severed, talks directed toward the drafting of a new treaty were initiated (see ch. 10, Foreign Relations).

Elections of 1964 and 1968

Seven candidates competed in the 1964 presidential elections, although only three were serious contenders. Marco Robles, who had served as minister of the presidency in Chiari's cabinet, was the candidate of the UNO, composed at that time of the PLN and seven smaller parties. After lengthy backstage maneuvers, he was endorsed by the outgoing president. Juan de Arco Galindo, former assemblyman and public works minister and brother-in-law of former President de la Guardia, was the candidate of the National Opposition Alliance coalition, comprising six parties headed by the CPN. Arnulfo Arias was fielded by his own Panameñista Party, already the largest single party in the country.

As usual, the status of the canal was one of the principal issues in the campaign. Both the PLN and the CPN coalitions cultivated nationalist sentiment by denouncing the United States. Arias, abandoning his earlier nationalistic theme, assumed a cooperative and conciliatory stance toward the United States, but he attracted lower class support by denouncing the oligarchy. The Electoral Tribunal announced that Robles had won over Arias by more than a 10,000-vote margin out of the 317,312 votes case. The CPN coalition trailed far behind the top two contenders. Arias' supporters, who had won a majority of the National Assembly seats, attributed Robles' victory to the "miracle of Los Santos"; they claimed that enough corpses voted for Robles in that province to enable him to carry the election.

The problems confronting President Robles were not unlike those of his predecessors but were aggravated by the consequences of the 1964 riots. In addition to the hardships and resentments resulting from the losses of life and property, the riots had the effect of increasing unemployment from 19 to 25 percent in the Metropolitan Area. Despite his nationalistic rhetoric during the campaign, the new president was dependent upon United States economic and technical assistance to carry on the development projects that Chiari's government, also with United States assistance, had initiated. Emphasis was placed on the building of schools and low-cost housing and on a limited agrarian reform program. Like his predecessor, President Robles sought to increase the efficiency of tax collection rather than to graduate taxes.

During the first two years of the Robles government negotiations for a new canal treaty went forward but, when the terms of the drafts were prematurely leaked to the press in June 1967, public reaction was adverse. Particularly unwelcome to Panamanians were provisions for the continuance of United States military bases in the canal area and for the establishment of an administrative board for the zone, of which five out of nine members would be appointed by the United States (see ch. 10, Foreign Relations). President Robles initially attempted to defend the terms of the drafts but, when it became apparent that he would be unable to obtain ratification and that his own coalition would be disadvantaged in the face of upcoming elections, he called for further negotiations.

By 1967 the coalitions were being reshuffled in preparation for the 1968 elections. By the time Arias announced his candidacy, he had split apart both of the coalitions that had participated in the 1964 elections. Among the faction leaders he had attracted from the PLN, for example, was Chiari, whose Independent Liberals joined the CPN, the Republican Party, the Third Nationalist Party, and the Democratic Action Party in a coalition headed by the Panameñista Party. Robles' endorsement went to David Samudio of the PLN. A civil engineer and architect of middle-class background, Samudio had served as an assemblyman and had held several cabinet posts, including that of finance minister under Robles. In addition to the PLN, he was supported by the National Liberation Movement, the Agrarian Labor Party, and the Progressive Party. A Christian Democratic candidate, Antonio Gonzalez Revilla, also entered the race.

As many of Arias' supporters continued to believe that the 1964 election had been rigged, the principal issue in the 1968 campaign became the prospective validity of the election itself. The credibility crisis became acute in February 1968 when the president of the Electoral Tribunal, a Samudio supporter, closed the central registration office in a dispute with the other two members of the tribunal, supporters of Arias, over electoral procedures. The government brought suit before the Supreme Court of Justice for the dismissal of the Arias' supporters on the grounds that each man had a son who was a candidate for elective office. Thereupon, Gonzalez Revilla, with the backing of Arias, petitioned the National Assembly to begin impeachment proceedings against President Robles for illegal interferences in electoral matters. Among other things, he was accused of diverting public funds to Samudio's campaign.

The assembly met in special session and appointed a commission to gather evidence. Robles, in turn, obtained from a municipal court a judgment that the assembly was acting unconstitutionally. The assembly chose to ignore a stay order issued by the municipal court pending the reconvening of the Supreme Court on April 1 and, on March 14, voted for impeachment. On March 24 the assembly found President Robles guilty and declared him deposed, but Robles and the National Guard ignored the proceedings, maintaining that they would abide by the decision of the Supreme Court when it reconvened.

The Supreme Court, with only one dissenting vote, ruled the impeachment proceedings unconstitutional. The Electoral Tribunal subsequently ruled that thirty of the parliamentary deputies involved in the impeachment proceedings were ineligible for reelection, and Robles, with the support of the National Guard, retained the presidency.

The election took place on May 12, 1968, as scheduled, and tension mounted over the succeeding eighteen days as the Election Board and the Electoral Tribunal delayed announcement of the results. Finally the Election Board declared that Arias had carried the election with 175,432 votes; Samudio received 133,887, and Gonzalez Revilla, 11,371. The Electoral Tribunal, senior to the board and still loyal to Robles, protested, but the commander of the National Guard, Brigadier General Bolívar Vallarino, despite past animosity toward Arias, supported the conclusion of the board.

Arias took office on October 1, demanding the immediate return of the Canal Zone to Panamanian jurisdiction and announcing that one of his first acts in office would be to change the leadership of the National Guard. He attempted to remove the two most senior officers, Vallarino and Colonel José María Pinilla, and appoint Colonel Bolívar Urrutia to command the force. On October 11 the National Guard, for the third time, removed Arias from the presidency. With seven of his eight ministers and twenty-four members of the National Assembly, Arias took refuge in the Canal Zone.

The National Guard in Power

The overthrow of Arias provoked student demonstrations and rioting in some of the slum areas of Panama City, and the peasants in Chiriquí Province battled guardsmen sporadically for several months, but the guard remained firmly in control. Urrutia was initially arrested but was later persuaded to join a two-man junta headed by Pinilla. Vallarino remained in retirement. The original cabinet was rather broad based, including several supporters of Samudio and even one of Arias. After the first three months, however, five civilian cabinet members resigned, accusing the new government of dictatorial practices.

The Provisional Junta Government moved swiftly to consolidate its control of the government. Several hundred actual or potential political leaders were arrested on charges of corruption or subversion. Others went into voluntary or imposed exile, and property owners were rendered acquiescent by threats of expropriation. The National Assembly and all political parties were disbanded, and the University of Panama was closed down for several months while its faculty and student body were purged. The communications media were brought under control through censorship, intervention in management, or expropriation (see ch. 7, Education, Culture, and Public Information).

Pinilla, who assumed the title of president, had declared that his government was provisional and that free elections were to be scheduled. It became apparent in January 1969, however, that power actually rested in the hands of Colonel Omar Torrijos and Colonel Boris Martínez, commander in chief and chief of staff, respectively, of the guard. In early March a speech by Martínez, promising agrarian reform and other measures radical enough to alarm landowners and entrepreneurs, provoked a coup within the coup. Torrijos assumed full control, and Martínez and three of his supporters in the military government were sent into exile.

Torrijos, who then promoted himself to brigadier general, stated that there would be "less impulsiveness" in government without Martínez. He did not denounce the proposed reforms, but he reassured Panamanian and United States investors that their interests were not threatened.

Torrijos became even more firmly entrenched in power after thwarting a coup attempt by colonels Amado Sanjur, Luis Q. Nentzen Franco, and Ramiro Silvera in December 1969. While Torrijos was on a trip to Mexico, the three colonels declared him deposed; but Torrijos rushed back to Panama, gathered supporters at the garrison in David, and marched triumphantly into the capital. The colonels followed earlier competitors of Torrijos into exile. Because the governing junta (Colonel Pinilla and his deputy, Colonel Urrutia) had not opposed the abortive coup, Torrijos replaced them with two civilians, Demetrio Bassilio Lakas, an engineer well-liked among businessmen, and Arturo Sucre, a lawyer and former director of the National Welfare Lottery. Lakas was designated provisional president, and Sucre was appointed his deputy.

The domestic program of the Torrijos government has emphasized public works, especially the construction of roads, bridges, and low-cost public housing, reform of the banking and tax collection systems, and agrarian reform. During the first two years after the overthrow of Arias, while the guard sought to consolidate its control of the government and Torrijos sought to disestablish his competitors within the guard, the canal issue was played down and generally held in abeyance. By late 1970, however, the government had adopted a more nationalistic stance, rejecting the three treaties drafted in 1967 as a basis for further negotiations (see ch. 10, Foreign Relations).

Sweeping cabinet reorganization and comments of high-ranking officials in 1971 portended a shift in domestic policy. Torrijos himself expressed admiration for the socialist trends in the military governments of Peru and Bolivia, and the new finance minister, José Guillermo Aizpu, for example, called for "a social reordering that will bring justice."

POLITICAL FORCES AND INTEREST GROUPS

Business and Professional Associations

Associational interest groups have never played a very important role in the country's political life. Commercial and industrial interests, like those of the landowners, have generally been expressed informally within the extended family systems that constitute the oligarchy. Resolution of interest conflicts within the oligarchy often takes place in the forum of social clubs, such as the Union Club of Panama City.

There are, nevertheless, a number of associations representing the particularistic interests of elite groups. The most important of these, including the Chamber of Commerce and its most recent offshoot, the Management Association, and also the Industrial Sindicate, the National Development Corporation, the Bankers' Association, and the National Cattlemen's Association, belong to a confederation known as the National Free Enterprise Council (Consejo Nacional de la Empresa Privada—CONEP).

The various groups within the council have had common interests in protection from encroachments by government in their affairs and in maintaining their positions vis-à-vis labor. There were strong disagreements, however, on other issues that immobilized the council in its role of influencing public policy. The Chamber of Commerce and the Management Association since the early 1960s have opposed integration into the Central American Common Market, but the Industrial Sindicate and the National Development Corporation have favored it. The former groups have advocated, as an alternative path to economic development, turning the entire country into a free zone, abolishing all import duties and quotas. This proposal has been vehemently opposed by the basically protectionist Industrial Sindicate.

Many individuals have membership in several of these associations, and some even have positions of leadership in more than one. In 1967, for example, the chairman of the board of the National Development Corporation was also president of the Industrial Sindicate. Nevertheless, a survey conducted in that year of the attitudes of interest group leaders indicated that such persons continued to rely more heavily on personal contacts than on collective pressure in their attempts to influence policy. Foreign businessmen in Panama also have a role in domestic policymaking. Their views on some issues tend to reflect the nationalistic aspirations of their local counterparts.

Among the professional groups that have taken stands on particular issues, the Panamanian Bar Association and the Teachers' Association have been the most outspoken. After the 1964 riots the Panamanian Bar Association issued a formal request for investigation to the International Commission of Jurists. A study commission appointed by the association in December 1967 branded the draft treaties relating to the Canal Zone "detrimental" to the sovereignty and territorial integrity of Panama. It particularly condemned the section that would have given the United States the right to deploy troops and armaments anywhere in the Republic. The Teachers' Association, a major base of support for the Christian Democratic Party, has strongly favored incorporation into the Central American Common Market. In general, however, a heavy reliance on government jobs has inhibited the development of organizations representing middle-class interests.

Organized Labor

The country's slow rate of industrial development has been reflected in weak labor union organization and only minor influence of labor, as such, on political affairs. There were no unions in the country until 1920. The Marxist-oriented Trade Union Federation of Workers of the Republic of Panama (Federación Sindical de Trabajadores de la República de Panamá—FSTRP), the country's strongest labor organization in the 1940s, had dwindled to a mere 622 members in 1968. The more moderate Confederation of Workers of the Republic of Panama (Confederación de Trabajadores de la República de Panamá—CTRP), formed in the mid-1950s through the merger of twenty unions, has attempted to organize the banana workers and has militated for equal pay for equal work for its affiliated local in the Canal Zone. In the late 1960s it had forty-five affiliated unions with a total membership of about 14,200.

In 1968 only about one-tenth of the members of the labor force of some 424,000 belonged to labor unions. The largest employer was the Panama Canal Company, with some 22,000 Panamanian employees, and most of the Canal Zone unions were affiliated with United States labor organizations. The rural workers, with the exception of those on the United States-owned Chiriquí Land Company plantations, have never been organized. Most of the farmers are squatters; only a small percentage own the land they work.

The government has made some attempts to win the support of organized labor. It has, for example, appointed a commission to draft a new labor code to replace that of 1947. The renewal in June 1971 of negotiations for a new canal treaty, which the government insists must recognize Panamanian sovereignty, has provided a rallying point for government and labor. An assemblage of labor leaders from all parts of the country, meeting in Chitré on July 13, resolved that "the Panamanian working class backs the patriotic position of the government's representatives for the new negotiations and will maintain a united front until we obtain the old aspirations of the Panamanian people."

The Roman Catholic Church

Traditionally, the Roman Catholic Church has not played a prominent role in politics. Weak organization and the absence of a native clergy generally prevented the development of strong hierarchical positions on social and political issues. As a result, Panamanian politics has been free of the anticlericalism that pervaded the political life of some of the other Latin American countries in the late nineteenth and early twentieth centuries. The church has always had some informal influence, however, and most candidates have taken the precaution of being photographed with a member of the church hierarchy.

Under the influence of the Social Christian movement, the church in the 1960s expanded its activities in the politically sensitive area of socioeconomic development, especially among the generally unorganized and politically inarticulate peasants. The Center for Study, Promotion, and Social Assistance (Centro de Estudio, Promoción, y Asistencia Social—CEPAS) and its affiliated organizations, for example, were responsible for the establishment of more than forty cooperatives in Veraguas Province. Among the achievements of these organizations have been the acquisition of services and material assistance from various international organizations and national agencies. Thus, the peasants involved in such projects have come to recognize the potential efficacy of bringing collective action to bear on government.

The alleged kidnapping in June 1971 of Father Hector Gallegos, who had been active in the rural cooperative program, had widespread political repercussions. Some members of the church hierarchy and some of the peasants of Veraguas Province maintained that he had been kidnapped by the National Guard, but the government attributed such accusations to "reactionary" elements and announced that an investigation of his disappearance was underway.

Students

The most influential and highly politicized groups in the society, other than the oligarchy and the parties, have been the students and, since 1936, the National Guard. As there has been a general lack of organizations capable of serving as spokesmen for the disadvantaged and the frustrated in the society, students, both at the secondary and university levels, have been the most vocal advocates of social and political reform. They have sought to arouse public opinion through contributions to newspapers, the distribution of printed materials and handbills, and strikes and demonstrations, and they have often clashed in the streets with the National Guard. When several students lost their lives in such an encounter in 1958, the government indemnified their families.

Traditionally, there have been two major centers of student politics—the University of Panama and the National Institute, a secondary school. A third was added with the establishment of the University of Santa Maria la Antigua in 1965. Before the 1968 coup d'etat there were at least six well-established student organizations, the largest of which was the Panamanian Federation of Students (Federación de Estudiantes Panameños—FEP).

At the university level, political activists have included advocates of immediate and sweeping social change on the order of the Cuban revolution and social democrats and Christian democrats with a less radical reformist orientation. Successive interviews conducted in elite high schools in 1961, 1963, and 1966 indicated that there had been a general decline within this group in support for the country's leaders and for its political processes. Strong majorities, however, opposed the use of violence to bring about change and felt that democracy was the appropriate form of government for developing nations.

Students in general are highly nationalistic and are particularly unified in advocacy of Panamanian exercise of sovereignty over the Canal Zone. Students were prominently involved in the 1964 riots (see ch. 10, Foreign Relations). In fact, the march into the Canal Zone, in response to the flag-raising by United States high school students in the zone, was planned at the National Institute. Students were also instrumental in undermining the position of the Robles government on the proposed new treaties.

An unauthorized student demonstration in December 1968 resulted in the closing of the University of Panama. When the school reopened in July 1969, some 2,000 students, about one-fourth of the 1968 enrollment, had been expelled allegedly for having failed to maintain a "C" average, and more than forty professors had been dismissed. The university had been administratively decentralized. Student representation on administrative boards had been numerically decreased, and participation had been limited to honor students. A ten-foot-high wire mesh fence topped with barbed wire had been constructed around the perimeter of the campus to keep the students in and agitators out (see ch. 7, Education, Culture, and Public Information).

Student reaction to the government's apparent shift to the left in 1971 has been generally favorable but cautious. A communiqué issued by the Panamanian Federation of Students contained the following analysis of the situation:

> The National Guard in the past was the loyal watchman of the oligarchy and imperialism. However, today the Panamanian National Guard is taking patriotic sides with the popular movement. However, CIA agents and the oligarchic fifth columnists continue to swarm in government circles and sabotage all progressive movements of the government, trying to isolate the popular movement from the democratic sectors within the government.

The National Guard

The National Guard assumed an important role in the country's political life after the United States, through the treaty revision of 1936, relinquished the role of arbiter in internal political affairs (see ch. 10, Foreign Relations). The identity of the guard as an autonomous power center became apparent for the first time during the 1948–52 period, when its commander, José Antonio Remón, installed and removed presidents with unencumbered ease. During that period he was able to increase salaries and fringe benefits for his men and to modernize training methods and equipment, all of which contributed to his election to the presidency, over oligarchic opposition, in 1952.

From the assassination of Remón in 1955 until its assumption of power in 1968, the guard appeared to have no definable political position other than a generalized support for the status quo, opposition to Arnulfo Arias and his supporters, and antipathy toward students because of their reformist militance and their disrespect for authority. The emphasis in the 1960s on training and equipping for internal security and antiguerrilla warfare, however, expanded its domestic political role. When Arias, upon assuming the presidency, dismissed the guard commander, Bolívar Vallarino, and, ignoring seniority within the institution, attempted to establish a command echelon loyal to him, several of the senior officers refused to accept the change and conspired to depose him.

Since assuming power the guard has expanded in size from about 5,000 to more than 7,500 and has adopted increasingly efficient means of controlling opposition. These have included the use of informants, telephone taps, and interrogation centers. Centralization of power within the guard has been accomplished through the arrest or banishment of more than seventy members of the officer corps.

SYMBOLS OF THE NATION

The coat of arms, designed by D. Nicanor Villalaz, was provisionally adopted in 1904, shortly after the founding of the republic, and became official in 1925. It consists of a shield draped with two national flags on each side. The escutcheon has a representation of the Isthmus of Panama in the middle with a setting sun and rising moon over it, two quadrant sections on top of the central representation and two below. The sections above depict a crossed sword and rifle, symbolizing alertness, and a crossed spade and hoe, signifying labor. The bottom sections depict an overflowing cornucopia and a winged wheel, symbolizing progress. The shield is set off against a field of green, denoting the tropical vegetation of the isthmus. Surmounting the shield is an eagle, its beak holding a streamer on which is inscribed the national motto, "Pro Mundi Beneficio" (For World Benefit). Above the eagle are nine stars representing the provinces of the Republic.

The flag is divided into four quarters. A white quarter on the upper half of the flag next to the staff contains a blue star in the center. The other white one, on the outer part of the lower half, has a red star in the center. The other quarters, solid red on the outer top half and solid blue on the lower quarter next to the staff, are unadorned. The national flag was originally conceived by Manual E. Amador, adopted provisionally by a law of 1904, and confirmed by legislation in 1925 and in 1941.

The music of the national anthem was composed by Jorge A. Santos, and the lyrics were written by Jerónomo de la Ossa. It was approved by action of the assembly in 1906 and was ratified in 1941. The chorus of the anthem declares:

> At last we have achieved victory
> On the happy field of union,
> With ardent torches of glory
> The new nation is illuminated.

Most of the national symbols and holidays relate to events that have meaning largely for the Spanish-speaking part of the population and often especially for the elite within it. Both independence days, for instance, refer to events that are triumphs for the ruling oligarchy and were directed almost solely by them. Nonetheless, some of them have obviously taken on considerable meaning for the rest of the population. The flag was readily accepted as a symbol for the entire nation's aspirations in the "flag" riots of 1959 and 1964. It is also interesting that an original design for the flag by Philippe Bunau-Varilla, the Frenchman who negotiated the original canal treaty, was rejected by the founding fathers as resembling too closely the flag of the United States. The flag, probably more than any of the other symbols, is closely associated with nationalist sentiment, particularly in respect to the dispute over Canal Zone sovereignty (see ch. 10, Foreign Relations).

CHAPTER 10

FOREIGN RELATIONS

The primary factors conditioning Panama's external relations have always been its size and strategic location and its economic dependence upon the canal and international trade. Provisions of the 1903 Hay-Bunau-Varilla Treaty, under which the United States was granted the Canal Zone "in perpetuity," made Panama a virtual protectorate of the United States until 1936. Relations with the United States in general, and the status of the Canal Zone in particular, have continued to be the overriding concern of foreign policymakers and have strongly influenced domestic political contests as well as relations with all other countries.

Despite the negotiation of a new treaty in 1955 and several lesser concessions by the United States, many of the goals Panamanians have sought in the relationship remain far from realization. Aside from the larger issue of jurisdiction over the zone, which bisects the territory of the Republic, Panamanians have complained that they have not received their fair share of the receipts from the canal, that commissaries in the zone have damaged commercial interests in the Republic, that Panamanian workers in the zone have been discriminated against in economic and social matters, and that the large-scale presence of the United States military in the zone and in bases outside the zone casts a long shadow over national sovereignty.

After serious rioting in 1964, which indicated the intensity of nationalistic aspirations concerning the status of the zone, the United States agreed to enter into negotiations for a new treaty. Meanwhile, studies relating to the construction of a new canal were undertaken. In June 1971, after a four-year interlude, negotiations were renewed but, as in the past, there were issues involved that were likely to generate controversy in both countries.

The country's small size and its general vulnerability to external economic and political pressures have caused it to take a legalistic approach to foreign relations, to advocate arbitration as a means of settling international disputes, and to champion such principles as the juridical equality of states, national self-determination, and nonintervention. In the Organization of American States (OAS)

217

and the United Nations, Panama has generally supported the initiatives of the United States on security issues. When it has felt that its own security or interests were jeopardized by the United States, however, it has not hesitated to appeal to international bodies.

The national self-image has placed the country in a category apart from both South America and Central America. Since the early 1960s it has moved toward a closer association in military and economic matters with the Central American states, but it has stopped short of incorporation into the Central American Common Market. Panama maintains diplomatic relations with only a few states outside the Western Hemisphere and Western Europe, but it maintains consular relations with most of the world's major shipping and trade centers (see ch. 13, Trade and Transportation). On a European tour in July 1971 President Demetrio Basilio Lakas intimated that Panama was contemplating extending its diplomatic relations within the socialist bloc as well as in Africa and Asia.

Since the coup d'etat of 1968, which resulted in the dissolution of the National Assembly, foreign policy decisionmaking has devolved upon the commander of the National Guard, General Omar Torrijos, and the governing junta and cabinet appointed by him. The National Council for Foreign Relations, including several former foreign ministers, continues to function in an advisory capacity, however, and commercial interest associations such as the Chamber of Commerce continue to exert considerable influence on foreign policy.

THE CANAL IN UNITED STATES-PANAMANIAN RELATIONS

Historical Background

The longstanding position of the United States in the Isthmus of Panama has been derived from its crucial interest in maritime transit there for both commercial and war vessels. The discovery of gold in California brought extensive contact in the 1850s and resulted in the construction of a transisthmian railroad. Naval operations during the Spanish-American War at the end of the nineteenth century served to convince President Theodore Roosevelt of the necessity of a United States-controlled canal somewhere in the area. This interest culminated in the Spooner Bill of June 29, 1902, providing for a canal through the Isthmus of Panama, and the Hay-Herrán Treaty of January 22, 1903, under which Colombia gave its consent to such a project in the form of a

100-year lease on a zone ten kilometers (6.2 miles) wide. This treaty, however, was not ratified in Bogotá, and the United States, determined to construct an isthmian canal, intensified its interest in the Panamanian separatist movement.

With Philippe Bunau-Varilla, a French national, playing a key role as representative of the New Panama Canal Company, the native Panamanian leaders conspired to take advantage of Washington's interest in a new regime on the isthmus. In October and November 1903 the revolutionary junta carried out a successful uprising against the Colombian government; the junta had the protection of United States military and naval forces, acting under the Bidlack-Mallarino Treaty of 1846 between the United States and Colombia. This agreement provided that United States forces could intervene in the event of disorder on the isthmus to guarantee Colombian sovereignty and an open transit route on the isthmus. Acting on this basis, the United States action paradoxically prevented a Colombian force—sent to suppress the insurrection—from moving across the isthmus to Panama City, the site of the revolution (see ch. 2, Historical Setting).

President Roosevelt speedily recognized the new junta as the de facto government on November 6; de jure recognition followed on November 13. Five days later Bunau-Varilla, as the diplomatic representative of Panama, concluded an isthmian canal treaty with Secretary of State John Hay in Washington. Isthmian patriots particularly were to resent the haste with which Bunau-Varilla concluded the treaty, an effort partially designed to preclude the objections an arriving Panamanian delegation might raise to its provisions.

The Hay-Bunau-Varilla Treaty, ratified by Panama on December 3, 1903, and by the United States on February 23, 1904, contained seeds of later dissension between the two partners. The rights granted to the United States were extensive. It received a grant "in perpetuity [of] the use, occupation and control" of a ten-mile strip of territory along with three-nautical-mile extensions into the sea from each terminal "for the construction, maintenance, operation, sanitation and protection" of an isthmian canal. Other important rights were conceded. The United States could acquire additional areas of land or water necessary for canal operation, along with the option of exercising eminent domain in Panama City. Bunau-Varilla's original choice of the term *lease* was replaced in the final draft by the word *grant*, thus laying the foundation for much future controversy. Within this territory, Washington gained "all the rights, power and authority . . . which the United States would possess and exercise if it were the sovereign . . . to the entire exclusion" of Panama.

The treaty also converted the Republic into a de facto protectorate of the larger country in two provisions whereby the United States guaranteed the independence of Panama and received in return the right to intervene in its domestic affairs. As compensation for the rights it obtained, the United States was to pay the sum of US$10 million and a yearly annuity, beginning nine years after ratification, of US$250,000 in gold coin. The provisions concerning the power of intervention were later written into the Panamanian constitution drafted early in 1904 and were thus thoroughly woven into the juridical structure of the Republic.

The harshest critic of United States policy at the time was, understandably, Colombia, with which a reconciliatory treaty providing an indemnity of US$25 million was finally concluded in 1921. Ironically, however, the friction resulting from the events of 1903 was to be greatest between the United States and its beneficiary—Panama. Major disagreements have related to the rights granted to the United States by the treaty of 1903 and the Panamanian Constitution of 1904. The United States government subsequently interpreted these rights to mean that it could exercise complete sovereignty over all matters in the Canal Zone to the total exclusion of the Panamanian government. Panama, however, admitting that the clauses were vague and obscure, later held that the original concession of authority related only to the construction, operation, and defense of the canal and that rights and privileges not necessary for these functions had never been relinquished.

The first ten years of United States presence on the isthmus were busy ones. Immigrants—many of them Negroes from the British West Indies—were brought in to work on the canal, which was completed in 1914. The nonprofit, official Canal Zone commissaries, which were to be a source of friction with Panamanian merchants, were opened (see ch. 13, Trade and Transportation). In the very first year of the treaty, however, dissension had already arisen over the sovereignty issue. Acting on its understanding of its rights, the United States had applied special regulations to maritime traffic at the ports of entry and had established its own customs, tariffs, and postal services in the zone. These measures were opposed by the Panamanian government.

Mounting friction finally led President Roosevelt to dispatch Secretary of War William Howard Taft to the Republic in November 1904. In a mission of great sensitivity, Taft produced a compromise agreement. The United States retained control of the ports of Ancón and Cristóbal, but their facilities might be used by ships entering Panama City and Colón. The Republic agreed to a reduction of the ad valorem duty on general imports, and the United States revoked the application of its own Dingley Tariff in the Canal Zone against Panama. The latter agreed to permit the free passage of persons and goods from the zone into the Republic. Similar compromises were reached in other areas, and both sides emerged with most of their grievances blunted if not wholly resolved.

Before the first year of independence had passed, the intervention issue also complicated relations. Threats to constitutional government in the Republic by the commander in chief of the country's one-battalion army had resulted in the disbanding of that army in 1904, at the suggestion of the United States diplomatic mission. Shortly afterward the United States obtained the abandonment of police use of high-powered rifles. By 1920 the United States had intervened four times in the civil life of the Republic. These interventions were relatively mild, involving little military conflict, and were, with only one exception, at Panamanian request (see ch. 14, National Security).

The internal dynamics of Panamanian politics encouraged appeals to the United States by any currently disgruntled faction for intervention to secure its allegedly infringed rights. The general policy was to intervene in the Republic's politics only if necessary to frustrate extraconstitutional changes in its government. At the same time, United States diplomatic personnel in Panama were often active in advising Panamanian officials—a policy resented by nationalists and still an active issue for many in the isthmus.

In 1921 the whole question of intervention was formally brought up by the government of the Republic. When asked for a definitive, written interpretation of the pertinent treaty clauses, Secretary of State Charles Evans Hughes pointed to the difficulty inherent in any such general interpretation and explained that the main objectives of the United States were to act against any threat to the Canal Zone or the lives and holdings of non-Panamanians in the two major cities.

Actual intervention took several forms. United States officials supervised elections at the request of the Republic. To protect American lives and property in Chiriquí Province, an occupation force was stationed there for two years over the protests of Panamanians who contended that the right of occupation could only apply to the two major cities. The United States also became involved in 1925 in an uprising of the San Blas Indians, incited by a North American. In the presence of the United States minister and of a United States Navy cruiser, the dispute was settled before disorder had spread. More serious was United States involvement in the 1925 rent riots in Panama City. After violent disturbances during October and at the request of the Panamanian government, 600 troops with fixed bayonets dispersed mobs that were threatening to take over the city. The detachment was quickly withdrawn with the reestablishment of order.

At the end of the 1920s traditional United States policy toward intervention changed. In 1928 Secretary of State Frank B. Kellogg reiterated the State Department's refusal to countenance illegal changes of government. In the same year, however, the United States declined to intervene during the national elections that placed Florencio H. Arosemena in office. The new government quickly became noted for its unusual degree of corruption and, when a conspiracy was soon organized to unseat it, the United States declined to intervene. Though no official pronouncement of a shift in policy was made, the 1931 coup d'etat—the first successful one in the Republic's history—marks a watershed in the history of intervention.

Meanwhile, sentiment for treaty revision on both sides had resulted in the Kellogg-Alfaro Treaty of 1926. The United States in this instrument agreed to restrictions on private commercial operations in the zone and also to a tightening of the regulations pertaining to the official commissaries. At the same time, however, the United States gained several concessions involving its security interests. Panama agreed to its automatic participation in any war involving the United States and to United States supervision and control of military operations within the Republic. These clauses, along with others, aroused strong opposition among nationalists, and amid considerable tumult and threats of violence the National Assembly on January 26, 1927, refused to consider the draft treaty.

The abortive Kellogg-Alfaro Treaty involved both countries in a critical incident with the League of Nations. The league assembly during the fall of 1927 insisted that Panama could not legally participate in the proposed arrangement with the United States because an automatic declaration of war would violate Panama's obligations under the league covenant to wait three months for an arbitral decision on any dispute before resorting to war. The discussion was largely academic, inasmuch as the treaty had already been effectively rejected, when Eusebio A. Morales, Panama's representative, seized the opportunity afforded by the debate to propose that the dispute over sovereignty in the zone be submitted to international arbitration. The United States Department of State denied that there was any issue to arbitrate.

The effects of this episode were felt the following year at the Sixth International Conference of American States in Havana, where the Panamanian delegation was identified with the bloc of Latin American nations that supported the adoption of a formal mode of nonintervention as a general rule for the conduct of hemispheric relations. Although such a code was not adopted, Ricardo Alfaro, who served as vice president of the conference, was openly skeptical of President Calvin Coolidge's personal pledge before the meeting that the United States would support without qualification the sovereignty of small nations.

This nadir in relations between the two countries was passed with the advent of the Hoover administration in 1929. Panamanians felt more sympathetic to the policies of President Herbert C. Hoover and his secretary of state, Henry Stimson, than to those of any previous administration in Washington. The Clark Memorandum, which renounced certain United States policies providing for direct intervention in Latin American nations, was a major step toward better relations.

These events, reinforced by the failure to intervene in the 1931 coup d'etat, presaged a decade of improvement in United States-Panamanian relations under Hoover's successor, Franklin D. Roosevelt. Roosevelt's Good Neighbor Policy, closely identified with Secretary of State Cordell Hull and Sumner Welles, and Hull's qualified renunciation of intervention in 1933 at the Seventh International Conference of American States together prepared the way for the first successful revision of the Hay-Bunau-Varilla Treaty. This revision, the Hull-Alfaro Treaty of 1936, further improved relations between the two countries, but it had grown out of immediate circumstances that were less than happy.

In the middle of 1932 a dispute arose over Panamanian opposition to the sale of 3.2 percent beer in the zone in competition with Panamanian beers. Tension rose when the governor of the zone insisted on formally replying to the protests, in the face of the Panamanian government's well-known view that proper diplomatic relations should involve only the United States ambassador. When unemployment in the Republic mounted to 50,000 from the delayed effects of the world depression and friction over the zone commissaries flared up again, President Harmodio Arias undertook a personal mission to Washington in October 1933.

The result was agreement on a number of issues. The United States pledged sympathetic consideration of future arbitration requests involving economic issues that did not affect the vital aspects of canal operation. Other forms of economic relief were provided or promised. Special efforts were to be made to protect Panamanian business interests from the smuggling of cheaply purchased commissary goods out of the zone. The United States also promised to seek appropriations from Congress to sponsor the repatriation of the numerous immigrant canal workers who were aggravating the unemployment situation.

Most important was President Roosevelt's acceptance, in a joint statement with Arias, that United States rights in the zone derived from the Hay-Bunau-Varilla Treaty could be applied only for the purposes of "maintenance, operation, sanitation and protection" of the canal. The resolution of this longstanding issue, along with a clear recognition of Panama as a sovereign nation, was a significant move in the direction of the Panamanian interpretation of the proper United States position in the isthmus.

A new problem arose with the devaluation of the United States dollar in 1934, which reduced its gold content to 59.6 percent of its former value. This meant that the value of the US$250,000 annuity was nearly cut in half. As a result, the Panamanian government refused to accept the annuity paid in the new dollars.

Roosevelt's visit to the Republic in the summer of 1934 prepared the way for the opening of negotiations on this and other matters. A Panamanian mission arrived in Washington in November, and discussions on a replacement for the Hay-Bunau-Varilla Treaty continued through 1935. On March 2, 1936, Secretary Hull and Assistant Secretary Welles joined the Panamanian negotiators, Ricardo Alfaro and Narciso Garay, in signing a new treaty and three related conventions. The conventions regulated radio communications and provided for the construction by the United States of a new transisthmian highway connecting Panama City and Colón.

The treaty itself provided a new context for relations between the two countries. It ended the protectorate by abrogating the 1903 treaty guarantee of the Republic's independence and the concomitant right of intervention. Thereafter the United States would substitute negotiation and purchase of land outside the zone for its former rights of expropriation. The dispute over the annuity was resolved by agreeing to fix it at B/430,000 (1 balboa equals US$1), which increased the gold value of the original annuity by US$7,500. This was to be paid retroactively to 1934, when the Republic had begun refusing the payments.

Various business and commercial provisions dealt with longstanding Panamanian complaints. Private commercial operations unconnected with the operation of the canal were forbidden in the zone. This policy and the closing of the zone to foreign commerce were to provide Panamanian merchants with relief from these sources of competition. Free entry into the zone was provided for Panamanian goods, and the Republic's customhouses were to be established at entrances to the zone to regulate the entry of goods finally destined for Panama.

The Hull-Alfaro revisions, though hailed by both governments, radically altered the United States special rights in the isthmus, and the United States was reluctant to accept the alterations.

Article X of the new treaty had provided that, in the event of any threat to the security of either nation, joint measures could be taken after consultation between the two. Only after an exchange of interpretive diplomatic notes had permitted the chairman of the United States Senate Foreign Relations Committee to advise his colleagues that Panama was willing under this provision to permit the United States to act unilaterally, did the Senate give its consent on July 25, 1939. The right to conduct military maneuvers in the Republic was also conceded in the notes to the United States.

After the ratification of the Hull-Alfaro Treaty in 1939, the chief problem in the two countries' relations was preparation for, and collaboration in, the coming war effort. Cooperation in this area proceeded smoothly for more than a year, with the Republic participating in the series of conferences, declarations, and protocols that solidified the support of the hemisphere behind United States efforts to meet the threat of Axis aggression.

This cooperation came to a halt with the inauguration of Arnulfo Arias, a severe critic of the United States, as president in 1940. Friction first arose over Arias's opposition to the arming of United States-owned merchant vessels sailing under the flag of Panama. Threats also were made to prevent such ships from entering declared war zones. At the same time, the pro-Axis Falangist Party, supported largely by Panamanians of German and Italian ancestry, became active on the isthmus. The prospect of espionage and infiltration of such a vital security zone was viewed with great concern in the United States. Impatience with President Arias's policies increased as the United States shifted from a policy of neutrality for the hemisphere to one of more open support for the Allies.

Arias was actually supporting a policy of strict neutrality quite close to the one the United States itself had fostered in the hemisphere only a year before. He was in office when negotiations for the acquisition by the United States of military bases outside the zone were begun but was overthrown by a coalition of pro-Allied Panamanian political factions in October 1941. An agreement on the war bases request was concluded with Arias's successor, Ricardo Adolfo de la Guardia, on May 18, 1942. Facilities granted to the United States under its terms included a large airfield at Río Hato, several radar stations, and a naval base on the island of Taboga in the Bay of Panama.

The close of World War II brought another treaty misunderstanding. The original agreement for the bases had provided for their return "one year after the date on which the definitive treaty of peace . . . shall have entered into effect." After the end of the

225

war, however, Panama demanded relinquishment of the bases, resting its claim on a subsidiary provision of the treaty permitting renegotiation after the cessation of hostilities. Although insisting on the basic terms of the treaty, the State Department took cognizance of growing nationalist dissatisfaction and sent the United States ambassador to propose in December 1946 a twenty-year extension of the leases on thirteen facilities. The authorization of a draft treaty by President Enrique A. Jiménez over the opposition of the foreign minister only exacerbated latent resentment. When the National Assembly met to consider ratification, a mob of 10,000 Panamanians armed with stones, machetes, and guns opposed it. Under these circumstances the deputies voted unanimously to reject the treaty.

The next episode in United States-Panamanian negotiation began in 1953, when President José A. Remón visited Washington and discussions of basic revisions of the 1936 treaty were opened. Panamanian requests were made in several areas of longstanding concern. First, officials of the Republic hoped to get a larger share of the canal tolls. Merchants on the isthmus continued to be unhappy with the competition from the nonprofit commissaries in the zone. Demands were also made that the discriminatory wage differential in the zone, favoring United States citizens over Panamanians, be abolished.

After lengthy negotiations a treaty was signed on January 23, 1955. Under its provisions commercial activities in the zone not essential to the operation of the canal were to be cut back. An enlarged annuity of US$1.93 million was agreed on. The principle of "one basic wage scale for all . . . employees . . . in the Canal Zone" was accepted, and provisions for its implementation were made. The Republic's request for the replacement of the "perpetuity" clause in the zone grant by a ninety-nine-year renewable lease was, however, rejected, as was the proposal that its citizens who were accused of violations in the zone be tried by joint United States-Panamanian tribunals.

Panama's contribution to the 1955 accord was its consent, which it had withheld a few years earlier, to United States occupation of the bases. Twenty thousand acres of the Republic's territory were leased rent free for fifteen years for United States military maneuvers. The Río Hato base, a particularly important installation in defense planning, was thus regained for the United States Air Force. With the strong support of President Ricardo Arias, who had succeeded to the office after Remón's assassination, the National Assembly this time approved the treaty with little hesitation.

The Egyptian nationalization of the Suez Canal in 1956 stimulated a reaction in the Republic, as the two canal situations were widely compared in the world press. Fearful of the Republic's conduct under the circumstances, Britain and the United States failed to invite Panama to the London Suez conference of the major world maritime powers. President Arias criticized this exclusion, pointing to the Republic's large maritime fleet, the sixth greatest in the world. As an indication of its resentment, the isthmian government joined ten communist and neutral nations in a rival Suez proposal.

Panama-United States relations were further disturbed by Secretary of State John Foster Dulles's unqualified statement in a press conference on the Suez issue on September 28, 1956, that the United States did not fear similar nationalization of the Panama Canal because it possessed "rights of sovereignty" there. This was interpreted in the Republic as an unqualified claim to sovereignty itself, and the foreign minister, Aquilino Boyd, contested Dulles's statement and reasserted Panama's own claim to sovereignty.

A second area of disagreement in 1956 related to the ending of wage discrimination in the zone. Isthmian public opinion was aroused by an army department statement in the summer that implied that the 1955 treaty had not in fact envisaged a total equalization of wage rates. The Canal Zone governor attempted to clarify the issue by explaining that the zone government did intend that all workers would be paid the United States rate. He explained that the only exception to the "equal pay for equal labor" principle would be a 25-percent differential that would apply to all citizens brought from the continental United States.

The last years of the de la Guardia government were the setting for an extreme intensification of resentment toward the United States. In May 1958 student demonstrations led by anti-United States nationalists were directed against the National Guard. The violence of these riots, in which nine lives were lost, was a forecast of the far more serious difficulties that were to follow a year later. In November 1959 nationalists of many different backgrounds combined to produce anti-United States demonstrations during the two Panamanian independence holidays of that month. Aroused by elite-controlled papers, particularly those owned by Harmodio Arias, Panamanians began to threaten a "peaceful invasion" of the zone in order to raise the flag of the Republic there as tangible evidence of Panama's sovereignty.

Confident they could control the course of events, elite politicians were active in stimulating popular feeling through the press and radio. When, on Independence Day and Flag Day, it appeared that Panamanian mobs might actually force entry into the zone, United States troops were called out. Several hundred Panamanians crossed barbed wire restraints and clashed with Canal Zone police and troops. A second wave of Panamanian citizens was repulsed by the Republic's own National Guard, supported by United States troops.

Extensive and violent disorder followed. The United States Information Service library was attacked by a mob, and its windows were smashed. The United States flag was torn from the embassy residence and trampled. Aware that public feeling was dangerously exceeding expectations and turning into general vandalism, elite politicians attempted to regain control over their followers but were unable to do so. Relations between the two governments were critically strained. United States authorities erected an eight-foot fence on the border of the zone. Partly from resentment of Panamanian actions, North Americans resident in the zone observed a voluntary boycott of the Republic's merchants, who traditionally depended on them for much of their trade.

Feelings remained tense through March 1, 1960, Panama's Constitution Day, when student and labor groups threatened another march into the Canal Zone. Apprehension arose that violence would result once more. The widespread disorders of the previous fall, however, had had a sobering effect on elite politicians, who seriously feared that new rioting might be transformed into a larger expression of internal Panamanian dissatisfaction directed against the social system itself. Both major coalitions contesting the coming elections seemed to wish to avoid further difficulties, and most elements in the population, particularly influential merchants who had been hard hit by the November 1959 riots, seemed genuinely apprehensive. Reports that the Canal Zone government and some influential members of the United States Congress were willing to fly the Republic's flag in a special site in the zone also served to ease tensions, and serious disorders were averted.

For some time the dispute over flying the Republic's flag in the zone had been seriously complicated by differences of opinion on the issue within the United States government. The press in the United States reported serious policy conflict between the State Department and the Department of Defense. The military opposed accepting a Panamanian flag, emphasizing the strategic importance of unimpaired United States control in the zone and the dangerous precedent that appeasement of the rioters' demands would set for future United States-Panamanian relations. The State Department, however, supported the flag proposal as a reasonable concession to Panamanian demands and a method of avoiding major embarrassment before hemispheric and global opinion. Diplomatic officials also feared that the stability of Panamanian institutions themselves might be threatened by extensive violence and mob action over the flag issue. Also involved in the intragovernment disagreement was the question of meeting Panamanian requests concerning the policy of purchasing zone supplies in third countries, a practice that the United States, in the 1955 treaty, had promised to avoid where feasible.

Differences of opinion over policy toward the Republic also divided the members of the United States Congress. A tentative statement by President Dwight D. Eisenhower at a press conference supported some "visible evidence" recognizing the Republic's claim to "titular" sovereignty over the Canal Zone. Gradually, in the early months of 1960, the United States came to favor not only permitting the Panamanian flag to fly symbolically in the zone but also making concessions in several areas of policy regarding Panamanians employed in the Canal Zone.

In April 1960 President Eisenhower announced a nine-point program aimed at meeting Panamanian demands for better pay and access to supervisory jobs in addition to the unskilled and semiskilled positions to which they were traditionally restricted. Included was a 10-percent salary increase for teachers and the lower ranks of Panamanians employed by the zone government. The construction of 500 new homes for Panamanians in the zone was promised, along with other improvements in the status of such groups. The promise to do away with discrimination in the zone was once again reaffirmed. Agreement on the flag question, however, was withheld.

In 1960 a concerted effort was also made by United States authorities in the zone to improve relations with the Republic, on both popular and official levels. The new military commander of the United States Army Caribbean Command inaugurated a program, widely publicized as Operation Friendship (Operación Amistad), to encourage friendly and affirmative contacts between military personnel in the zone and their Panamanian neighbors. The new United States ambassador extended his contacts and circle of acquaintances among Panamanians far beyond those traditionally maintained by North American diplomats, traveling to provincial capitals and deep into the interior where even Panamanian leaders had seldom gone. The United States community in the zone made greater goodwill contacts with Panamanians both through increased support of Panamanian philanthropic causes and on a less formal basis. Both the military commander's and the ambassador's efforts to promote understanding received extensive and sympathetic coverage from Panamanian newspaper publishers, now sincerely concerned at the prospect of any further public disorder threatening both the United States position and the interests of the elite.

On September 21, 1960, the goodwill campaign of the United States authorities was climaxed by the simultaneous raising of the Panamanian and United States flags side by side in the zone. The special ceremony at the zone's Shaler Triangle was attended by the new governor of the zone, along with all high United States military and diplomatic officers and the entire Panamanian cabinet. Even this incident, however, which marked official recognition of Panama's "titular" sovereignty, was marred by President de la Guardia's refusal to attend the ceremony after his request to raise the flag personally was rejected. As a retaliatory measure, invitations to the presidential reception following the ceremony were extended only to Ambassador Joseph Farland and his diplomatic associates; United States Canal Zone officials were excluded.

The acceptance of the daily flying of the Panamanian flag at this one site was accompanied by the transfer to the Republic of extensive properties in Panama City and Colón owned by the United States government, as called for in the 1955 treaty. Additional progress was made toward the abolishment of racial segregation in United States facilities, and a regulation requiring Panamanian drivers to have a Canal Zone license to drive through the zone was no longer to be enforced.

In spite of the beneficial effect of these policy changes on Panamanian opinion, anti-United States feeling continued to be expressed throughout 1961. Marchers in the May Day parade through the center of Panama City carried signs attacking the United States, and speakers at the rally that followed excoriated Washington's policies in the zone toward Cuba. This time the authorities, haunted by the specter of the previous fall's disorders, took rigorous security precautions, and disorders did not occur.

The year 1961 also witnessed the announcement of a major aid program by the United States for all Latin America—the Alliance for Progress. No regular United States government development loans or grants had been available to Panama through the late 1950s, although the United States-sponsored Inter-American Cooperative Public Health Service (Servicio Cooperativo Inter-Americano de Salud Pública) had been active in the isthmus (see ch. 4, Living Conditions). On August 5 Washington announced that Panama would share in the initial large-scale loans under the program to support self-help housing.

Friction continued, however, in 1961 between the two countries on issues that, although not central to their relations, involved troublesome differences. Panamanian officials were alarmed at the Kennedy administration's proposed change in the internal United States tax structure affecting United States-owned corporations domiciled outside the country. Panama had long been

230

attractive to United States businesses seeking the advantages of its incorporation regulations. Panamanian officials feared changes in the United States tax structure might lead to a damaging flight of such companies from the isthmus.

Another point at issue between the two governments was Panama's claim to legal jurisdiction over the waters extending twelve miles beyond its shores. This claim directly affected United States control of the waters adjacent to the zone, as Washington's jurisdiction was limited to a three-mile extension by the terms of its treaty with Panama. The Republic's claim, if accepted, would thus give it control of the maritime entrances to the canal. In late August 1961 the Republic's Ministry of Foreign Affairs, in protesting a ruling of the United States National Labor Relations Board affecting a labor dispute on a ship owned by a Panama-domiciled firm, seized the opportunity to reiterate its claim to a twelve-mile limit. The protest stated pointedly that jurisdiction over such territorial waters included "waters near the Panama Canal."

The next major episode in United States-Panamanian relations was opened with President Roberto Chiari's state of the nation address to the National Assembly on October 1, 1961. In it he formally requested a general revision of the terms under which the United States held the canal and the Canal Zone. Chiari said that the new treaty arrangements would be necessary if Panama were to be "treated as an equal despite its limited territorial and economic position . . . a free and sovereign nation in command of its own destiny." Informing the assembly that his request for negotiations had already been forwarded to Washington, he called for a "sincere, cordial and comprehensive coexistence" between the two countries on the basis of their equal interest in the canal. Shortly after this announcement, President Kennedy replied in a letter expressing United States willingness to conduct mutually beneficial negotiations between the two countries.

The prospect of negotiations for a new canal arrangement appeared against a background of extensive discussion within the Republic of its relations with the United States. A wide variety of Panamanian leaders, representing every shade of political opinion, had aired the subject extensively during the year; although they differed on details, their views reflected a basic similarity of approach. Revision of both economic and political arrangements for the zone was demanded. In the economic sphere enlargement of the annuity was envisaged; suggested figures ranged from US$5 million through US$30 million to half of the gross receipts of the canal. Because of the widespread belief that Panama's resources were not extensive enough to permit it to operate the canal alone, nationalization of the canal was infrequently mentioned. Demands called for abolition of the 25-percent wage differential and "security" classified positions, which continued to restrict Panamanian employees in the zone to nondecisionmaking jobs at lower rates of pay. In the political sphere politicians called for the removal of the "perpetuity" clause, the recognition of operative as well as titular Panamanian sovereignty in the zone, and a sharing by the two countries of jurisdiction over the zone's courts, customs, operations, schools, health and sanitary measures, and, most important of all, the canal itself.

President Chiari visited Washington on June 12 and 13, 1962, at which time he and President Kennedy agreed to appoint high-level representatives to discuss controversies between their countries regarding the Canal Zone. The results of the discussions were disclosed in a joint communiqué issued by the two governments on July 23, 1963.

Agreement had been reached on the creation of the Bi-National Labor Advisory Committee to consider disputes arising between Panamanian employees and zone authorities. The United States had agreed to withhold from its Panamanian employees taxes to be remitted to the Panamanian government and, pending congressional approval, to extend to Panamanian employees the health and life insurance benefits available to United States citizens in the zone. Several other controversial matters, however, remained unresolved. The United States agreed to increase the wages of Panamanian employees in the zone but not as much as the Panamanian government requested, and no agreement had been reached in response to the Panamanian requests for jurisdiction over a corridor linking the two segments of the country and the licensing of two piers in Cristóbal to the Colón Free Zone.

The 1964 Riots and the Aftermath

Discontent over the status of the canal reached a climax in January 1964. An agreement had been reached between President Kennedy and President Chiari that at certain points in the Canal Zone the United States and Panamanian flags should be flown side by side. United States citizens residing in the zone were reluctant to abide by this agreement, however, and the students of an American high school, with adult encouragement, on two consecutive days hoisted the United States flag alone in front of their school.

Word of the gesture soon spread across the border and, on the evening of the second day, January 9, about 200 Panamanian students marched into the zone with their own flag. A struggle ensued in which the Panamanian flag was allegedly torn. With that provocation, thousands of Panamanians stormed the border fence, and the rioting that persisted for three days resulted in more than twenty deaths, serious injuries to several hundred persons, and more than US$2 million in property damage.

At the outbreak of the fighting, Panama charged the United States with aggression, severed relations, and appealed to both the OAS and the United Nations. The controversy smoldered for almost a year until President Lyndon B. Johnson announced that plans for a new canal would be drawn up and that an entirely new treaty would replace the 1903 one governing the Canal Zone.

Negotiations were carried on throughout the first half of the presidency of Marco Robles, but when the terms of three draft treaties concerning the existing lock canal, a possible sea-level canal, and defense matters were revealed in 1967, Panamanian public reaction was strongly adverse. The new treaties would have abolished the resented "in perpetuity" clause in favor of an expiration date of December 13, 1999, or the date of the competion of a new sea-level canal if that were earlier. Furthermore, it would have compensated the Panamanian government on the basis of tonnage shipped through the canal, an arrangement that could have been expected to increase the annuity to more than US$20 million.

The intensity of Panamanian nationalism, however, was such that many among the elite contended that the United States should abandon the isthmus altogether. Provisions for the continuance of United States military bases in the canal area, for the right of the United States to deploy troops and armaments anywhere in the Republic, and for a joint board of nine governors for the zone, five of whom were to be appointed by the United States, were particularly unpopular. President Robles therefore placed the matter in abeyance by announcing that further negotiations were necessary.

One of Arnulfo Arias's first statements after assuming the presidency in October 1968 asserted Panamanian sovereignty over the Canal Zone, but after twelve days in office he was deposed by the National Guard. The guard commander, General Torrijos, who soon emerged as the effective head of the military government, initially assumed a conciliatory stance on the issue, maintaining that Panama had no desire to take operating control of the canal away from the United States.

By 1970, however, his control over the National Guard and the country having been consolidated, Torrijos had begun to move toward identifying his government with Panamanian nationalistic aspirations. In September he publicly rejected the treaties that had been drafted in 1967. In early 1971 he refused to renew an agreement on United States use of the Río Hato air base and terminated the Peace Corps program that had been in the country since 1962. Relations were further strained when the Panamanian government accused two United States servicemen from the Canal Zone of attempting to kidnap two other United States servicemen who had defected from the Canal Zone and had been offered political asylum in Panama. The charges were later dropped.

Meanwhile, the Interoceanic Canal Commission appointed by President Johnson in December 1964 to study alternative routes for a new canal had announced in November 1970 that it would not recommend any routes that might be developed outside of Panama. The following month the Panamanian foreign minister, Juan Antonio Tack, asserted in a speech to the American Society of Panama that all the causes of conflict between the United States and Panama were to be found in "the existence within our own territory of a structure and form of government totally foreign to the central national government." When negotiations concerning new treaties were renewed in Washington in June 1971, he announced that "Panama will not negotiate a revision of existing treaties; it will negotiate for a new treaty to replace the abhorrent 1903 treaty, with its opprobrious and illegal perpetuity clause."

Some Areas of Reciprocal Interest and Cooperation

From 1946 through 1970 Panama received a net total of US$266 million from the United States in economic and military assistance. Diplomatic relations and military assistance were suspended briefly after the guard assumed power in October 1968, but economic assistance was increased to US$11.8 million for 1970, as compared to US$9.1 million for the previous year, and US$279,000 was extended in military assistance. In 1971, as negotiations concerning the Canal Zone were resumed, the United States proposed an increase in Panama's quota in the United States sugar market of 20,000 tons for a three-year period (see ch. 13, Trade and Transportation).

Another important development in United States-Panamanian relations in 1971 was the conclusion of an agreement for cooperation in the construction of the Panama segment of the Darién Gap Highway. This agreement and a similar one between the United States and Colombia, both of which were signed in Washington on May 6, were directed toward filling in the missing link in the Pan-American Highway. It was estimated that the project would be completed in five to ten years.

RELATIONS WITH NEIGHBORING COUNTRIES

For most isthmian statesmen, Panama's position vis-à-vis the United States was a consideration of overwhelmingly greater importance than any problem that might arise in other international arenas. The extremely close ties that until 1936 bound the Republic's internal political system directly to United States policy and that have continued to relate Panama's economy to the United States-administered Canal Zone have tended to divert Panama's attention from other parts of the world. Panama's peculiar location has set the country apart, even from close neighbors. Situated on the bridge between the South American continent and Central America, Panama has not been an integral part of either region. It has exhibited ambivalent feelings toward the south—Colombia, Venezuela, and Ecuador—and the five Central American states to the north.

Originally a part of Colombia, Panama had always lacked a feeling of real unity of interests—political, economic, or cultural—with that country. The difficulty of communication and transportation during the period of colonial development had created a different set of goals and loyalties in Panama City that set it off from Bogotá. This sense of difference led to continual attempts at separation in the nineteenth century, culminating in the successful attainment of independence in 1903 (see ch. 2, Historical Setting).

A similar sense of difference has been present in the Republic's relations with the five countries to the north. Costa Rica, El Salvador, Honduras, Nicaragua, and Guatemala had for some time shared a history of common institutions. They were actually united in a federation from 1823 to 1838, and various attempts to renew the federation were made throughout the nineteenth century. This trend tangibly persisted during the first years of Panama's independence in the form of the Central American Court of Justice. Panama had relations with these countries both on a bilateral basis and multilaterally through the inter-American movement in which all participated. Other than in special areas of common interest, such as education and health, Panama in the past demonstrated little desire for any arrangement joining its interests formally with the Central American bloc.

In the 1960s this attitude underwent modification. Panama had for some time been increasingly aware of the importance of movements toward multinational trade associations. Of particular importance to the Republic was the Central American Common Market, which included among its members Nicaragua, Guatemala, El Salvador, Honduras, and Costa Rica. Always sensitive to questions involving international trade and commerce, the

Republic's policymakers came to favor some form of association with the group, with the particular hope that expanded trade within the area would bring heavy rewards to Panama through its Colón Free Zone, the Republic's duty-free redistribution and assembling center. Finally in November 1960 it was announced that Panama hoped to associate itself with the Central American Common Market. In 1963, however, the five members of the group rejected Panama's bid for associate membership. Thereafter, important interest groups in Panama, including the Chamber of Commerce and the Management Association, withdrew their support for the incorporation of Panama into the common market.

The course of the common market's development in the 1960s was somewhat uneven, and the so-called soccer war between El Salvador and Honduras in 1969 seriously disrupted trade and resulted in the partial withdrawal of Honduras. In 1971 there was an agreement among the members of the common market providing for an open-ended invitation to Panama to join, but Panama did not accept the invitation. Panama's external trade was indirectly linked to the market, however, through a tripartite agreement with Costa Rica and Nicaragua signed in 1958 and various bilateral arrangements. In mid-1971 a treaty was being negotiated with Guatemala, product lists for mutual tariff reduction were being drawn up with Costa Rica and El Salvador, and similar talks with Honduras were being planned.

Panama has also participated since the early 1960s in several multilateral discussions of Central American defense problems. The Central American Defense Council was formally established in 1964 by Guatemala, Honduras, Nicaragua, and El Salvador, with United States technical and material assistance, as a subsidiary organ of the Organization of Central American States. In 1966 it modified its constitutional act to include not only armies but also "the Ministries of National Security" in order to incorporate Costa Rica and Panama.

The only instance of armed conflict between Panama and another state in the region occurred in 1921 on the Costa Rican frontier, when hostilities erupted between the two nations' forces over the disputed Coto region, now a part of Costa Rica. Since then, relations with Panama's immediate neighbor to the north have generally been satisfactory. Encounters between the Panamanian National Guard and peasant insurgents in Chiriquí Province after the overthrow of Arnulfo Arias heightened tensions in the border areas for several months. Costa Rica appealed to the Inter-American Peace Committee to investigate alleged violations of its territory by the National Guard, but the Panamanian government refused to allow an on-the-spot investigation and accused the Costa Rican communications media of exaggerating the scope of the conflict. In 1970, however, an agreement was signed by the two countries for the integrated development of industry and agriculture in the frontier region.

The stabilization of Panama's relations with Colombia was more problematical because of the long association of the countries and the circumstances of separation in 1903 (see ch. 2, Historical Setting). The Colombians were understandably bitter for several years over the loss of their Panamanian department. An agreement demarcating the boundary between the two countries was concluded in 1909, but it became the subject of an internal dispute between political factions in Bogotá and was consequently rejected by the Colombian government. Finally, a treaty was concluded between the two countries in 1924, resolving the boundary question and establishing diplomatic relations. Since then, Colombia and its former isthmian province have enjoyed, for the most part, mutually satisfactory relations. A series of cooperative agreements were signed in 1960, when the Colombian president visited Panama.

REGIONAL AND GLOBAL RELATIONS

Panama's relations with its neighbors in the hemisphere and with other parts of the world have emphasized the principle of absolute equality among nation states, full respect for the sovereignty and rights of smaller nations, and the importance of international law as a force for ordering relations among states. Panama's early interest in establishing formal diplomatic relations with as many nations as were willing to recognize its separation from Colombia has a counterpart today in the extensive list of countries with which it maintains relations and in its participation in many international organizations.

In regional affairs Panama signed, in 1947, in Rio De Janeiro, the Inter-American Treaty of Reciprocal Assistance, which provides for collective security against attack from within or beyond the hemisphere against a signatory state. It joined the OAS at its formation in Bogotá in 1948 and the Inter-American Development Bank in 1959 and signed the 1961 Charter of Punta del Este, formalizing the Alliance for Progress, and the 1967 Latin American Nuclear Free Zone Treaty. In 1971 it had observer status in the Latin American Free Trade Association and the newly formed Andean Common Market.

Panama's role in multilateral organizations has largely reflected the status of its relations with the United States. On January 9,

1964, the day of the outbreak of conflict between Panamanians and American forces in the Canal Zone, Panama severed diplomatic relations, charged the United States with aggression, appealed to the OAS, and called for an urgent meeting of the United Nations Security Council.

The OAS referred the case to the Inter-American Peace Committee the following day. When the United Nations Security Council met, United States Ambassador Adlai E. Stevenson pointed out that the Inter-American Peace Committee had already scheduled an on-the-spot investigation and urged that the problem be considered in the regional forum. A proposal of the Brazilian delegate that the president of the council address an appeal to the two parties to exercise restraint was agreed upon, and no further action was taken by the United Nations.

The United States had hoped to confine the controversy to the Inter-American Peace Committee but, when negotiations broke down, Panama insisted that the Organ of Consultation under the Inter-American Treaty of Reciprocal Assistance be convoked. The OAS Council, acting provisionally as the Organ of Consultation, appointed an investigating committee consisting of all of the members of the council with the exception of two disputants. A joint declaration recommended by the committee was signed by the two countries in April, and diplomatic relations were restored, but the underlying issues, including that of sovereign rights in the Canal Zone, remained unresolved in 1971.

The only other occasion on which Panama initiated a convocation of the Organ of Consultation under the Inter-American Treaty of Reciprocal Assistance was in 1959. At that time Panama informed the OAS Council that the country had been invaded "by forces composed almost entirely of foreign elements." Although it was known that the vessel carrying eighty armed men led by Roberto Arias, son of Harmodio Arias and nephew of Arnulfo, had embarked from Cuba, Panama did not prefer charges against the Cuban government. The Cuban government formally denied any association with the Arias force and offered its full cooperation in dealing with the threat to the Panamanian government. Rubén Miró, a co-conspirator and cousin of Arias, was placed under precautionary arrest in Havana, and two Cuban army officers were dispatched by the Castro government to persuade the invasion force to surrender.

The procedure of the OAS in this case was for the most part routine but, as there were persistent rumors of additional invasion forces en route to Panama, naval and air patrols were established to observe and identify vessels in the area. OAS members were not willing at this point, however, to authorize the patrols to detain any vessel, even in waters claimed by Panama. The rebels, isolated in Nombre de Dios, abandoned their attempt and surrendered to an OAS observation team, and Roberto Arias sought political asylum in the Brazilian embassy.

On security issues that have not directly involved Panamanian interests the country has consistently supported United States initiatives in international forums. It supported, for example, the exclusion of the Cuban government from the OAS in January 1962 and the use of armed force to stop the emplacement of Russian missiles in Cuba in October of that year, the diplomatic and economic sanctions adopted by the OAS against Cuba in 1964, and the creation of the ad hoc Inter-American Peace-Keeping Force following the United States unilateral intervention in the Dominican Republic in 1965. In 1971 it supported an OAS resolution providing for the extradition of persons accused of abducting or terrorizing foreign diplomats.

In a more general sense, however, Panama has joined other Latin American countries in opposing United States dominance of the OAS and in urging greater United States economic aid for Latin America. At OAS conferences in 1965 and 1966 the country proposed a "graduated income tax" as a means of redistributing the wealth of the hemisphere, and in 1971 the president stated, "We believe that the OAS should take a position closer to Latin American interests."

Along with eight other Latin American countries, Panama in 1971 was claiming that its territorial waters extended 200 nautical miles from its coastline. This claim, which Panama had maintained since 1967, was not recognized by the United States and constituted a potential source of friction between the two countries.

Participation in multilateral organizations has included charter membership in the former League of Nations and in the United Nations. Panama has consistently looked to such organizations as a source of protection and a means of strengthening its bargaining position vis-à-vis the United States. The country's expectations in this regard, however, have often met with frustration. In 1921, for example, the league refrained from involvement in Panama's boundary dispute with Costa Rica, allowing the United States to impose a solution unfavorable to Panama, and in 1927 the league shelved Panama's proposal that the question of sovereignty over the Canal Zone be submitted to arbitration.

The strengthening of the United Nations has been a major tenet of the country's foreign policy. It served on the United Nations Commission on Palestine in 1947 and on the Security Council from 1958 to 1960, and a Panamanian has served as a member of the International Court of Justice. On cold war issues, such as the seating of the People's Republic of China and the Korean conflict, it has in the past supported United States initiatives, although on issues of less ideological import it has tended to defend the rights of small states. It has proposed, for example, international recognition of four basic rights of states: independence, self-defense, juridical equality, and territorial jurisdiction.

Panama has on several occasions made use of the United Nations as a forum for airing its grievances against the United States. Its charge of aggression that followed the 1964 riots was the most serious one, but in 1957 it complained to the United Nations that it was not receiving its fair share of the profits from the canal, and in 1962 it attacked the canal treaty as "humiliating, injurious, unjust, and inequitable."

Panama was an early participant in the work of the International Labor Organization, the Hague Convention, the Pan-American Sanitary Bureau (now the regional branch of the World Health Organization), and the International Commission of Jurists. The country has also been active in most of the specialized agencies of the United Nations. In 1971 it was a member of the Food and Agriculture Organization (FAO); the United Nations Educational, Scientific and Cultural Organization (UNESCO); the International Monetary Fund (IMF); the International Bank for Reconstruction and Development (IBRD) and its affiliates, the International Finance Corporation (IFC) and the International Development Association (IDA); the International Telecommunications Union (ITU); the Universal Postal Union (UPU); the International Atomic Energy Agency (IAEA); the International Civil Aviation Organization (ICAO); the Intergovernmental Maritime Consultative Organization (IMCO); the United Nations Development Program (UNDP); the United Nations Council on Trade and Development (UNCTAD); and the Economic Commission for Latin America (ECLA).

Since the mid-twentieth century Panama has exhibited increasing interest in international politics beyond the Western Hemisphere. The Republic has also attracted the attention of several nations that for various reasons considered Panama's international position relevant to their own national interests. After the seizure of the Suez Canal by the government of Egypt, Cairo vigorously sought to extend its influence in the isthmus. During 1960 the diplomatic mission of the United Arab Republic (UAR) was reported to be the most active in the Republic, and its minister, Mohammed el Tabei, cultivated acquaintances in a wide variety of political circles but with heavy emphasis on the anti-United States nationalists. As part of a general expansion of its relations with

Latin American countries, the UAR offered Panamanian students a special program of postgraduate scholarships for study in its universities.

Its legation in Panama was also active in offering advice on problems concerning canal management. At that time, still reacting strongly to the European attack of 1956, the Cairo overseas radio directed Spanish programs to Panama, attacking the treatment the Republic had received in the zone at the hands of the United States.

Increased contact with the Soviet bloc was another indication of Panama's growing importance on the world scene. In May 1959 an opportunity for exploratory talks was provided in the biennial meeting of ECLA in Panama City. Delegations from the Soviet, Polish, Hungarian, and Czechoslovakian governments attended as official observers. The Republic also sent observers to the conference of neutralist nations at Belgrade in the summer of 1961.

The country maintained diplomatic relations in 1971 with all of the Western Hemisphere states except Cuba, relations with that country having been severed in 1961. Its closest ties outside the Western Hemisphere were with the Western European countries and Japan, but it also maintained diplomatic relations with Israel, Lebanon, the Arab Republic of Egypt, India, and the Republic of China (Nationalist China). It did not maintain relations with the Soviet Union, but the Polish and Yugoslav ambassadors to Mexico were accredited to Panama, and there was a Polish trade office in Panama City. Panama's interest in shipping and trade has also led it to establish a system of consular facilities in most of the shipping and trade centers of Africa, Asia, and the South Pacific, even though expenses or other considerations have precluded the establishment of diplomatic relations. The 1967 report of the comptroller general listed 192 consulates.

Interchanges with the Soviet Union in recent years have been primarily in cultural affairs. In 1970, for example, a Sovet pianist performed in Panama, and Soviet art prints were exhibited under the auspices of the National Institute of Culture and Sports. Several Latin American and Western European countries engage in cultural exchange programs with Panama. France, West Germany, Spain, Brazil, Chile, and Mexico have been prominent among those countries offering scholarships to Panamanians. Great Britain, Spain, France, Italy, Chile, Colombia, Ecuador, and El Salvador maintain binational cultural associations. France and Spain have been particularly influential in the country's universities through the placement of teachers and books. France has assisted in the establishment of an educational television program, and Israel and Nationalist China have extended technical

assistance in the form of agricultural projects. The United States, in addition to the many projects of the Agency for International Development, maintains an extensive communications and cultural exchange program under the auspices of the United States Information Service (see ch. 7, Education, Culture, and Public Information).

FOREIGN POLICY DECISIONMAKING

The general responsibility for the conduct of foreign affairs is delegated by the 1946 Constitution to the president of the Republic. As the head of state, he directs the nation's foreign relations generally and has the task of accrediting and receiving diplomatic representatives. Article 144 vests the president with the treaty-making power, which he is to wield in association with the National Assembly. The role of the legislative branch in foreign affairs is outlined in detail by Article 118, which grants it a veto power over treaties, in addition to the functions of declaring war and of formally authorizing the executive to enter into peace negotiations.

The legislative branch has not functioned since the National Guard assumed control of the government in 1968, and the decisionmaking role has been filled by General Torrijos and those to whom he has delegated such authority. An issue frequently raised by opponents of the military government is that, even if a new canal treaty were negotiated, in the absence of a National Assembly it could not be ratified and therefore could not be considered legitimate.

Constitutional provision for the office of the minister of foreign affairs is quite general. Under the delineation of general ministerial function, the minister is the director of his department and an "indispensable" collaborator of the president in the making of foreign policy. The foreign minister in 1971 was Juan Antonio Tack, a former professor of diplomatic history at the University of Panama.

Within the Ministry of Foreign Affairs immigration and naturalization affairs fall under the supervision of a special department; the three other major sections are the Department of Consular Affairs, the Department for International Political Affairs, and the Department for Protocol Affairs. The attention given to the conduct of relations with the United States is reflected in the internal organization of the Department for International Political Affairs. There, one office is responsible for international organizations, conferences, and treaty affairs; another supervises United States-Panamanian relations; and the third has the responsibility for all the other countries with which the Republic has relations.

The Office of the Negotiating Mission (**Oficina de la Misión Negociadora**) has been established as a result of the reopening of negotiations in June 1971 for a new treaty on operations of the Panama Canal and the administration of the Canal Zone. Panama was being represented in these negotiations by Ambassador José Antonio de la Ossa, former Foreign Minister Carlos López Guevara, and former Minister of Commerce and Industry Hernando Manfredo. The United States delegation was headed by Robert Anderson, secretary of the treasury under the Eisenhower administration.

Statutory enactments significantly affecting the Ministry of Foreign Affairs were passed in 1955 and 1957 and provided for a consultative group, the National Council for Foreign Relations, composed of seven members and seven alternates. This council has been maintained by the military government. Its members, officially appointed by the governing junta, include several former foreign ministers. Galileo Solis, for example, was foreign minister under the Chiari government and under the most recent, short-lived presidency of Arnulfo Arias.

Unofficial influence on foreign policy is exercised by industrial, commercial, and professional groups. The Panamanian Bar Association, for example, was among the groups opposing the canal treaty revisions negotiated by the Robles government. The Teachers' Association has advocated the incorporation of Panama into the Central American Common Market, but membership in that body has been blocked in part by the opposition of other powerful groups, such as the Chamber of Commerce. The commercial interests of the country's political elite have been reflected in the maintenance of consular relations with major trading centers all over the world and in the longstanding policy of curtailing commercial competition from the commissaries in the canal zone.

Public demonstrations and riots, such as occurred in 1927, 1947, 1959, and 1964, have also been effective in influencing foreign policy, especially in relation to the country's stance vis-à-vis the United States. National leaders have alternately responded to and contributed to an explosive climate of public opinion. Whether in response to such a climate or in an attempt to generate popular support, government spokesmen in late 1970 and early 1971 were forcefully articulating nationalistic aspirations and frustrations. In December 1970, for example, the foreign minister alleged that "efforts have been made to weaken the Panamanian state as a results of excessive concern for the security of the canal, which leads to the belief that the security is obtained solely by controlling not only the canal zone but the Republic itself in many aspects."

CHAPTER 11

CHARACTER AND STRUCTURE
OF THE ECONOMY

Two different economic systems have developed. One is the highly sophisticated urban economy of Panama City, Colón, and their environs—based upon domestic and foreign trade and services—that provides a comparatively high standard of living for most of the residents of those areas. The other is an agriculture-based economy that provides a subsistence or low-income standard of living.

The dichotomy is accounted for in large part by the geographical circumstances that historically made the isthmus a transit zone and resulted in a concentration of income in the terminal cities of the isthmian crossing. Although a gradual change toward greater diversification of the economy has started, the role of the urban areas will probably be overwhelming for a long time to come.

Agriculture, which involves the largest precentage of the population, produces an ever-decreasing percentage of the gross domestic product (GDP). The majority of the farmers do not own or rent land but simply occupy a plot owned by the state or a private landowner and use it mainly for family subsistence, producing little for the market. The five most important crops in terms of value are bananas, rice, sugarcane, corn, and coffee (see ch. 12, Agriculture and Industry).

Low output in the agricultural sector and costly domestic transportation make it possible to buy products more cheaply on the world market than from the interior of the country. Bananas, refined petroleum products, and shrimp make up the bulk of the exports. Panama has never been an exporting country, and exports make up less than 11 percent of gross national product (GNP) annually, much lower than the average percentage for Latin America. Imports are usually much larger than exports, but the sizable trade deficit is offset by income from the sales of services and goods, including labor, to the Canal Zone and to tourists.

Industry has been one of the faster growing sectors but is characterized by a geographical concentration in the terminal cities and by the domination of a few large enterprises in each branch.

Manufacturing is starting to grow away from simple mixing, processing, or packaging operations into more complex activities, such as metalworking. Industrial activity is stimulated by very generous incentives under an industrial development law.

Mainly because of the highly advanced urban economy, Panama has one of the highest per capita incomes in Latin America, the equivalent of more than US$664. The distribution, however, is highly unequal. The GNP grew at a rate higher than that for most countries—an average of 6.3 percent from 1960 to 1969. In 1968 a slowdown began because the private sector, lacking confidence in the new government, refrained from making new investments; but in 1970 and 1971 private investment again started to increase. From time to time, as in 1970, the economy is hurt by extensive crop damage caused by rains and floods, but the government may be able to maintain the growth-rate, as it did in that year, by increased public spending on public works. Panama was judged by international economists to have favorable prospects for continual economic development during the 1970s.

The country has been able to adhere to a tradition of total absence of monetary controls. It has been able to attract incoming foreign capital to the banking system for relending both to residents and to foreigners. The United States dollar and the Panamanian balboa are both legal tender. The balboa is on par with the dollar but exists only in the form of coins. Banking services are well developed in the urban areas and starting to expand into the rural areas. Credit policies generally are conservative.

National fiscal policy as expressed in the annual budget has been characterized by small deficits in the operating budgets but by large deficits in the capital budgets, caused by excessive spending of the autonomous agencies, with the result that the public debt has been rapidly increasing. The tax system has been reorganized, and direct and indirect taxes contribute almost equally to government revenues. Nontax revenues, mainly from gambling activities controlled by the government, also bring in a considerable share of revenue. Municipalities enjoy partial fiscal independence.

NATIONAL ACCOUNTS

The GNP at current market prices rose at an average annual rate of 6.3 percent during the 1960s to reach more than B/1 billion (1 balboa equals US$1) in 1970. For some of the years the country had the highest GNP growth rate in all of Latin America (for example, 9.5 percent in 1967), and the average rate for the decade ranked it tenth highest of forty-one developing countries studied by the United States Agency for International Development. A dynamic external demand, mostly for services to the Canal Zone, was one of the main elements of economic growth during the 1960s. Investment, which grew at a rate of almost 14 percent annually, was another important factor, and the public sector's share of investment began to increase during the later part of the decade. Public sector consumption also rose relatively fast during the same period (see table 9).

The GDP adjusted for constant prices to reflect real rather than inflationary changes in the economy, grew at a higher rate than the GNP, something that few countries achieve. The relative importance of the contributions of different sectors of the economy to the GDP portion of the GNP has been changing since 1950 and has come to be diversified rather than dependent upon two sectors as it was previously (see table 10). Agriculture, forestry, and fishing have been steadily decreasing as contributors to the GDP. The low productivity of land and labor for staple crops for domestic consumption is the main obstacle to increased agricultural production, although livestock and fishing production has been increasing. Commercial fishing contributes about 2 percent of the total share

Table 9. *Gross National Product of Panama at Current Market Prices, 1960 and 1966–70*
(in millions of balboas)[1]

National Account	1960	1966	1967	1968	1969 [2]	1970 [2]
Consumption expenditure:						
Private	322.9	492.9	536.2	551.8	606.0	692.0
Government	46.9	86.7	102.6	109.7	116.0	131.0
Total	369.8	579.6	638.8	661.5	722.0	823.0
Gross domestic investment:						
Private	56.4	137.1	139.9	158.7	170.0	214.0
Government	11.4	20.1	28.5	33.2	49.0	60.0
Total	67.8	157.2	168.4	191.9	219.0	274.0
Net goods and services from abroad	−47.0	−64.6	−57.7	−49.1	−54.2	−119.8
Gross domestic product	390.6	672.2	749.5	804.3	886.8	977.2
Net factor income from abroad [3]	12.8	30.5	28.5	31.8	32.7	38.8
Gross national product	403.4	702.7	778.0	836.1	919.5	1,016.0

[1] 1 balboa equals US$1.

[2] Preliminary.

[3] Investment income and earnings to the country of residents working abroad less corresponding factor payments made abroad. This is mainly wages and salaries of Panamanian residents working in the Canal Zone.

Table 10. *Gross Domestic Product of Panama by Sector at Constant Prices, 1950, 1960, and 1970*

Sector	Value (in millions of balboas at 1960 prices)[1]			Percentage of Total			Average Annual Growth Rate (in percent)		
	1950	1960	1970	1950	1960	1970	1950-60	1960-69	1969-70
Agriculture, forestry, and fishing	74.5	95.7	167.7	30.9	24.7	20.3	2.5	6.1	2.6
Manufacturing	23.5	54.5	155.6	9.8	14.1	18.8	8.8	12.0	5.1
Miscellaneous services	49.1	69.4	125.8	20.3	17.9	15.2	4.3	5.3	13.7
Wholesale and retail trade	34.9	57.9	125.2	14.4	14.9	15.2	5.1	8.0	8.4
Ownership of buildings	23.3	34.5	61.2	9.7	8.9	7.4	4.0	5.6	9.1
Construction	10.6	22.9	57.1	4.4	5.9	6.9	8.0	9.2	12.8
Transportation, warehousing, and communications	10.0	21.5	52.1	4.2	5.5	6.3	8.0	9.8	4.4
Banking, insurance, and real estate	4.5	10.3	33.5	1.9	2.7	4.1	8.6	8.2	33.5
Public administration	6.7	11.4	24.2	2.8	2.9	2.9	5.5	8.2	4.3
Electricity, gas, and water	3.2	8.4	20.8	1.3	2.2	2.5	10.1	9.8	6.7
Mining	0.6	1.1	2.3	0.3	0.3	0.3	6.2	16.3	-46.5
TOTAL	240.9	387.6	825.5	100.0	100.0	99.9[2]	5.0	7.9	8.3

[1] 1 balboa equals US$1.
[2] Does not total because of rounding.

for **agriculture,** forestry, and fishing but provides the third most important export by value. Another reason for the slow growth of agriculture is that the demand for rice and corn, the two main staples, is not increasing as fast as the population (see ch. 4, Living Conditions).

Manufacturing has developed well in excess of the average increase in the GDP during the 1960s and has become the second most important economic sector. A major reason was the establishment of a refinery near Colón in 1962 to supply ships in transit through the Panama Canal with bunker fuel and to produce refined petroleum products for export. The refinery's activities account for 5 percent of the GDP. The food-processing industry and the metalworking industry also have been expanding, and the government encourages foreign investment by the use of liberal industrial incentive laws.

Miscellaneous services and wholesale and retail trade each contribute over 15 percent to the GDP. Activity in the free trade zone of Colón and the growing tourist industry have helped these sectors (see ch. 13, Trade and Transportation). Some Panamanian government statistics include the wages and salaries of Panamanians working in the Canal Zone as part of the services sector of the GDP but this is not in accordance with standard United Nations national accounts statistical practices. Such income is usually treated as factor income from abroad in the GNP rather than the services account in the GDP. If this income were to be included in the GDP as suggested by Panama, then the services sector, instead of agriculture, would be the leading segment of the economy

Rental income as a share of the GDP has been declining, whereas the contribution of construction, transportation, banking, and utilities have been increasing. The share of public administration has more or less remained stable. Banking has been experiencing the fastest growth rate, and construction was booming in 1970 and 1971 because of new hotels being erected or expanded.

Per capita GNP rose at an average annual rate of 4.5 percent from 1960 through 1969 and by 5 percent in 1970 to a provisional figure of B/664, whch was the third highest in Latin America and double the 1960 figure. The per capita income, however, is considered to be unevenly distributed. About 79 percent of the population is estimated to be receiving less than the per capita average, whereas 8 percent receive more than double the average. The unequal distribution is more evident in rural areas; about 6,000 farmers are estimated to earn over B/1,000 annually, whereas 84,000 have annual incomes under B/100. During the early 1960s, when the per capita GNP was about B/400, about one-third of all farmers were earning less than B/50 annually.

DEVELOPMENT PLANNING

Economic and financial experts agree that the country could produce almost all of the foodstuffs it needs (wheat is an important exception), as well as many of the agricultural raw materials for industrial use, and could simultaneously enlarge its industrial base considerably. Nevertheless, it would always be dependent on the import of more specialized manufactured goods because it does not possess adequate minerals, fuels, and markets to develop competitive industries of great refinement.

Movement toward an integrated and developed economic system depends upon changes that would deeply affect the traditional sociopolitical structure. Fear of such changes have been one of the reasons why even the more sophisticated and responsible members of the wealthy upper class attempted to focus public interest on a revision of the treaty with the United States rather than on sweeping economic reforms. They argued that higher income from the canal and from preferential terms of export to the United States could improve economic conditions temporarily and act as stopgap measures to counter unemployment without endangering the present delicate socioeconomic equilibrium but that large segments of the rural population had little comprehension of the values of long-range development planning and the benefits it might ultimately bring. Even some members of the political opposition resisted sweeping development plans because they feared that the extension of governmental control necessary for an extensive development program might so strengthen the party in power as to render effective opposition difficult or impossible.

The military government that came into power in 1968 and was still governing in late 1971 recognized the need to play a more effective role in solving the country's development problems. It improved public administration and prepared a public investment program to diversify the economy, to expand the production of traditional export products, and to develop activities that had been partially exploited. The tax collection machinery was improved, and some new fiscal measures were adopted to increase government revenues.

The success of the development plan in changing the structure of the economy and raising standards of living depends heavily on sociopolitical and psychological factors. The strong traditional attitudes that advise spectacular short-range solutions in business as well as in politics, as opposed to long-range planning and persistence, continue and have to be reckoned with in any attempted prediction of success or failure.

In the field of public investment planning, the most decisive administrative move toward economic planning on a national scale was the creation in 1961 of the Directorate General of Planning and Administration attached directly to the Office of the Presidency. The head of this office attended cabinet meetings but was without voting power. Before 1961 the government's efforts to stimulate economic development consisted mainly of the granting of tax exemptions to new firms, a small road program, and some extension of health and educational services outside the Metropolitan Area (see Glossary). The Planning Department of the office was in charge of preparing the development plans, and it enabled its government to be the first to present specific plans and projects to be pursued within the framework of the Alliance for Progress at the conference of American states at Punta del Este in August 1961.

Soon after the conference the government published outlines of the Preliminary Five Year Investment Program for the 1961–66 period. This formed the nucleus of the more ambitious Economic and Social Development Program 1963–70, which emphasized the development of agriculture and agriculture-related industries. Priority was to be given to research and extension services, irrigation, better transportation, and marketing facilities. The plan called for total government expenditures of B/310 million and an average annual increase in GNP of 5.5 percent and offered incentives to the private sector to develop specific industries. The plan was not initiated, however, until 1965 because of the political events of 1964 (see ch. 10, Foreign Relations). It became only a two-year program for the period 1964–66; investments were lowered to B/95 million. The plan was further revised to be made applicable to the period 1965–67, and the volume of public investments was then set at B/110 million. Transportation and electric power were given increased emphasis, as were education and housing.

The results of the planning efforts were limited because public investments actually were about half the projected figures; and agriculture, which was originally to be emphasized, was neglected, more attention being given to housing and highways instead. Frequent staff turnovers (with the best talents moved to other positions of authority) and internal political pressures were responsible for the difficulties. In 1967 the new Four Year Development Plan was under preparation for implementation in 1968.

The government that took over in late 1968 gave the Planning Department more responsibility. The result was the Public Investment Program for 1969–72, built over the already existing Four Year Development Plan. It was soon realized that the new plan was too optimistic, although it had been well prepared and feasibility studies had been completed on some of the proposed projects.

The investment program's expenditures, therefore, were revised downward, and the time period was extended through 1974. The program was again revised in 1970 to include new suggestions from various ministries and extended this time through 1975. The final revision called for an average gross domestic product growth rate of 8 percent annually, and primary emphasis was again given to agriculture. Health, education, transportation, and electrification were other important areas given priority. Total public investment through 1975 was projected at about B/550 million, with most of the outlays to come from foreign borrowing.

In addition to the Public Investment Program, the Planning Department prepared the Ten-Year Strategy for National Development, setting forth priority goals for the 1970s but without detailed plans or analyses. The strategy assumes that increased revenues will come from the Canal Zone and from a growth in tourism. It is also assumed that the Colón Free Zone will double its capacity during the 1970s. More emphasis is given to expanding agriculture, particularly export products such as livestock, fish, fruits, and vegetables. Isolated rural areas would be opened up via roads, electrification, and an intensified agrarian reform program.

BUDGET

Until World War II each branch of government spent public funds according to its own judgment, and it was not until 1941 that an overall budget for the central government was established. Before 1960 the overall budget was prepared by the comptroller general, who submitted it directly to the National Assembly. Budget control was exercised by the comptroller general, who thus had de facto veto power over the fiscal operations of the executive branch. Since 1960, and as of late 1971, the Budget Department in the Office of the Presidency prepared the budgets, which ran on a calendar-year basis. Separate operating and capital budgets were prepared, and program budgeting was followed in both budgets. All operating budgets were carefully prepared, and only small deficits occurred; larger deficits occurred in the capital budget. Deficits usually are carried over into the next year and paid from current revenues, a bond issue, or a loan.

The operating budget was B/130 million in both 1968 and 1969, B/163 million in 1970, and almost B/196 million in 1971. The capital budget in 1969 was about B/50 million; it increased to B/94 million in 1970 and rose to B/121 million in 1971. In the late 1960s not all of the proposed expenditures were in fact made. Most of the operating budget is spent by the central government, but part is transferred to various autonomous agencies and institutions, such as the Institute for Housing and Urbanization and the National Water Supply and Sewerage Institute. The fact that the major share of the capital expenditures was spent by autonomous entities caused the public debt to increase. The central government has been exercising stricter control of the finances of the autonomous entities since the mid-1960s. In addition to transfers from the central government, revenue for the autonomous entities comes from their own operations and from loans, both foreign and domestic. It has been estimated that the combined budgets of all twenty autonomous agencies total over B/100 million annually.

Expenditures

Budgeted expenditures have been characterized by an emphasis on the social and economic ministries. Since the mid-1960s the Ministry of Education has received the largest single allocation, over 23 percent in 1970 (see table 11). Appropriations for the University of Panama are treated separately, mainly to emphasize the significance of the university as a symbol of national educational advance. By law the annual appropriation for the university cannot be less than the previous year, and salaries must be increased by 15 percent annually. If the university allocation is added to that of the Ministry of Education, the share of education in the 1970 budget rose to 26.6 percent.

Amortization of the public debt (foreign and domestic), which has been increasing, took the second largest share in the 1969 and 1970 budgets. The amounts and percentages are expected to be even higher in future budgets because of heavy debts incurred from 1968 through 1971. The Ministry of Government and Justice, which received the next largest amount, spent most of it on the National Guard. Local government, communications, and other domestic services received the remainder of this ministry's share. The Ministry of Health disbursed in 1970 the fourth largest percentage of government revenue—over 12 percent. Until 1969 it received the second largest amount, but it had been combined with the Ministry of Labor and Social Welfare. It is also responsible for the administrative costs of the Red Cross and several other services.

Transfers of funds to the autonomous institutions, international organizations of which Panama is a member, and the Social Security Fund have been taking an increasing percentage annually and in 1970 amounted to 7.6 percent of the total budget. The Ministry of Public Works receives varying amounts, depending upon planned government construction projects. The largest part of its budget goes for the maintenance of public buildings. Expenditures of the Ministry of Finance and Treasury also fluctuate.

Table 11. Panamanian Central Government Operating Budget, 1970
(in balboas)*

Revenues	Amount	Percent	Expenditures	Amount	Percent
Tax Revenues:			National Assembly	126,482	0.1
Direct taxes	59,867,000	36.8	Comptroller general	3,341,630	2.0
Indirect taxes	59,211,000	36.4	Presidency	3,287,162	2.0
Total	119,078,000	73.2	Ministries:		
Nontax Revenues:			Government and Justice	23,619,736	14.5
Rent and sale of government			Foreign Affairs	3,190,097	2.0
assets	2,366,000	1.4	Finance and Treasury	4,949,493	3.0
Public services	9,867,000	6.0	Education	37,769,676	23.2
Profits of state enterprises	17,690,000	10.9	Public Works	7,900,000	4.9
Transfers to government	2,706,000	1.7	Agriculture and Livestock	5,606,721	3.4
Other miscellaneous	11,000,000	6.8	Health	20,054,712	12.3
Total	43,622,000	26.8	Commerce and Industry	2,012,687	1.2
			Labor and Social Welfare	1,783,925	1.1
GRAND TOTAL	162,700,000	100.0	University of Panama	5,500,000	3.4
			Judicial branch	2,045,227	1.3
			Public Ministry	1,138,249	0.7
			Electoral Tribunal	907,070	0.6
			Foreign debt	13,196,244	8.1
			Domestic debt	13,600,495	8.4
			Current transfers	11,483,307	7.1
			Capital transfers	881,557	0.5
			Office of Price Control	305,530	0.2
			GRAND TOTAL	162,700,000	100.0

* 1 balboa equals US$1.

Source: Adapted from Republic of Panama, Contraloría General de la República, Dirección de Estadística y Censo, *Estadística panameña, año XXIX: Hacienda pública y finanzas, año 1969* (Series "E", No. 1), Panama City, 1970, p. 2.

The Ministry of Agriculture and Livestock receives over 3 percent of the budget annually, but agriculture as an economic sector actually receives a much larger share of total government expenditures because of the agricultural activities of the autonomous entities, such as the Institute for Economic Development (Instituto de Fomento Económico—IFE).

The comptroller general, the Office of the Presidency, and the Ministry of Foreign Affairs each receive about 2 percent of the budget. The comptroller general's office includes the active and efficient Directorate of Statistics and Census, which collects and publishes current economic data. The expenses of the Office of the Presidency are attributable to increased planning activities of the Directorate General for Planning and Administration. About half of the expenses of the Ministry of Foreign Affairs are for diplomatic representation in foreign countries. All other ministries, the legislature, and the judiciary receive smaller percentages.

In the 1970 capital budget the largest share of public investment was 22 percent for housing. This was followed closely by transportation, 20 percent, and agriculture, 19 percent. Health and sanitation absorbed 15 percent; electrification, 10.5 percent; and all other activities, smaller percentages.

Revenue

The main sources of government income changed radically after a large-scale tax reform was implemented in 1964. Before then the bulk of income had come from import and export duties, excise taxes on alcohol, and gambling activities. Income and property tax rates were low, and enforcement of tax collection was lax and uneven. Since 1964, and as of 1971, the income tax had become the most important source of revenue, and customs duties and nontax revenues had become less important (see table 12). Total revenue increased at a rate of nearly 12 percent annually from 1965 through 1969 and by over 20 percent in 1970. About half the 1970 increase came from amendments to the income tax law, some new import charges, and a change in the basis of calculating cigarette taxes. Revenue for 1971 was expected to rise by about 15 percent because of the new tax measures of 1970 and more vigorous tax enforcement procedures.

The system of revenue administration was highly centralized. The General Directorate of Revenues of the Ministry of Finance and Treasury collected all taxes and revenues, including customs duties at ports of entry. The Panama City tax office, one of four regional tax offices, handled 80 percent of all tax collections. In 1970 the tax auditors were given the power to make searches, seizures, and arrests without a judicial order, and the penalties for

Table 12. Panamanian Central Government Current Revenues, 1966–70
(in millions of balboas)*

Account	1966		1967		1968		1969		1970	
	Amount	Percent	Amount	Percent	Amount	Percent	Amount	Percent	Amount	Percent
Direct Taxes:										
Income	29.6	29.5	34.2	30.3	37.3	31.2	41.0	30.8	54.5	34.0
Property, gift, and										
inheritance	4.9	4.9	5.0	4.4	5.5	4.6	7.1	5.3	7.6	4.8
Total	34.5	34.4	39.2	34.7	42.8	35.8	48.1	36.1	62.1	38.8
Indirect Taxes:										
Foreign trade	24.8	24.7	27.8	24.7	27.7	23.2	31.0	23.3	37.5	23.4
Production and sales	14.4	14.4	15.4	13.6	16.4	13.7	18.9	14.2	22.8	14.3
License fees and stamp taxes	4.4	4.4	4.8	4.3	5.1	4.3	6.0	4.5	6.3	3.9
Total	43.6	43.5	48.0	42.6	49.2	41.2	55.9	42.0	66.6	41.6
Nontax revenue	22.2	22.1	25.5	22.7	27.4	23.0	29.1	21.9	31.4	19.6
TOTAL	100.3	100.0	112.7	100.0	119.4	100.0	133.1	100.0	160.1	100.0

* 1 balboa equals US$1.

tax violations were increased. All tax violations are categorized as either delinquency, fraud, or violation and omission. Delinquency is defined as late payment of taxes and in 1971 incurred a 10-percent surcharge of the amount owed plus 7 percent interest until paid. If the case goes to a tribunal, the taxpayer incurs an additional surcharge if he loses the case.

Old tax debts could be cancelled by a payment of 50 percent of the amount owed and the balance in monthly installments. Fraud, however, was penalized by a fine of either five or ten times the amount of the fraud or by imprisonment for one month to one year. Violations and omissions, such as the lack of proper account books, were penalized only by fines ranging from B/10 to B/1,000; but if the fine was not paid, the taxpayer could be imprisoned by the order of the ministry at the rate of one day for every B/2 owed. In addition, all taxpayers needed a tax clearance certificate in order to perform certain legal acts, to enter into contracts, or to acquire a passport. Panama has been the headquarters of the Inter-American Center of Tax Administrators since its formation in 1967 and thus receives the benefits of new ideas in tax administration earlier than other countries.

Gambling, particularly the National Welfare Lottery, was the most important source of the nontax revenues. The popular lottery, which started in 1850, provided as much as 10 percent of the total annual revenues of the government, and drawings took place weekly. Several government-owned casinos were located in tourist hotels, and the government operated horseracing. Income from public services includes the sale of water, postal services, airport fees, and public registry fees. The principal income from government assets is the Panama Canal annuity. Loans are another source of revenue, but most of it is used for public investments under the capital budget.

Taxation

Before 1964 the government's fiscal policy was based upon a belief that low taxes would stimulate savings and private investment. After 1964 the governmental policy was that the public sector should stimulate investment and that the tax burden for the necessary projects should be redistributed in a progressive manner. The 1964 reforms and the 1970 adjustments have produced an adequate tax system, according to outside experts, and the government was continuing to study further tax revisions in 1970. The tax burden on the population, higher than the average for Latin America, was 14.4 percent of the GNP in 1970; however, the government recognized that higher revenues were required to sustain the momentum of the previous decade's economic development.

Income taxes are the most important direct tax and accounted for 34 percent of total revenue in 1970. The first such tax dates from 1934, but until 1964 there were no detailed regulations, and interpretation of the basic law varied over the years. Tax evasion also was common until 1965, when the auditing section of the Ministry of Finance and Treasury was expanded. As of 1971 only income from Panamanian sources was taxable, and income from the following activities was exempt: billing from a Panamanian-based office for the sale of commodities negotiated outside the country, directing of business operations abroad from Panama, and dividends from income not produced in the country.

All individuals earning over B/600 a year and all married persons earning over B/1,000, as well as all businesses, must file an income tax return. Since withholding is in effect for many individual taxpayers, they usually do not owe much at the end of the tax year. A number of items are deductible, and some are nontaxable for both individuals and businesses. Interest on government bonds, savings accounts, prizes, and gambling profits, for example, are not taxable. For individuals, an exemption of B/150 per dependent is allowed and medical expenses over 5 percent of taxable income, as well as donations and interest paid on loans and mortgages, are deductible. After all deductions and exemptions are allowed, only about 2 percent of the population actually pays an income tax, with most of the income tax being paid by businesses.

In general only two tax tables, each with progressive rates, are used to determine tax liability. One is for individuals, with rates ranging from a low of 2.5 percent on the first B/1,000 of taxable income to a high of 56 percent on taxable income over B/200,000. The other tax table is for corporations and partnerships, and the rates range from 10 percent on taxable income under B/15,001 toto 50 percent on income over B/500,001. The upper rate is the second highest corporation tax rate in the Western Hemisphere. Some special income tax rates exist for certain activities. Transportation companies pay only on income attributable to operations in Panama; therefore, most of the foreign-owned registered vessels do not pay a tax even if the contracts are signed in Panama. Those transportation companies that are subject to the Panamanian income tax may elect to consider 10 percent of their gross income as taxable income in Panama to simplify their accounting. All subsidiaries of foreign corporations submitting profit remittances to their head offices abroad pay a 10 percent dividend income tax on the amount of the remittance.

The two other direct taxes levied are a property tax and a gift and inheritance tax. The property tax is levied on all land and buildings having an assessed value of more than B/500. In order to stimulate the construction industry during the business recession following the 1968 political disturbances, property taxes were exempted for a period of ten years on new buildings constructed between December 1, 1968, and February 28, 1970. In principle an additional tax is levied on idle, privately owned rural lands over 500 hectares (1 hectare equals 2.47 acres) in size. The tax, however, is almost never levied because, for every hectare being worked, five idle hectares are exempt from the tax. Farmers working land to which they had no title were assessed 50 centesimos (1 centesimo equals US$0.01) per hectare as of 1971. A cadastre, or registration, of rural lands, scheduled for completion in 1972, was expected to provide a better basis for assessing rural land taxes.

The inheritance and gift tax is levied on proceeds to the recipients rather than on the estate. The rates are progressive and range from 4 percent on the first B/5,000 to 33.75 percent on properties valued over B/400,000. They also vary according to the degree of relationship involved, being higher for distant relatives and unrelated persons.

The principal indirect taxes are import duties. Since the income tax has assumed a greater role, many imported items are granted free entry under the various investment incentive laws. In 1969, for example, one-fifth of all imports were exempt from duties. In addition, most customs duties are very low, ranging from 5 to 20 percent on most items, with a high of 50 percent for wood products. A general ad valorem surcharge of 6 percent of the duty assessed is levied on all goods except foods, medicines, and a few other items, and 3.5 percent is levied on all imported foods. Some export duties are also levied, with the most important applicable to bananas: B/0.02 per stem. Consular fees amount to over 12 percent of total foreign trade tax revenue.

Production and sales taxes were the next most important indirect taxes. They are applicable only to selected items and are not general. The most important in terms of producing revenue are those on the sale of gasoline and the manufacture of alcoholic beverages, cigarettes, and a few other luxury items. Other indirect taxes are derived from revenue stamps and stamped paper, which must be used on most documents, and from business license fees. Business and industrial license fees are levied in proportion to the capital of the enterprise and must be paid during the first three months of every year. Some minor indirect taxes are levied on insurance premiums, admissions to public entertainment, raffles and other games of chance not run directly by the government, livestock slaughtering, and the rental of stalls in privately owned public markets. A new education tax to become effective September 1, 1971, was to be levied on business payrolls in order to finance the training of skilled workers.

Local Finances

Provinces have no fiscal independence. The costs of provincial administration are included in the budget of the Ministry of Government and Justice. The sixty-five municipalities, however, are entitled by law to collect taxes and fees for their own use, although the national government provides for virtually all their public services through the appropriate central ministries.

Municipal finances are managed by the municipal treasurer, appointed by the district council for a period of four years. He prepares the annual budget and submits it to the council, which approves and forwards it to the mayor for signature and execution. The Planning Department of the Office of the Presidency offers advice to municipal governments on fiscal operations.

The combined revenue of all municipalities amounted to B/7.78 million in 1969, and only thirteen of them had budgets of more than B/50,000, with Panama City accounting for more than half of the total. During the 1960s the combined municipal budgets were balanced every year except 1968, when a small deficit occurred.

General administration of the municipalities absorbs nearly 60 percent of the total municipal expenditures. Twenty percent is spent on education; a 1954 law requires 15 percent of total municipal revenues to be spent on general education and 5 percent on physical education. About 15 percent is spent on public works (mostly maintenance of streets, buildings, parks, and cemeteries); 4 percent, on health and sanitation; and the balance, on miscellaneous expenditures.

About 55 percent of municipal revenues come from local taxes; 25 percent, from municipal services; 10 percent, from national government grants; and the balance, from miscellaneous sources. Municipal services include the supply of electricity and water, income rental for use of municipal property, and the sale of municipal property. Although on an overall basis the national government provides only a limited amount of fiscal assistance, certain smaller cities are very dependent upon this source, which may account for from 50 to 80 percent of their total revenues.

Law 8 of February 1, 1954, which governs municipalities, lists forty-eight different categories of items that may be taxed by municipalities. Each municipality imposes its own fees and taxes at rates that are revised every four years, with the taxpayer having the right to appeal the revision. The two leading taxes are the vehicle license tax and business licenses for commercial and industrial establishments.

PUBLIC DEBT

Although Panama started its era of independence with practically no debt, by 1960 it had accumulated over B/87 million. As a result of extensive borrowing during the 1960s, the total public debt had soared to over B/434 million by the end of 1970, of which B/280 million was external and the balance domestic. The rapidly rising debt has been caused by increased expenditures for public investment not covered by current revenues. Panama has established a good international credit standing by meeting its obligations and, on occasions, paying even before the debt was due.

The internal debt of over B/154 million was the result of a combination of about eighty different bond issues, several short-term treasury bills, plus the floating debt on unpaid obligations. Bond issues had been well received by the investing public until 1963, when enthusiasm for them began to diminish, and after that were sold at a discount from face that reached a high of 35 percent following the 1968 political disturbances. The government also aggravated the situation by paying contractors and suppliers in bonds instead of cash. The bonds were then dumped on the market in order to obtain working capital. Private individuals held about half of the outstanding bonds, the Social Security Fund held 45 percent, and banks held the rest. Interest on the bonds ranged from 1 to 7 percent, with almost 70 percent of them paying 6 percent. The treasury bills, which were sold for the first time in 1969, mature in three or six months. They are interest-tax free and sold only to banks. The floating debt varies annually and consists primarily of unpaid central government obligations to the Social Security Fund and unpaid bills of contractors and suppliers. From time to time the floating debt is converted into longer term bonds.

The external debt consists mainly of over seventy loans from foreign private and public institutions, including international organizations, plus three outstanding bond issues sold on the United States market between 1960 and 1962. A small amount is owed for the purchase of equipment from abroad. About 30 percent of the total foreign was contracted by autonomous institutions, all in the form of long-term development loans paying a relatively low rate of interest, mostly under 4 percent. Although most of the central government's loans are also long-term low interest, some of its short-term debt is high interest—over 8 and 9 percent. Some of the short-term loans were refinanced in 1970 and 1971, but it was estimated that as much as 25 percent of the government's anticipated revenues for 1972 would have to be used to pay off the short-term loans falling due in that year if they could not be further refinanced.

BANKING AND CURRENCY

Panama has adequate banking and financial facilities in the

urban centers and a growing network of credit institutions in the rural areas. The geographic spread of banking services, however, has not been accompanied by as great an extension of credit facilities to the lower income groups who do not share substantially in the money economy. The commercial banks have had notable freedom of action and recorded rapid growth from 1960 through 1967. The political disturbances of 1968 temporarily brought bank growth to a halt (see ch. 9, Political Dynamics and Values). The expansion resumed in 1969, however, particularly in deposits from foreign banks to Panamanian banks.

The banks are becoming a haven for foreign-owned capital because of higher interest rates being paid on deposits, numbered accounts that provide secrecy for the owners, and the country's geographic position in Latin America, with daily air contacts with all capital cities. A number of foreign banks are also transferring some of their assets to their branches in Panama for relending to other Latin American customers. Of the total deposits of nearly B/490 million in the banking system in 1969, foreigners owned about B/273 million, or 56 percent.

The country has no central bank with regulatory powers and, because of the absence of adequate controls, foreign interest groups on occasion have established temporary bases in Panama and withdrawn after their transactions have been completed. Such operations, as in the case of one bank that disappeared in 1961 with B/4 million in assets, have often led to doubts about their ultimate intention and legality. In 1970 the government, determined to improve the image of the banking industry and to ensure a sound banking system, created the National Bank Commission with full powers to regulate reserve requirements, interest rates, and financial practices. The commission is composed of seven members who are representatives of the government and of private banks. The law creating the National Banking Commission classified all banks as one of three kinds; those incorporated to operate in Panama, those organized in Panama but operating abroad, and foreign banks maintaining only a resident representative in the country. As of mid-1971 all foreign banks were required to have at least B/1 million in capital plus a capital reserve of 5 percent of assets; 85 percent of checking account deposits must be re-lent for productive purposes; 50 percent of savings account deposits must be used for home mortgages; 12 percent of the checking accounts and 6 percent of the savings accounts must be held as reserves, with 30 percent of the total reserve in legal tender and 70 percent on deposit in the National Bank of Panama/or in Panamanian treasury securities.

Banks

In 1971 about ninety corporations were registered as banks, but many of them were not active. The new banking law of 1970 was partially designed to force them to act as banks or dissolve. By mid-1971 there were two official banks and twenty-one private banks, most of them foreign owned, in operation (see table 13). Seventeen of the banks were opened between 1963 and 1971, and another six were seeking permission during 1971 to begin operations. The combined assets of the existing banks at the end of 1969 totaled almost B/578 million, of which B/434 million, or 75 percent, constituted outstanding loans (see table 14).

The National Bank of Panama (Banco Nacional de Panamá— BNP) is one of the two government-owned banks. The oldest bank in the country, it began as a mortgage loan bank and was reorganized as a full commercial bank in 1956. In 1969 it absorbed another government institution, the Bank of Popular Credit (Banco Crédito Popular), which had been created in 1962 to make small loans to low-income workers. Although not a central bank, it exercises some fiscal functions and is the official depository and fiscal agent of the central government, the provinces, the munici-

Table 13. Panamanian Banking Institutions, June 30, 1971

Bank	Year Established	Number of Branches and Agencies	Total Establishments
National Bank of Panama	1904	32	33
Savings Bank	1934	18	19
First National City Bank	1904	14	15
The Chase Manhattan Bank	1915	6	7
Bank of Colombia	1964	6	7
Panama Bank and Trust Company	1948	5	6
Bank of America	1964	5	6
Foreign Bank	1967	5	6
United States Investment Bank	1969	3	4
National Savings and Loan Company	1963	2	3
Bank of London and Montreal	1966	1	2
Mercantile Bank of Panama	1966	1	2
Coffee Bank	1966	1	2
Bank of Santander and Panama	1967	1	2
Bank of Commerce	1967	1	2
Bank of Bogotá	1967	1	2
Philanthropic Bank	1969	1	2
General Bank	1955	0	1
First National Bank of Chicago	1971	0	1
German-Panamanian Bank	1970	0	1
Spanish Bank of Credit	1970	0	1
Swiss Bank Corporation	1970	0	1
Bank of Tokyo	1971	0	1
TOTAL		103	126

Table 14. Summary Balance Sheet of Panamanian Banking Institutions, 1965–69

(in thousands of balboas)[1]

Account	1965	1966	1967	1968	1969
Assets:					
Cash and other monetary assets	29,735.5	33,748.6	34,040.2	40,723.6	37,772.4
Net bank deposits[2] ..	16,114.2	26,461.3	29,980.2	41,191.3	76,372.7
Loans	184,302.2	240,818.7	263,263.5	302,614.9	433,920.6
Securities	2,382.0	3,081.5	4,993.6	6,779.6	8,612.4
Other assets[3]	9,229.4	17,930.6	17,057.6	15,534.1	21,079.7
TOTAL	241,763.3	322,040.7	349,335.1	406,843.5	577,757.8
Liabilities:					
Demand deposits	84,698.3	89,195.1	104,033.5	111,671.6	128,319.7
Time deposits	90,412.1	106,925.5	132,325.5	150,156.7	198,131.4
Interbank deposits[4] ..	34,528.2	79,395.0	66,935.2	92,772.4	163,104.7
Other liabilities	13,182.3	26,027.9	25,822.4	31,081.1	58,610.2
Capital	15,194.8	16,594.8	17,562.8	18,212.9	21,912.6
Reserves	3,747.6	3,902.4	2,655.7	2,948.8	7,679.2
TOTAL	241,763.3	322,040.7	349,335.1	406,843.5	577,757.8

[1] 1 balboa equals US$1.
[2] Deposits into other banks, both locally and abroad, and in the International Monetary Fund.
[3] Real estate, equipment, and receivables.
[4] Mostly foreign banks making deposits into Panamanian banks.

Source: Adapted from Republic of Panama, Contraloría General de la República, Dirección de Estadística y Censo, *Estadística panameña, año XXIX: Hacienda pública y finanzas, año 1969*, (Series "E", No. 1), Panama City, 1970, pp. 64, 66–72.

palities, and the autonomous agencies. The bank is managed by a manager and a five-man board of directors, of which the finance minister is a member. From 1968 to 1970 the bank experienced frequent changes in management. In 1968 many private depositors withdrew their funds at the same time that the government was borrowing heavily from the bank, and it was not until the end of 1970 that the bank's deposits and assets were rebuilt to the 1968 level. Still, the BNP is the largest bank and held about 20 percent of the total banking system assets in 1970. It has numerous branches throughout the country, and the policy is to open additional branches in smaller localities.

The other government-owned bank is the Savings Bank (Caja de Ahorros), founded in 1934. By 1970 it had about 5 percent of the total assets in the banking system. Accumulated savings of its depositors are used for granting loans on real estate and on tangibles with open market value. It has made important contributions to the economy, making over B/100 million in loans from its inception through 1970, and in one way or another has served about half the population of the country.

The oldest private bank, the First National City Bank, first began operations in 1904 as the International Bank. The Chase Manhattan Bank, started in Panama as the Commercial National Bank of Washington, has a large technical staff aiding its customers. The Panama Bank and Trust Company (Banco Fiduciario de Panama) is a subsidiary of the National Bank for Commerce and Industry (Banque Nationale pour le Commerce et l'Industrie) of Paris with a large participation of Panamanian capital. Many other banks are subsidiaries of German, Swiss, Spanish, Colombian, British, Japanese, and United States institutions. All the banks are headquartered in Panama City except the Coffee Bank (Banco Cafetero), which has its headquarters in Colón and maintains weekly B/100 lotteries based upon passbook numbers in order to stimulate deposits.

Other Financial Institutions

There were twenty-four finance companies operating in 1970, with total assets of about B/36 million. Thirteen of them were commercial credit companies, mainly financing automobile and home appliance purchases; five were in the business of granting small personal loans; four were home loan savings and loan associations; and two were industrial development institutions. The most important of these finance companies is Industrial Development, formed jointly in 1963 by the government and private individuals with the assistance of the United States Agency for International Development. By 1971 it was totally privately owned by 281 Panamanian stockholders, and its authorized capital was B/14 million. It was authorized to grant medium- and long-term loans to new industries. The Industrial Development corporation prefers to lend for equipment and buildings but also will make loans for working capital if they are tied to equipment and building loans. All loans must serve to increase employment, increase exports, utilize national raw materials, or substitute for imports. Loans are granted for up to fifteen years plus a three-year grace period at 9 percent interest. As of June 1970 the Industrial Development corporation had authorized 152 loans for a total of B/12 million. It also has created a subsidiary corporation to develop idle land for industrial parks.

About twenty-four insurance companies were operating in 1969, having total assets of over B/41 million. Most of the investments of the insurance companies are in real estate, but increasing amounts are starting to go into industrial development. The Social

Security Fund, although not a banking institution, is authorized to use funds accumulated from its insured members to purchase government bonds and to make loans to industry and housing, the amount of the loan depending upon the security offered by the borrower. Also engaged in credit operations is IFE, which obtains the bulk of its funds from the central government's budget and a smaller part from its own operations. IFE grants loans to agriculture, housing, and industry.

Decree Law 17 of 1954 established the National Council of Cooperatives to help promote agricultural and credit cooperatives. By June 1970 there were nearly 200 functioning cooperatives with over 22,000 members. The largest number, 115, were credit cooperatives; twenty-eight were consumer cooperatives; twenty-two were agricultural cooperatives; and the others were miscellaneous. The credit cooperatives are located mainly in urban areas and are the fastest growing. Seventy-five of them belong to the Federation of Credit Cooperatives (Federación de Cooperativas de Crédito), which was financially strengthened in 1971 by the receipt of a B/2 million loan from the United States Agency for International Development for relending to members. Twenty-three of the consumer cooperatives are located on banana plantations and help to lower the cost of goods brought in from the urban areas. Many of the agricultural cooperatives were in financial difficulties because of poor management.

No established stock market existed as of 1971, but securities issued by private business and the government were sold directly to the buyer or through an intermediary, such as a bank or a stockbroker, or by advertisement in the various means of mass communication. The Stock Brokers Association of Panama publishes daily in the press the prices of about 100 domestic securities. To encourage the development of a capital market and the creation of a formal stock exchange, a new securities law was passed in 1970, and the National Securities Commission was created to supervise the registration, issue, sale, and transfer of securities. The commission, which is composed of the minister of commerce and industry, the manager of the BNP, and three private members, was starting to issue its regulations in 1971. Mutual funds in particular are more strictly regulated; all foreign mutual funds must have at least B/5 million paid-up capital before commencing operations in the country, whereas Panamanian mutual funds require only B/200,000 in capital. One-third of all mutual fund sales must be invested in Panama.

Credit

Financial policies have had the effect of making adequate capital available for production and investment at home and for relending abroad. In addition to the incoming foreign deposits, domestic demand and time deposits have been increasing steadily. Savings habits of the people have been fostered by a high degree of confidence in the currency and the banks and by government insurance of up to B/10,000 on all savings accounts. The number of savings accounts grew from 89,000 in 1960 to over 225,000 at the end of 1969. The two government banks have more accounts than all the other banks combined, but the private banks had more funds on deposit, as the government Savings Bank caters to the small saver in particular. Over 171,000 of the total accounts held less than B/250 apiece.

Banks are conservative in granting medium- and long-term loans except for mortgages and industry. Most loans are short term— under three years. Although the credit granted is diversified, commercial activities receive the largest amount. Loans to foreign borrowers have assumed increasing importance as the international operations of the banks expand. Personal consumption loans have become more important to some banks and are also provided by the small finance companies and savings and loan associations. The increase in personal loans is due in part to the liberalized credit policies of the official banks and the greater job security attained by many persons, such as teachers, who have increased the number of credit-worthy borrowers.

The BNP is the most active bank in lending for activities not usually covered by other banks, such as fishing and forestry. Most of the loan portfolio of the BNP is in commercial credits and personal loans. It makes many small loans, particularly since its takeover of the Bank of Popular Credit in 1969. Over 50,000 small consumer loans were made by the BNP in 1970. In the late 1960s the BNP started to place more emphasis on loans to agriculture and industry, but it is handicapped by a lack of sufficiently qualified professionals to appraise the merits of the development projects. Out of a staff of 900 persons in 1971, only four were economists, and eighteen were technical specialists.

The large agricultural producers have access to the private banks for loans to finance livestock, cash crops, and the processing of products for export. The Ministry of Agriculture and Livestock and IFE concentrate on the small and medium farmers through a supervised credit system. The Ministry of Agriculture and Livestock will make loans only to farmers whose production is less than B/1,000 annually. IFE grants credits via rural credit boards and does not duplicate any program of the Ministry of Agriculture and Livestock. In 1970 IFE made 4,500 loans, and its total outstanding portfolio was about B/11 million. The Chase Manhattan Bank was the first private bank to initiate, in 1950, a program of agricultural credits coupled with technical assistance to the farmer. As of 1970 it had lent over B/80 million to farmers, mostly for livestock development.

Currency

Panama has a double currency system. Both the balboa, created in 1904, and the United States dollar are legal tender and circulate freely in the country. The balboa is divided into 100 centesimos and is at par with the dollar. In mid-1971 it was one of five world currencies with the longest lifespan since its value was last altered —over thirty-seven years. There are no paper balboas, only coins that correspond exactly in size and metallic content to United States coins. The number of coins in circulation is limited by a monetary agreement with the United States. A silver balboa is commonly called a rucano, and the ten-centesimo coin is frequently referred to as a real. The only paper currency is the United States dollar.

Ownership of gold is legal, and the balboa and the dollar can be freely exchanged into gold. There are no foreign exchange restrictions, and no black market exists. All foreign exchange transactions are based on New York money market quotations, and gold and foreign exchange can be shipped anywhere, giving the residents the greatest currency freedom in the world.

Since there is no paper balboa, the government cannot increase the stock of money by artificial means via the printing press, and this helps the country in experiencing a high degree of price stability. Panama is one of five countries in the world without government control over the amount of currency in circulation. Some foreign economists believe this lack of control is good for the economy. Although the gold and foreign exchange reserves of the banking system were at a historic high of over the equivalent of US$304 million at the end of 1970, the total amount of money in circulation is not known because of substantial private holdings of United States notes and coins.

The cost-of-living index did not rise by more than 2 percent in any year during the 1960s, and the average annual increase for the 1960–69 period was 1.2 percent. Inflationary pressures, however, became noticeable in 1970—mainly because of the higher prices of imported products and increased domestic building costs—and the index rose by over 3 percent in that year.

CHAPTER 12

AGRICULTURE AND INDUSTRY

Agriculture, forestry, and fishing engaged the labor of the largest segment of the economically active population in 1970, about 40 percent, but contributed only about 20 percent to the gross domestic product (GDP). Industrial activity, which included manufacturing, mining, construction, and energy, employed 18 percent of the labor force but contributed almost 29 percent to the GDP (see ch. 11, Character and Structure of the Economy).

Nearly 30 percent of the country's total area of 18,685,000 acres serves agriculture, but only about 6.6 percent is used for crop production. Almost 16 percent is in pastures, and the balance of the agricultural land is used for miscellaneous purposes or left fallow. Although there are over 100,000 farms, there are only a few dozen large holdings with a high degree of technical development and about 30,000 farms utilizing varying degrees of modern practices and producing for the market. The vast majority are small subsistence farms still using traditional methods and producing less than B/100 (1 balboa equals US$1) annually. Only 4,200 farms have annual sales of more than B/1,000.

Most farmers do not own the land they cultivate. The largest number—about two-thirds—are squatters on state or private land. The others are renters, paid agricultural laborers, and owners. Twenty percent of all farmland is included in 224 large holdings of over 1,250 acres, including some owned by the state. More than half of all farms are under 12.5 acres. Little social pressure had resulted from the uneven distribution of land, however, because relatively large amounts of virgin tracts of arable land belonging to the state are available for distribution to those who want land. Under an agrarian reform program, the granting of legal titles to squatters working government land was underway in 1971.

The major food products are bananas, the leading export, and rice and corn, which are the primary food staples. Shrimp, sugar, and beef make growing contributions to export. Other important products are coffee, beans, cacoa, tubers, tobacco, tomatoes, citrus fruits, other fruits and vegetables, eggs, poultry, and fishmeal.

In general, the productivity of land and agricultural labor is low.

A study by the government in 1967 indicated that the per capita value of production by workers in agriculture was B/780 per year, whereas the per capita value of production by workers in nonagricultural activities was B/2,614. The average value of production per acre was less than B/30. Using the average annual production of the 1961–65 period as a base of 100, the index of total agricultural production as well as that of food production had risen to 136 by 1970, mainly because of rapid increases in the production of bananas, rice, and livestock. The per capita index of each in 1970, however, was much smaller—108—because of the rapid population growth, which was nearly outpacing agricultural production.

The government gives priority to stimulating the production of certain crops, such as rice, beans, and corn, and livestock; grants technical assistance and loans; provides marketing services; and guarantees to purchase stipulated products at a fixed price. Its role in industry is less direct, except for power production, which is the exclusive right of an autonomous government entity. The government stimulates industrial production mainly by granting the industries fiscal benefits under an industrial development law, and since the mid-1950s the industrial sector has been one of the most dynamic elements of the economy. Between 1950 and 1970 the value of manufacturing more than tripled.

Manufacturing contributed almost 19 percent to the gross domestic product in 1970; construction, almost 7 percent; power, about 2.5 percent; and mining, a negligible amount. Discoveries of minerals, particularly copper ore, in the 1968–71 period may lead to an expansion of mining.

Data on the number of industrial establishments vary, but 2,358 productive enterprises were registered with the government in 1969, the majority in manufacturing. Most companies were small; total capital investment of all companies as declared for tax purposes was about B/125 million, with 73 percent declaring less than B/10,000 capital investment. The Panama Refinery (Refinería Panamá) and five other companies accounted for B/94 million of the total.

The 424,000 persons aged fifteen and over who were economically active during 1969 constituted some 30 percent of the population, about the same proportion as that recorded during 1960. More than one-fourth were girls and women, one-half were wage and salary earners, and two persons in five were engaged in agriculture and related occupations.

The important changes that occurred in the composition of the labor force during the 1960s were in large part consequences of the massive urban migration taking place during those years. In 1971,

270

although farming continued to occupy more workers than either the industrial or the services sector of employment, its relative strength had suffered a sharp decline. At the same time, a sharp rise in the rate of female participation in the labor force came as a consequence of the migration to urban centers of young farm-women seeking better job opportunities.

A relative increase in the number of wage and salary earners that occurred during the period and a corresponding decrease in the number of self-employed persons and unpaid family workers consisted principally of a relative decline in the number of subsistence farmers and working members of their families, together with an increase in the number of persons working for wages in urban stores and factories and in urban service occupations. Skills remained in generally short supply, but the level of skills was far higher in urban than in rural occupations, and an upward trend in their incidence was more pronounced in urban localities.

Organized labor gained somewhat in membership during the 1960s, but in 1969 only a small fraction of the labor force belonged to the unions. A level of wages much higher than in most Latin American countries limited the appeal of militant activists, and strikes were few. During earlier years communist influence in the labor movement had been strong, but during the 1960s labor's relations with both owners and the government were generally harmonious. The largest of the three central labor organizations was represented on the council of the principal management association.

GOVERNMENT ROLE IN AGRICULTURE

The jurisdiction and inner structure of the Ministry of Agriculture, Commerce, and Industry were altered several times after its inception in 1940, and some functions related to agriculture were assigned to other departments of the government. In 1969 the Ministry of Commerce and Industry was created, and the old ministry was renamed the Ministry of Agriculture and Livestock. The reorganized Ministry of Agriculture and Livestock had nine operations divisions, including research and extension, agricultural engineering, marketing, and animal and vegetable health. Subordinate to the ministry were six regional offices and an agricultural school. The division of research and extension operated several experimental farms and ranches; in the late 1960s it was concentrating on research in corn, pastures, hog feeding, vegetables, rice grown under irrigation, and crops grown under semiarid conditions.

The ministry had seventy veterinarians to help ranchers eliminate livestock diseases. It provides seeds, cattle, and pigs from its experimental farms to farmers at reasonable prices and, along with related agencies, grants credits to farmers for certain purposes. The most important of the other agencies is the Institute for Economic Development (Instituto de Fomento Económico—IFE). Established in 1953 by the merging of three governmental credit institutions, the IFE is a semiautonomous entity responsible for all economic development programs outside the jurisdiction of other government agencies. It offers farm credits, especially to small farmers in areas where credit facilities do not exist; administers silos, warehouses, cold storage facilities, and grain mills; and maintains price supports on selected products, such as rice, beans, corn, and coffee. Products that are price-supported must be sold at designated buying stations to the IFE, which stores and then markets the commodities at later dates.

The Directorate of Statistics and Census has been making a notable contribution to agricultural research and planning since World War II by providing statistical data related to agriculture. Fairly extensive and reliable data were obtained in the 1950 and 1961 agricultural censuses. Complete results of a 1970 census were not available in mid-1971.

LAND UTILIZATION AND TENURE

Topography and soil quality limit utilization of the more than 18.6 million acres of land. About one-fifth of the land lies above 2,500 feet on steep, heavily wooded mountain slopes that do not provide adequate level space for extensive settlement and farming (see ch. 3, Physical Environment and Population). A belt between 1,000 and 2,500 feet has a limited use for agriculture; coffee is grown, and some livestock is raised at these elevations. Most farming, however, is carried on at elevations lower than 1,000 feet, on the hills and plains of the lowland that covers over half of the country's surface.

Land is plentiful in relation to population, but only a small portion of the potential cropland is utilized. According to a 1966 agricultural survey, about 29.3 percent of the land, or 5.5 million acres, was in farmland (see fig. 3). Clear lines of demarcation between the lands used for different agricultural purposes cannot be drawn because of overlapping farming practices.

Land utilization varies with the topography and climate. The bulk of the dry lands and volcanic soils are located in the five provinces of Coclé, Herrera, Veraguas, Los Santos, and Chiriquí, where about 54 percent of the total land is in agricultural use. In Herrera, which lies entirely in a dry zone, 81 percent of the total area is used. These provinces constitute the center of agricultural activity, with focal points at David, Santiago, and in the general vicinity of the Gulf of Parita.

Along the Atlantic only a narrow strip of coastal land, about 9.5 percent of total land in this area, is used. Its largest area is in the northern part of Bocas del Toro Province, near the Costa Rican border, where banana and cocoa plantations dominate. There is also some concentration of farming near the canal, north and west of Gatún Lake in Colón Province.

In Darién and Panama provinces 13 percent of the land is used agriculturally. A growing agricultural nucleus exists in the immediate vicinity of the Canal Zone, but most of eastern Panama Province and all of Darién Province constitute a vast reservoir of only partially explored land suitable for agricultural expansion if soil conservation were to be practiced. Detailed surveys of used lands are not available, but foreign observers estimate that potential cropland encompasses about 36 percent of the country's surface, much of it lying east of the canal.

Because the country was settled not by immigrants seeking land to work but rather by merchants and adventurers, most of the land remained in the hands of the state. Further, all land titles issued previously had to be revalidated when the Republic of Panama was established in 1903. Unvalidated land reverted to the state, and it is estimated that the government owns from 88 to 90 percent of the country's surface.

In colonial times the Spanish crown recognized squatters' rights, and this ruling was not in conflict with Indian land tenure practices, which generally recognized not private ownership but rather the use of communal land by individual families. These traditional elements, together with a relative abundance of land in a sparsely populated area and the lack of a general land policy, are chiefly responsible for the prevailing land tenure system.

The 1966 agricultural survey showing that 224 out of 107,000 farms accounted for 20 percent of all farmland also reported that, of the 224 farms, thirty were over 6,000 acres. More than half of the farms over 1,250 acres are operated not by the owner but by administrators who report to the absentee owner. About 63 percent of all farms were cultivated by squatters, and the 1966 survey revealed that only slightly more than 4,200 farms had annual sales of over B/1,000 and could therefore be classified as commercial farms. These were the cattle ranches, coffee, rice, sugarcane, and banana producers, and fruit and vegetable growers. About 23,000 farms had annual sales of between B/100 and B/1,000, and the rest were subsistence farms, 35 percent of all farms reporting no cash income at all.

Acquisition of legal rights to land involves some financial obligations, such as payment of land survey services and payment of the purchase price or rent. Consequently, the penniless farmer uses a piece of land without authorization. Since they are usually forced off privately owned land when discovered, most squatters use state land to which their right can be established in at least three ways: by gaining official permission for their land occupancy, by renting, or by purchase. The procedure by which squatters occupy land is simple: the prospective shifting cultivator chooses some land, clears a small patch of it, builds a temporary makeshift house from building materials available in the area, and plants various crops that insure the subsistence of his family until he moves again (see ch. 5, Social System).

In response to Alliance for Progress precepts and because of the large number of squatters, the government in 1962 passed the Agrarian Code, which entered into force on March 1, 1963, and created the Agrarian Reform Commission, whose main function is to legalize landownership and titles and to resettle squatters. The application of the law has been slow. From its inception through 1970 the Agrarian Reform Commission had granted about 4,500 titles to a total of 167,000 acres and had resettled 3,100 squatters' families on fifty-seven settlement sites to be worked on a cooperative basis. In 1969 there were about 25,000 applications from squatters still pending, and for the titles already granted the average time from the date of filing to the granting of title was almost ninety-five weeks.

Before the passage of the Agrarian Code, landless poor farmers could obtain the right to free use of a specified plot of land on the government-owned farms for an unspecified length of time. Beginning in 1968 the land on these farms was subject to sale and redistribution to the farmers working on it. Over 185,000 acres of land occupied by indigenous "uncivilized" or "semicivilized" people, coastal lands, islands, lands on the banks of navigable rivers, and other specified lands are not open to redistribution or allotment. Foreign nationals may not buy land in a ten-kilometer (6.2-mile) belt along the national borders.

For those farmers who can afford to rent, up to 1,200 acres of surveyed state land may be rented for one-tenth of its assessed value for a renewable ten-year period. Unsurveyed land rents for 20 centesimos (1 centesimo equals US$0.01) per acre for a maximum of twenty years. Private land is usually leased under contracts for one to five years for 15 to 20 percent of the gross product. Some farmers purchase private land, but generally prices are high, especially where farm roads have been built. The highest priced land is found in Herrera Province and Los Santos Province, where the soils are excellent for livestock pasturage. Cleared land throughout the country costs from B/60 to B/400 per acre, and uncleared land, from B/10 to B/20. Since land valued for as much as B/1,000 can be rented for as little as B/15 per year, considerably more private land is rented than purchased.

The government also makes attempts to force large landowners to use their land more intensively, but a major loophole exists. A tax of 40 centesimos per acre was placed on land kept uncultivated in tracts of more than 1,240 acres, but for every acre of land under cultivation five idle acres are permitted to be exempt from the tax.

PATTERNS OF FARMING

Although farming methods have been evolving more rapidly since the early 1950s, the majority of persons engaged in agriculture still practice a traditional slash-and-burn type of shifting cultivation, often referred to as machete farming or *roza* farming. *Roza* means land sown in rice or corn. Its basic tools are the machete, a large heavy knife with an eighteen-inch blade used in clearing land and in harvesting, and a digging or planting stick (*coa* or *chuzo*) to loosen the soil and make a hole for seeds, usually at two-feet intervals. Girdling and fire are used to destroy trees and heavy overbrush, and a knife or no tools are used in harvesting rice and other produce picked by hand.

In this system of shifting cultivation the farmer clears and plants a plot and, when the productivity of the soil is nearly exhausted, usually after one or two years of use, he moves to clear another patch nearby, leaving the formerly used land to secondary overgrowth and natural regeneration. He may return to the first patch and clear it again after several years. The government estimates that about 75,000 acres of forested land are cut annually under this method.

Machete farming requires the cooperation of the family and also, at the crucial clearing and harvesting times, the help of neighbors and friends. Clearing of virgin forest land or secondary overgrowth is done in the dry season following mid-December. Planting is done immediately after burning and clearing during March and April and, by the time the rain becomes heavy, most of it is completed. Under the influence of the hot and humid climate, crops mature rapidly and can be harvested toward the middle of the wet season. In many instances a second crop can be planted, then harvested toward the end of the wet season or early in the dry months. More than one product is usually planted in the same field.

The history of the slash-and-burn type of farming goes back to pre-Colombian times. The sub-Andean Indians who settled in the relatively dry lands of the isthmus, and for whom agriculture was of signal importance, applied it extensively. After clearing the land they planted maize, beans, yuca, peppers, and squash, supplementing their diet with fruits and game from nearby forests. The tropical forest Indians, who gained most of their food from hunting, fishing, and gathering, practiced agriculture only to a limited extent but applied the same slash-and-burn techniques. Ecological conditions for both types of Indian culture were similar enough to justify the use of the slash-and-burn system in an area where land seemed to be available without limitation, soils were of modest fertility, and growth of vegetation was extremely rapid.

The Spanish conquerors of Panama were not agriculturists and had little interest in the soil because the favorable location of the colony provided more lucrative rewards in other activities. The only new agricultural practice introduced by the Spanish was livestock raising, which could be exercised by absentee landlords with the help of a small number of Indians or slaves. Some new crops were added to the extensive list of native species, but the agricultural practices of the subsistence farmer were not changed, the plow was not introduced, and overall agricultural production was never raised to a level sufficient to feed the urban population of the country.

The country is relatively poor in volcanic deposits; soils are low in phosphorus, nitrogen, and organic matter and high in acidity. Erosion is particularly damaging on grazing lands, where sandy loams are washed off as a result of overgrazing. Only 47 percent of the total land area had been surveyed for soil types by 1970. Most soils in Bocas del Toro and Darién had not been studied. In 1969 only about 13,000 tons of fertilizers were used in the entire country, mostly by the banana and sugarcane growers. Practically all farms under twenty-five acres and even larger units that engage in commercial production or combine livestock raising with crop farming rotate crops on part of their land.

To perform urgent tasks that the farmer and his immediate family cannot accomplish in due time farmers join together in two traditional forms of communal labor: the *junta* and the *peonada*. Both institutions have social and economic significance. The *junta* is usually a short-term (one-day) but extensive cooperative effort by several persons and families for the purpose of clearing land, harvesting, or building a house. No money or work is exchanged, but good entertainment at the end of the day is expected. The host usually invites good workers and attractive women, but almost everyone in the area is free to participate. The event is characterized by a competitive spirit in both work and fun.

276

The *peonada* usually lasts longer than one day and is attended by fewer people, who expect the host to return the services when they are needed. In regional variations the *junta* and the *peonada* are often indistinguishable, characterized by the same competitive spirit and providing an excuse for a fiesta.

The more progressive small-scale farmer who also produces for the market economy may replace the machete with machinery, plant fruit trees on part of his land, raise poultry and pigs, and sell his produce in the nearby village or to truckers. Crop farming may also be combined with livestock raising.

Some farmers own a mule or a pony, which is used to transport produce. Some use oxen to pull carts, but fewer than 10 percent of all farmers use draft animals in the field. Plowing has not become an accepted practice, partly because of the topography and the tradition of machete cultivation and partly because of the expenses involved in the purchase and maintenance of draft animals and equipment.

Lack of cash or credit prevents most farmers from buying mechanical equipment. Fewer than 2 percent of the farms are mechanized. Most of the 2,000 tractors in the country are used on banana and sugar plantations, some for rice production and pasture management. The greatest progress in mechanization of recent years has been made by the farmers engaged in mechanical rice production on the dry plains of Chiriquí Province and south of Penonomé in Coclé Province. Extensive use of fertilizers and mechanization, as practiced on these farms, is an exception rather than the rule in the country.

The government operates several machine stations, which rent machinery for land clearing, plowing, and harvesting. Some of the small farmers producing for commercial purposes have equipped themselves with machinery, which they also lease to other small farmers in their vicinity. Credit for machinery purchase is limited.

The climate generally favors agriculture. Lands where the annual rainfall does not exceed seventy inches and the dry season lasts four to five months are considered more suitable for agriculture than the wetter areas where annual rainfall may be as much as 140 inches and the dry season of four months' duration or less. Lack of water constitutes a considerable danger to both crops and stock, however, during the longer dry seasons under tropical conditions.

The prevailing northerly and northeasterly winds deposit the heaviest rains on the northern slopes and higher elevations of the mountains, a phenomenon that bears major responsibility for the distribution of cultivated lands (see ch. 3, Physical Environment and Population). To conserve moisture during the dry months, irrigation has been developed and applied by about 1,000 farmers on about 30,000 acres, chiefly on banana and sugarcane plantations and on ricefields. The government also began an irrigation program in 1969 in various dry areas. Over 2,200 acres were under government irrigation by 1971, and plans existed for an eventual 50,000 acres to be irrigated.

Prevailing high temperatures and the high relative humidity promote the rapid spread of weeds, insects, and diseases that retard agricultural development. Much greater usage of pesticides is reported, however, even by some of the smallest farms.

CROPS

Rice

Rice is a staple food of the population and is grown on almost every farm, on a total of over 310,000 acres. The development of dry-land rice production has ranked at the top of government programs, and as a result the country has been self-sufficient in this commodity in several years since 1953. Two crops per year are grown. Expansion of rice production has been stimulated by protective import tariff and price support policies and by government support of the processing and marketing organizations. New and improved varieties were introduced after World War II, and mechanization and fertilization have been promoted with very good results. Farmers, however, must contend with a rice-eating wild bird called the arrocero, which is more of a pest than insects.

Nevertheless, about 80 percent of the rice is produced by small farmers who seed untilled soil with a digging stick. The remaining 20 percent of the national output comes from mechanized rice farms, located mainly in the southern part of Coclé and Chiriquí provinces. Because of the abundant domestic supply, only token amounts are imported. The average yield shows a slow improvement from 1,000 pounds an acre in the 1930s to 1,175 pounds in the late 1960s. When fertilizers are used in mechanical farming, yields of 1,600 pounds an acre are not unusual. Between 1960 and 1970 rice production increased by about 50 percent to 170,000 tons (see table 15). About one-third of the production comes from Chiriquí Province. The gradual provision of adequate storage facilities, the extension of loans to producers, and continued price support by the government seem to insure sufficient production to continue to meet the domestic demand in the future and to meet the government's desire to export rice by 1974.

Table 15. *Production of Selected Agricultural Products in Panama,*
1960 and 1970

Product	Unit	1960	1970
Rice	Metric tons	113,262	170,000
Corn and corn products	........do........	77,293	88,000
Beans	........do........	6,000	5,000
Potatoes	........do........	11,000	6,000*
Yucca	........do........	15,000	22,000*
Bananas	........do........	6,800,000	670,000
Coffee	........do........	4,082	5,000
Sugar			
Centrifugal	........do........	27,216	69,000
Noncentrifugal	........do........	9,072	5,000
Tobacco and tobacco products	........do........	601	828*
Cacao	........do........	1,000	1,000
Tomatoes	........do........	16,000	21,000*
Oranges	........do........	39,000	41,000
Pineapples	........do........	4,000	5,000*
Cattle	Head	748,000	1,200,000
Hogs	........do........	224,000	174,000*
Poultry	Each	2,700,00	3,000,000
Eggs	Dozen	8,666,000	9,416,000
Milk and milk products	Metric tons	53,000	85,000
Meat and meat products	........do........	28,000	32,000

* 1969.

Adapted from: U.S. Department of Agriculture, Economic Research Service, *Indices of Agricultural Production for the Western Hemisphere. Revised 1961 through 1969. Preliminary 1970,* Washington, 1971, p. 71; and Organization of American States, Instituto Interamericano de Estadística, *América en cifras, 1970. situación económica, I:* agricultura, ganadería, silvicultura, caza and pesca, Washington, 1970.

Corn

Corn, grown on about 68 percent of all farms on a total of about 250,000 acres, is the second most important item in the rural diet. The output was 88,000 tons in crop year 1969/70 and 90,000 tons in 1970/71, but small imports are still required. Chiriquí and Veraguas are the leading corn-producing areas. Corn is used widely to manufacture cornmeal and *chicha,* the popular local drink, and as feed by the growing poultry industry. It is cultivated by hand on slopes where the practical value of machinery is limited at best. The average yield per acre has remained at about 800 pounds but, according to non-Panamanian experts, provision of the storage and drying facilities, better cultivation practices, and improved seed qualities may eventually increase the output.

Beans

Various kinds of beans are grown in small lots totaling 42,000 acres on about 36,000 farms, with 35 percent of the total production in Veraguas Province. Only about 8 percent of the 5,000-ton annual production enters the market, the rest being consumed on the farm. The high protein content of beans makes them a valuable part of the local diet, but the lack of storage facilities and of insect control keeps production and yield low and necessitates imports. To eliminate the annual import of from 1,500 to 2,000 tons of beans, the government makes continuous efforts to introduce improved varieties and to popularize the cultivation of beans as a rotation crop with rice and maintains high price supports.

Root and Oil Crops

Irish potatoes are grown only in small quantities, and urban demand must be satisfied by imports. About 60 percent of the farms produce yuca, a favorite food with high starch content. Yams (*ñames*) are produced on a smaller scale than yuca and are consumed widely.

Edible oil production does not meet the growing domestic demand. The provinces of Colón and Veraguas produce some coconuts, but the largest producers are the San Blas Indians, who gather an estimated 24 million coconuts annually but smuggle the major share to Colombian copra producers in exchange for salt, sugar, cloth, or other supplies on terms more favorable than the domestic price.

There are attempts to popularize peanut production, and experiments on Chiriquí ricelands resulted in good yields. Experiments with sesame were also in progress on a few hundred farms, but no large-scale production had been started as of 1971.

Bananas

The principal export crop, constituting the major portion of the total value of agriculture, is bananas. A high degree of technology is utilized in banana production. About 69,000 acres are planted in bananas, half of the total acreage being in two plantations of the Chiriquí Land Company, a subsidiary of the United Fruit Company, which began operations in 1899. Both plantations are near the Costa Rican border in western Panama. The leading plantation, comprising some 22,000 acres, is situated in the general area of Puerto Armuelles in Chiriquí Province, on the Pacific, where bananas of the best quality are produced. The second largest plantation, with 12,000 acres, lies near Almirante in Bocas del Toro Province on the Caribbean coast; it was reactivated in 1953 after Panama disease destroyed the crop in 1936. Although the company engages in other agricultural activities, such as cacao, palm oil, and timber production, its main contribution to the national economy comes from the banana industry.

The large-scale banana production also faces hazards of considerable dimensions. Windstorms and rainstorms occasionally destroy millions of plants, as they did in late 1970, and fungus diseases, such as sigatoka and Panama disease, make repeated inroads despite intensive preventive measures. A new variety of banana, introduced in the Bocas del Toro plantation, has proved resistant to blight. The stems are encased in plastic bags while growing to prevent insect damage, and yield per acre has risen steeply.

Because of growing labor difficulties arising from social pressures, the Chiriquí Land Company since 1962 has been selling land to Panamanians while retaining buying and distributing rights of their production. In 1970 there were twenty-seven such independent producers. In addition, the company has given or sold to the government over 14,000 acres of other lands it held for redistribution to landless farmers.

Local markets are supplied by 60,000 small banana growers concentrated mainly in the Gatún Lake area and in eastern Darién near El Real. Few small producers sell to exporters, and transportation as well as marketing organizations have to be improved before they can enter the international market on a competitive basis.

Coffee

Over 66,000 acres, or about 7 percent of total cropland, is planted in coffee, on about 35,000 farms in practically every province in the country. Most coffee farms are small; only 200 are larger than twenty-five acres. One-third of the total crop is grown on a few plantations near El Volcán and Boquete in Chiriquí Province, where 90 percent of the export coffee is grown, and on small farms in Herrera, northern Coclé, and Veraguas provinces, particularly near Santa Fé. The mild taste of the Chiriquí coffee is well received on the world market, especially in the Federal Republic of Germany (West Germany), the Netherlands, and the United States. The country has a small export quota of 24,000 bags under the International Coffee Agreement.

Over two-thirds of the coffee produced is consumed domestically, with some regular sales to the Canal Zone. The balance is exported, but overproduction by the large coffee-producing countries and a consequent accumulation of surplus coffee on the world market places high-cost Panamanian coffee in a precarious and highly vulnerable position. Hence, the government protects the industry through price support. Both the government and the coffee growers promote the expansion of the industry, which was producing from 4,500 to 5,000 tons annually during the 1960s. The government provides seedlings from its nurseries at Concepción and Penonomé; the extension service of the Ministry of Agriculture and Livestock emphasizes improvements in processing methods; and business-minded producers attempt the opening of new production areas. A government agency called the Coffee Institute, created in 1961 to give technical advice, was given authority in 1969 to purchase all coffee for export and handle all export sales.

Cacao

The climate and soils are extremely favorable for cacao production, and no cacao disease had been reported by 1971. Cacao is grown by the Indians of Darién Province and San Blas. Over 9,000 farmers raise cacao in the country on about 10,000 acres. The largest producer is the Chiriquí Land Company, which devotes about 3,000 acres to cacao production but rents most of this to individuals to manage in Bocas del Toro. In adjacent lands there are some 600 small-scale producers, over 200 of whom are organized in a marketing cooperative.

Sugar

Sugarcane is grown throughout the country by about 21,000 farmers for use in *panela* (a homemade brown sugarcake), for syrup sold to alcohol-manufacturing enterprises, for sale to commercial sugar factories, and for livestock feed. More than one-half of the production is concentrated in Coclé Province. The two leading sugar mills near Aguadulce in Coclé Province produce about one-half of their requirement on their own irrigated and fertilized land and buy the other half from small producers. The sugar content of the cane is relatively low, about 9 percent of the weight. Irrigated cane produces a higher percentage. The relatively short maturing period allowed by the seven to eight months of favorable weather is the principal reason for the low sugar content. Production, stimulated by exemption of taxes, doubled during the ten years before 1961 and by that year exceeded domestic demand. Growth after 1961 was stimulated by increased domestic demand and a United States sugar quota. Further growth during the 1970s should be stimulated by the construction of a new 40,000-ton-capacity sugar mill in 1971.

Fruits and Vegetables

A staple food item of the rural population is the plantain, a variety of banana not affected by the common banana diseases and grown by 44,000 of the small farmers. A fairly large quantity of plantains is marketed mostly from the Darién area, and some, from Chiriquí. Mangoes are widely grown but are of inferior quality. Pineapples of excellent quality are grown on 35,000 farms, and papayas are also popular. Navel oranges are grown with very good results on higher elevations of Veraguas and Chiriquí provinces by coffee farmers and in a few commercial orchards. Native oranges are widespread on about 64,000 farms and are grown for commercial purposes mainly in the La Chorrera-Arraiján-Campana area, southwest of Panama City.

Commercial investment of about B/5 million in 10,000 acres of orange groves and a juice-processing plant was in progress in 1971 in the El Volcán area by the Chiriquí Citrus Company (Compañía Chiriquana de Citrios). With improvement in the quality of fruits, an official grading system, and organized marketing, the fruit potential could be exploited to a much larger extent. Limes are produced widely, but few grapefruit and even fewer lemons are grown, even though conditions for the production of most citrus fruits are considered favorable.

Vegetables are produced in a few areas near the two terminal cities of the zone and along the highways. Many of the 4,000 small vegetable gardens are operated by Chinese growers. Truck vegetables come from Pacora, Chitré, El Valle, and El Volcán. Tomatoes are grown in large quantities. About 30,000 farms raise peas. Peppers, avocados, and watermelons are other leading products, but eggplant, okra, green beans, squash, and other minor vegetables form an unexploited potential.

Minor Industrial Crops

Tobacco production, confined to 200 acres on 1,200 farms in the dry lands, meets only about one-half of the domestic demand and is able to supply only three cigarette factories. Production varies greatly from year to year. In crop year 1968/69 it was under 1,000 tons. A rubber plantation established as a demonstration farm has shown excellent results. Pita, a cactus that grows wild in many areas, may be utilized by industry for its fibrous content.

LIVESTOCK

Cattle

Most cattle ranches are small. Eighty percent of cattle are

raised on farms under 250 acres, and only 8 percent, on farms larger than 2,500 acres. Large cattle ranches specialize in either steer or calf raising. The general pattern of cattle raising is like that of the open range farm.

The native type of cattle used to predominate, but by 1971 more than half of the stock consisted of the native crossed with the imported zebu, or brahman. The cattle inventory of the country increased by 30 percent between 1950 and 1960 to almost 800,000, despite a high rate of calf mortality, and then by 50 percent to 1.2 million head by 1970, making the country self-sufficient in beef. Almost 30 percent of the total are located in Chiriquí Province, and 20 percent, in Los Santos Province. Both slaughter cattle and fresh frozen beef are exported.

There is little separation of beef and dairy cattle, except on large dairy farms. Many farms own some cattle for their own needs, but during extensive dry seasons small farmers are forced to sell their livestock in the absence of supplementary feed. Only the large ranchers possess means for supplementary feeding. Most cattle are free from disease.

The government provides breeding stations, artificial insemination, tick baths, pasture improvement, and dairy management training. The IFE, some of the commercial banks, and the Panamanian Cattle Institute extend credit for the improvement of pasture and cattle. Substantial numbers of pureblood bulls have been imported. The Cattle Institute, an autonomous agency established in 1958 to organize the export market, has since assumed other functions including the granting of subsidies to producers, and it has been criticized by government planners for duplicating the work of other agencies.

Milk is produced on about 9,000 farms, but only a few are specialized dairy farms. The specialized farms are located near Colón and Panama City where fresh milk is consumed in large quantities in a steady upward trend. Milk is also produced near Natá for the Nestlé condensing plant; near Aguadulce, where a pasteurizing plant purchases milk for the United States Army and its markets in Panama City; and in the area of Concepción, where another plant processes evaporated milk, butter, and powdered milk.

According to foreign technicians and observers, the potential for the expansion of the cattle industry, particularly on higher elevations of Chiriquí and Coclé provinces, is considerable. As prerequisites for expansion, domestic production of supplementary feed, provision of more adequate transportation, and additional refrigeration facilities are needed.

Other Livestock

Pig production has been decreasing since 1960 because of high production costs, and import of pork products and lard has cost an annual B/1.5 million to the national economy. Pigs, numbering about 150,000 in 1971, are common on many farms, but large-scale commercial production exists on a few specialized farms mainly in Veraguas and Los Santos provinces. The native breed is most common and has an average weight of 120 pounds.

The situation is quite different in the case of poultry and poultry products, in which the country became self-sufficient during the decade 1950–60. The country imported only hatching eggs because the 3.9 million chicken in 1971 supplied sufficient quantities of fresh eggs for local consumption. About 69,000 farms raise poultry. Commercial poultry farms are modern and large. Some have as many as 40,000 chickens. About 35,000 turkeys and 113,000 ducks are also raised. There are about 160,000 horses and 5,000 mules and donkeys in the country.

FISH AND FOREST PRODUCTS

Fishing

The natural setting of the country provides it with the fish and marine resources of two oceans. More than fifty species of commercially valuable fish and crustaceans, among them shrimp, Spanish mackerel, anchovy, tuna, snook, and groupers, are present in large quantities. They are caught mainly within a 100-mile radius of Panama City but also all along the two sides of the isthmus. Game fishing is also excellent in both fresh water and deep seas. Panama's Pacific coast is considered one of the world's best game fishing areas, and the government stocks the inland streams and lakes. Several projects are reported to be planned to stimulate tourism for fishing enthusiasts.

As of 1970 about B/20 million was invested in the fishing industry, mostly in vessels and freezing plants, and over 4,600 persons were employed in some branch of the industry. The government is actively pursuing the full development of the country's fisheries capacity but at the same time is limiting the fleet size in order to prevent overexploitation. The absence of a good sheltered fishing port on the Pacific has caused costs within the industry to increase, and the government had plans in 1971 for the eventual construction of a modern fishing port.

The total landed catch of fish and crustaceans soared from 30 million pounds in 1961 to over 165.6 million pounds by 1968. The catch dropped to less than half in 1969, however, because one of the major fishmeal plants ceased operations. It reopened in 1970, and production again started to climb. The largest catch is of anchovies and thread herrings, which are processed into fishmeal and fish oil; although the annual catch of these two species fluctuates widely, the annual average between 1965 and 1970 was 112.4 million pounds, caught by a twenty-vessel fleet.

A much larger fleet is engaged in shrimping, which is well organized and developed and has grown rapidly from an insignificant eight fishing boats in 1951 to 238 licensed trawlers in 1971 and six freezing plants. The shrimp catch averaged over 13.2 million pounds annually from 1960 to 1970 and amounted to 15.2 million pounds in 1970; the value averaged B/9 million from 1965 to 1970, almost all of which was exported, making shrimp the third leading export (see ch. 13, Trade and Transportation).

Three main types of shrimp are found in Panamanian waters—white, pink, and a small variety called sea bob. The white is the most valuable because of its larger size. In 1971 the government recognized the need to modernize the shrimp boats. Half of the licensed number were wooden trawlers over ten years of age with high operating and maintenance costs, and a loan program was being set up to enable the boatowners to modernize their vessels.

The food fish catch, which averaged 7.8 million pounds during the 1968–70 period, is caught almost equally by 250 inshore small boats and by the shrimpers and anchovy fishermen. Sixty of the small boats supply the fish markets of Panama City. Between B/1.5 million and B/2 million of fish products are imported annually—mainly tuna, salted cod, and sardines. According to fishing experts there are great resources of tuna and sharks, which could replace the imports if adequately exploited. There are also large resources of spiny lobsters only slightly exploited.

Forestry

A comparatively small portion of the vast forest resources is exploited (see ch. 3, Physical Environment and Population). Inaccessibility actually limits the commercial forest area to some 9 million acres located mainly in Darién and Bocas del Toro provinces. Mahogany production is the most important. Of the estimated 75 million board feet of mahogany resources, some 60 million board feet are in Darién.

A balsa-like softwood, the *cuipo*, is abundant, as is *cativo*, suitable for plywood production. Small quantities of Spanish cedar, mangrove, sapodilla, tagua, and a dozen other industrially valuable species have been logged and exported; hundreds of other species are present. Dyewoods also exist in abundance.

286

In the absence of coal and oil, wood is the sole rural source of fuel. Over 95 percent of all timber removed from the forests is used for fuel. Over 1.8 million cubic meters is estimated to be cut annually. Nevertheless, forest management is poorly organized, and large quantities of timber and fuelwood are destroyed annually by the prevailing slash-and-burn cultivation system in farming and the exploitation methods of the sawmill operators. Concessions for exploitation of forest land are being granted by the government on plots of up to 250 acres and for a maximum of five years. The government has a reforestation program, which includes demonstration plots. Over 1 million pine trees were being planted in parts of Veraguas, where shifting cultivation farmers have cut down all ground cover and rains have eroded the soil. The Food and Agriculture Organization of the United Nations had been helping with a forestry inventory, which in 1971 was estimated to be 80 percent completed.

GOVERNMENT ROLE IN INDUSTRY

In the industrial sector the government role has been mainly the encouragement of investments by private domestic and foreign capital. Investment incentive laws passed in 1950 and 1957 were designed to attract capital to industry by granting privileges and concessions for up to fifteen years and providing tariff protection against competitive imports (see ch. 13, Trade and Transportation). About 250 companies had taken advantage of these laws by the end of 1970, when the new Industrial Development Law classified all companies in two categories—those producing mainly for export and those producing for the domestic market. Different incentives and benefits are granted to the two categories, with the greater benefits accorded to export-oriented industries, and additional benefits are granted to firms locating in certain designated geographical zones outside the Metropolitan Area (see Glossary). All privileges and benefits of the new law are limited to a fifteen-year period.

The Center for Development and Industrial Productivity (Centro por el Desarrollo y Productividad Industrial—CDPI), established in 1955, makes feasibility studies for various industries, conducts research in productivity, and offers technical consultations. A private entity called the Panamanian Institute for Development (Instituto Panameño de Desarrollo—INPADE), formed in 1964 as a nonprofit organization by the government but financed by businessmen, works closely with the center, offering management training courses, technical assistance, and courses in labor relations. The government selects businessmen to attend the

Central American Institute of Business Administration, located in Nicaragua and assisted by the Harvard Business School, which is a regional center for graduate research training and consultation in management.

MINING

Crude salt, which is a government monopoly, is obtained from sea water in sufficient quantities to meet domestic demand; lime, clay, stone, and gravel are produced for the construction industry. No other significant exploitation of minerals was in progress in early 1971. Only thirty-one mining companies were operating in 1969, and sixteen of them were extracting salt, sand, gravel, and stone. Several industrially valuable minerals are known to exist and, when full exploitation of them commences, mining activities should contribute much more to the economy. The government was revising the mining code in 1971 in order to stimulate mining activities by private industry.

The most important mineral is copper. Three large deposits, which also contain molybdenum, had been discovered by 1971 by a United Nations minerals survey team, which was continuing its prospecting. The largest deposit was discovered in 1968 in a twenty-two-square-mile area near Petaquilla in Colón Province, twelve miles inland from the coast, and preliminary estimates indicated at least 30 million to 40 million tons of copper-bearing ore. Negotiations for its exploitation were going on in 1971 between the government and foreign mining companies. The second deposit is located at Cerro Colorado in Chiriquí Province, and a local company to which this concession was granted was negotiating with a Canadian mining firm in 1971 for its exploitation. The third mineral belt was discovered in 1971 along the San Blas coast at the Pita River near the Colombian border. This deposit was reported to contain zinc and gold in addition to copper and molybdenum.

Manganese of very good quality was mined intermittently during World War II and in the late 1950s in the Nombre de Dios area in the province of Colón, but controversial property claims forced suspension of production in 1960. Production began again in mid-1971. Construction of mining installations also began in 1971 on the Pacific sand beaches to extract magnetite and ilmenite from the sand for the extraction of iron and titanium.

In early colonial times the country was called Castilla del Oro (Golden Castile) because the Indians had large quantities of gold. The Spanish themselves mined gold and silver in commercial quantities as early as 1570. Known gold reserves in 1971 did not warrant the large investment that would be necessary for exploitation and transportation on a commercial basis. Nevertheless, the hope of finding large quantities of gold is cherished by many, and concessions for exploration are granted annually, although most of them later revert to the state because they are not being worked. The little gold produced usually comes from panning in rivers and streams. Coal finds in Bocas del Toro Province have evoked interest in the past, but the veins have turned out to be too narrow and the carbon content too low.

Salt is produced mainly in the tidal lowlands on the east side of the Azuero Peninsula. Some 16,000 to 20,000 tons of solar salt are produced annually, but the present exploitation only scratches the surface of the total potential, which is estimated to be about 500,000 tons a year.

Relatively large deposits of low-grade bauxite have been discovered in western Panama; but since aluminum is one of the world's most common metals and exploitation of any bauxite deposit depends upon cost and accessibility, much is available elsewhere at lower cost. In the late 1960s Panama had an estimated reserve of 70 million tons of bauxite, as against total known world reserves of over 8.7 billion tons.

ENERGY

As late as the 1950s fuelwood had provided more than half of the total energy consumed in the country, but by the end of the 1960s this source provided less than 20 percent of total energy. Fuelwood had been supplanted by electricity, gas, and petroleum. Petroleum finds of neighboring countries and oil showings on the surface within Panama fired the imagination of many Panamanians, but extensive exploration since 1919 had brought no economically valuable results by 1971. In 1970 the Mobil Oil Company signed a ten-year contract with the government to conduct oil exploration in the Gulf of Panama.

The Panama Refinery, representing United States and Panamanian private interests—the largest single industry in the country—has a B/36-million plant on Payardi Island in Las Minas Bay, near Colón. It began operations in 1963; by 1971 it had the capacity to refine 70,000 barrels of crude oil a day and was producing about 2 percent of all refined petroleum products in Latin America. Most of the supply of crude oil comes from Venezuela, and most of its market consists of ships transiting the Panama Canal. In 1971 plans also existed for a petrochemical complex and a second refinery to be built by another company, the Panama Petrochemical Company (Petroquímica Panamá), also near Colón.

An oil pipeline transiting the isthmus east of Chepo, being built by private foreign firms in 1971, with completion scheduled for 1973, was to be used to move petroleum between giant tankers on both coasts that are too large for passage through the canal. The capacity of the pipeline eventually was to be 700,000 barrels a day, and the government would acquire ownership of it after twelve years of operation by the private companies to recover their costs. The cost was estimated at the equivalent of US$80 million.

The failure to find commercially valuable coal and oil in the country and the demand for power by households and industry, which was rising at a rate of about 10 percent annually, stimulated several surveys of hydraulic power resources and the prevailing conditions of power production. These revealed that power was generated mainly by thermal plants and was high priced and that generating capacity was not sufficient to meet future demands. Only the two major cities and western Chiriquí Province had adequate electrical services. The residential cost of electricity in 1969 was 3.9 centesimos per kilowatt-hour. More than 50 percent of the population in 1970 still lacked access to electricity. About 87 percent of the total electricity generated was being consumed in the Metropolitan Area. Almost 40 percent of the total was used by commercial stores; about 34 percent, by residences; 15 percent, by industry; and the balance, by government.

The heavy rainfall, which in some parts of the country is never less than 100 inches a year and occasionally reaches 200 inches, is favorable for the establishment of hydroelectric plants (see ch. 3, Physical Environment and Population). The crest of the high mountains is relatively near the seacoast and, although the volume of water in each of the numerous rivers is not large, the water level is almost constant the year round, and the fall of water is considerable. Sixteen rivers are capable of hydroelectric projects with capacities between 5,000 and 125,000 kilowatts. Some rivers, like the Bayano, have a larger capacity, and even waters of small streams can be diverted into single channels to provide a larger volume, as has been demonstrated by hydroelectric installations in Chiriquí Province. Total hydroelectric potential is estimated at 2.4 million kilowatts by the United Nations.

Generally the utility industry of the country is characterized by a few large and many small powerplants, which are not interconnected by transmission lines and therefore serve isolated areas of individual industrial plants. Total generating capacity in 1970 outside of the Canal Zone was 155,000 kilowatts, provided by twelve companies to over 100,000 consumers. The capacity of the Canal Zone was 168,000 kilowatts, all generated by the Panama

Canal Company. The Canal Zone and Panama frequently exchange electricity.

The leading producer in 1971 was the Panamanian Power and Light Company (Compañía Panameña de Fuerza y Luz), a private company supplying Panama City and Colón. In 1970 it had fixed assets of about B/32 million and total installed capacity of 89,000 kilowatts. In 1969 it generated over 80 percent of the 550 million kilowatt-hours of electricity consumed in Panama City and Colón.

The government-owned Electrification and Hydraulic Resources Institute (Instituto de Recursos Hidráulicos y Electrificación— IRHE) had 50,000 kilowatts of generating capacity in numerous small and medium-sized plants in 1970. The IRHE originally was set up in 1961 to provide power to small communities in the interior and in the Metropolitan Area not served by private companies. In 1970 it had 19,000 customers in fifty locations. In 1969 the government gave the IRHE the exclusive right to construct and operate all new facilities and to sell electricity to the private utilities. In 1969 the IRHE also signed a long-term contract with the Panama Canal Company to supply the zone's future requirements when IRHE's new facilities are built. The IRHE was expected to become the major electric power utility in the country by 1975, with 287,000 kilowatts of generating capacity. Its largest project in 1971 was the Bayano River hydroelectric plant, which initially was to be completed in 1975. Other medium-sized and smaller plants were also under construction for the IRHE in 1971.

Some of the other principal producers of electricity in 1970 were the Chiriquí Electric Enterprises (Empresas Eléctricas de Chiriquí), which served the principal urban areas of Chiriquí Province and had 9,000 kilowatts of generating capacity, including a 7,000-kilowatt hydroelectric plant at Caldera; the Santiago Electric Company (Santiago Eléctrica), which served the Santiago district in Veraguas Province with 1,000 kilowatts; the El Valle Company (Compañía de El Valle), which served the city of El Valle in Coclé Province with 340 kilowatts; and the La Chorrera Hydroelectric Company (Hidroeléctrica de La Chorrera), with 1,330 kilowatts for the city of La Chorrera in Panama Province. A number of industries outside the Metropolitan Area also generate their own electricity.

Until 1971 over 700 million cubic feet of gas was produced annually, most of it by the Panamanian Power and Light Company, which had 17,000 customers in Panama City and Colón receiving gas by pipeline. Most of the gas was for residential use, with very little used by industry and commerce. In mid-1971 the company announced the suspension of such service because of excessive costs, making it necessary for gas users to shift to bottled gas, kerosine, electricity, or charcoal.

MANUFACTURING

Manufacturing enterprises are relatively small. Some 2,070 enterprises registered with the government in 1969, but only eight declared a capital of B/1 million or more, and only one had more than 1,000 employees. Sixty-five percent of the plants are located in the province of Panama. Because of the limited domestic market and the early stage of industrialization, a few plants dominate each branch of industry, especially in sectors where heavy initial investment is required. This monopolistic tendency can be observed in such industries as brewing, edible-oil production, cement making, and plywood and clay manufacture. Textiles and footwear, soft drinks, marine products, and bakery products are more competitive.

The National Brewery Company, with a plant valued at B/11 million, in 1971 had the largest number of employees—over 1,000; the Panamanian Power and Light Company had nearly as many. Ten companies had between 200 and 500 employees, thirty-five had between 100 and 200, forty-nine had between fifty and 100, and the remainder had fewer than fifty. The total number of employees in the manufacturing sector was about 47,000 in the late 1960s.

Industrial and construction enterprises, as a rule, are privately owned by individual entrepreneurs, by partners, or by a small number of shareholders. Only about 900 enterprises were incorporated. In general, family groups or groups of close friends own most of the corporations, and only a few of the largest have a reasonably wide distribution of shares. The government appears to have little intention of participating in industry directly.

Foodstuffs, Beverages, and Tobacco

Food-processing enterprises, using both domestic and imported raw materials, constitute the most active sector of manufacturing (see table 16). Milk, tomatoes, and sugar are the basic raw materials. Milk-processing enterprises used 8 million gallons of raw milk to produce 10,000 tons of condensed evaporated and powdered milk in 1968. The leading food enterprise—the Panamanian Food Company (Compañía Panameña de Alimentos), established at Natá, Coclé Province, in 1938, has its own tin can factory and produces fruit juices, catsup, tomato juice, and instant coffee during the slack milk season.

The second largest milk-processing enterprise is the Chiriquí Milk Company (Compañía Chiriquana de Leche) at Concepción, (in millions of balboas) [1]

Industrial Activity	1960	1964	1968	1969 [2]	1970 [2]
Mines and quarries	1.1	1.8	2.1	4.3	2.3
Construction	22.9	28.1	46.3	50.6	57.1
Electricity, gas, and water	8.4	12.0	18.9	19.5	20.8
Manufacturing					
Foodstuffs	17.0	25.7	37.6	39.9	n.a.
Beverages	8.4	11.4	15.4	17.6	n.a.
Tobacco	2.6	3.3	3.7	3.8	n.a.
Shoes and apparel	5.4	5.4	10.0	12.1	n.a.
Lumber, furniture and					
wood products	4.3	7.3	10.7	12.6	n.a.
Paper and paper products	0.8	3.2	5.3	5.9	n.a.
Printing	3.6	5.6	8.5	12.4	n.a.
Leather products	0.5	0.8	0.6	0.7	n.a.
Rubber and chemicals	2.0	3.1	3.7	3.9	n.a.
Petroleum derivatives	0	6.4	7.1	7.1	n.a.
Nonmetallic mineral products	5.2	6.8	10.5	11.2	n.a.
Metals and metal products	2.1	8.6	13.0	14.3	n.a.
Other manufacturing	2.4	3.9	5.6	6.1	n.a.
Total Manufacturing	54.3	91.5	131.7	147.6	155.6
GRAND TOTAL	86.7	133.4	199.0	222.0	235.8

n.a.—not available.
[1] 1 balboa equals US$1.
[2] Preliminary.

which also cans foods, such as tomatoes and carrots. Among the
fruit processing and canning plants, the National Products of
Panama (Productos Nacionales de Panamá) began operation in
1955 with an initial investment of over B/1 million. This company
applies a canning technique that eliminates the process of cooking
the sealed cans by placing sterilized foods into sterilized cans.
This is said to preserve the flavor of such delicate tropical products
as banana puree, mango puree, and orange juice concentrates
without freezing. Other companies engaged in fruit processing
and canning are: the Chiriquí Citrus Company, the Libby, McNeil
and Libby Company; and a number of small plants concentrated
mainly in Panama Province. Production of tomato derivatives
(pastes, sauces, juices, and soups) rose to 4,000 tons annually by
the end of the 1960s.

Increasing amounts of refined sugar are produced in three refineries. The two largest are the Star Sugar Refinery Company
(Compañía Azucarera La Estrella) and the National Sugar Refinery (Azucarera Nacional), both located in the Natá-Aguadulce

region of Coclé Province. The third is in Panama Province, and in mid-1971 a fourth refinery was scheduled to begin operations in 1972 in Veraguas Province. Numerous small mills produce *panela,* a less refined sugarcake that is often a product of household industries.

Adjacent to the Star Sugar Refinery Company is the Natá Industries (Industrias de Natá), which produces candy and feed concentrates. In line with the expanding dairy and poultry industry of the country, the demand is growing for feeds consisting of a mixture of imported mineral concentrates, oats, alfalfa, barley, domestic corn, and coconut cakes.

There are enterprises that produce edible oil, margarine, and soap from domestic and imported fats and copra. Largest of these companies is the Panama Boston Industrial Company (Industrial Panamá Boston), which has a modern plant in Panama City. Other companies make fruit-flavored syrups, vinegar, laundry products, and cosmetics, mainly from domestic raw materials.

Thirteen coffee roasters process domestic green coffee. The milling of corn, rice, oat, banana, and yuca starch flours and the repacking of imported wheat flour have been carried on by numerous small companies. Almost 200 rice millers existed in 1970.

Seven slaughterhouses and seven meatpackers operate in Chiriquí and Panama provinces. Armour has a meat producing and packing plant in Panama City. The National Abbatoir (Abbatoir Nacional) owns and operates a modern slaughterhouse in Panama City with a capacity of about 250 cattle and 150 hogs per day. Refrigeration and freezing vaults are available, though most of the meat is sold unchilled on the local market. Byproducts, with the exception of some hides, are locally consumed. Beef and veal production reached 70,000 pounds in 1970.

Processing of the large shrimp and fish catch consists of grading, washing, peeling, deveining, and packing done by twelve companies, eight of which are located in Panama City and Taboga Island. The Panamanian Cooperative Fishing Company is the largest, with a declared investment of about B/5 million, of which B/4 million is in fishing vessels and B/1 million in the processing plant. Freezing units to store 3,000 to 4,000 pounds of shrimp and cold storage units for as much as 100,000 pounds of shrimp are available.

The domestic production of beer, rum, whiskey, and soft drinks rose rapidly during World War II, and the National Brewery Company was formed during the war by the merger of three small breweries. It produces over 3 million gallons of beer annually. A number of distilleries produce 400,000 gallons of rum and alcohol from molasses and sugarcane juice, and wineries produce a variety of wines. The inexpensive popular fermented drinks of the interior are *seco* and the homemade *chicha*. Anisette, cognac, and liqueurs are also produced in small quantities. Soft drinks are produced by eighteen enterprises.

Bread is baked by 200 small bakeries all over the country and two modern plants in Panama City. A large quantity of bread produced by the leading plant is purchased by the United States Army. Crackers and cookies of all types are produced in a large, fully mechanized plant and several small enterprises. Noodles, macaroni, spaghetti, and other wheat products are also made in ten plants with a capacity much larger than the demand. Four companies produce ice cream, and there are several candy and chocolate processing enterprises, which supply the domestic market.

Three cigarette factories, all located in Panama City, supply a considerable portion of the domestic demand of 1.8 million pounds of tobacco products. There are plans to develop the growing of a broadleaved tobacco that could be used for the manufacture of cigars.

Construction and Construction Materials

The construction industry in 1971 consisted of about 240 small contractors and six or seven larger construction companies with their own engineering and planning departments, transportation facilities, machinery, and a nucleus of permanent employees. The growth of the industry is indicated by the rising annual investment in construction—from less than B/10 million in 1950 to over B/57 million in 1970. Panama City accounts for an estimated 60 percent of total construction.

Construction is basically dependent on domestic or foreign credit. After World War II, when wartime savings became available for investment, construction entered a period of boom; when private investment seemed to fade out, large-scale public work projects kept the industry working at its peak capacity. Foreign loans have enabled the government to take up the slack in construction by engaging in such public works as the construction of highways, airports, port facilities, sewerage systems, schools, and hospitals. Private construction is mainly residential and commercial.

Cement and cement products, which once were costly imports, have become a profitable line of export. The fifth largest industrial enterprise in the country is the Panama Cement Company, located some twenty-eight miles north of Panama City in Colón Province. The plant, which began operation in 1948, had an annual production capacity of 10 million bags of cement (ninety-four pounds each) in 1971, which is more than the local construction industry can use. The establishment of the industry enabled the country to begin cement export in 1952. A new asbestos-cement plant was opened in 1960, and two years later an abaca fiber-cement plant also began operations.

Drainage, roof, floor, and hollow clay building tiles, brick, and pottery are produced by over sixty small firms, which supply almost the entire need of the domestic construction industry. A large plant in Panama City plus three smaller ones manufacture a full line of vitreous products and fixtures.

The country has sixty-five sawmills and lumberyards and one plywood and veneer mill, owned by the Panama Plywood Corporation (Plywood de Panamá). This mill is able to supply almost the entire local demand for plywood, veneers, and railroad ties. It is also engaged in the manufacturing of prefabricated houses and semifinished lumber for carpenter shops and construction companies. Over sixty small plants are making furniture of low quality; furniture of good quality is still imported. About twenty companies make other wood products.

Seventeen boatbuilders engage in the construction of vessels for the fishing industry. One of them is a large shipyard with an annual capacity of twenty steel trawlers. The others build smaller boats, most of them of wood. One small plant processes mangrove bark for tanneries.

Other Industries

The five largest tanneries are in Panama City, Chitré, and David. One of the tanneries in Panama City specializes in tourist articles made from alligator skin. Representatives of tanneries continually complain about the poor quality of domestic hides attributable to careless branding practices and damage caused by the torso fly. Such damage to the hides reduces the quality and usable portions of the hides and increases the production cost of leather. Fifteen other companies make small leather goods.

Six small textile factories manufacture a variety of fabrics. Readymade dresses and suits are made by sixty-five clothing firms, mostly from imported textiles, and more than 100 tailor shops make clothes to order. Some 500,000 pairs of shoes, most of them of low-to-fair quality, are produced by thirty-six mechanized shoe factories and 100 individual shoemakers. Some of the upper leather is imported, but all sole leather is obtained from domestic sources. About the same number of shoes—mainly of rubber and cloth—are imported. *Alpargatas* (light shoes made of fiber soles and canvas tops), popular in the interior, are also manufactured domestically.

Seventeen firms that repair and retread tires serve both the domestic market and the United States forces in the Canal Zone. Batteries are produced domestically from imported parts by six companies. About 100 shops repair vehicles, ten shops repair and make machinery, and about forty shops make and repair electrical equipment.

Several shops use light metal to manufacture tanks, bins, sinks, and other metal commodities. Imported paper is used to manufacture bags and sanitary paper by fifteen companies. Paints and varnishes, produced according to United States specifications by four firms, are sold mostly in the Canal Zone. The local market imports two-thirds of its paint needs. Oxygen and acetylene are produced for welding, and carbon dioxide is produced for use by beverage plants.

The Panama Steel Mill (Siderúrgica Panamá) was established in 1958, although many economic experts opposed its construction because steel consumption is small and no good sources of iron ore and coal exist locally. Between 11,000 and 13,000 tons of steel are produced annually by the steel plant. An aluminum extrusion plant produces several hundred tons of pipes, tubes, and bars annually.

Handicrafts

The government classifies all establishments with fewer than five employees as small scale. Most of them are operated by the owner and members of his family. An estimated 15,000 families devote themselves solely to these cottage-type industries. They make such items as wood articles, leather, clay products, fiber and straw articles, paper articles, rubber articles, and glass articles. Most of these small industries have difficulties in financing expansion or operating costs. In an effort to promote and encourage diversified handicrafts and small-scale industry, the government created the National Service for Handicrafts and Small-Scale Industry (Servicio Nacional de Artesanías y Pequeñas Industrias —SENAPI) in 1966. The United Nations and the International Labor Organization helped with its financing and technical assistance. SENAPI is emphasizing its activities in the interior of the country.

The subsistence farmer of the interior has little cash to spare for the purchase of consumer goods. Many families therefore prepare their own beverages, grind their own flour, and make their own eating utensils, agricultural implements, and much of their furniture, clothing, and recreational equipment as part-time occupations. The most common containers are made of gourds. Such items as storage bins, measuring cups, plates, and spoons are easily made by any member of the family by cutting a gourd of approximate size and form in half or into the desired shape and drying it in the sun. Wood products, such as benches, stools, spoons, and mortars, are usually made by the male members of the family, but in larger communities carpenters are not uncommon. Persons skilled in woodwork may also produce musical instruments, such as violins, guitars, and drums.

Baskets of various sizes and shapes are also made at home by the men. There is little specialization in basketry, although there are communities that sell their surplus to neighboring settlements. Baskets are needed to carry produce and to strain *chicha;* straw mats, hammocks, net bags, and other fiber products are also made for the household. Such items are also for sale near tourist centers. Men make leather bags to carry produce on horseback or muleback, as well as chairs with leather seats and leather sandals. The *chuspa,* a pouch for tobacco made of snake or iguana skin, can still be seen in Los Santos Province.

Women used to make their own yarn almost exclusively, but both spinning and weaving have almost completely disappeared as household industries. Women still sew their own dresses from purchased textiles and prepare bed linen and men's shirts in the home. They also crochet the *chácara,* a traditional traveling bag or purse, and make straw hats for the family, and some produce for sale. Only in a few isolated areas do men make their own clothes.

Pottery is also made by women. Cooking jars, storage bins, and water containers are commonly produced in the family, but some women specialize in pottery and supply the entire community with their products. Although there are a few remote communities—mainly Indian settlements in Darién and San Blas—that produce their own weapons, fuel oils, and soap, in most areas even the poorest *campesino* (small farmer or peasant) purchases these items commercially.

Construction of homes, storage places, and fences is also a family affair. Friends with special skills are often asked to help, but carpenters and contractors are employed by those economically better off for the construction of projects that are beyond the capabilities of the family unit.

LABOR

Composition of Labor Force

The labor force in 1969 was reported provisionally to number about 424,000 persons, as compared with 330,000 in 1960 (see table 17). These figures do not include tribal Indians or persons seeking work for the first time. The totals are not fully comparable because those for 1969 do not include workers under the age of fifteen (there had been some 11,000 of these in 1960). Between 1960 and 1969 the size of the labor force fifteen years of age and older increased from about 30 to 30.2 percent of the population as a whole. This slight gain, however, was probably more than offset by a decline in the proportion under the age of fifteen because of the progressively greater number of young people remaining in school for a greater number of years.

In 1971 the most recent data available concerning the age of the labor force were those presented in the 1960 population census. For the force as a whole, the rate of participation increased progressively from 2.6 percent of the population under the age of fifteen to 63.4 percent between the ages of thirty and forty-nine before decreasing progressively in older age groups, although

Table 17. Labor Force in Panama by Sector of Economic Activity and Sex, 1960 and 1969

(in thousands)

Sector of Economic Activity	1960[1]			1969 [1] [2]		
	Total	Male	Female	Total	Male	Female
Agriculture, forestry, hunting, and fishing..	156	151	5	164	157	7
Mining and quarrying	—[3]	—[3]	—[3]	—[3]	—[3]	—[a]
Manufacturing	26	19	6	47	31	16
Construction	14	14	—[3]	21	20	—[3]
Electricity, gas, water, and sanitary services	2	1	—[3]	3	3	—[3]
Commerce	31	21	10	53	33	19
Transport, warehousing, and communications	10	9	1	16	14	2
Services	68	27	41	100	35	65
Canal Zone	19	15	4	22	17	6
Activities not well specified	5	4	1	—[4]	—[4]	—[4]
TOTAL	330	261	69	424	310	114

[1] Because of rounding, columns do not necessarily total.
[2] Preliminary data.
[3] Reported as greater than 0 but less than 501.
[4] None reported.

Source: Adapted from Republic of Panama, Contraloría General de la República, Dirección de Estadística y Censo, *Panamá en cifras*. (*Compendio Estadístico, años 1965 a 1969*), Panama City, 1970, pp. 148–149; and U.S. Department of Labor, Bureau of Labor Statistics, *Labor Law and Practice in Panama*, Washington, 1970, p. 10.

32.3 percent in the nominal retirement-age group of those over sixty-five years of age continued to be active economically (see table 18).

For males the maximum rate of participation—96.9 percent— was attained in the age bracket between the ages of thirty and forty-nine, but for females the maximum was attained at the substantially earlier age of twenty to twenty-four years, a reflection of the larger number of young women leaving the labor force because of the responsibilities of marriage and family. About three-fourths of all employed females during 1960 were single, and the unmarried proportion was not substantially lower in the older age brackets; apparently, few women continued to work after marriage.

The proportion of females in the labor force rose from 19.5 percent in 1950 to 20.9 percent in 1960 and to 26.9 percent in 1969. The phenomenal increase in the rate of female participation, particularly during the 1960s, was a direct consequence of the country-to-town migration, in which well over half of the participants were females. Young women for the most part, they had been unable to find jobs in agriculture, where in 1969 they represented less than 5 percent of all agricultural employment. After arrival in urban localities many found jobs—for the most part, unskilled ones in the services sector of employment—and for the first time were counted as members of the labor force. Between 1960 and 1969 female participation increased at a rate faster than that of males in all major occupational sectors. In

Table 18. Rate of Participation of Population of Panama in Labor Force by Age and Sex, 1960

(in percent)*

Age	Male	Female	Total
Under 15	4.0	1.1	2.6
15 to 19	63.2	23.5	43.2
20 to 24	92.3	31.2	62.0
25 to 29	96.5	28.3	62.8
30 to 49	96.9	27.1	63.4
50 to 54	95.0	21.8	60.8
55 to 59	92.4	17.4	55.6
60 to 64	81.8	12.9	48.6
65 and over	57.5	6.6	32.3
All ages	51.4	14.5	33.3

* Based on totals including persons seeking work for the first time.

Source: Adapted from *Yearbook of Labour Statistics*, 1970 (30th issue), Geneva, p. 33.

1969 females far outnumbered males in personal services because of the predominance of female domestic servants; in the sector of professional and related workers, they were in a large and increasing majority because of the considerable number of female schoolteachers in this category (see table 19).

Between 1960 and 1969 the proportion of workers employed in the primary, or agricultural, sector declined from about 50 to 41 percent of all employment excluding the Canal Zone. During the same period secondary, or industrial, employment rose from 13 to 18 percent, and tertiary, or commercial and services, employment was up from 37 to 41 percent.

The number of wage and salary earners rose from 168,000 to 217,000, or from 48 percent to 51 percent of the labor force, between 1965 and 1969. During the same period the number of employers and self-employed persons increased moderately, but their proportion declined, and the actual number of family work-

Table 19. Labor Force in Panama by Occupation and Sex, 1960 and 1969

(in thousands)

Occupation	1960 [1]			1969 [1][2]		
	Total	Male	Female	Total	Male	Female
Professional, technical, and related workers	16	7	9	22	9	13
Administrative executive, and managerial workers	8	7	1	15	14	2
Clerical workers	21	10	11	32	14	18
Sales workers	18	12	6	31	18	13
Farmers, fishermen, hunters, loggers, and related workers	152	148	4	159	152	7
Miners, quarrymen, and related workers	—[3]	—[3]	—[3]	—[3]	—[3]	—[3]
Transport and communication workers	12	12	—[3]	18	18	—[3]
Craftsmen, production process workers, and laborers not elsewhere classified	52	45	7	80	64	16
Service and related workers	43	14	29	66	20	46
Workers not classifiable by occupation	7	5	2	—[3]	—[3]	—[3]
TOTAL	330	261	69	424	310	114

[1] Because of rounding, columns do not necessarily total.
[2] Preliminary data.
[3] Reported as greater than 0 but less than 501.

Source: Adapted from Republic of Panama, Contraloría General de la República, Dirección de Estadística y Censo, Panamá en cifras (Compendio Estadístico, años 1965 a 1969), Panama City, 1970, pp. 150–151; and U.S. Department of Labor, Bureau of Labor Statistics, Labor Law and Practice in Panama, Washington, 1970, p. 10.

ers suffered a small decline (see table 20). The 1965 and 1969 data do not distinguish between employers and self-employed persons. Figures for 1950 and 1960, however, show the proportion of employers in the labor force to have remained stable at about 2 percent of the total.

In 1969 some 46,000 persons were employed by government entities. This was almost 60 percent more than the number employed in 1960, a growth rate twice that of the labor force as a whole. In 1969 about 75 percent of the public employees were employed by the central government, and the balance were divided about equally between autonomous public agencies and local administrations.

Between 1960 and 1969 employment in the Canal Zone increased from about 19,000 to 22,000, but during this period its proportion as a component in the labor force declined from 6 to 5 percent of the total. A large proportion of the personnel are West Indians or descendants of West Indian people who came to Panama for employment in the construction of the canal; women occupy about one-fourth of the jobs, including many of the better paid white-collar positions. Employment in the zone tends to be permanent, and the average worker is in his late thirties, somewhat older than the labor-force average. The labor force is concentrated principally at the Pacific and Atlantic terminals of the canal, and most live in Panama City and Colón. The remainder are housed in the zone in Gamboa, Rainbow City, and other towns scattered along the course of the canal.

Skills

The labor force is generally deficient in skills and, as in most Latin American countries, the incidence of skills is lowest in agriculture. In particular, skills are few among the subsistence farmers; they are virtually without education, and the large number who practice shifting agriculture feel little incentive to abandon their traditional methods. The average level of proficiency among farm laborers is somewhat higher because of the fairly high pay and on-the-job training available to the 15,000 workers on the banana plantations.

The incidence of skills in the industrial sector is much higher. Productivity is three times that in agriculture, and skill shortages are gradually being met, largely through adult and on-the-job vocational training. Most of the blue-collar skills are found in this sector, but most of them are limited ones, and the growth of employment in the sector has been so rapid that the relative number of totally unskilled workers has increased substantially.

Table 20. Agricultural and Other Employment in Panama by Category of Worker and Sex, 1965 and 1969

(in thousands)

Category of Worker	Total			Male			Female		
	Total	Agri-culture	Other	Total	Agri-culture	Other	Total	Agri-culture	Other
1965[1]									
Employers and self-employed	134	92	42	116	89	27	18	3	15
Wage and salary earners	168	27	141	114	26	88	54	1	53
Family workers	47	44	3	41	40	1	6	4	2
TOTAL	350	165	185	271	156	115	79	9	70
1969[1][2]									
Employers and self-employed	161	90	71	126	88	38	35	2	33
Wage and salary earners	217	33	184	145	31	114	72	2	70
Family workers	46	40	6	38	36	2	8	4	4
TOTAL	424	163	261	310	156	154	114	7	107

[1] Because of rounding, columns do not necessarily total.
[2] Preliminary data.

Source: Adapted from Republic of Panama, Contraloría General de la República, Dirección de Estadística y Censo, *Panamá en cifras* (*Compendio Estadístico, años 1965 a 1969*), Panama City, 1970, pp. 152–154.

303

The economy is generally oriented toward trade, where most of the relatively abundant supply of white-collar skills is found. In service occupations, the level of proficiency at the professional level is high, but the supply is limited. Most of the services sector, moreover, is made up of almost totally unskilled workers employed as custodians, street vendors, and domestic servants. Many or most of these are urban immigrants from the countryside.

A 1970 study based on population census data has attempted to determine the proportions of the labor force in 1950 and 1960 engaged in white-collar and unskilled work. The study does not furnish criteria for distinguishing between skilled and unskilled work and is of limited value as an indicator of the general prevalence of skills. It does, however, indicate trends in the several sectors of employment.

The proportion of unskilled labor in the primary, or agricultural, sector declined from 98.7 percent of the labor force in that sector in 1950 to 98 percent in 1960; the white-collar proportion rose moderately from 0.34 to 0.65 percent. In the secondary, or industrial, sector white-collar rolls were up from 6.45 to 8.2 percent, and unskilled were up from 6.72 to 11.9 percent of the total. In tertiary, or services, employment white-collar rolls rose from 21.8 to 26.3 percent; and unskilled labor, from 38.8 to 40.8 percent. In general, the pattern was one of an increase in the white-collar and the unskilled worker and a relative erosion in the number of blue-collar personnel listed as having acquired some skills.

The same study showed the skills of females to have increased much more rapidly than those of males between 1950 and 1960. In the labor force as a whole, the proportion of white-collar workers increased by 2.7 percent, including 1.1 percent for male and 8.8 percent for female workers. During the same period there was a proportional decline of 1.5 percent in blue-collar and 2.3 percent in unskilled employment. In both instances the rate of decline for females was about four times that for males.

The number of self-employed persons and family workers in the labor force declined progressively from 56.6 percent of the total in 1950 to 50.1 percent in 1960 and to an estimated 45.3 percent in 1969. Since workers in these categories tend to be unskilled or to possess skills of a traditional or obsolescent nature, their relative decline in number strongly suggests a rise in the average level of capabilities of the labor force.

In 1960 well over 40 percent of the labor force (and 70 percent of the farmers) were without formal education or had less than three years of primary school. Most of the remainder had no more than from four years to the full six years of primary school. The advantage to students resulting from completed primary schooling was higher in Panama than in all but one of five other countries reviewed in the 1970 study but was by far the lowest of the six with respect to the return to education resulting from secondary schooling.

Unemployment

The level of unemployment ranged irregularly downward from 9.1 percent of the labor force in 1960 to 5.1 percent in 1966 before veering upward to 6.7 percent in 1970. These proportions do not include persons seeking employment for the first time.

Overt unemployment has been consistently higher in urban than in rural localities. In 1969 the rate was 9.4 percent in the heavily urbanized Metropolitan Area and 3.6 percent in the predominant agricultural remainder of the country. In addition, unemployment has been considerably higher in moderately urbanized Chiriquí than in the agricultural region of Central Panama and lowest in the frontier regions of Atlantic Panama and Darién.

By sector of economic activity, unemployment in 1960 ranged from less than 2 percent in agriculture and related activities to in excess of 10 percent in all of the occupations in the industrial and services sectors. Underemployment has been extensive in agriculture, however, and a large proportion of the urban unemployed have been unskilled migrants from the countryside. Many of these have migrated because of inability to find rural employment and might have appeared as elements in the unemployment statistics had they remained part of the agricultural labor force.

The incidence of unemployment for females, already far higher than that for males, rose from a rate less than twice that for males in 1965 to one more than three times that for males in 1969. The higher rate among women occurs largely because of the relatively limited variety of jobs open to them, but the rise in the rate reflects the great number attempting to enter the labor force during recent years. In 1960, for example, only one-fifth of the labor force was female, but females seeking employment for the first time constituted virtually half of the total.

Data from the 1960 census show overt unemployment to have been lower among those without formal education and those with higher education than among those with some schooling. The lowest rate was registered by those without education, but this sector was made up in large part of subsistence farmers and other self-employed persons, many of whom were underemployed and had little cash income. The rate was much higher but still well under the average rate for the labor force in the case of persons with university backgrounds, a reflection of the limited supply and considerable demand for professionals and highly skilled technical and managerial personnel.

For persons with complete or incomplete primary education the unemployment rate was somewhat higher than the labor-force average, and it was almost twice that average for those with some secondary schooling. The much higher incidence of unemployment among those with more education relates to the fact that young people who have attended secondary schools tend to look not for blue-collar but for the white-collar commercial or office employment for which competition is heavy. Commercial skills are taught in the secondary schools, but industrial skills are more often acquired in training courses or on the job by workers with enough primary background to have made them capable of this training. The relatively small number of qualified blue-collar industrial workers encounter little difficulty in finding jobs.

Wages

The average level of wages is higher in Panama than in any of the other Central American countries and is among the highest in Latin America. Over half of the labor force is paid on a monthly basis, but most of the blue-collar force receives hourly or daily payments, and there are some weekly pay schedules. The Labor Code also recognizes piecework and commission payment, and payment in kind may be made for a portion but not all of the wage. Payments in money, however, must be in legal tender; the use of promissory notes or vouchers of any kind is forbidden.

Minimum wage legislation is an integral part of the Labor Code, and in 1971 there was a generally applicable wage floor of B/0.40 per hour for work in places with populations in excess of 20,000 and of B/0.25 per hour in the rest of the country. A general floor of B/2.00 per day was in effect for agricultural labor.

The minimum wages are fixed periodically for geographic regions and sectors of employment by the Ministry of Labor and Social Welfare on the basis of reports submitted by the National Minimum Wage Council, which also oversees enforcement of the minimums. For the years 1968 and 1969 in localities including most of the Metropolitan Area, the minimums in stated occupations in the industrial and services sectors of employment ranged from B/0.50 to B/0.65 per hour. For the years 1968 and 1969 the hourly minimums for occupations in the industrial and services sectors of employment in the cities of Panama and Colón and several other districts of the Metropolitan Area ranged from B/0.50 to B/0.70. The B/0.70 minimum applied only to electricity and gas workers.

Longevity wage increases are not required under the Labor Code. They are customary, however, and since the 1950s wages have moved sharply upward in a rise that reflected a considerable real as well as a nominal gain. Between 1956 and 1960 real wages in manufacturing rose 8.7 percent annually. Between 1961 and 1969 the average in six major employment sectors calculated on a basis of monthly payments rose more than 50 percent from B/129 to B/198 (see table 21).

Although minimum wages are the same for both sexes, the average wage for women is somewhat less than that for men. In 1969 it was more than 30 percent lower in the Metropolitan Area and 15 percent lower in the rest of the country. There is little, if any, correlation between age and level of wages. In Panama City during 1960 the average monthly wage for all workers between fifteen and nineteen was in the same range as that of workers between twenty and twenty-four and was slightly higher than that for persons over the age of thirty-five.

The level of basic wages paid in the Metropolitan Area is quite different from that prevailing in the rest of the country. For male workers in the agricultural sector of employment in the Metropolitan Areas, the basic wage in 1969 was reported as averaging under B/15 weekly (although 24 percent received between B/15 and B/24 and 13 percent received B/25 or more). In the rest of the country the average for males was B/15.20; the pay of farm labor outside the Metropolitan Area averaged higher because of the relatively high pay (more than B/30 weekly) of the banana plantation personnel. Wages for female workers in the agricultural sector in the Metropolitan Area were not reported. In the rest of the country they averaged B/19.50, substantially more than for males—probably because many women occupied office positions on plantations and commercial farms.

In the nonagricultural sectors of employment, male wages averaged B/36.20 per week in the Metropolitan Area and B/21.70 in

Table 21. Average Wages per Month in Panama, 1961, 1965, and 1969
(in balboas)*

	1961	1965	1969
Private enterprise	126	142	172
Banana plantations	116	102	145
Central government	120	145	183
Autonomous agencies	157	178	211
Local governments	78	86	102
Canal Zone	169	297	372
NATIONAL AVERAGE	129	157	198

* 1 balboa equals US$1.

the rest of the country. Wages for females averaged B/23.30 and 17.10, respectively. For both sexes in both parts of the country the highest wages were paid by gas and electricity producers, banking and financial institutions, and the national government. The lowest salaries were paid to females engaged in personal services, who received wages reported as averaging less than B/10 per week both in the Metropolitan Area and in the rest of the country.

During the 1960s the Canal Zone workers enjoyed both the highest and fastest rising pay of the several sectors of employment as a consequence of upward adjustments made in accordance with United States minimum wage requirements. In 1967 fewer than 1 percent earned less than B/1 per hour; 73 percent earned between B/1 and B/2; over 17 percent earned between B/2 and B/3; and 8 percent earned B/3 or more. One percent of the workers—most of them women—were paid on a monthly basis and received B/500 or more a month.

On the basis of a forty-hour week, Panamanian workers employed by United States government agencies in Panama City received salaries of up to about B/10,000 annually. Compensation ranged from B/8,610 to B/10,220 for a consulting senior engineer, from B/5,405 to B/6,525 for an auditor, from B/2,575 to B/3,415 for a clerk-stenographer, from B/1,680 to B/3,415 for a photo-lab technician, from B/1,680 to B/2,870 for a switchboard operator, and from B/1,645 to B/3,130 for a chauffeur (fifty hours).

These wage levels are comparable to those paid to officeworkers in foreign-owned enterprises in Panama, as recorded in a 1967 survey conducted by the Chase Manhattan Bank. An average of B/4,627 was paid to executive secretaries, B/3,430 to junior examiners, B/2,644 to stenographers, B/1,919 to file clerk-typists, and B/1,619 to janitors and watchmen.

There is no Labor Code provision for severance pay or bonus payments, although many individual employers give *aguinaldos* (Christmas bonuses) and some employers offer supplemental incentive payments and cash prizes. The basic pay for urban workers within the lower paid sectors of employment, however, is often insufficient to enable them to maintain their households. As a consequence, moonlighting is fairly common; custodial personnel, in particular, tend to hold two jobs.

In 1969 only about half of the economically active population worked for wages or salaries. Some 90,000—about 21 percent of the labor force—were farm operators whose cash incomes were derived principally or solely from the sale of their produce. A 1966 government survey found that fewer than 4 percent of the farms produced cash incomes in excess of B/1,000 annually and about 21 percent produced between B/100 and B/1,000. The

remaining 75 percent produced less than B/100, and nearly half of these had no recorded cash income. The operators of these farms, who made up nearly 10 percent of the labor force, were true subsistence farmers, who probably engaged in considerable barter but who remained entirely outside the cash economy except to the extent that some received some money as seasonal workers on plantations.

Conditions of Employment

Employment procedures are not well developed. Few facilities exist for verifying qualifications of job applicants, although urban private agencies reported in 1971 that they had commenced requiring applicants to submit previous employment records, police records, and other personal data.

Private employment agencies are concentrated in Panama City, where some thirty offices are concerned with the placement of domestic servants. A government labor exchange that operated in Panama City and Colón during the early 1960s and a national exchange in existence from 1964 to 1968 were replaced by the Employment Service of the Ministry of Labor and Social Welfare. During the late 1960s, however, word of mouth and newspaper advertising remained the most common means of finding work.

Conditions of employment are prescribed by the comprehensive Labor Code of 1947, as modified by subsequent legislation. A comprehensive revision of this code had been prepared as early as 1969 but had not been promulgated by mid-1971.

Labor matters are the responsibility of the Ministry of Labor and Social Welfare, an entity created in 1969 by a separation of the functions of the previous Ministry of Labor, Social Welfare, and Public Health. Laws and regulations in the ministry's areas of competence are administered by inspectors who function under the Inspectorate General of Labor, with headquarters in Panama City and offices in provincial capitals. In 1968 there were nine inspectors assigned in Panama Province and six inspectors assigned elsewhere in the country.

The maximum regular workweek consists of forty-eight hours divided into eight-hour days for daytime work and forty-two hours divided into seven-hour days for night work. A daily rest period of thirty minutes is mandatory for all workers. For minors the week may not exceed forty-two hours, and the day is limited to seven hours. No general limitation on work periods for women is imposed. There are certain exceptions to the general maximum of eight hours for a rgeular day's work, but a general limitation of eleven hours including overtime is prescribed.

In practice, the number of hours actually worked in the manufacturing industry is reported by the International Labor Organization as having varied irregularly between forty-two hours weekly in 1958, forty-seven hours in 1963, and forty-three hours in 1968. In the agricultural sector, banana companies strictly observe the regular eight-hour-day limitation, but practices are reported to vary for migrant workers on the coffee, rice, and other agricultural plantations, and self-employed farmers work a day of twelve hours or more during peak periods.

Overtime is paid at the rate of time and one-quarter for daytime employment. Night overtime is at the rate of time and one-half if it is a continuation of daytime work and time and three-quarters if it is a continuation of night work.

A mandatory weekly day of rest should occur on Sunday, but another day of rest may be designated to avoid interruption of necessary work. Workers are also entitled to the ten national holidays (see ch. 4, Living Conditions). After every eleven months of continuous employment, workers are eligible for one month's vacation with pay. For daily- and hourly-wage personnel, compensation for the vacation period is on the basis of the days during which they were actually engaged in work. These workers are not necessarily paid for the weekly days of rest, but the draft revision of the Labor Code is reported to contain provision for Sunday pay, a perennial demand of organized labor.

Wage and salary earners are entitled to eighteen days of paid annual sick leave, which may be accumulated during a period of two consecutive years. In addition, women are entitled to leave for six weeks preceding and eight weeks following childbirth. When wages covering this period are not payable under the country's social security program, the employer is liable for their payment.

No general restrictions apply to the employment of women. Children under the age of sixteen, however, are under the protection of the government's Institute for Vigilance and Protection of Children and are not permitted to engage in certain occupations. Under the age of fifteen, they are permitted to work only if they have completed primary school. The regular employment of children under this age is rare except in rural areas, where the minimum age is twelve years for those engaged in farming and livestock activities.

An increasing number of workers, principally urban, participate in a retirement and disability program funded by 5 percent of their taxable incomes supplemented by a 7-percent employer contribution. In addition, a 1970 decree extended a previously limited occupational injury and illness insurance program to include employers and self-employed persons (see ch. 4, Living Conditions). Some fringe benefits, such as the requirement that day nurseries be established by larger firms, are required by law, and some foreign firms offer group life insurance programs. In general, however, fewer fringe benefits are conditions of employment than in most Latin American countries.

There is a general rule that a minimum of 75 percent of the workers in every commercial or industrial enterprise be Panamanian citizens and that 75 percent of the wages be paid to them. Foreigners resident for twenty years or more as well as those married to Panamanians are considered citizens for this purpose. Exceptions with respect to personnel in certain highly qualified categories may be made by the minister of labor and social welfare. The 75-percent formula is more or less standard in the labor law of Latin American countries, but a mandatorily higher percentage of Panamanian participation has been a continuing demand of organized Panamanian labor.

Labor Relations

Title I of the Labor Code regulates the individual contracts that cover most of the wage- and salary-earning population. They are customarily for an indefinite period but may also be for a limited time. They need not be written when they concern farming or livestock activities, domestic services, occasional or temporary work not exceeding three months, work for services contracted in a place with no more than 500 inhabitants, or work of a specified nature involving no more than a total cost of B/100.

There is no probationary period for new employees. During the first three months of employment, the workers may be separated after a notice period of twenty-four hours. After longer periods of employment, the notice period increases progressively to a maximum of six months after more than twenty-five years. There is no provision for terminal pay, but the worker on receiving or giving notice has the option of working during the notice period or of receiving immediate payment equivalent to the pay for work during it.

The requirement of advance notice applies both to dismissal and to voluntary resignation of the worker, and a schedule of penalties is prescribed for its nonobservance. There are also schedules of causes justifying either dismissal or voluntary resignation without notice.

Although comparatively rare, collective contracts usually supplement individual contracts and usually involve the larger foreign-owned firms. They are negotiated on a local rather than an industrywide basis and are applicable to nonunion as well as to union personnel. In general, the contracts negotiated have concerned wage-hour and social matters to the near exclusion of such considerations as job qualifications, job retention, and union prerogatives.

The principal tribunal for the settlement of labor disputes is the Superior Labor Court, an autonomous judicial agency quartered in Panama City. Under it are five sectional labor courts—one for the provinces of Panama and Darién, one for the four provinces of Central Panama, and one for each of the three remaining provinces. The Superior Labor Court acts on resolutions submitted to it by the sectional courts. Disputes not resolved by it within five days and appeals in matters involving amounts in excess of B/500 are referred to the Supreme Court of Justice.

In enterprises that have not been unionized, grievances are usually first handled directly with the owner of a small establishment or with the shop superintendent of a larger concern. A 1963 Labor Code amendment, however, specifies that all stock companies (*sociedades anónimas*) having ten or more workers who are employed for three or more months must see to the naming of a representative for workers in that locality. This representative assumes responsibility before the proper court for any claims presented by a worker.

Initially, all collective disputes are subject to direct negotiation between employers and worker committees established under the supervision of the Inspectorate General of Labor. Should no agreement be reached as a result of direct negotiation, the dispute is subjected to conciliation by a tripartite board established by and presided over by the competent court judge under procedures specified by law. If no settlement has been reached after ten days, the board must terminate its intervention. The dispute may then be subjected to compulsory arbitration under procedures similar to those for conciliation. Recourse to arbitration is, however, rare.

In the absence of a settlement or a decision to refer the dispute to arbitration, the sectional labor judge may propose the declaration of a strike or lockout if 60 percent of all workers affected support the strike call. The proposal is then referred to the Superior Labor Court for final decision with respect to the legality or illegality of the proposed action, and workers are granted a twenty-day time period in which to declare a strike. For lockouts, the time period is three days following a fourteen-day period during which workers may terminate their contracts.

Secondary or sympathy strikes and strikes by public employees are prohibited. Major strikes involving both of these elements, however, occurred during 1965. A sympathy strike involving the strong Typographers' Union (Sindicato de Tipográficos y Artes Gráficas) resulted in mass discharges and the substantial weakening of the union, and a strike of public services workers was settled by compromise. An exact count of the number and severity of strikes of all kinds occurring during recent years is not available. In general, however, strikes have been discouraged by the government, and few have taken place.

Worker and Employer Organizations

The Constitution guarantees to both workers and employers the right to organize unions or associations for the protection of their economic and social interests. In order to qualify for official recognition (*personería jurídica*), a workers' union must have at least twenty members, and an employers' association must be made up of at least five independent employers.

The types of union organizations recognized by the government are the craft union, formed by workers engaged in the same occupation or trade; the plant union, formed by workers of various occupations or trades in the same enterprise; the industrial union, formed by persons of various occupations or trades employed by two or more enterprises of the same kind; and the mixed union, formed by workers engaged in various or unconnected activities in a province or in an enterprise where the number of workers in one craft is not sufficient to meet the legal minimum requirement for organization. Federation of workers may be formed by two or more unions.

Organized labor's collective membership is of moderate size. In 1963 it was estimated at less than 20,000, or about 6 percent of the labor force. It enjoyed some gains during the late 1960s but in 1971 probably remained substantially less than 10 percent of the total. Many Panamanians are reluctant to join unions that include West Indian members, with whom they have been accustomed to compete vigorously for jobs in the major cities and the Canal Zone. Union membership is predominantly urban, and the wage- and salary-earning sector of the labor force that represents nearly all of the potential union membership makes up only about half of the labor force. Many of these are commercial and office employees, who are often seeking middle-class status and are, accordingly, not eager for the identification with the laboring class that would result from union membership.

Unions are anxious to attract new members, and a unionized labor elite has not developed. The general level of skills is insufficiently high for unions to insist on high occupational qualifications, and a scarcity of labor qualified for the skilled blue-collar jobs of primary concern to union members virtually precludes any union attempt to control the employment of this skilled manpower. The Labor Code's prohibition of union activity that restricts the freedom to work by preventing nonmembers from engaging in their occupations appears to proscribe the closed shop. Moreover, unions are receptive to vocational training programs, and their nominal reluctance to accept the installation of labor-saving machinery appears to be underlaid by a recognition that in the long run they will benefit from the resulting higher productivity.

Discipline is often lax and, in most unions, attendance at meetings is more regular than dues payment. As yet unaware of the potential strength of organized labor, workers seldom support their organizations to the extent necessary for fully effective operation. In general, local unions are so small that shop stewards are unnecessary; presiding officers usually handle grievances and approach the memberships directly with requests for support.

Union positions with respect to such matters as the closed shop and conditions of employment are often ambiguous, and organized labor has never presented a united front either in its political orientation or in its economic and social goals. In this connection, General Omar Torrijos late in 1969 urged the formation of a general union of workers embracing the entire labor force and modeled on the organized labor program of Mexico.

A series of sixteen demands presented to the government by the country's largest national labor organization in 1971 suggested an increased concern over union organization as well as over conditions of employment. In addition to demands for reform of minimum-wage legislation, a forty-hour week, retirement at the age of fifty-five, and other economic and social considerations, the list included many demands aimed specifically at the strengthening of organized labor. Among these were more effective enforcement of collective bargaining, the establishment of labor courses in school curricula, immunity from dismissal for officers of labor federations and confederations, payroll deductions of union dues, effective labor participation in Panama Canal treaty negotiations, and the establishment of facilities for extending unionization to rural activities.

The first labor unions, organized soon after World War I, were heterogeneous groups in which labor mingled with intellectuals who saw in the workers a means for political expression, often communist in its orientation. At the end of World War II a labor congress held in Panama City led to establishment of the Trade Union Federation of Workers of the Republic of Panama (Federación Sindical de Trabajadores de la República de Panamá—

314

FSTRP), a leftist organization that for a short time was able to claim the support of most of organized labor.

During the 1940s communism also made substantial gains among Panamanian workers in the Canal Zone through the establishment of the leftist-directed Local Union 100 of the United Public Workers of America, a United States-based entity affiliated with the Congress of Industrial Organizations (CIO). In 1949, however, the parent CIO expelled the United Public Workers of America as communist-dominated and reorganized its Canal Zone affiliate as a unit free from communist influence.

By 1950 communist leadership in the trade union movement had faltered. The General Union of Workers (Unión General de Trabajadores) and several other smaller noncommunist central labor organizations came into existence to challenge the FSTRP, which by 1954 had lost the allegiance of all but three of its constituent unions. In 1956 the Confederation of Workers of the Republic of Panama (Confederación de Trabajadores de la República de Panamá—CTRP) was organized as a politically moderate national organization. It survived a 1963 secessionist move by four member federations, which was declared illegal by the government, and by 1968 its membership of about 14,200 represented half or more of the country's organized labor.

In 1968 the CTRP dwarfed the two other national labor organizations then in existence. Its approximately forty-five member unions included some craft organizations, but the majority were plant or industrial. Slightly over half of its membership came from two Canal Zone unions, both made up principally of Panamanian workers and affiliated with the American Federation of State, County, and Municipal Employees. Local 900 was made up of employees of the zone government and private business, and Local 907 was made up of Panamanian employees of the United States armed forces. United States citizens employed in the Canal Zone were organized in numerous locals all affiliated with the Metal Trades Council of the American Federation of Labor (AFL). Among the other major elements in the CTRP were unions representing the transport workers, the banana workers of the Chiriquí Land Company in Bocas del Toro Province, hotel workers, and petroleum workers and unions of various kinds associated in two Colón-based federations.

Internationally, the CTRP is associated with the Inter-American Regional Workers' Organization (Organización Regional Interamericana de Trabajadores—ORIT), a regional branch of the International Confederation of Free Trade Unions (ICFTU). Various unions of the CTRP are affiliated with six of the international trade secretariats, and its unions have worked closely with the American Institute for Free Labor Development (AIFLD) in the establishment and execution of that organization's union leadership and development training program in Panama. The AIFLD is an organization sponsored jointly by the United States government, organized labor, and private industry to assist in the development of organized labor in the Americas.

A second national labor organization, the Isthmian Federation of Christian Workers (Federación Istmeña de Trabajadores Cristianos—FITC), in 1968 claimed eight craft union affiliates and a membership in excess of 2,000. Its effective membership, however, was limited to a little over 600 workers in a federation of rural workers and a barbers' union. It had not received government recognition. The organization is affiliated internationally with the International Confederation of Christian Unions.

The third national labor organization is the FSTRP, which in 1968 survived with a membership reduced to about 600 in two unions—one of clothing manufacture workers and one of construction workers. Because of its continued association with the Panamanian Communist Party and its consequent ability to muster support from party members and sympathizers, however, it was probably much stronger than indicated by its limited membership. The FSTRP is a regional affiliate of the communist-oriented World Federation of Trade Unions (WFTU).

In 1964 the country's thirteen management associations representing some 1,400 members united to form the National Free Enterprise Council (Consejo Nacional de la Empresa Privada—CONEP). By 1970 the organization's rolls included the 350-member Panamanian Association of Business Executives; the 300-member Chamber of Commerce, Industries, and Agriculture of Panama; the 300-member Association of Real Estate Owners of Panama; the 200-member Union of Industrialists of Panama; and several smaller organizations.

The organization conducts studies in a variety of fields of interest to business. Its researchers are professional specialists in their fields, and it has worked with the government on studies of such matters as tax reform. One of the CONEP organizations, the Panamanian Institute for Development (Instituto Panameño de Desarrollo—INPADE), serves as its technical secretariat. INPADE collaborates with the government's autonomous Center for Development and Industrial Productivity (Centro por el Desarrollo y Productividad Industrial—CDPI) on national planning for industrial development, and a combined CDPI-INPADE office has the responsibility for executing the plans evolved.

Although the attitudes of the upper and middle income groups toward organized labor are changing, there remains a tendency to look upon it as, at best, a necessary evil that must be tolerated. On their part, the unions are uncertain about the degree of cooperation that may be expected from employers. In order to improve this climate of labor relations, CONEP has brought the president and the secretary general of CTRP into its governing council.

CHAPTER 13

TRADE AND TRANSPORTATION

Trade, particularly international trade, has been an important element of the economy historically. From colonial days to the present time the Isthmus of Panama has been a focal point of world trade, and the transisthmian route, whether by foot, muleback, railroad, or canal, has had a profound impact upon the country. It has brought into being a sophisticated urban economy focused on commerce and services at Panama City and Colón, which is integrated into the world market but which is different and partially isolated from the economy of the rest of the country.

Trade is the mainstay of the Metropolitan Area (see Glossary) but plays only a minor role in the interior. Difficult and costly overland transportation between the urban centers and the interior has been one of the principal reasons for the slower development of domestic trade. A growing road network, however, is slowly making urban markets more accessible to rural people.

Urban marketing centers offer all domestic products and a large variety of imported goods. The centers of trade in the smaller communities are general stores, grocery stores, and bars, which maintain limited stocks of goods. Many of the smalltown store owners also act as wholesalers' purchasing agents for agricultural products from the surrounding areas. Truckdrivers also act as middlemen, and some farmers sell their produce directly to the retailer or consumer.

The government engages in trade directly through a few monopolies and through the purchasing and reselling of selected agricultural products. It maintains price supports for some farm products and exercises price control on various consumer commodities and services. All businesses must be licensed by the government, and it is difficult for a foreigner to obtain a license to open a new retail outlet.

A key factor in the economy is the Canal Zone. The income flow to the Republic, principally in the form of wages to Panamanians, purchases by United States government agencies, and expenditures of zone residents, was estimated to equal 16 to 18 percent of the gross domestic product during the 1960s. In 1970 this income was about B/150 million (1 balboa equals US$1).

The Colón Free Zone is another important prop to the economy. Several hundred firms store, process, assemble, and reexport goods and give employment to over 2,500 Panamanians. Foreign firms have made the Colón Free Zone a major distribution center for Latin America, and activity there brings millions of balboas into the economy annually.

Foreign investment is stimulated by generous investment incentive decrees. An overwhelming percentage of total foreign investment has been made by United States firms, but most companies' individual investments are small. Foreign economic assistance is received from several sources, the United States providing the largest amount.

The United States is also the principal trading partner, taking as much as 80 percent of Panama's exports and supplying from 30 to 50 percent of all imports annually. Bananas, refined petroleum, and shrimp account for between 80 to 90 percent of the exports, and a wide range of consumer goods constitute the bulk of the imports.

Although imports far exceed exports every year, the country's balance of payments situation is not critical. The invisible income provided to the economy by the Canal Zone, the Colón Free Zone, tourist expenditures, and incoming new capital usually make up the deficit in the trade account.

ROLE OF GOVERNMENT

The government has shown intensive interest in regulating business activities, influencing prices of selected commodities, and improving the transportation facilities. It has plans to expand agricultural storage facilities and complete the Pan-American Highway in order to open up new agricultural marketing areas. It operates a free zone at Colón that has attracted hundreds of foreign firms.

The government owns several commercial enterprises, among which the salt monopoly is the oldest. Since 1903 it has produced, transported, and distributed all the salt in the country. The distribution of alcohol is government operated, although the manufacture of alcoholic beverages is in private hands. The government owns and operates all airports, several of the electricity plants, and part of the domestic communications systems. It also owns and operates several hotels and related tourist services. According to the Constitution, the government has the exclusive right to conduct games of chance and activities on which wagering is done, and under these articles it runs the National Welfare Lottery, gambling casinos, and horse racetracks.

Although the economy is based on the principle of free competition, the government exercises control over the wholesale and retail prices of a score of articles. Many foodstuff prices, including those of vegetables, meats, and poultry, are regulated, but the regulations have little effect outside the principal urban centers. More effective is the influence of the Institute for Economic Development—(Instituto de Fomento Económico—IFE), which regulates the prices of corn, rice, coffee, sugar, tomatoes, and coconuts through its buying activities. As a result, these agricultural products are not subject to individual bargaining, as is the case with all other foodstuffs. Occasionally the government places limits on profits as a gesture of concern for certain public goals. Price policies, however, are designed to serve national interests, such as self-sufficiency or higher government revenue; the socioeconomic effects they may have on the small producer are not considered.

No one may engage in trade without a license from the government except the farmer, who may sell his crops, but not his livestock, without permission. Licenses are of three classes, two of which restrict the holder to certain types of activities. A general license available only to Panamanian citizens entitles the person to engage in any commercial activity. Various laws have been passed since the 1930s tending to restrict the activities of foreigners in trade as part of a desire to "nationalize" commerce. Although the "nationalization" of commerce continues to be used as the theme for a slogan, the 1946 Constitution formulated more lenient policies toward foreigners than previously had existed. A special provision permits citizens of countries operating an enterprise in the isthmus to carry on business activities, a provision that, in fact, affects only United States citizens since the United States government is the only foreign government operating an enterprise in the isthmus.

In general, with the exception of United States citizens, foreigners can engage in retail trade only if they were so occupied before the promulgation of the 1946 Constitution. No foreigner, however, may invest in radio stations, and only 49 percent of aviation companies can be owned by foreigners. There are no restrictions, however, regarding wholesale activities, in which foreigners and nationals share the same rights and privileges.

One restriction that affects foreigners regulates the proportion of foreign labor in enterprises employing five or more persons. Such establishments must hire at least 75 percent Panamanian labor and cannot devote more than 25 percent of their expenses in wages and salaries to foreigners. Exceptions are made for jobs requiring unusual training or special skills, but employees with such skills must be recognized as experts and technicans by the Panamanian government (see ch. 12, Agriculture and Industry).

FOREIGN ECONOMIC RELATIONS

Trade

The country has one of the highest foreign trade growth rates in the world. Between 1960 and 1969 the value of exports grew by an average rate of 13 percent annually, and imports rose by nearly 11 percent annually. In 1970 exports fell slightly below those of 1969 to almost B/106 million, whereas imports soared to nearly B/323 million (see table 22). The large annual trade deficit is not as serious as it would be in other countries because

Table 22. Composition of Foreign Trade of Panama, 1968–70 [1]

(f.o.b. in millions of balboas) [2]

Product	Value			Percent of Total		
	1968	1969	1970	1968	1969	1970
Exports:						
Bananas	53.0	61.2	62.0	56.5	56.2	58.5
Refined petroleum	18.9	24.1	21.7	20.1	22.1	20.5
Shrimp	9.7	9.7	9.8	10.3	8.9	9.3
Sugar	4.6	5.4	4.9	4.9	5.0	4.6
Beef (live and meat)	1.7	1.3	1.3	1.8	1.2	1.2
Coffee	0.6	1.1	0.8	0.7	1.0	0.8
Cacao	0.2	0.4	0.4	0.3	0.4	0.4
Other	5.1	5.7	5.0	5.4	5.2	4.7
TOTAL EXPORTS	93.8	108.9	105.9	100.0	100.0	100.0
Imports:						
Manufactured goods	83.2	95.2	n.a.	33.8	35.1	n.a.
Vehicles and transportation equipment	58.5	59.3	n.a.	23.8	21.8	n.a.
Fuels and lubricants	52.9	60.6	n.a.	21.5	22.3	n.a.
Chemical products	24.0	26.7	n.a.	9.8	9.8	n.a.
Foodstuffs	19.9	20.7	n.a.	8.1	7.6	n.a.
Beverages and tobacco	2.4	2.9	n.a.	1.0	1.2	n.a.
Raw materials	1.6	1.6	n.a.	0.6	0.6	n.a.
Oils and fats	0.5	0.4	n.a.	0.2	0.1	n.a.
Other	2.9	4.1	n.a.	1.2	1.5	n.a.
TOTAL IMPORTS	245.9	271.5	322.5 [3]	100.0	100.0	100.0 [3]

n.a.—not available.

[1] Trade between Colón Free Zone and Panama included; trade with Canal Zone not included except for petroleum exports.

[2] 1 balboa equals US$1.

[3] Exact categories not known as of mid-1971—only totals available.

the sale of goods and services to the Canal Zone, tourist expenditures, and incoming capital make up most of the deficit in the country's balance of payments.

For statistical purposes most trade with the Canal Zone is not included as part of foreign trade except for petroleum exports and some imports subject to customs taxes, such as used vehicles sold by zone residents to Panamanians. Colón Free Zone trade is not included unless the products enter or leave the domestic market; then they are listed as exports or imports. Shipments to and from bonded warehouses are accorded similar statistical treatment.

Panama is one of the few Latin American countries without a general protectionist trade policy. The average duty of the Customs Tariff of 1957, still in force in 1971, was only 22 percent on the f.o.b. (free on board) value. The commercial policy is to use tariffs and quantitative controls as little as is necessary to stimulate development of domestic industries. Imports of capital goods and construction materials are encouraged by low duties, but some competitive consumer products and food items are subject to high duties or restrictive quotas.

Import licenses are required for some goods, such as foods, drugs, and cosmetics, and all items subject to import quotas. About 140 commodities were subject to quantitative restrictions as of 1971. Export licenses are required for several commodities, such as coffee, coconuts, copra, and beef cattle, and also for items having an export tax, such as bananas. The export of wheat flour, firearms, and ammunition is completely prohibited. Several government offices are responsible for issuing import and export licenses according to the nature of the goods. Most licenses, however, are issued by the Office of Price Control, established in 1952 with authority to set prices, control weights and measures, and limit trade of selected goods.

Exports

Four products account for over 90 percent of all exports. Historically, the most important has been bananas, and the country usually contributes between 6 and 7 percent to the total world banana market. In 1969 it accounted for 9 percent of world exports and became the third leading exporter of the product. Favorable world prices and new varieties stimulated banana exports during the 1960s, but floods in the banana plantations during 1970 hampered growth in that year, and reduced shipments were expected in 1971 (see ch. 12, Agriculture and Industry).

Petroleum products have been the second leading export since 1962, when the oil refinery began operations. In addition to the export of refined products, large quantities of bunker fuel are sold to vessels transiting the canal; such fuel sales are not listed as exports in the balance of payments but as income from transportation services. In the late 1960s increased domestic demand for petroleum products started to cut into the supply available for export, but the expansion of the refinery in 1970 promised a resumption of increased exports (see ch. 12, Agriculture and Industry).

Shrimp was the second leading export from the early 1950s until the country began exporting petroleum and, since then, has been third, with between 9 and 12 percent of total annual exports. Sugar has been the fourth most important export since 1962, but sales depend almost entirely upon the United States sugar import quota. High costs of production prevent sales to other markets. Increased beef exports are hindered by government export controls designed to assure an adequate domestic supply and the failure of some of the slaughterhouses to meet sanitary standards. Although Panama has been able to sell most of its coffee production, coffee is no longer an important export item, and the annual export earnings from coffee are the smallest of all Latin American countries. Cacao is another declining export. Before 1950 cacao was the second most important export after bananas, but the world price has decreased to the point that in some years production is not remunerative. Other exports include fishmeal, lumber, cement, coconuts, hides, skins, strawhats, and other commodities of minor significance.

Imports

The country has one of the highest per capita import figures in the hemisphere, and the composition indicates some basic characteristics of the economic structure. One-half of all imports are consumer goods, composed mainly of manufactured items, such as paper products, tires, and clothing, and transportation equipment, such as vehicles. About one-fifth is fuels and lubricants, but industrial raw materials make up less than 1 percent because of the low level of heavy industrial activity. The principal chemical products imported are insecticides, fertilizers, patent medicines, and cosmetics. Nine percent of its imports are foodstuffs and beverages, which reflect the need for a higher output in agriculture and the expansion of the food-processing industries.

A Panamanian government study in 1970 indicated that half of all food imports could be produced in the country. The main foodstuffs imported are wheat, butter, ham, cheese, and salted fish. Some of the other items, not common to the diet of the average family and beyond the means of most Panamanians, are

324

related to the tourist industry, along with the import of luxury and semiluxury consumer goods.

Trading Partners

The United States is the principal trading partner. During most of the 1960s it took over 60 percent of all Panamanian exports annually and supplied from 30 to 50 percent of all imports (see table 23). In 1968, for example, the United States bought almost 80 percent of the exports, including virtually all bananas, shrimp, cacao, beef, and sugar and half the petroleum. Most of the remaining exports went to a few European and Latin American countries.

Italy is the second major market for bananas and purchases almost nothing else. Almost all exports to Canada consist of refined petroleum products. The Federal Republic of Germany (West Germany), the leading coffee buyer, also purchases bananas and petroleum products. Costa Rica takes numerous items, the

Table 23. Direction of Panamanian Trade, 1969

(in percent)

Countries	Export to	Import from	Countries	Export to	Import from
United States	64.7	35.7	Spain	0.1	0.5
Venezuela	—*	21.8	Mexico	1.6	0.9
Colón Free Zone	0.3	12.4	Switzerland	0	0.7
Japan	0.2	5.8	Sweden	0.2	0.6
West Germany	13.8	2.9	Denmark	0	0.7
Italy	1.1	1.2	Ecuador	0.3	0.1
United Kingdom	—*	2.5	Honduras	—*	0.2
Netherlands	3.3	1.6	Guatemala	0.1	0.5
Costa Rica	2.2	1.6	Nicaragua	0.2	0.3
Canada	4.5	1.6	Netherlands Antilles	0.1	0.2
Colombia	0.5	1.0	Norway	0.2	0.2
Hong Kong	0	1.1	India	0	0.2
Belgium	—*	1.0	Argentina	0	0.2
Panama Canal Zone	4.5	0.8	El Salvador	0.1	0.2
France	—*	0.9	Dominican Republic	0.1	—*
New Zealand and			Republic of China	—*	0.1
Australia	0	0.5	Others	1.9	2.0

* Less than 0.1 percent.

Source: Adapted from Republic of Panama, Contraloría General de la República, Dirección de Estadística y Censo, *Estadística panameña, año XXIX: Anuario de comercio exterior, año 1968* (Series "K"), Panama City, 1970, pp. 6–13; and International Monetary Fund, *Direction of Trade: Annual 1964–68*, Washington, n.d., p. 28.

more important being petroleum, aluminum products, paper products, and food products.

Although the United States plays the leading role, with a long list of items, about thirty other countries provide some imports. Venezuela contributes over 20 percent; almost all of it is crude petroleum for the refinery. The Colón Free Zone is listed in third place, but a large portion of the items imported from there originate in the United States, thus increasing that country's predominance in the import trade. European countries contribute about 14 percent, West Germany, the United Kingdom, Italy, Belgium, and the Netherlands being in the lead. Vehicles, ships, and chemicals are the principal items from West Germany, and the United Kingdom provides mainly beverages and transport equipment.

Most of the imports from Asia originate in Japan. In the Western Hemisphere, apart from the United States and Venezuela, only Canada, Colombia, and Costa Rica contribute 1 or more than 1 percent each. All other trading partners provide less than 1 percent each.

Illegal Trade

Uncontrolled illegal trade has always existed with crews of transient ships as well as with neighboring countries. Most of the transactions in goods and services with the Canal Zone take place without any official control or intervention. It is well known that the San Blas Indians sell or barter most of their coconuts in Colombia and import manufactured consumer goods in return. The government is aware of the situation and attempts to reduce its loss by means of stricter enforcement of existing customs regulations and controls, but a long tradition of illegal practices hampers government efforts, and no major improvements have been made in recent years.

International Commercial Agreements

The country has not negotiated many commercial or economic agreements and in 1971 was a member of only one multilateral pact and a few bilateral agreements. Nevertheless, the National Commission of Foreign Commerce (Comisión Nacional de Comercio Exterior) was created in 1970 to study, advise, and issue concepts regarding Panamanian participation in economic integration movements and foreign trade treaties. The commission is a consultative organ composed of nine members headed by the minister of commerce and industry.

The one multilateral agreement in force is a free trade treaty with Costa Rica and Nicaragua, signed in 1961, called the Treaty for Free Trade and Customs Preferences Between Panama, Costa Rica, and Nicaragua, and the three countries periodically negotiate lists of items to be granted free entry. As of 1971 about 200 items were on the Panama-Costa Rica list; and 100, on the list between Panama and Nicaragua. Total trade between the three members has been growing annually but, although the trade between Nicaragua and Panama has been nearly in balance, that of Costa Rica and Panama is continually in Costa Rica's favor. In early 1970 Panama and Costa Rica signed a bilateral agreement for the joint development of agriculture and industry of their respective border areas, including a small free trade zone at the Costa Rican town of Paso Canoa.

The Central American Common Market was formed during the 1950s between Guatemala, Honduras, Nicaragua, El Salvador, and Costa Rica. Membership was offered to Panama, but as of 1971 it had not joined, though it may do so if it so desires. Historically, Panama has never had a common bond with the countries of Central America except for Costa Rica, and whether or not membership would benefit the country had not been resolved. As a member of the Central American Common Market, preference for imports would have to be granted to member nations, and many of the Panamanian tariffs would have to be raised to be in line with the common external tariff policy of the members. Most of the country's importers oppose the concept of joining, whereas most of the industrialists, whose market would be widened, favor it. Panama signed a bilateral agreement with El Salvador in 1970 that would eventually lead to free trade between the two countries.

Role of the Canal Zone

The strip of land that includes the interoceanic waterway and railroad represents a vital interest to the United States and is the largest single source of income to the Panamanian economy. The Panama Canal, through which over 14,800 vessels carrying more than 118 million long tons of cargo passed in 1970, is of immense value to all maritime nations and of unique importance to the economic development of Latin America.

The zone—its active property, plants, and equipment—represented a capital investment of B/739.7 million as of June 30, 1970. Of this, the equity of the United States government was US$577.4 million, of which US$217.2 million bore interest at a rate of 3.6 percent a year. The zone, operated by the joint efforts of the Canal Zone government and the Panama Canal Company, both under the direct supervision of the president of the United States through the secretary of the army, derives its income from tolls levied on transient vessels. The rates for merchant vessels, military transports, tankers, and yachts are B/0.90 a displacement ton for laden ships and B/0.72 a displacement ton for ships in ballast. Warships and other floating craft pay at the rate of B/0.50 a displacement ton. Vessels of the governments of Panama and Colombia are given free transit.

Although the balance sheet of the Panama Canal Company shows an annual profit, which during the past ten years has fluctuated between US$11 million and US$15 million, expenses of maintenance and operation included in the budget of the United States Department of Defense are in excess of the profit and make the zone a deficit item in the United States budget. Lack of resources to maintain and operate such an enterprise is the principal reason why the Panamanians do not want sole operation of the canal themselves but advocate an increase in United States annuities to be supported from increase in tolls (see ch. 10, Foreign Relations).

The zone provides several different sources of income to the Panamanian economy. The largest amount—about B/70 million to B/80 million a year—comes through wages and salaries paid to almost 23,000 Panamanian citizens employed by the United States agencies and firms on contract with the various institutions in the zone. Their income affects a larger number of Panamanians than any other economic activity because most of it is spent in Panama proper.

Another source is the purchases of United States agencies in Panama. The Panama Canal Company, the armed forces, and various subordinate agencies satisfy an increasing share of their need by purchasing Panamanian merchandise, particularly petroleum. After the Treaty of 1955 the zone government gradually eliminated most of its own processing industries, and in 1971 it procured numerous products from the Panamanian economy (see ch. 10, Foreign Relations; ch. 12, Agriculture and Industry).

Zone residents, mostly United States citizens, spend some of their income in Panama on both services and locally made or imported goods, such as souvenirs and food. Fluctuation in the number of employees and strength of the armed forces in the zone affects government revenue, especially from horseraces, liquor sales, and the lottery (see ch. 11, Character and Structure of the Economy). The combined foreign exchange income derived from purchases of zone agencies and personnel amounts to about B/35 million to B/40 million per year. Crews of foreign ships and tourists spend another B/30 million.

Another source of income is the annuity of the United States government paid directly to the Panamanian government. The rights and concessions granted in the Treaty of 1903 obligated the United States, among other conditions, to pay an annuity of B/250,000, subsequently increased to B/430,000 in 1936 and to B/1,930,000 in 1955 (see ch. 2, Historical Setting). In addition to this formal commitment, the armed forces spend considerable sums for the maintenance and operation of their installations; these are not included in the budget of the Panama Canal Company and are not publicized. The United States government also pays for the maintenance of the transisthmian highway, built by the United States on Panamanian territory.

The total annual gross income derived from the Canal Zone is estimated to exceed B/150 million, a small portion of which is returned in the form of payments for purchases in the zone, for utilities provided by the zone, for tolls and repairs of private Panamanian vessels passing through the zone, and for services rendered to Panamanian citizens in the zone. The combined amount of these visible and invisible imports is B/14 million to B/15 million, leaving a net income of about B/135 million to Panama.

Colón Free Zone

The Colón Free Zone, a 120-acre enclosure in the city of Colón, has no resident population or retail trade, which are prohibited; it provides space and services to store, process, assemble, grade, clean, pack, manufacture, and exhibit imported goods and has facilities for reexport. Because goods are handled free of duty, the free zone has become an important distribution center for Latin American trade.

Established by Executive Decree No. 18 of 1948, the Colón Free Zone began operation in 1953 and has grown steadily since its inception. It functions as an autonomous agency of the government of Panama and is administered by a board of directors and a managerial staff. By 1970 it accommodated over 600 firms and employed over 2,500 persons. During the same year the trade of the free zone reached B/500 million, making it one of the world's largest distribution centers. It contributes about B/30 million to the national economy in the form of salaries, taxes, and fees, although this is partially offset by imports from the Colón Free Zone.

Companies may erect their own buildings, lease space in a free zone-owned building for from one to twenty years, use the facilities of the public warehouses to store merchandise on a monthly basis, or contract with a customs warehouser to perform all merchandising services without having to maintain an office or a staff. Goods can be shipped anywhere in Latin America within fourteen hours by air, and about one-fourth of all outgoing shipments are made that way. The Colón Free Zone has become such a success that by 1971 it was approaching its physical saturation point, and the government was seeking the use of some land within the Canal Zone for additional space.

The Panamanian government levies no taxes on operations within the Colón Free Zone except a social security tax on the payrolls of Panamanians. On income earned from the export or re-export of goods abroad, beneficial income tax rates are applied, which has meant that most firms pay at less than a 4-percent rate. Profits made from export to Panama are taxed at the full domestic rate, however.

Foreign Investment

The government is receptive to foreign investment and has passed several incentive laws since the 1950s. The one in effect in 1971, promulgated in late 1970, provided numerous benefits for new companies. Firms producing for the domestic market have a 50-percent income tax exemption if the profits are reinvested; a 100-percent exemption from import duties for machinery, equipment, and parts; partial exemption of duties on raw materials and containers not made locally; a 12.5-percent depreciation on machinery and equipment; and, if the plant is located outside the Metropolitan Area, additional income tax exemptions of 10 percent of the salaries of personnel and 50 percent of the cost of utilities. Those companies producing for the export market receive total exemption from income, export, sales, assets taxes, and import duties on machinery, equipment, parts, raw materials, containers, fuels, and lubricants. In addition, government export credit is available for new industries.

One-third of all foreign investment is in manufacturing. A study by the Panamanian government published in 1970 indicated that there were ninety-six foreign firms in the country, not counting banks, with total direct investment of over B/192 million. Most of the companies were small—sixty-two had made investments of under B/500,000—but nineteen had investments of over B/1 million. United States firms accounted for 91 percent of the total foreign investment, which was concentrated in oil refining, power generation, transportation, manufacturing, agriculture, and commerce. The United Kingdom and Switzerland each had about 3 percent of the total; the Netherlands, about 1 percent; and all other countries, the balance.

Other estimates for foreign investment in Panama include the firms operating in the Colón Free Zone and firms domiciled in the country but operating elsewhere. Under this definition nearly B/1 billion is estimated to be invested in the country, United States firms accounting for about B/800 million.

Foreign Assistance

As of mid-1971 foreign assistance in the form of grants, loans, and programs extended since the end of World War II totaled the equivalent of over US$460 million. More than US$70 million was still being negotiated in 1971. The close economic ties with the United States have made that country the major source of assistance, although several international organizations, other foreign countries, and private banks have also made substantial contributions. Total United States economic and military financial assistance by mid-1971 was about US$280 million, of which US$100 million was in the form of grants. The Agency for International Development and its predecessor agencies provided the largest amount, about US$177 million in grants and loans, for numerous projects, such as roads, agriculture, education, urban renewal, and sewer systems. The Export-Import Bank had provided about US$36 million in long-term loans, about US$10 million for emergency relief and food-for-peace programs, nearly US$14 million for the Social Progress Trust Fund administered by the Inter-American Development Bank, and the balance for various other programs. In addition, a peace corps program was in operation from 1962 until 1971.

The second major source of foreign assistance was the International Bank for Reconstruction and Development (World Bank), which had made loans totaling over US$80 million since 1959. No loans were granted from 1962 to 1970, however, because of administrative problems caused by domestic political pressures in connection with previous loans. The two largest loans were made by the World Bank in 1971. A US$20-million loan was allotted for the Tocumén Airport improvement project, and an additional US$42-million loan was for electricity projects (see ch. 12, Agriculture and Industry). An associated agency of the World Bank, the International Finance Corporation, also lent US$1 million for construction of a tourist hotel.

The role played by the Inter-American Development Bank has been rapidly increasing. About US$52 million in loans had been approved, and almost US$70 million more was under negotiations in mid-1971. The largest amounts were for farm feeder roads, housing, water systems, and livestock improvement. About US$48 million was obtained by the government from a group of private foreign banks in the 1969–71 period to be used for public works in agriculture, health, and rural resettlement projects. Several United Nations projects in the country totaled US$11 million; voluntary assistance from the United Kingdom for educational projects totaled about US$2 million; five private United States

331

voluntary agencies were providing about US$1 million annually in food and medical supplies; and the French government agreed in 1970 to finance the construction of a new slaughterhouse in David and a cold-storage warehouse in the Colón Free Zone. In addition, the International Monetary Fund had signed several standby agreements in keeping with the government's desire to maintain a stable financial climate. Such an agreement, for US$14 million, was signed in March 1971, against which the government could draw in case of need. Some of the previous standby agreements were only partially utilized.

Tourism

The government, through its Panamanian Institute of Tourism, is pursuing a vigorous tourist promotional campaign and finances numerous studies relating to possibilities for tourism in the country. The tourist industry has benefited from tourism in neighboring countries, as many persons stop off in Panama. In 1969 about 143,000 persons visited the country in addition to brief stopovers by thousands of in-transit travelers. An estimated B/30 million was spent by all the tourists, and this amount is expected to increase, although it is partially offset by expenditures of Panamanians traveling abroad.

In an attempt to attract more tourists, the two old Spanish towns of Portobelo and Panamá Viejo are to be reconstructed. An annual three-month-long international deep sea fishing tournament is sponsored by the government, and scheduled "minicruises" on small modern liners were started in 1971 through the canal and in the bays and islands of both coasts. In 1971 there were fifty-one hotels in the country, of which sixteen were in Panama City; five of these were first class. All hotels have a high occupancy rate: 70 to 80 percent on an annual basis and higher occupancy during the months of November and December, when the climate is at its best. In keeping with the projected increase in the number of tourists, additional first-class hotels were being planned for the 1970s.

In early 1971 the government issued an incentive decree valid for five years to stimulate investments in tourist facilities. All firms dedicated to the tourist industry were to be exempt from customs duties on the import of automobiles, buses, boats, ships, and aircraft and taxes on airport or dock facilities.

Balance of Payments

Balance of payments problems do not affect Panama in the same way that they affect other countries, mainly because the United

States dollar is the de facto currency (see ch. 11, Character and Structure of the Economy). A loss of reserves does not put pressure on the exchange rate of the balboa, and there is no central bank to expand money supply. Instead, decline in exports and incoming capital only tends to reduce the available money supply and thereby reduces the demand for further imports. Because of the sizable deficits in the trade of goods, the country has always suffered from an apparent shortage of dollars to pay for its imports. Even when the transactions with the Canal Zone and the Colón Free Zone are included, the balance of transactions in goods and services shows a deficit, which reached over B/80 million in 1970 (see table 24). The record high deficit in 1970 was caused by exceptionally high imports, a small decline in exports, and a leveling off of earnings generated by the Canal Zone. Most annual deficits in goods and services are offset by incoming capital, both private investment and government borrowings.

In the balance of payments, under transactions with the Canal Zone, recorded trade, for the most part, represents petroleum products and other items sold to Canal Zone agencies. Earnings of Panamanian residents include wages plus the sale of goods and services to Canal Zone contractors and private residents in the zone. Figures on expenditures by Canal Zone residents are based upon a comprehensive survey done in 1968 by Canal Zone authorities and include expenditures in Panama by both civilian and military personnel. Expenditures of Canal Zone agencies reflect expenditures by United States military installations and the Panama Canal Company in Panama on other than merchandise. Other transactions with the Canal Zone are payments for freight and insurance on merchandise sold and passenger fares on the Panama Railroad.

Transactions with the Colón Free Zone are processing services performed by Panamanian residents for firms in the Free Zone. The definitions for exports and imports are self-evident. Tourism and travel are the receipts from expenditures of tourists not from the Canal Zone, minus expenditures of Panamanians traveling abroad. Freight and insurance of goods expenditures are also self-evident, but the entry for other transportation includes the sale of bunker fuel oil to ships transiting the canal, aircraft fuels, and ships' crew expenditures. Investment income is the interest paid abroad on the public debt and on private loans. Government services is the B/1.9 million annuity from the United States for use of the Canal Zone plus foreign government expenditures in Panama, less Panamanian government expenditures in other countries. Nonmonetary gold is the export of gold by private

Table 24. Balance of Payments of Panama, 1967–70

(in millions of balboas)[1]

	1967	1968	1969	1970[2]
Goods and Services:				
Transactions with the Canal Zone[3]				
Recorded trade	17.3	17.6	18.9	n.a.
Earnings of Panamanian residents	63.0	72.5	78.5	n.a.
Expenditures of Canal Zone residents	30.7	33.8	35.8	n.a.
Expenditures of Canal Zone agencies	5.0	4.8	6.4	n.a.
Other	−0.8	−0.9	−0.9	n.a.
Total transactions with the Canal Zone	115.2	127.9	138.7	n.a.
Transactions with the Cólon Free Zone	16.6	16.7	16.9	n.a.
Other goods and services				
Exports, f.o.b.	8.8	96.2	112.0	129.9[4]
Imports, f.o.b.	−228.5	−241.5	−277.8	−331.5[4]
Tourism and travel	9.3	9.5	13.0	56.5[4]
Freight and insurance of goods	−21.5	−23.4	−28.9	−33.5
Other transportation	10.5	18.6	23.1	15.5
Investment income	−22.8	−25.4	−30.0	−28.2
Government services	−2.2	−1.6	−1.8	7.4[4]
Nonmonetary gold	−0.7	−0.7	−0.8	−0.5
Other	6.1	10.5	14.1	121.6[5]
Total other goods and services	−161.0	−157.8	−177.1	n.a.
Total goods and services	−29.2	−13.2	−21.5	−80.5

Transfer Payments:				
Private[6]	−6.9	−6.1	−6.9	−4.0
Official	8.7	6.4	8.0	6.6
Total transfer payments	1.8	0.3	1.1	2.6
Capital Movement:				
Direct private long-term investment	3.7	12.7	9.5	20.3
Other long-term private	6.8	8.2	2.6	
Short-term private	1.7	−5.9	−7.0	
Official loans received	6.0	4.4	15.6	23.6
Official loans repaid	−3.6	−6.6	−4.0	n.a.
Banking system assets	29.2	27.1	41.7	188.5
Banking system liabilities	−14.7	−22.0	−20.4	−124.6
Total capital movement	29.1	17.9	38.0	77.9[7]
Errors and Omissions	−1.7	−5.0	−17.6	n.a.

n.a.—not available.

[1] 1 balboa equals US$1.

[2] Preliminary.

[3] Except United States annuities, which are included in government services.

[4] Includes transactions with the Canal Zone for 1970.

[5] Includes transactions with Colón Free Zone and earnings of Panamanians in Canal Zone for 1970.

[6] Figures may include some remittances to Canal Zone residents, some capital transactions, and some payments for goods and services and may duplicate entries made under other headings. Such considerations explain in part the sums under errors and omissions.

[7] Includes errors and omissions.

Source: Adapted from *Balance of Payments Yearbook, 1965–69*, *XXII*, Washington, 1971; and Republic of Panama, Contraloria General de la República, Dirección de Estadística y Censo, *Panamá en cifras (Compendio Estadístico, años 1965 a 1969)*, Panama City, 1970, pp. 80–83.

persons, and other transactions are nonfreight insurance and miscellaneous items.

Private transfers are generally pensions received by former employees of the Canal Zone, minus bank drafts sent abroad by Panamanian residents. Official transfers are grants from foreign governments and international organizations and the fees from foreign-owned vessels flying the Panamanian flag.

Direct private long-term investment is new foreign investment. Other long-term private capital are loans to the private sector and the purchase of Panamanian securities. Short-term private capital reflects the changes in export and import credits extended or received by Panamanian individuals and firms. Official capital loans received and official loans repaid cover drawings on, and repayment of, foreign loans. Banking system assets are deposits made by foreigners into Panamanian banks; banking system liabilities are the repayment for loans in foreign currencies, International Monetary Fund drawings, and changes in foreign securities and currency held by the banks.

DOMESTIC TRADE

Organization of Trade

The law distinguishes between wholesale and retail business mainly on the basis of operating capital. Thus barbershops, bars, filling stations, and many other businesses that would be considered retail in the United States are classed as wholesale establishments if their capital investment exceeds B/2,500. About 1,650 establishments of the almost 13,000 trade establishments were called wholesale in 1968 (see table 25).

Like all commercial activities, wholesale trade is centered in Panama City and Colón, where many businessmen engage in multiple activities as export-import agents, manufacturers' representatives, and wholesalers. In the interior, wholesale activities are exercised by the sugar refineries, canneries, and large cattle ranches, which buy from small producers and sell their processed goods to retailers or exporters. Truckdrivers and owners may act as agents for the wholesalers or may sell directly from the producer to the retailer or consumer. The retailers buy their food products either from the producer or from the truckers. Imported merchandise and manufactured domestic goods are bought by the retailer from the importer or from the manufacturer's agent.

Importers use the public warehouse in Panama City, the storage facilities of the railroad depots in Cristóbal and Panama City, the warehouses in the Colón Free Zone, or the three bonded gov-

Table 25. Domestic Trade Establishments and Transport Companies in Panama, 1968

	Number
Trade Establishments:	
Wholesale grocers	98
Liquor wholesalers and retailers	304
Soft-drink wholesalers	5
Wholesalers of agricultural products, including meat and fish	34
Pharmaceutical wholesalers	73
Hardware stores, wholesale and retail	71
Electrical articles sales, retail and wholesale	119
Gasoline and mineral oil sales, wholesale and retail	311
Bookstores and office supply sales, wholesale and retail	107
Import-export agencies, agents and wholesalers	618
Bazaars and clothing stores, retail and wholesale	702
Retailers of meat, fish, and fowl	456
Retail grocers, including stands	2,536
General stores, including bars and supermarkets	4,220
Refreshment and fruit stands	219
Machinery for industry, commerce and agriculture	67
Department stores	16
Shoestores	101
Leather stores	6
Drugstores and pharmacies	239
Furniture stores	311
Music stores	37
Swap shops	91
Construction materials	140
Auto and auto accessories sales and motorcycles	160
Photographic materials sales	15
Jewelers	146
Flower shops	19
Tobacco specialty shops	7
Other wholesale and retail enterprises	1,166
TOTAL	12,394
Transport Companies:	
Bus and taxi companies	84
Other transport companies	72
Shipping companies	25
Air transport companies	66
Services connected with transport	51
Warehousing	5
Communications	10
Other	15
TOTAL	328

Source: Adapted from Republic of Panama, Contraloría General de la República, Dirección de Estadística y Censo, *Estadística panameña, año XXVII: Industrias, año 1968* (Series "F," No. 1), Panama City, 1969, pp. 58–61.

ernment warehouses. Goods stored in the government warehouses for more than six months without payment of storage fees are considered abandoned. The Colón Free Zone and the government warehouses are popular because the payment of customs duties can be postponed until the merchandise is removed from the warehouse. Panama City, Colón, David, and Chitré have the only modern cold-storage facilities for perishables, and the food-processing establishments have their own refrigeration facilities.

Commercial activities may be conducted under three different types of business organization: individual proprietorships, partnerships, and corporations. Individual ownership is most common on the retail level. Over 10,000 of the total trade establishments licensed in 1968 were individually owned. The individual proprietors usually conduct the business with the help of family members. Partnerships vary in form. In a general partnership the partners are liable jointly and without limit. One or more of the partners' liabilities may be limited, but this must be included in the basic agreement, and the word *limitada* must be added to the firm's name. Other forms of partnerships are stock-issuing limited partnerships and cooperatives. If the firm issues stock, this fact must be reflected in the title. Silent partners cannot be included in the title of the firm, but other designations, such as "and brothers" or "and sons," may be indicated.

Incorporation is governed by Law 32 of 1927 and various articles of the commercial code that contain regulations regarding the formation, financing, and management of corporations. At least two persons are required for incorporation, but no limitations exist as to the number, domicile, or nationality of board members and their place of meeting. There is no minimum capital requirement and no limit on the duration of the life of the corporation. Most foreign-owned enterprises use this form of business.

Marketing and Distribution

Panama City plays the preeminent role as the center for collecting and distributing all types of goods. About 90 percent of all fresh fruits and vegetables are marketed there; 40 to 45 percent of all cattle are butchered in its slaughterhouse; and 75 percent of all imported goods pass through its gates. Agricultural, forest, and marine products are brought to the city by road from areas along the road network, by water from coastal settlements, and occasionally by air from places not accessible by surface transportation. Water transportation is used to a greater extent in Darién and Bocas del Toro provinces than those on the Pacific coast.

Such items as bananas, sugar, bottled milk, and processed foods are distributed to Panama City and the other cities by the major producers themselves. Nonperishables, such as rice, coffee, corn, and beans, are distributed to consumers through hundreds of small retail establishments and a growing number of supermarkets. Perishables are sold mainly in public markets by both retailers and wholesalers. There is no separate central wholesale market in the entire country. Panama City has four major public markets where wholesalers, retailers, truckers, and consumers congregate. The largest market is held in an open square in the center of the city next to the waterfront. Although well supervised, it is ill equipped for storing perishables. The sellers rent space from the city, and the market is open six days a week from 5:00 A.M. to 1:00 P.M.

Similar open markets are located in the Calidonia District of the capital. A new market on Via España is enclosed, has refrigeration facilities, and houses some retail stores. Smaller public markets exist in other parts of Panama City. Livestock is marketed in a special market in the San Francisco District. The city has several supermarkets, department stores, such as Sears and Roebuck, and a variety of specialized stores concentrating on tourist items and imports from all parts of the world. Supermarkets are growing in importance as an outlet for merchandise. A 1965 government survey indicated that about 30,000 customers daily were patronizing the cities' supermarkets, which was almost as many as the number of persons frequenting all Panama City's public markets.

The second largest distribution and market center is Colón. Products are received from the San Blas and Gatún Lake areas by boat and from the surrounding farms by pushcart or truck. The open market in the heart of the business district resembles the Panama City market, although it does have some refrigeration facilities. Supermarkets and specialized stores are abundant, but business is somewhat slower than in the capital because many passengers discharged at Colón by ships take the transisthmian railroad to Panama City, where they spend more time and money because of its larger size and somewhat drier weather.

In the interior almost every town and city has public markets on three or more days of the week. Aguadulce, Boquete, and Chorrera have modern sanitary buildings for their public markets, but most town have no buildings at all. David, which serves nearly the entire Chiriquí Province, has modern shops, grain mills, and a slaughterhouse. It is also an important stopover for truckers transporting produce from the surrounding areas to Panama City and Colón.

Chitré is in the heart of a fast-growing agricultural district and is a center for livestock raising and grain milling and storage.

Santiago, Aguadulce, and Penonomé are important collection points for agricultural products of the central provinces as well as stopovers for truckers commuting between the Metropolitan Area and the western part of the country. These three towns, however, have few modern shops and limited storage facilities. The larger towns of the interior have stores carrying a limited variety of high-priced consumer products. In smaller villages the basic stock of a typical store is rice, beans, kerosine, bread, cigarettes, coffee, and spaghetti—all items that can sell quickly. Canned goods are limited in variety and may have been on the shelf for several years. In the larger cities there are ambulatory vendors of miscellaneous products.

The lack of adequate storage and refrigeration facilities on farms, at collection points, and in markets constitutes the most serious handicap to the marketing of agricultural products. Secondarily, the lack of all-weather roads hampers marketing during the rainy season. A Panamanian government study in 1967 indicated that from 37 to 66 percent of the retail price of selected items was marketing costs and included the markup for the large number of intermediaries between the farmer and the consumer, such as commission agents, truckers, wholesalers, millers, processors, and retailers, as well as covering losses from spoilage.

Storage facilities in the rural household are few and inadequate. Water and grains are stored in large pottery containers, discarded five-gallon cans, bottles, or wooden containers that often expose their contents to rodents and moisture damage. Consequently, most farmers sell indiscriminately to the various intermediaries at harvesttime, when competition is highest and prices are lowest. Near the urban centers the farmers themselves often sell their products directly to the consumer. Horses, mules, and donkeys are used as pack animals; oxcarts are seen in flat areas; and boats are used along both coasts. Since many farmers do not possess these means of transportation, it is not unusual for them to carry as much as 100 pounds to market on their backs. Often the entire family goes along, and small children are carried atop the baskets.

Farmers in the interior, located far from market centers, may transport their produce to a collection point of the Institute for Economic Development (Instituto de Fomento Economico—IFE), where it is purchased and forwarded to a city market or to an IFE storage facility. IFE silos could handle about 14,000 tons of grains in the late 1960s—only 7 percent of average annual grain production. The price supports granted by the government through IFE purchases provide some encouragement for the farmer to produce more than for his personal need.

Occasionally a farmer in the interior may transport his produce to the large cities on a small bus or converted truck for carrying passengers and freight. Such trips, however, are uneconomic because the selling price in the city often fails to compensate for the cost of transportation. Trips of long duration are exceptions and are usually motivated by a need or desire to visit friends or relatives, to conduct an important business transaction, or make a sizable purchase.

The farmer must obtain a permit from the local authorities for the transport of livestock. Cattle are driven long distances or are transported by truck or boat. About one-third of all cattle marketed in Panama City are hauled by boat, tied in groups of four, and thrown overboard to swim ashore, a practice that results in considerable loss from drowning. A beaching charge is collected by the city. The slaughtering of livestock is subject to a local tax even if done on the farm for the farmer's own use. Abattoirs, with the exception of the few modern ones in Panama City, Colón, and David, are usually simple buildings with a killing floor, hoist, and racks but no storage and refrigeration facilities. The abattoirs do not engage in livestock trading themselves but slaughter cattle belonging to butchers or other retailers.

The lack of uniform standards and measures handicaps marketing. Only certain exports, such as shrimp, cacao, sugar, and some fruits and vegetables, are inspected for quality by a government or private organization, and there are no official quality standards for the domestic marketing of products. As a result, large quantities of substandard produce are moved and sold. Although the metric system is the official system for weights and measures, United States measures are frequently used by supermarkets and other stores in the Metropolitan Area, and dozens of local systems exist in the interior. Units of measurement for the same quantity may differ in name, and often the same denomination signified different quantities when used to measure another product. Rice, for example, is measured by twenty different units, one of which is called the *lata,* equal to twenty-five pounds. One *lata* of coffee, however, weighs thirty-five pounds, and one *lata* of corn weighs thirty-three pounds. Whereas the different measurements are fairly well known and comprehended in the area of their use, they create difficulties when the produce is sold in another area.

TRANSPORTATION

Roads

The few roads in the country are found in the southern part, mainly west of Panama City. There were only twenty-five miles of roads in Bocas del Toro Province and only ten miles in Darién Province in 1970. Many areas are completely unreachable during the rainy season as gravel and dirt roads become inundated. The government, fully conscious of the need for feeder roads leading into agricultural areas, has negotiated numerous foreign credits in order to extend the farm-to-market roadnet.

In 1970 paved roads, either concrete or asphalt, totaled 950 miles. The key route was the 304-mile Inter-American Highway running from the Costa Rican border to Panama City. Extension of this axial route to the Colombian border as part of the Pan-American Highway system is to be financed by the United States, Panama, and Colombia according to an agreement signed in 1971. Up to that time, only a thirty-two-mile stretch from Panama City to Chepo had been finished. Other paved roads include the forty-seven-mile United States-built Boyd-Roosevelt Trans-Isthmian Highway from Panama City to Colón, largely outside the Canal Zone; coastal roads on the Azuero Peninsula; the road from David to Boquete; and some branch roads leading to resort areas.

All-weather roads, improved with gravel and stone, totaled 705 miles in 1970. These included a twenty-seven-mile feeder road from Concepción, in Chiriquí Province, to Cerro Punta, near the Volcán de Chiriquí; over 160 miles of feeder roads on the southern coast west of Panama City; and a road from Colón to Portobelo opening up that historic town to tourism. About 2,500 miles of dirt roads, usable only in dry weather, also existed in 1970. In roadless areas there are horse and foot trails over which goods and produce are transported by pack animals or on farmers' backs.

Over 55,300 motor vehicles, not counting those owned by the government, were registered in 1969. Almost 37,000 were automobiles, and the balance were trucks, jeeps, buses, and *chivas*. The *chivas* (literally goats) are small, varicolored buses that actually butt their way through traffic and operate independently of the regular buslines. Most towns and cities are served by connecting buslines, and many trucks make scheduled runs and take passengers. Many private automobiles are for hire—apart from those that are taxis.

Railroads

There are four railroad lines in the country, one owned by the Panamanian government, one by the United States government, and two by the Chiriquí Land Company. The only transisthmian line is the 47.6-mile Panama Railroad connecting Colón and Panama City and generally paralleling the canal within the zone. Owned and operated by the United States government, it has a five-foot gauge, and its rolling stock and equipment are of United States manufacture. Although large sections were moved to accommodate the canal and Gatún Lake, the line is the lineal descendant of the original railroad completed in 1855 to provide a transisthmian transportation link between the east coast of the United States and California during the gold rush days (see ch. 2, Historical Setting). The railroad has twenty-four passenger cars and 280 freight cars and runs from twelve to fourteen trains daily between the terminal cities. It carries nearly 1 million passengers annually and 250,000 tons of freight.

The government-owned National Railway of Chiriquí (Ferrocarril Nacional de Chiriquí) is a thirty-six-inch narrow-gauge system of 124 miles connecting David and Puerto Armuelles with spur lines to Potrerillos, Pedregal, and San Andrés. The railroad owns ten passenger cars and 250 freight cars and carries about 17,000 short tons of cargo annually, mostly fertilizer from the seaport to the farming areas.

The Chiriquí Land Company Railways operate the Northern Line in northwest Bocas del Toro Province and the Southern Line in Chiriquí Province. Both lines, which carry passengers and freight, are thirty-six-inch narrow-gauge track and are used to connect the company's plantations in Panama and Costa Rica with the nearby ports. The Northern Line has 100 miles of track in Panama and five miles in Costa Rica, and the Southern Line has ninety-one miles in Panama and twenty-five miles in Costa Rica. Between them the two lines own eighteen passenger and over 1,000 freight cars.

Shipping

Communication along the Atlantic coast is almost entirely dependent on coastal shipping: steam, motor, and sail. The principal deepwater ports outside the Canal Zone are Almirante, Bocas del Toro, Portobelo, and La Bahía de las Minas on the Atlantic and Puerto Armuelles on the Pacific. Cristóbal and Balboa in the Canal Zone have modern port facilities, as does Puerto Armuelles, and all three can accommodate large freighters and passenger liners. The port of La Bahía de las Minas, where the petroleum refinery is located, handles mostly tankers, although other vessels sometimes discharge there.

Almost two dozen ports are used only for cabotage or fishing boats, and most of the minor ports are on the Pacific coast. The only means of surface travel to the east of Panama (beyond Chepo) is by water. La Palma is a port of supply for the Darién area, and large launches can proceed eighty miles above it on the

Tuira River and also for thirty miles on the Chucunaque above its mouth at El Real. Vessels drawing no more than ten feet can proceed up the Bayano River for fifteen miles from its mouth. On many rivers along the south coast, especially in the east, there is much local traffic by means of *cayucas* (small fishing boats) and balsa rafts. Aguadulce is the chief sugar shipping port.

Sixty-four of the world's steamship lines maintain regular schedules from Colón (Cristóbal) or Balboa, and most of the ships in cabotage also maintain scheduled service. In 1971 a ferry service for vehicles and passengers began regular operations between Colón and the port of Turbo in Colombia. On paper, Panama has one of the worlds largest international shipping fleets, 2,100 vessels totaling over 5 million deadweight tons in 1969, equivalent to almost 3 percent of the world's total merchant marine tonnage. One thousand of these, however, were foreign owned and flew the Panamanian flag for convenience because of lenient regulations. The country permits ownership of vessels by noncitizens with easy registration, small annual fees, and no income tax on profits. Most of these ships never call at Panamanian ports. About 1,000 vessels are classified as private recreational boats, yachts, and launches, and presumably many of these are also foreign owned. In addition, almost 500 small vessels are engaged only in cabotage and fishing, and these are all Panamanian owned.

Aviation

Air transportation is well developed. There are about 240 airports, airstrips, and landing grounds, of which 115 are used commercially, although only four have paved runways. All airports are owned and operated by an autonomous government agency, the Directorate of Civil Aeronautics (Dirección de Aeronautica Civil). The country's principal international airport is that of Tocumen, fifteen miles east of Panama City on the Pan-American Highway. It is one of the busiest airports in Latin America and handled 400,000 incoming and outgoing passengers in 1969 plus about 200,000 in-transit travelers. The airport is being enlarged and modernized with World Bank financial assistance to take advantage of its location as a storage, processing, and assembly point for goods to be reexported to South America. The new facilities should be finished by 1975.

A smaller airport at David, rated as an international port of entry, is used principally for traffic originating in the Central American countries. A few hundred international passengers enter and leave annually via small aircraft from some of the lesser airfields. Domestic flights carried over 145,000 persons and 15 million pounds of cargo in 1969. About twenty-five towns and cities have scheduled domestic flights, and nonscheduled charter service is available to the other minor fields and landing strips. About twelve domestic airlines and twenty-one foreign airlines provide domestic and international service.

COMMUNICATIONS

All communications systems are under the control of the government, which may grant private enterprise concessions to operate them. As of 1971 the government itself was operating the postal system, the long-distance telephone service, the domestic telegraph system, and several radio communications stations. Private firms were providing local telephone service and international telephone and telegraph service. In 1970 there were over 73,500 telephones in the country, of which more than 69,000 were in Panama City and Colón. Among the more than 250 towns with telephone service, eight had automatic service, and most had only one telephone, located at the post office. Many of the towns in the interior are connected to the Metropolitan Area by microwave.

About fifty towns and cities have telegraph service. International telegraph and telephone service is provided both by radiotelephone and radiotelegraph and by undersea cables. In 1971 an earth satellite station was being built near Panama City for communication with cities in North America and Europe. Over 200 towns have postal service.

CHAPTER 14

NATIONAL SECURITY

In 1971 the country's only military or police force, the National Guard, had the capability of maintaining public order, and there appeared to be no significant internal or external threats to the provisional governing junta that had been in power since 1968. Sporadic activity by small bands of guerrillas in the western part of the country near the Costa Rican border was easily suppressed. The Panamanian Communist Party had been declared illegal in 1953, and Cuban radio propaganda had little apparent success in affecting the country's politics (see ch. 7, Education, Culture, and Public Information).

When the country gained its independence in 1903, a small unit of the Colombian army—about one battalion of infantry—was stationed in the territory and became the Panamanian army. As a consequence of conflict between the commander and the president, the army was disbanded in 1904, and the Corps of National Police (Cuerpo de Policia Nacional, also referred to as the National Police Corps) was established for the maintenance of public order (see ch. 2, Historical Setting). During its first thirty years of independence the country did not require a large police force since the United States military forces were depended on to maintain public order in case of emergency, as provided in the 1903 treaty concerning the construction of the canal. The police force, renamed the National Guard (Guardia Nacional) in 1953, has remained, and an army as such has never been reestablished.

Before 1930 (when the United States established a policy of nonintervention) the number of police rarely exceeded 1,000 for the whole country. Officials of successive administrations generally followed a policy of choosing top police officers from among supporters of the faction that had placed them in power, with the result that during most of the first half of this century the police never attempted to seize political power or to establish a military dictatorship. The first overt entrance into politics on the part of the police took place in 1949 as a result of conflict between its commandant and the president.

When, in 1953, the name of the police was changed to the National Guard, its functions remained the same. The elections of 1960 and 1964 showed no signs of National Guard intervention but, when Arnulfo Arias was elected in May 1968, it became obvious that he planned some changes in the command structure of the National Guard after he assumed office in October. He became president on October 1 and was deposed by the National Guard on October 11 (see ch. 2, Historical Setting).

In 1971 the strength of the National Guard was more than 6,000; the greater part of its personnel was concentrated in the Panama City-Colón-Tocumen Airport area. The remaining units were assigned to the ten zones into which the country is divided.

The administration of justice initially resembled that of Colombia, and Panamanian judicial codes were not drafted until 1917. At the apex of the court system was the Supreme Court of Justice (also known as the Supreme Court), followed by superior tribunals, circuit courts, and municipal courts. The Penal Code was approved by the National Assembly in 1922. The death penalty is outlawed by the Constitution, and the maximum prison sentence is twenty years for a single offense.

The incidence of crime increased between 1965 and 1969, and the number of persons arrested for various offenses in 1969 had increased 30 percent over that for 1965. Riots occurred during the 1960s, in some cases said to be instigated or condoned by government officials in order to achieve political aims.

THE NATIONAL GUARD

Development

In 1971 power in Panama was centered in the National Guard, commanded by Brigadier General Omar Torrijos. At the time of the dissolution of the army in 1904, the only police force in the country was a small force of forty-five policemen in Panama Province, organized under a Colombian decree of April 1903. The new government established the National Police Corps by a decree of December 1904 at a strength of 700. The Provincial Police were incorporated in the national force but apparently functioned autonomously until 1914, when they were disbanded.

In 1908 the strength was raised to a little over 1,000, and the force was organized into seven sections, each corresponding to one of the existing provinces. The heaviest concentrations of police were allotted to Panama and Colón. From 1908 until 1932 strength varied in accordance with budgetary allotments, and the police forces of successive administrations ranged between a maximum of 1,150 in 1915 and a minimum of 960 in early 1931.

During the same period the police force continually added to its functions, creating special branches to perform new duties. A body of sanitary police had a brief existence in 1908 and 1909. Created at the request of the Canal Zone's health department, the unit of twenty-two men was employed in sanitary inspection to prevent or report the strewing of garbage, waste, and trash. The effort proved impractical, and Canal Zone personnel took over the duty. A small section designated as frontier police was stationed in 1909 at the extreme eastern end of the San Blas coast to prevent illegal entry of Colombians and to cooperate with customs officials. Despite the country's long coastline and many islands and the prevalence of smuggling, a maritime police force was not organized until the 1960s.

The necessity for mounted police in rural areas, particularly in the southwestern provinces, was early recognized because of the prevalence of cattle rustling. Again, for reasons of economy, such a force was not organized until 1919. It is unclear when the rural mounted police were disbanded, but by 1932 the only mounted unit was the Cavalry Squadron, stationed in the capital and used there and at Tocumen Airport for crowd control, riot duty, and ceremonial purposes. It still existed in 1971.

A small detachment called the Colonial Police was formed in 1919 to maintain order in the San Blas region. According to some observers, misconduct by members of this force had much to do with the Indian uprising in 1925, and among the ensuing reforms was the incorporation into the local police of a number of Cuna Indians of San Blas, who were supervised directly by the Ministry of Government and Justice rather than by the commandant of the National Police Corps.

The Traffic Police was first organized in 1927, when the first traffic regulations were published. From small beginnings (a few officers, twenty men, and a dozen motorcycles) the force has steadily grown and is equipped with radio patrol cars as well as motorcycles. The completion of the Inter-American Highway from the Costa Rican border to the town of Chepo, thirty miles east of Panama City, and the Bridge of the Americas across the canal have resulted in a great increase of motor travel. Accordingly, the Traffic Division of the National Guard has placed greater emphasis on the training of its members in highway safety and traffic control.

Organization

According to Articles 143 and 144 of the Constitution of 1946, the president of the Republic, without consulting anyone, had the power: "To supervise the regular functioning of the administration and the preservation of public order; to appoint and dismiss freely the chiefs and officers of the Public Force and of the National Police Corps"; and "to dispose of the Public Forces of the Nation." This, in effect, makes the president the commander in chief of the National Guard, and he may freely appoint and dismiss its senior officers and direct its operations.

When, by the terms of a 1953 law, the National Police Corps became the National Guard, but without essential change in organization or functions, the president was authorized to direct operations and to assign officers through the minister of government and justice.

The chain of command went from the president of the Republic to the Ministry of Government and Justice and from that ministry to the Headquarters Command. This command had as its principal officers the commander (a brigadier general), the deputy commander (a colonel), and the secretary general (a lieutenant colonel). Directly subordinate to the Headquarters Command were two organizations, the Office of the Zone Commander and the General Staff. The zone commander directed the National Guard units in the ten zones into which the country was divided. The General Staff had five sections: G–1, personnel; G–2, intelligence; G–3, operations; G–4, logistics; and G–5, civic action. The G–3 section was responsible for the administration of the Police Academy and for the supervision of the Traffic Division and of recruit basic training. It also supervised the operations of the coast guard and the air force. Special units of the National Guard were the Presidential Guard, the Bay Guard, the Cavalry Squadron, the Tocumen Airport Guard, the Public Order Company (Compañía de Orden Público), and the National Department of Investigation (Departamento Nacional de Investigación—DENI).

The coast guard was equipped with several patrol craft (lanchas patrulleras), two of which were built in England and joined the naval service in June 1971. They are used for coastal patrol and antismuggling operations. The air force has C–47 type cargo and passenger aircraft, light aircraft, and UH1D Huey helicopters. The headquarters and main base of the air force is at Tocumen Airport, and officers and enlisted personnel have been trained in Venezuela and Colombia and at the Inter-American Air Force Academy in the Canal Zone.

The civic action section of the General Staff was responsible for project maintenance, engineering, architecture, community development, and rural development. In addition to its police functions, the National Guard maintains five infantry companies, specially trained for emergencies. These were formerly under the supervision of the G–3 section of the General Staff, but in 1971 they came directly under the Headquarters Command.

When Arnulfo Arias was elected president in May 1968, to take office October 1 of that year, he sought to exercise the powers granted him by the Constitution. The commander of the National Guard was Brigadier General Bolívar Vallarino, who had headed the organization for seventeen years. General Vallarino resigned, and the president directed the minister of government and justice to issue orders transferring several senior officers from positions of importance in the guard headquarters to posts of less importance in the interior of the country and to posts on foreign soil. Torrijos, then a lieutenant colonel, who was secretary general in the office of the guard commander, was to be transferred to San Salvador as military attaché to El Salvador and Guatemala. These orders were to be effective October 11, but on that night President Arias was deposed.

Personnel

In 1971 there was no lack of applicants for enlistment in the National Guard, which consists entirely of volunteers. The provision in Article 248 of the Constitution of 1946 that requires obligatory military service "whenever so demanded by public necessity" has never been applied. Recruits must be Panamanians and have a sixth-grade education, and this policy is generally followed, although schools to promote literacy have been reported. Recruiting is local, though centrally controlled as to numbers.

Since Panamanian statistics do not indicate race, except in the case of the tribal Indians, the racial composition of the force cannot be accurately determined, but there is no discrimination as far as race is concerned in enlistment or in attaining noncommissioned and commissioned ranks. For most of its members the National Guard is a career job, and it is not unusual to see a forty-year-old guardsman walking a police beat as a private. Most of the officers have entered the commissioned ranks directly, usually after graduating from one of the military academies of the other American republics. Former guard commanders José Antonio Remón and Vallarino entered the service this way, as did the 1971 commander and deputy commander, General Torrijos and Colonel Rodrigo García, both of whom graduated from the El Salvador Military Academy.

Training

Until 1957 systematic training was at best sporadic. A United States citizen was engaged in 1917 as instructor and in 1919 was made inspector general in charge of the entire force. Remaining as inspector until 1927, he is credited with improving the discipline and training of the police.

Commandants and ministers of government and justice from time to time recommended the establishment of training schools but were not able to secure funds for the necessary personnel and installations. Even Colonel Remón does not appear to have been able, either as commander of the National Guard or later as president, to install schools on any continuous or systematic basis; nevertheless, the discipline and training improved during his time. In 1954 a Venezuelan military mission helped establish a basic training school for recruits, the National Guard Orientation School (Escuela de Formación de Guardias Nacionales). The contractual relationship with Venezuela ceased early in 1958, but the school has continued.

Newly enlisted guardsmen are sent to the school in groups of about fifty and pursue a course of about three months in military and police training, including a brief familiarization with the Constitution and Panamanian history, National Guard regulations, and police theories and responsibilities.

An officers' school (the Police Academy) was started in 1960; and one for sergeants, shortly thereafter. These schools are not prerequisites for promotion, but newly appointed lieutenants and sergeants are sent to them for instruction in their new duties. National Guard officers have attended the command and general staff courses at the School of the Americas, given by the United States Army Caribbean Command at Fort Gulick in the Canal Zone. General Torrijos is a graduate of this course. Noncommissioned officers have also attended schools in the Canal Zone where courses in radio and motor operation and maintenance are given.

Operations

In 1971 the total strength of the National Guard was about 6,500, and of this number at least half were assigned to the Panama City-Colón-Tocumen Airport area. The nerve center of National Guard operations is located at the central barracks (*cuartel central*) in the capital city. Besides the headquarters and staff, it houses the communication center under which the radio patrol cars operate, the Traffic Division, the armory, the clinic and pharmacy, detention cells for persons arrested and those with light sentences, and rooms for off-duty or reserve guardsmen.

Conventional police duty is performed by policemen on regular beats twenty-four hours a day. Beat duty is rotated with days in reserve and days of free time. The periods of assigned patrol in the radio cars are coordinated with the regular shifts, though the police cars are controlled by a different section in headquarters. The traffic police, both dismounted and mobile (radio cars and motorcycles), are directed by a third section of the Traffic Division. The communication section, to which the radio patrol is attached, operates not only the net control of the mobile stations but also that of the radio net that links provincial stations with headquarters as well as the central police switchboard.

Other sections stationed in or near Panama City are the Presidential Guard, the Bay Guard, the Cavalry Squadron, and the Tocumen Airport Guard. The Presidential Guard, with quarters in the palace, mounts guard over the grounds and controls traffic in the adjacent streets. It has special uniforms for both daily duty and ceremonies and is responsible for the personal safety of the president. The Bay Guard is attached to the Presidential Guard and is responsible for order in the wharf area where coastal vessels dock. The Cavalry Squadron is maintained for ceremonial occasions and for crowd control. When not so employed, the members perform ordinary dismounted police duty. The National Guard is also charged with the security of the central jail and has a special detachment at Tocumen Airport. This detachment performs normal watchman service and is prepared to cooperate with customs personnel when necessary.

The penal farm colony on Coiba Island is administered by the National Guard with the assistance of employees from the Department of Correction under the Ministry of Government and Justice.

Two other National Guard organizations are the Public Order Company and the National Department of Investigation. In 1931, after the armed coup that deposed President Florencio H. Arosemena, proposals were made to create a police reserve of approximately battalion strength to cope with serious disorders. For political and budgetary reasons nothing came of the project. In 1959, however, a plan was brought forward to create the Public Order Company as a police reserve organized along tactical lines, to be available not only for internal disorders but for emergency field use as well. Members of this organization have attended United States Army schools in the Canal Zone.

An organization usually called the Secret Police has existed in Panama since 1909. For the most part, it has been simply a detective force, and devices have been employed to conceal the number and identity of its operatives. Until 1941 it was a special section of the National Police Corps, but at that time it was separated, although it still came under the supervision of the Ministry of Government and Justice. By terms of its basic decree, its duties were to follow up and investigate infractions of the laws and to prevent attempts against the institutions of the state and against national security.

By a decree-law of May 1960 the name of the Secret Police was changed to the National Department of Investigation (Departamento Nacional de Investigación—DENI) and was removed entirely from the Ministry of Government and Justice and placed under the Public Ministry (see ch. 8, Governmental S stem). Its functions, still focused primarily on crime detection, appear to be unchanged, though it has some potential as an antisubversive auxiliary through its accumulation of dossiers on suspected persons. It was also authorized to establish a universal fingerprint file. In 1968 DENI, within the area of police-community relations, initiated a program designed to improve relations with high school students. This was done by giving a series of lectures to explain how DENI as a law enforcement agency works within the society. In 1971 it was estimated that DENI numbered about 300 agents.

Civic Action

During the 1960s the National Guard was engaged in civic action, particularly in the fields of health, sanitation, and education. Newspapers emphasize this with articles and photographs depicting members of the National Guard awarding scholarship prizes, constructing schools and other public buildings, working on road construction, erecting water purification systems, digging wells, and providing medical assistance to residents of rural communities.

Budgetary and Administrative Matters

During the 1960–70 period the annual allocation of funds for national security had not placed a burden on the country's economy. The National Guard constituted 0.5 percent of the total population and did not adversely affect the nation's labor force. Between 1967 and 1970 the budget for national security and the maintenance of public order averaged between 7 and 10 percent of total government expenditures. This included the amount needed for the penitentiary service.

Data for the annual budget of the National Guard are prepared by its general administration (*intendencia general*) department, whose personnel are responsible for the expenditure of all funds, whether for pay, operations, or the acquisition of equipment and property. It maintains both financial and property records, which must eventually be submitted to the comptroller general of the Republic.

The annual appropriation for pay for members of the National Guard increases regularly because of the greater amounts necessary to take care of the increments for length of service. This increase indicates that the guard is a long-service unit, especially in the commissioned and noncommissioned grades. Another indication of this is the authorization of awards for increments of twenty, fifteen, ten, and five years' service. For 1969 the Ministry of Finance and Treasury reported a raise in pay for officers. The three senior officers received monthly salaries of B/1,360, B/1,068, and B/878 (1 balboa equals US$1), respectively.

There are no appropriations for rations, no allowances for rations and quarters, and no guardsmen's messes except for recruits in basic training. In the 1966 budget for the National Guard the largest item was for pay and allowances, and the next largest was for shoes and clothing, indicating that these are issued free.

No provisions for medical care are known to have existed before 1950. At that time an arrangement was made for the establishment of a clinic at the headquarters building in Panama City, to be served by a number of civilian doctors (given honorary officer rank), for the purpose of treating guardsmen and their families without personal cost. Dental attention is similarly provided. At about the same time a ward in Santo Tomás Hospital in Panama City was reserved for the National Guard. In case of retirement for disability, members are eligible for social security plus a special increment. National Guard units stationed in the interior, if they are equipped with medical facilities, provide medical treatment for the civilians in the area as part of the civic action program.

A commissary was established to sell food, clothing, and minor household items at prices somewhat reduced from retail. Sales are both for cash and by a credit-book system. Profits are expended on barracks amenities and help support another convenience, the Savings and Loan Fund (Caja de Ahorros y Préstamos). From that agency guardsmen receive interest on deposits, made either in cash or in allotment, and may take out small loans in emergencies. Supervision of the clinic, the commissary, and the loan fund are among the duties of the secretary general in the Headquarters Command.

Awards and Rank Insignia

The government of Panama has three decorations that may be awarded to nationals or foreigners for outstanding service rendered to the Republic in the fields of scientific research, education, and literature or accomplishments of a civic or humanitarian nature. These are the Order of Manuel Amador Guerrero, the Order of Vasco Núñez de Balboa, and the Order of Octavio Méndez Pereira. Each may be awarded in one of five different degrees. There is an additional award, the Honor for Merit.

In 1956 the government authorized the award of several decorations to commissioned and enlisted members of the National Guard. These awards are named for National Guard General Remón who was assassinated while he was president of the Republic and other officers who lost their lives while on active duty with the National Guard. The highest of these is the José Antonio Remón Cantera gold medal, which may be awarded to members of the National Guard or to civilians for meritorious service. The second is the Lieutenant Colonel Alfredo Lezcano Gómez silver medal for completing twenty years' service in the National Guard. The others are Major Juan C. Comparez bronze medal for fifteen years' service, the Captain Juan E. Flores bronze bar for ten years' service, and the Second Lieutenant Ernesto Meril bronze bar for five years' service. There are also six lesser awards for meritorious acts.

Officer rank insignia, which are the same for all Central American armed forces, conform to the designs adopted in 1968 by the Central American Defense Council (Consejo de Defensa Centroamericana—CONDECA). The insignia are the same for all officers, including those assigned to the air force and coast guard. Insignia are worn on the shoulder straps of the blouse or on the collar of the uniform shirt. The insignia consist of gold-colored bars, stars, or three laurel leaves—the latter being reserved for the commander of the National Guard if he is a general officer. Field Grade officers wear one, two, or three stars, and company grade officers wear one, two, or three bars. Noncommissioned officers wear sleeve insignia of colored cloth.

ADMINISTRATION OF JUSTICE

The court system and criminal procedure derive largely from Colombian law, which at the time of independence was left in force, except where manifestly inapplicable, until Panamanian codes could be drafted. The first codes, which came into force in 1917, left little leeway to the judges or officers of the courts in the matters of procedure, delays, or degrees of guilt. One feature of Anglo-Saxon origin not found in some Latin American codes is the right of habeas corpus, guaranteed by Article 24 of the Constitution of 1946.

The Public Ministry, headed by the procurator general, furnishes prosecuting attorneys at all levels of the court system except the lowest. The municipal courts are served by prosecutors called *personeros*, appointed and paid by the municipality but nevertheless subject to the supervision of the procurator general. The prosecuting attorneys are also responsible for the investigation and preparation of cases. Investigation is accomplished by a combination of the efforts of the National Guard in its police function and DENI.

Arrest may be the result either of a complaint made to the National Guard (the normal case) or of the direct action of a guardsman or detective on the spot. The Constitution recognizes the right of any citizen to arrest a person seen in the act of committing a crime. It also guarantees that no person may be detained for more than twenty-four hours before being informed in writing of the legal reason for the detention. The investigating prosecutor must be promptly informed and must complete the investigation within a set period of time, though delay for specified causes is permissible.

During the course of the investigation, the accused and all witnesses are questioned (the latter under oath). The accused, by constitutional right, may not be compelled to incriminate himself or his close relations by blood or marriage. If it is necessary, the scene of the crime is visited, but domiciles can be searched only with the owner's consent or by court order. In general, all testimony is reduced to writing and signed by all concerned. The case, if a true bill is found, is then referred to an appropriate court. Bail is permissible in certain cases, but the privilege is subject to many restrictions dependent on the seriousness of the offense; at the discretion of the Public Ministry its representative may intervene to give cause for denying bail.

Municipal courts exercise jurisdiction in minor cases up to the level of seriousness of minor assaults or robbery and theft involving amounts less than B/100. A special type of municipal court is the traffic court, which tries minor traffic cases not involving serious injury to persons and property. To the circuit courts go more serious cases, including aggravated assault, mayhem, negligent homicide, preventable damage to person or property by fire, and robberies and thefts of over B/100. The superior tribunals receive all the most serious cases except those specifically reserved for the Supreme Court, which in general tries only cases involving high government officials.

Trial by jury, unless the accused waives his right to it, is held in superior tribunal courts in specified types of cases, such as murder and robberies and larcenies of over B/2,000. Juries, drawn from a panel from which clergymen and most government officials as well as relatives of the parties involved are excused, may have five or seven members. Challenges for cause are permitted to both defense and prosecution.

Testimony is taken under oath, and the opposing sides question witnesses on the facts related and on any discrepancies between their testimony in court and earlier signed statements made at the investigation. The accused has the opportunity to testify in his own behalf. Trial is customarily open to the public but may be in closed court in cases where public morality may be offended or sometimes in consideration of the grief of injured persons. The jury, if any, considers only the verdict of guilt or innocence as charged. Any questions concerning the degree of guilt or the accused's previous conduct or character are in the purview of the court when it passes sentence.

PENAL CODE

The country's first penal code was approved by the National Assembly on November 17, 1922. It describes the penal code in general and details the various punishments—*reclusión* (imprisonment in a penitentiary), *prisión* (prison), *arresto* (arrest), *confinamiento* (confinement), *multa* (fine), suspension of the exercise of rights, and subjection to vigilance by the authorities. The definitions and penalties for felonies (*delitos*) are found in the Penal Code; and those for misdemeanors (*faltas*), in the Administrative Code. The different types of felonies defined are crimes against public order, the administration of justice, public security, good morals, the person, and property.

The death penalty is outlawed by the Constitution, and the maximum sentence for a single offense is twenty years. *Reclusión* is the most severe type of punishment and may be adjudged for from thirty days to twenty years. Prison labor is required, and it is served at the Coiba Penal Colony. *Prisión* sentences may be from thirty days to eighteen years and are usually served in the central prison in Panama. An individual who has completed three-fourths of a *reclusión* sentence or two-thirds of a *prisión* sentence may be freed if he has a record of good conduct, unless he was convicted of robbery, extortion, or being a member of a criminal gang.

Arresto is a penalty assessed for relatively minor offenses and may extend to eighteen months, usually served in a local jail. The prisoner is required to work. *Confinamiento,* a punishment that, despite its name, does not imply physical restraint, is a requirement that the offender reside in a specified place, which must be a minimum of thirty kilometers (18.65 miles) from the place where the offense was committed or where the injured party lives. The time limit is at the judge's discretion unless stated in the law.

Multa is the least severe of the stated penalties and may in some instances be added to a jail sentence. If an offender cannot pay, or later defaults, fines are convertible to *arresto* on a basis of one day for each balboa fined. There also are some penalties in addition to the principal ones named. In some cases, these are automatic: *reclusión*, for example, involves the loss of civic rights for the terms of the sentence, and in some cases for longer. Thus, an offender's loss of the right to vote may extend beyond his penitentiary term. Another additional penalty is the loss of his rights of control as the head of a family, applied when the conduct of the offender indicates wrongdoing or gross negligence in that regard.

A type of suspended sentence (*condena condicional*) is given at the discretion of the judge in minor cases of first offense. It involves the registration of a fixed residence, frequent reports to the court, and checkups by police or welfare officials. Misdemeanors, the long list of which includes many minor offenses and pays special attention to vagrancy and begging, may be punished by short sentences of *arresto*, but more often only fines or periods of directed labor on public works without confinement are adjudged.

Many types of cases require automatic review in a higher court, and provisions for appeals exist; time limits are set on the preparation of, and action upon, appeals. Few cases can be appealed to the Supreme Court, and these usually must be on the grounds of error. Reversal is rare.

The government began to take official action in the matter of juvenile offenders in the 1940s by organizing the Institute of Child Welfare, but the worsening of conditions caused a spreading of concern, and in 1951 the Correctional Court for Minors (Tribunal Tutelar de Menores) was established. The court's services come into play through reports from the National Guard, DENI, or interested individuals on cases of juvenile delinquency, vagrancy, and abandonment that are referred to the court's Department of Social Investigation.

The report is then submitted to the court for disposition, and this may be conditional release, release under surveillance, or commitment to the Observation Center. Physical and psychological examinations are also made. The Observation Center combines the functions of restraint, observation, and training for rehabilitation; and restraint is graduated according to observed behavior. The center receives assistance from the ministries of public health and education and maintains a small agricultural colony for inmates.

PENAL SYSTEM

Before the country gained its independence in 1903, prisoners were incarcerated in the old Presidio of Chiriquí, which was built into a corner of the seawall in Panama City. The cells were dark, damp and unventilated. The inscription over the entrance door read: *"Entran bravos como leones y salen mansos como corderos"* (They enter fierce as lions and leave mild as lambs).

In 1919 a penal colony was founded on the island of Coiba, fifteen miles off the southwestern coast of the Veraguas Province. The island has an area of about 600 square miles, most of which is jungle. The prisoners are housed in a main compound, as well as in several small camps scattered around the island. Farming and animal husbandry are the principal occupations of the inmates, who also make various articles, which are sent to the mainland for sale. In addition to convicted felons, political prisoners have been sent to the Coiba colony. Between 1919 and 1944, in the many attempts to escape, only nine convicts have not been recaptured.

The Carcel Modelo (Model Jail) was established in Panama City in 1920. This is where most of the serious offenders are sent before being transferred to Coiba Island. Those awaiting trial are confined to their cells, and frequently there have been long periods of waiting. There are jails in each of the provincial capital cities, a reformatory for women at Los Santos, and an agricultural colony at Divisa, at the intersection of the three provinces of Coclé, Veraguas, and Herrera.

The Ministry of Government and Justice is charged with the administration of prisons through its Department of Correction, established in 1940. The object was to place the penal institutions under the department rather than directly under the national police. The small number of personnel assigned to the department, however, precludes effective supervision, and the actual administration of prison operations falls largely upon the National Guard (formerly the National Police Corps).

The president by constitutional authority may "grant pardons for political offenses, reduce penalties, and grant paroles to persons guilty of common offenses." Conditional liberty (*libertad condicional*) is possible under the law after a major portion of some specified severe sentence is served with good conduct. It resembles parole in that the person released must register his place of residence with the National Guard and either report periodically or be subject to investigation of his conduct for a determined period.

INCIDENCE OF CRIME

The number of persons arrested for various offenses between 1965 and 1969 increased from 27,854 to 36,080, the latter figure constituting a ratio of twenty-five for each 1,000 of the country's inhabitants. The province in which the greatest number of arrests occurred was Panama, with 17,741, and Panama City accounted for 14,679 of these. Over 6,000 were arrested in Chiriquí Province and 3,159 in Colón Province, the city of Colón accounting for all but 304 of those arrested.

In 1969, 3,951 persons stood trial, seventy-three before superior tribunals, 2,415 in circuit courts, and 1,463 in municipal courts. Of these, 1,130 were sentenced to various terms of confinement. Of the total number of persons tried, 1,882 were in the city of Panama.

An official breakdown of the various charges against persons arrested is available for 1966. Of the total of 28,440, 25 percent were detained for traffic violations; and 25 percent for crimes against persons, including homicide (205 cases) and armed assault (1,052 cases). There were 3,391 arrests for crimes against public morals and 2,950 for crimes against property, 50 percent of these being for theft. During that same year there were seventy-five suicides. More than 25,000 of those arrested were male; most of these were young males between the ages of twenty and thirty-nine.

SUBVERSIVE POTENTIAL

In 1971 there appeared to be no internal political force that could pose a threat to the provisional governmental junta established in October 1968. The country had long been a target for communist penetration because of the importance of the canal, and Panamanian concern over its position in relation to the United States had been a primary object of communist appeals. The Communist Party had been proscribed, however, in 1953; and, even after the advent of Fidel Castro in Cuba, the substantial pro-Castro sentiment that had at first been manifested was diminished by subsequent changes in Cuban political philosophy to the point of breaking off diplomatic relations, which had not been reestablished by mid-1971.

During the rioting that occurred in Panama City in January 1964, at the time of the flag-raising incident, members of the

Communist Party are reported to have participated actively in the disturbances and to have attempted to organize and lead the anti-American campaign (see ch. 2, Historical Setting; ch. 10, Foreign Relations). Their goals were said to be to force a protracted confrontation of United States troops with armed Panamanians, to produce civilian martyrs, and to stimulate "Hate America" agitation in all quarters.

Membership of the two illegal communist organizations was estimated to number about 250 in 1971. These were the People's Democratic Party and the Movement of Revolutionary Unity (Castroite). The parties are weak and disorganized and have suffered from arrest, imprisonment, exile, and death of their top leaders. After the coup of October 1968, the junta government continued its pressure on these parties, and neither group has mounted any serious opposition to the new government.

In December 1968 the government closed and then reorganized the University of Panama. It was reopened in July 1969. This effectively neutralized a traditional center of communist agitation. Student political activity has been curtailed, and a campus security unit enforces the new regulations. Furthermore, practically all communist activity in the National Institute and other secondary schools has ceased.

Incidents between Panamanian and United States personnel, some of which have resulted in serious riots, have long formed a special case in the history of local disorders owing to the growing nationalism and the desire on the part of all Panamanians for complete sovereignty over the Canal Zone.

The socioeconomic system has been marked by inequalities that have caused various degrees of disaffection and tensions between social groups. Communist agitation has been directed at the social and economic problems of the proletariat. The Communists have also attempted to control the labor union movement but have had little success. The labor union movement in Panama has not been integrated into a single overall organization, making it difficult for any political party to penetrate the movement far enough to gain complete control. In 1969 and 1970 General Torrijos traveled about the country urging the merger of unions into a single national organization, but by 1971 this had not been accomplished.

Government measures have reduced the flow of both Cuban and Sino-Soviet propaganda and have continually countered its effects by pointing out the ways in which Soviet or Castro policies threaten Panamanian national interests. During the three years that the provisional junta has been in power, the government has shown an awareness of the problems of labor and of the lower economic strata that, if translated into visible action, may go far toward dissipating sources of discontent within the society. The government's interest in these problems has been made evident by the speeches and many trips to the countryside made by General Torrijos.

BIBLIOGRAPHY

RECOMMENDED SOURCES

Adams, Richard N. *Cultural Surveys of Panama-Nicaragua-Guatemala-El Salvador-Honduras.* (Scientific Publications, No. 33). Washington: Pan American Sanitary Bureau, 1947.

Alexander, Robert J. *Communism in Latin America.* New Brunswick: Rutgers University Press, 1957.

Amado, David. *La Administración pública como instrumento del desarrollo, Panamá.* Washington: Secretaría General. Organización de los Estados Americanos, 1966.

Anderson, Charles William. *Political Ideology and the Revolution of Rising Expectations in Central America, 1944–1958.* Madison: University of Wisconsin Microfilms, 1960.

Anderson, C. L. G. *Old Panama and Castillo del Oro.* Washington: Sudwarth, 1911.

Arias, Harmodio. *The Panama Canal.* London: King and Son, 1911.

Baldwin, Hanson W. "New Currents in the Panama Canal," *New York Times Magazine,* May 26, 1957, 14–15.

Baxter, Richard R., and Carroll, Doris. *The Panama Canal: Background Papers and Proceedings of the Sixth Hammarsköld Forum.* (Ed., Lyman M. Tondel, Jr.), Dobbs Ferry: Oceana, for the Association of the Bar of the City of New York, 1965.

Bemis, Samuel Flagg. *A Diplomatic History of the United States.* (Rev. ed.) New York: Holt, 1942.

Biesanz, John. "The Economy of Panama," *Inter-American Economic Affairs,* I, Summer 1952, 3–28.

———. "Social Forces Retarding Development of Panama's Agricultural Resources," *Rural Sociology,* XV, No. 2, 1950, 148–155.

Biesanz, John, and Biesanz, Mavis. *The People of Panama.* New York: Columbia University Press, 1955.

Biesanz, John, and Smith, Luke M. "Panamanian Politics," *Journal of Politics,* XIV, No. 3, 1952, 386–402.

"Bonfires in Panama," *Economist* [London], CXCIII, No. 6067, December 5, 1959, 984.

Brenes, Gonzalo C. "El Teatro nacional casa de la cultura, 1908–1958," *Lotería* [Panama City], II, No. 35, 1958, 40–56.

Camarano de Sucre, Yolanda. *Los Capelli.* Panama: Talleres de la Estrella de Panamá, 1967.

―――. *La dona del paz.* Panama: Imprenta Nacional, 1966.

Cameron, Duncan H. "The Panama Canal Policy of the United States," *Midwest Quarterly*, XI, No. 2, January, 1970, 141–152.

Campbell, Carolina de, and Hooper, Ofelia. "The Middle Class of Panama," In Theo R. Carvenna (ed.), *Materiales para el estudio de la clase media en la América Latina*, IV. Washington: Pan American Union, 1950.

"Canal Politics," *Economist* [London], CXCV, No. 6091, May 21, 1960, 733.

Candanedo, César A. *La otra frontera.* Panama City: Imprenta Nacional, 1966.

Castedo, Leopoldo. *A History of Latin American Art and Architecture from Pre-Columbian Times to the Present.* (Trans. and ed., Phyllis Freeman.) New York: Praeger, 1969.

Castillero Calvo, Alfredo. *La sociedad Panameña: historia de su formación e integración.* Panama City: Dirección General de Planificación y Administración de la Presidencia, May 1970.

Castillero Reyes, Ernesto J. "Los Panameños y los estudios históricos," *Lotería* [Panama City], II, No. 27, 1958, 20–29.

Chidsey, Donald Barr. *The Panama Canal: An Informal History.* New York: Crown, 1970.

Cochrane, James D. "Costa Rica, Panama, and the Central American Economic Integration," *Journal of Inter-American Studies*, VII, No. 3, July 1965, 331–344.

Davis, Harold Eugene. *Government and Politics in Latin America.* New York: Ronald Press, 1958.

Denton, Charles F. "Interest Groups in Panama and the Central American Common Market," *Inter-American Economic Affairs*, XXI, No. 1, Summer 1967, 31–48.

Diamond, Walter H. *Foreign Tax and Trade Briefs.* New York: Fallon, 1960.

Dominguez, Caballero, Diego. "Panamá y la historia de las ideas en Latinoamérica," *Revista de historia de las ideas*, [Quito], I, November 1959, 217–235.

Dubois, Jules. *Danger over Panama.* Indianapolis: Bobbs-Merrill, 1964.

Duval, Miles P., Jr. *Cadiz to Cathay.* Stanford: Stanford University Press, 1947.

―――. *And the Mountains Will Move: The Story of the Building of the Panama Canal.* Stanford: Stanford University Press, 1947.

Ealy, Lawrence O. *The Republic of Panama in World Affairs, 1903–1950.* Philadelphia: University of Pennsylvania Press, 1951.

Echeverri Herrera, Carlos. *Tendencias económicas de América Latina.* Madrid: Sucs. de Rivadeneyra, 1956.

Editor and Publisher International Year Book. New York: Editor and Publisher, 1971.

"Fears in Panama," *Economist,* [London], CLXXXII, No. 5919, February 2, 1957, 384.

Fitzgibbon, Russell H. (ed.) *The Constitutions of the Americas (as of January 1, 1948).* Chicago: University of Chicago Press, 1948.

Foreign Broadcast Information Service. *Broadcasting Stations of the World, Part I:* Amplitude Modulation Broadcasting Stations According to Country and City. Washington: January 1971.

————. *Broadcasting Stations of the World, Part IV:* Television Stations. Washington: January 1971.

Fuentes Irurozqui, Manuel. *Economía Hispanoamericana.* Madrid: Monographias de Industria y Comercio, 1948.

Fuson, Robert H. "Communal Labor in Central Panama," *Rural Sociology,* XXIV, No. 1, 1959, 57–60.

Garcia-Mora, Manuel R. "The Panama Canal Controversy," *Vital Speeches of the Day,* XXX, No. 13, April 15, 1964, 412–416.

Gillin, John. "Ethos Components in Latin American Culture," *American Anthropologist,* LVII, No. 5, 1955, 488–500.

Goldrich, Daniel. "Panama." Chapter 8 in Martin C. Needler (ed.), *Political Systems of Latin America.* (2d ed.) New York: Van Nostrand, 1970.

Goldrich, Daniel, and Scott, E. W. "Developing Political Orientations of Panamanian Students," *Journal of Politics,* XXIII, No. 1, 1961, 84–107.

Gorban, Samuel. *Integración económica de América Latina.* Rosario, Argentina: Editorial Rosario, 1951.

Goytía, Victor F. *Las constituciones de Panamá.* Madrid: Ediciones Cultura Hispánica, 1954.

Great Britain. Board of Trade. *Panama.* (Economic and Commercial Conditions in Panama, Overseas Economic Surveys.) London: HMSO, 1951.

Guzmán, Luis E. *Farming and Farmlands in Panama.* (Research Paper No. 44.) Chicago: University of Chicago Press, 1956.

Hall, Clarence W. "Panama: The Crisis We Could Have Avoided," *Reader's Digest,* LXXXIV, No. 504, April 1964, 84.

Hanson, Simon G. *Economic Development in Latin America: An Introduction to Economic Problems of Latin America.* Washington: Inter-American Affairs Press, 1951.

Harding, Earl. *The Untold Story of Panama*. Mt. Clemens, Michigan: Bookmailer, 1959.

Harris, Louis K. "Panama." Chapter 5 in Ben G. Burnett and Kenneth F. Johnson (eds.), *Political Forces in Latin America*. Belmont, California: Wadsworth, 1968.

Herring, Hubert. *A History of Latin America*. New York, Knopf, 1968.

"Highways in Latin America," *Latin American Business Highlights* (Chase Manhattan Bank), X, No. 4, 1960, 7–9.

Hirschman, Albert O. *Latin American Issues*. New York: Twentieth Century Fund, 1961.

Horn, Paul V., and Bice, Hubert E. *Latin American Trade and Economics*. New York: Prentice-Hall, 1949.

Institute for the Comparative Study of Political Systems, 1968. *Panama Election Factbook*. Washington: 1968.

James, Preston E. *Latin America* (4th ed.) New York: Odyssey Press, 1969.

Johnson, John J. *The Military and Society in Latin America*. Stanford: Leland Stanford Junior University, 1965.

Kantor, Harry. *Patterns of Politics and Political Systems in Latin America*. Chicago: Rand McNally, 1969.

Langley, L. D. "U.S.-Panamanian Relations Since 1941," *Journal of Inter-American Studies*, XII, No. 3, July 1970, 339–366.

Liss, Sheldon B. *The Canal: Aspects of United States-Panamanian Relations*. Notre Dame: University of Notre Dame Press, 1967.

Lodge, George C., and Gudeman, Stephan F. *The Veraguas Report: A Study of the Organization of Change in Rural Latin America*. (Report submitted to the U.S. Agency for International Development; FAR 7798.) Boston: Harvard University Graduate School for Business Administration, November 13, 1967.

López, Georgian Jiménez de. "Panama in Transition: Period 1849 to 1940." (Ph.D. dissertation, University Microfilms Publication #6640). New York: Columbia University, 1953.

Lothrop, Samuel Kirkland. *Coclé, An Archaeological Study of Central Panama*, VII. Cambridge: Peabody Museum of Archaeology and Ethnology, Harvard University, 1937.

McCain, William D. *The United States and the Republic of Panama*. Durham: Duke University Press, 1937.

Martínez, Ortega, Aristides. "Avant-Garde Poetry in Panama," *Américas*, XVI, No. 7, July 1964, 12–19.

Martz, John D. *Central America: The Crisis and the Challenge*. Chapel Hill: University of North Carolina Press, 1959.

May, Stacy, and Plaza, Galo. *The United Fruit Company in Latin America*. Washington: National Planning Association, 1958.

Merrill, John C.; Carter, R. Bryan; and Alisky, Marvin. *The Foreign Press*. Baton Rouge: Louisiana State University Press, 1964 (2d printing, 1966).

Milne, Jean. *Fiesta Time in Latin America*. Los Angeles: Ritchie Ward Press, 1965.

Miró, Rodrigo. *La Cultura colonial en Panamá*. Mexico City: n.pub., 1950.

————. "Panamá, 50 años de república," *Hispanic American Historical Review*, XXXV, No. 1, 1955, 128–129.

Moscote, J. D. *El Derecho constitucional panameño*. Panama City: Panama Star & Herald, 1943.

"Murder in Panama," *Economist*, [London], CLXXIV, No. 5812, January 15, 1955, 200.

Naughton, William A. *Panama: A Foreign Policy Analysis*. Washington: School of International Service, The American University (unpublished paper), 1968.

————. "The Rails that Linked the Oceans," *Américas*, XVII, No. 2, February 1965, 11–17.

"No Flag for Panama," *Economist*, [London], CXCV, No. 6088, April 30, 1960, 421.

Organization of American States/International Development Bank, Joint Tax Program. *Fiscal Survey of Panama: Problems and Proposals for Reform*. Baltimore: Johns Hopkins Press, 1964.

Organization of American States. General Secretariat. *Young Poetry of the Americas, I: Cultural Themes*. Washington: 1964.

Organization of American States. Instituto Interamericano de Estadística. *América en cifras, 1970. situación económica, I: agricultura, ganadería, silvicultura, caza y pesca*. Washington: Secretaría General de la OAS, 1970.

"Our Girl in Panama," *Economist*, [London], XCXI, No. 6035, April 25, 1959, 318.

Padelford, Norman J. *The Panama Canal in Peace and War*. New York: Macmillan, 1942.

"Panama—No U.S. Backdown," *U.S. News & World Report*, LVI, No. 4, January 27, 1964, 29–31.

"Panama." Pages 67–110 in Amos J. Peaslee (ed.), *Constitutions of Nations, III: Nicaragua to Yugoslavia*, (2d ed.). The Hague: Martinus Nijhoff, 1956.

"Panama, The Atlantic Report," *Atlantic*, CCVII, No. 3, 1961, 24–30.

Pan American Union. *América en cifras 1965; situación cultural: educación y otros aspectos culturales*. Washington: Organization of American States. 1967.

Porras, Demetrio A. *Problemas vitales panameños.* Panama City: Ministerio de Educación, Departamento de Belles Artes y Publicaciones, 1960.

Publishers' International Directory (3d ed.) Munich: Verlag Dokumentation, 1967.

"Record of U.S. in Panama as a New Era Begins," *U.S. News & World Report,* LVI, No. 20, May 18, 1964, 42–44.

Republic of Panama. Comisión del Atlas de Panamá. *Atlas de Panamá.* Panama City: Dirección de Estadística y Censo, 1965.

Republic of Panama. Junta Nacional del Cincuentenario. *Panamá: 50 años de república.* Panama City: Imprenta Nacional, 1953.

Republic of Panama. Laws, Statutes, etc.
> *Códigos Penal y de Minas.* Panama City: 1944.
> *Constitution of the Republic of Panama, 1946.* Washington: General Secretariat, Organization of American States, 1968.
> *Industrial Incentives Law: Decree Law No. 413 December 30, 1970.* New York: 1971.

Republic of Panama. Ministerio de Agricultura y Ganadería. *Memoria, 1969–1970.* Panama City: 1970.

Republic of Panama. Contraloría General de la República. Dirección de Estadística y Censo. *Estadística panameña, año XXVII: Demografía.* Panama City: 1967.

————. *Estadística panameña, año XXVII: Empleo, año 1967.* (Series "M".) Panama City: 1967.

————. *Estadística panameña, año XXVI: Estadísticas vitales, 1966.* (Series "B1", No. 1.) Panama City: 1966.

————. *Panamá en cifras. (Compendio Estadístico, años 1965 a 1969).* Panama City: November 3, 1970.

————. *Panamá en cifras.* Panama City: October 1961.

Republic of Panama. Presidencia de la República. Dirección General de Planificación y Administración. Departamento de Planificación. *Estudios de estructuras agrarias panameñas y análisis de la reforma agraria.* (Estudios Esp. no. 3.) Panama City: Industrial Gráfica, 1970.

————. *Estudios sectorales: sector agropecuario diagnóstico, 1960–1968.* Panama City: Industrial Gráfica, 1970.

Rodman, Selden. *The Road to Panama.* New York: Hawthorne, 1966.

Rodriguez Bou, Ismael. *Estudio del sistema educativo de la república de Panamá.* Panama City: Ministerio de Educación, 1957.

Sinan, Rogelio. "Rutas de la novela panameña," *Lotería* [Panama City], II, No. 23, 1957, 103–110.

Soler, Ricaurte. *Pensamiento panameño y concepción de la nacio-nalidad durante el siglo XIX*. Panama City: Imprenta Nacional, 1954.

Tamames Gómez, Ramón. *Aspectos económicos de la vinculación de Panamá al mercado común centroamericano*. Panama City: Imprenta Nacional, June 1966.

Teichert, Pedro M. *Economic Policy Revolution and Industrialization in Latin America*. Oxford: University of Mississippi, Bureau of Business Research, 1959.

Turner Morales, David. *Estructura económica de Panamá*. Mexico City: Editorial América Nueva, 1958.

United Nations Educational, Scientific and Cultural Organization. *World Communications—Press, Radio, Television, Film* (2d ed.) New York: 1966.

United Nations. Economic and Social Council. Economic Commission for Latin America. *Análisis y proyecciones del desarrollo económico, VII, el desarrollo económico de Panamá, part II apendices*. Panama City: May 12, 1959 (mimeo).

U.S. Agency for International Development. *Summary of Economic and Social Indicators, 19 Latin American Countries 1961–1968*. Washington: Office of Development Planning, Bureau of Latin America, 1968.

U.S. Congress. 89th, 2d Session. House of Representatives. Committee on Banking and Currency. *Food for Progress in Latin America*. Washington: GPO, 1967.

U.S. Congress. 86th, 2d Session. House of Representatives. *United States Relations with Panama*. Washington: GPO, 1960.

U.S. Congress. 86th, 2d Session. House of Representatives. Committee on Foreign Affairs. Sub-Committee on Inter-American Affairs. *Report on United States Relations with Panama*. Washington: GPO, 1960.

U.S. Congress. 86th, 2d Session. Senate. Committee on Foreign Relations. Subcommittee on American Republics Affairs. *United States-Latin American Relations*. Washington: GPO, 1960.

U.S. Department of Agriculture. Economic Research Service. *The Agriculture and Trade of Panama*. (ERS-Foreign 179.) Washington: 1967.

U.S. Department of Commerce. Bureau of Foreign Commerce. *Establishing a Business in Panama*. (World Trade Information Service: "Economic Reports," Pt. 1, No. 58–15.) Washington: GPO, February 1958.

U.S. Department of State. "President Restates U.S. Position on Panama and Canal Zone," *Department of State Bulletin*, L, No. 1285, February 10, 1964, 195–196.

U.S. Department of State. "U.S. and Panama Announce Results of Canal Zone Talks," *Department of State Bulletin;* XLIX, No. 1259, August 12, 1963, 246–247.

U.S. Embassy in San José. Agricultural Attaché. *Panama: Agricultural Situation.* San José: 1971.

University of Arkansas Agricultural Mission to Panama. *Marketing Panamanian Agricultural Products,* Pts. 1 and 2, n.pl.: n.pub., January 1953 (pamphlets).

"Verdict: The U.S. Was Not Guilty," *Time,* LXXXIII, No. 25, June 19, 1964, 30.

Wechsler, Sally (ed.). *Publisher's World 68/69.* New York: R. R. Bowker, 1968.

"Why Panama Erupted," *U.S. News & World Report,* LVI, No. 2, January 13, 1964, 32–33.

Wilgus, A. Curtis (ed.). *The Caribbean: Its Economy.* Gainesville: University of Florida Press, 1954.

The World and Its Peoples: The Caribbean Region and Central America. New York: Greystone Press, 1969.

Worldmark Encyclopedia of the Nations, II: Americas. (3d ed.) New York: Harper and Row, 1967.

Woytinsky, W. S. *The United States and Latin America's Economy.* (Taniment Institute Public Service Pamphlet.) New York: Taniment Institute, 1959.

Wythe, George. *Industry in Latin America.* New York: Columbia University Press, 1949.

Zárate, Doria P. de. "De nuestro folklore: instrumentos para el canto," *Tierra y Dos Mares,* [Panama City], VII, No. 38, 1968, 18, 64–65.

Zárate, Manuel F. *Tambor y socavón: un estudio comprehensivo de dos temas del folklore panameño, y de sus implicaciones históricas y culturales.* Panama: Ediciones del Ministerio de Educación, Dirección Nacional de Cultura, 1968.

OTHER SOURCES USED

Abad, Pablo (ed.). *Directorio comercial e industrial de Panamá.* Panama City: n.pub., 1959.

Alba C., M. M. *Geografía descriptiva de la República de Panamá.* Panama City: Editora Panamá América, 1950.

Alba, Victor. *Politics and the Labor Movement in Latin America.* Stanford: Stanford University Press, 1968.

Alexander, Robert J. *Organized Labor in Latin America.* New York: Free Press, 1965.

———. *Today's Latin America.* Garden City, New York: Doubleday (Anchor Books), 1962.

"All Clear," *Time*, LXV, No. 26, June 27, 1955, 32.

Alvarez Rubiano, Pablo. *Pedrarias Dávila*. Madrid: Instituto Gonzalo Fernández de Oviedo, 1954.

Anstey, Robert L. "The Physical Environment of the Canal Zone in Panama," *Revista Geográfica* [Rio de Janeiro], No. 66, June 1967, 163–188.

Arce, Enrique J., and Castillero, Ernesto J. *Guía Histórica de Panamá*. Panama City: Cía. Editora Nacional, 1943.

Armbrister, Trevor. "Panama: Why They Hate Us," *Saturday Evening Post*, 237th year, No. 9, March 7, 1964, 75–79.

Armstrong, Walter J. *Industrial Development in Panama*. Washington: International Bank for Reconstruction and Development, May 1957 (mimeo).

Azcárate C., Fermin. *Vida (la novela de un joven)*. Panama City: Cía. Editora Nacional, 1944.

Backus, Richard C., and Eder, Phanor J. *A Guide to the Law and Legal Literature of Colombia*. (The Library of Congress Latin American Series No. 4.) Washington: Library of Congress, 1943.

Balance of Payments Yearbook, 1965–69, XXII. Washington: International Monetary Fund, 1971.

Baxter, Glaister. *The Agricultural Problem of Panama*. Panama City: Imprenta Nacional, 1937.

Bemis, Samuel Flagg. *The Latin American Policy of the United States*. New York: Harcourt, Brace, 1943.

Benítez, Enrique Nrey. "The Remón-Eisenhower Treaty of 1955." Unpublished master's thesis, George Washington University, 1959.

Biesanz, John. "Cultural and Economic Factors in Panamanian Race Relations." Pages 245–251 in Olen E. Leonard and Charles P. Loomis, *Readings in Latin American Social Organization & Institutions*. N.pl.: Michigan State College Press, 1953.

————. "Inter-American Marriages on the Isthmus of Panama." Pages 43–47 in Olen E. Leonard and Charles P. Loomis, *Readings in Latin American Social Organization & Institutions*. N.pl.: Michigan State College Press, 1953.

Biesanz, John, and Smith, Luke M. "Adjustment of Interethnic Marriages on the Isthmus of Panama." Pages 48–51 in Olen E. Leonard and Charles P. Loomis (eds.), *Readings in Latin American Social Organization & Institutions*, N.pl.: Michigan State College Press, 1953.

————. "Race Relations in Panama and the Canal Zone." Pages 251–258 in Olen E. Leonard and Charles P. Loomis (eds.), *Readings in Latin American Social Organization & Institutions*. N.pl.: Michigan State College Press, 1953.

Billard, Jules B. "Panama: Link Between Oceans and Continents," *National Geographic*, CXXXVII, No. 3, March 1970, 402–440.

Blakemore, Harold. *Latin America*. London: Oxford University Press, 1966.

"Boston Firm to Survey Panama's Power Potential," *Pre-Investment News* (United Nations Development Program.) June 1971, 1, 7.

Bunau-Varilla, Philippe. *Panama: The Creation, Destruction and Resurrection*. London: Constable, 1913.

Busey, James L. *Latin American Political Guide*. Maniton Springs, Colorado: Juniper, 1971.

"The Business Outlook: Panama," *Business Latin America*, June 3, 1971, 172.

"The Business Outlook: Panama," *Business Latin America*, March 15, 1970, 92.

Butland, Gilbert J. *Latin America, A Regional Geography* (2d ed.) New York: John Wiley and Sons, 1966.

Butler, Charles, and Springer, Stewart. *A Program for the More Effective Use of Panama's Fishery Resources*. (P10/T 525–29–060–3–10037, Bureau of Commercial Fisheries.) Washington: International Cooperation Administration, June 30, 1961 (mimeo).

Cabeza, Berta María. "El trumpo de tres artistas panameñas," *Lotería*, [Panama City], II, No. 18, 1957, 14–16.

Carlos, Rubén Darío. *La gente de "Allá Abajo."* Panama City: n.pub., 1947.

Castillero, Alfredo. "Breves apuntes para una historía del pensamiento panameño," *Lotería*, [Panama City], III, No. 37, 1958, 81–95.

Castillero Reyes, Ernesto J., and Arce, Enrique J. *Historía de Panamá*. Buenos Aires: A. Ruiz, 1948.

Castillero Reyes, Ernesto J., and Behrendt, Richard F. "El Sistema monetario de Panamá," *Boletín* [Panama City], (Universidad de Panamá, Instituto de Investigaciones Sociales y Económicas), II, July 1945, 833–869.

Centre de Recherches Socio-Religieuses. *Encyclopédie Catholique du Monde Chrétien, II:* Bilan du Monde. Brussels: Casterman, 1960.

Centro Interamericano de Administradores Tributarios. *Documentos y actas de la primera asemblea general 1967*, Panamá. Buenos Aires: Compañía Impresora Argentina, 1968.

Centro Interamericano de Administradores Tributarios. *Tax Incentives in the American Countries*. (Doc. V–A/1.) Rio de Janeiro: CIAT Executive Secretariat, 1971.

Chaloner, W. H. "The Birth of the Panama Canal, 1869–1914," *History Today*, [London], IX, No. 7, 1959, 482–492.

Chardkoff, Richard. "The Cuna Revolt," *Américas*, XXII, No. 7, July 1970, 14–21.

———. "Journey into the Tropics," *Américas*, XXII, No. 7, July 1970, 35–42.

Clagett, Helen L. *The Administration of Justice in Latin America*. New York: Oceana, 1952.

Coker, William. "The Panama Canal Tolls Controversy: A Different Perspective," *Journal of American History*, LIII, No. 3, December 1968, 555–564.

Colón Free Zone. *Colón Free Zone*. New York: n.pub., 1971.

Condon, Richard. "Lightning Guide to Panama," *Holiday, XXXIV*, No. 5, November 1963, 82–83.

Considine, M. M., John J. (ed.). *The Church in the New Latin America*. Notre Dame: Fides, 1964.

———. *Social Revolution in the New Latin America*. Notre Dame: Fides, 1965.

Conway Research Inc. *Latin America's Industrial Incentives*. Atlanta: 1967.

Core, Sue. *Ravelings From a Panama Tapestry*. New York: Westchester, 1933.

Cowes, Robert A. "The Gold of Coclé," *Américas*, XVIII, No. 2, February 1966, 18–25.

Coyner, Mary S. "Central American Economic Integration on the Way," *Foreign Agriculture*, XXV, No. 6, 1961, 19–20.

———. "Panama Links Its Agricultural Policies to Self-Sufficiency," *Foreign Agriculture*, XXI, No. 11, 1957, 10–12, 20.

Crawford, William R. *A Century of Latin American Thought*. Cambridge: Harvard University Press, 1961.

Dalla Chiesa, Romeo. *Public Finance of Panama*. Washington: International Bank for Reconstruction and Development, 1957 (mimeo).

———. *Some Aspects of the Economy of Panama*. Washington: International Bank for Reconstruction and Development, May 1957 (mimeo).

"A Deal on the Panama Canal: Rough Transit Ahead," *U.S. News & World Report*, LXIII, No. 2, July 10, 1967, 41.

Demographic Yearbook, 1969. New York: United Nations, 1970.

Diamond, Walter H. "How the Colón Free Zone in Panama Saves Tax Dollars for United States Business," *Foreign Tax and Trade Briefs*. New York: n.pub., 1958 (pamphlet).

Díaz E., Manuel Antonio. *La Jurisdicción contencioso-administrativo en Panamá*. Panama City: Republica de Panamá, 1947.

Dye, Ira. "Flag of Convenience; Maritime Dilemma," *US Naval Institute Proceedings,* February 1962, 76–87.

Ealy, Lawrence O. "The Development of an Anglo-American System of Law In the Panama Canal Zone," *American Journal of Legal History,* II, 1958, 283–303.

"The Economic Development of Panama," *Economic Bulletin for Latin America* [Santiago], IV, No. 2, 1959, 48–59.

Economic Intelligence Unit. *Quarterly Economic Review: Central America, Annual Supplement, 1970.* London: 1970.

Elmore, R. B. *Completion of Assignment Report.* Knoxville: University of Tennessee, Technical Assistance Unit in Panama, May 29, 1961 (typescript).

"Energy in Latin America," *Economic Bulletin For Latin America* (U.N.), XV, No. 2, Second Half 1970, 3–92.

Escala, Virginia. "La Planificación en Panamá," *Sociedad Interamericana de Planificación* [Cali, Colombia], III, March/June 1969, 33–38.

The Europa Yearbook, 1971, II. London: Europa Publications, 1971.

"Exclusive Interview: President Ernesto de la Guardia," *Latin American Report,* II, No. 7, 1958, 14–19.

Export-Import Bank of the United States. *Cumulative Record by Country, February 12, 1964 to June 30, 1970.* Washington: 1970

Exquemelin, Alexander O. *The Buccaneers of America.* London: Allen and Unwin, 1951.

Fábrega, J. *Código de Trabajo de la República de la Panamá (Ley 67 de 1947) y Leyes que lo Reforman.* Panama City: Editorial Jurídica Panameña, 1966.

Fábrega P., Jorge (ed.). *Legislación maritima panameña.* Panama City: La Imprenta de la Academia, 1957.

Fábrega, Ramón E. (ed.). *Constitución de la República de Panamá.* Panama City: Editora Pública, 1961.

Family Planning in Five Continents. London: International Planned Parenthood Federation, January 1969.

"Fleeing Capital Finds Refuge in Panama," *Times of the Americas,* XV, No. 29, July 28, 1971, 1.

Food and Agriculture Organization. *Government Marketing Policies in Latin America.* Rome: 1967.

Fox, Hugh. "Latin American Report. Panama: The Place Between Places," *North American Review,* V, No. 6, November-December 1968, 2–4.

Freeburger, Adela R. *Guide for the Evaluation of Academic Credentials from the Latin American Republics.* (Studies in Comparative Education, OE–14055.) Washington: U.S. Department of Health, Education and Welfare, February 1957.

Fry, George, et al. *Industry in Panama.* (Survey and Action Report to the International Cooperation Administration of the United States Government.) Chicago: n.pub., July 14, 1961 (mimeo).

Fuson, Robert H. "Land Tenure in Central Panama: A Case Study of an Aspect of the Latino Mythology," *Journal of Geography,* LXIII, No. 4, April 1964, 161–168.

Garay, Narcisco. "El arte en Panamá," *Lotería,* [Panama City], No. 49, June 1945, 11–14.

———. "Elogío de don Roberto Lewis," *Lotería,* [Panama City], VII, No. 102, 1949, 18–20.

Gause, Frank A., and Carr, Charles Carl. *The Story of Panama— The New Route to India.* New York: Arno Press and the New York Times, reprinted 1970.

Geyelin, Philip. "The Irksome Panama Wrangle," *Reporter,* XXX, No. 8, April 9, 1964, 14–17.

Glade, William. "Social Backwardness, Social Reform and Productivity in Latin America," *Inter-American Economic Affairs,* XV, No. 3, 1961, 3–32.

Goldrich, Daniel. *Sons of the Establishment—Elite Youth in Panama and Costa Rica.* Chicago: Rand McNally, 1966.

Gorgas, Marie D., and Hendrick, Burton J. *William Crawford Goya—His Life and Work.* Garden City: Garden City Publishing, 1924.

Great Britain. Commercial Relations and Export Department. *Panama.* (Overseas Economic Surveys.) London: HMSO, January 1955.

Grunwald, Joseph and Musgrove, Phillip. *Natural Resources in Latin American Development.* Baltimore: Johns Hopkins Press, 1970.

Gutierrez, Samuel A. *El problema de las "barriadas brujas" en la ciudad de Panamá.* Panama: Librería Cultural Panameña, 1961.

Hale, H. C. *Notes on Panama.* Washington: GPO, 1903.

Haring, C. H. *The Spanish Empire in America.* New York: Oxford University Press, 1947.

Harris, Louis K. *Political Force in Latin America.* Belmont, California: Wadsworth, 1968.

Hedrick, Basil C. and Hedrick, Anne K. *A Historical Dictionary of Panama.* Metuchen, New Jersey: Scarecrow Press, 1970.

Henao, Jesús María, and Arrubla, Gerardo. *History of Colombia.* (Ed. and trans., J. Fred Rippy.) Chapel Hill: University of North Carolina Press, 1938.

Hobson, Dr. Jesse E. *Prospectus of the International Tropical Research Institute.* Washington: n.pub., March 13, 1961 (mimeo).

Holguin, Beatrice de. "Picturesque Panama," *Travel,* CXXVII, No. 1, January 1964, 40–44.

Hooper, Ofelia. "Land and Rural People on the Isthmus Link," *Land Policy Review,* VI, No. 2, 1943, 12–15.

Hoselitz, Bert F. *Theories of Economic Growth.* Glencoe, Illinois: Free Press, 1960.

Howarth, David. *Panama—Four Hundred Years of Dreams and Cruelty.* New York: McGraw-Hill, 1966.

————. "Panama." Pages 227–240 in Claudio Véliz (ed.). *Latin America and the Caribbean: A Handbook.* New York: Praeger, 1968.

Hudson, James. *Law and the Judicial System of Nations.* Washington: World Peace Through Law Center, 1968.

"Income Tax Raised; Stamp Tax Set," *Foreign Commerce Weekly,* LV, No. 12, February 20, 1961, 20.

Institute of Inter-American Affairs. Food Supply Division. *The Agriculture of Panama, Present and Potential.* Washington: November 1945.

Inter-American Center of Tax Administrators. *Report on Technical Seminar on Tax Audit, San José, Costa Rica, January 25 to February 2, 1969.* Washington: GPO, 1969.

Inter-American Committee for Agricultural Development. *Inventory of Information Basic to the Planning of Agricultural Development in Latin America.* Washington: Pan American Union, 1965.

Inter-American Development Bank. *Activities 1961–1964.* Washington: n.d.

————. *European Financing of Latin America's Economic Development.* Washington: 1966.

————. *Social Progress Trust Fund: Fifth Annual Report, 1965.* Washington: 1966.

————. *Social Progress Trust Fund: Fourth Annual Report, 1964.* Washington: 1965.

————. *Social Progress Trust Fund: Second Annual Report, 1962.* Washington: 1963.

————. *Social Progress Trust Fund: Third Annual Report, 1963.* Washington: 1964.

————. *Socio-Economic Progress in Latin America: Social Progress Trust Fund: Eighth Annual Report, 1968*. Washington: 1969.

————. *Socio-Economic Progress in Latin America: Social Progress Trust Fund: Ninth Annual Report, 1969*. Washington: 1970.

————. *Socio-Economic Progress in Latin America: Social Progress Trust Fund: Seventh Annual Report, 1967*. Washington: 1968.

————. *Socio-Economic Progress in Latin America: Social Progress Trust Fund: Sixth Annual Report, 1966*. Washington: 1967.

————. *Socio-Economic Progress in Latin America: Social Progress Trust Fund: Tenth Annual Report, 1970*. Washington: 1971.

————. *Tenth Annual Report, 1969*. Washington: 1970.

International Bank for Reconstruction and Development. *List of National Development Plans*. (2d ed.) Washington: September 1968.

————. *News Release No. 70/13*, March 11, 1970.

————. *Report of the Bank Mission to Panama*. Washington: IBRD Loan Department, June 19, 1952 (mimeo).

————. *The World Bank Group in the Americas*. Washington: 1967.

International Financial Statistics, XXIV, 5, May 1970, 268–270.

International Labor Organization. International Labor Office. *Indigenous Peoples: Living and Working Conditions of Aboriginal Populations in Independent Countries*. (Studies and Reports, New Series, No. 35.) Geneva: 1953.

International Labor Organization. Ninth Conference of the American states members of the International Labor Organization, Caracas, April 1970. *Report IV—Remuneration and Conditions of Work in Relation to Economic Development, Including Plant-Level Welfare Facilities and the Worker's Standard of Living*. Geneva: 1970.

International Monetary Fund. *Annual Report, 1969*. Washington: 1969.

————. *Direction of Trade: Annual 1964–68*. Washington: IMF/International Bank for Reconstruction and Development, n.d.

————. *Twenty-First Annual Report on Exchange Restrictions, 1970*. Washington: 1970.

International Monetary Fund. Research Department. Statistics Division. *Paper on International Financial Statistics, No. 17, Panama*. Washington: IMF, February 7, 1952 (mimeo).

International Yearbook of Education, 1967. Geneva: International Bureau of Education and United Nations Educational, Scientific and Cultural Organization, 1968.

International Yearbook of Education, 1968. Geneva: International Bureau of Education and UNESCO, 1969.

International Yearbook of Education, 1969. Geneva: International Bureau of Education and UNESCO, 1970.

"La intervención estatal es una necessidad," *Revista de economía,* [Panama City], II, No. 2, 1960, 1–3.

Jane's World Railways. London: B.P.C. Publishing, n.d.

Jiminéz, Georgia Isabel. *Panama in Transition, 1849–1940.* Washington: George Washington University Microfilms, 1954.

Johansen, O. Lund (ed.). *World Radio, TV Handbook: Broadcasting-Television 1961.* (15th ed.) Copenhagen: 1961.

Karnes, Thomas L. *The Failure of Union: Central America, 1824–1960.* Chapel Hill: University of North Carolina Press, 1961.

Keeler, Clyde E. *Land of the Moon-Children, The Primitive San Blas Cultures in Flux.* Athens: University of Georgia Press, 1956.

Kemble, John Haskell. *The Panama Route, 1848–1869.* Berkeley: University of California Press, 1943.

Kirk, William W. *The First Literary Periodicals of the Republic of Panama.* Ann Arbor: University of Michigan Microfilms, 1956.

Koster, R. M. "New Riots in Panama?" *New Republic,* CLI, No. 22, November 28, 1964, 9–10.

Lamb, F. Bruce. "The Forest of Darién, Panama," *Caribbean Forester* [Río Piedras, Puerto Rico]: XIV, Nos. 3 and 4, 1953, 128–135.

Larravide, Alvaro E. "Monetary Discipline and Growth—The Case of Panama," *Finance and Development,* VII, No. 2, June 1970, 44–50.

Latham, Herald. "Panama: 'Crossroads of the World' for Industry," *Industrial Development and Manufacturers Record,* CXXXIV, No. 3, March 1965, 8–38.

Latin American Business Highlights (Chase Manhattan Bank), II, No. 2, 2d Quarter, 1961.

Leland, Simeon E. *A Report on the Revenue System of Panama.* (Submitted to the Economic and Fiscal Commission, Republic of Panama.) N.pl.: n. pub., June 15, 1946.

Lewis, Richard S. "Panama Junction," *Science and Public Affairs: Bulletin of the Atomic Scientists,* XXIV, No. 5, May 1968, 12–16.

Limosin, Febo de. *Estrellita de Taboga, novela panameña.* Panama City: Imprenta Nacional, 1927.

MacDonald, Austin F. *Latin American Politics and Government.* (2d ed.) New York: Crowell, 1954.

MacEoin, Gary. *Revolution Next Door—Latin America in the 1970s.* New York: Holt, Rinehart, and Winston, 1971.

McMullan, Frank. "Theatre, Panama," *Theatre Arts,* XLIV, June 1960, 66–68.

Mallory, Walter H. (ed.) *Political Handbook of the World, 1952–61.* New York: Harper, for Council on Foreign Relations, 1952–61.

Mander, John. *The Unrevolutionary Society; The Power of Conservatism in a Changing World.* New York: Knopf, 1969.

Mangham, Herbert. "Cruising Along the Panama Coast," *New York Times,* July 2, 1961.

Mansfield, Mike J. *The Panama Bases.* Washington: GPO, 1948.

Martini, José A.; Chu, Ricardo Ah; Nel Lezcano, Pedro. "Forest Soils of Darién Province, Panama," *Tropical Woods,* CXII, April 1960, 28–39.

Mellander, G. A. "Magoon in Panama." Unpublished master's thesis, George Washington University, 1960.

—————. *The United States in Panamanian Politics: The Intriguing Formative Years.* Danville, Illinois Interstate Printers and Publishers, 1971.

Mendoza, Carlos Alberto. "La Constitución panameño de 1946: sus fundamentos sociales," *Lotería,* [Panama City], II, No. 44, 1959, 65–79.

Mercado Villar, Olga, and de la Puente Lafoy, Patricio. *Características del Proceso Migratorio en América Latina, Estudios Preliminares.* Santiago: Centro Para el Desarrollo Económico y Social de América Latina, 1968.

Methvin, Eugene H. "The Anatomy of a Riot: Panama 1964," *Orbis,* XIV, No. 2, Summer 1970, 463–489.

Miner, Dwight Carroll. *The Fight for the Panama Route: The Story of Spooner Act and the Hay-Herrán Treaty.* New York: Columbia University Press, 1940.

Minerals Yearbook, 1968: IV—Area Reports, International. Washington: GPO, 1970.

Miró, Ricardo. *Flor de María; ensayo de novela.* Panama City: Talleres gráficos de "El Tiempo," 1922.

Miró, Rodrigo. *La literatura panameña.* Panama City: n.pub., 1946.

—————. *Teoría de la patria.* Buenos Aires: n.pub., 1947.

Mori, Arturo. *Treinte años de teatro hispanoamericano.* Mexico City: Editorial Moderna, 1941.

Moss, Harold. "Experiences Under the U.S. Foreign Tax Assistance Program." (Speech before National Tax Association.) Washington: Internal Revenue Service, October 1967 (mimeo.).

"National Economy of Panama," *Commercial Pan-America,* XVI, No. 1, 1947.

Needler, Martin C. "Political Development and Military Intervention in Latin America." Pages 229–248 in Arpad Von Lazar and Robert R. Kaufman (eds.). *Reform and Revolution: Readings in Latin American Politics.* Boston: Allyn and Bacon, 1969.

———. *Political Development in Latin America: Instability, Violence, and Revolutionary Change.* New York: Random House, 1968.

Needler, Martin C. (ed.) *Political Systems of Latin America.* New York: Van Nostrand, 1970.

Niemeier, Jean Gilbreath. *The Panama Story.* Portland, Oregon: Metropolitan Press, 1968.

Olsen, Jack. "A Mob of Marlin in the Bays of Panama," *Sports Illustrated,* April 22, 1963, 63–72.

Oppenheim, L. *The Panama Canal Conflict Between Great Britain and the United States of America.* Cambridge: Cambridge University Press, 1913.

Organization for Economic Cooperation and Development. *Statistics of the Occupational and Educational Structure of the Labour Force in 53 Countries.* Paris: 1969.

Organization of American States. *Panama.* (American Republics Series No. 16.) Washington: 1964 (reprinted 1971).

Organization of American States. Departamento de Asuntos Sociales. *Datos básicos de población en América Latina, 1970.* Washington: Pan American Union, 1970.

Organization of American States. General Secretariat. *Motoring in Central America and Panama* (Rev. ed.) Washington: 1969.

"The Other Canal," *Economist* [London], CLXXXIII, No. 5931, April 27, 1957, 297.

"Outcries of Panama's President Leave Washington Unfrightened," *Business Week,* No. 1444, May 4, 1957, 135.

"Panama: A Brief Parenthesis," *Newsweek,* LXXII, No. 18, October 28, 1963, 63.

"Panama: A Revolutionary Development Plan," *Latin America,* [London], III, No. 33, August 15, 1969, 260–261.

"Panama Boosts Corporate Tax Burdens," *Business Latin America,* March 26, 1970, 102.

The Panama Canal, Funnel for World Commerce. N.pl.: Panama Canal Company, n.d.

"Panama Canal Troubles," *Economist,* [London], CLXXX, No. 5899, September 1, 1956, 724.

"Panama: Crossroads of the Hemisphere," *Latin American Report*, II, No. 7, 1958, 14–19.

"Panama in Hand," *Economist* [London], No. 5815, February 5, 1955, 457

"Panama: More 'Nasserists'?" *Latin America*, [London], III, No. 10, March 7, 1969, 78–79.

Panamanian National Tourist Commission. *The Republic of Panama and the Panama Canal Zone*. Panama: 1944.

"Panama: Passing a Test," *Time*, LXXXV, No. 4, January 22, 1965, 30.

"Panama—Playground of Latin America," *Panama Canal Review* (Special Issue) [Balboa Heights, Canal Zone], n.d.

"Panama Primes Economy for Further Growth," *Commerce Today*, I, No. 21, July 26, 1971, 47–48.

"Panama: Rule of the Whitetails," *Time*, LXXXIII, No. 7, February 14, 1964, 32.

"Panama's 1971 Budget to Stimulate Economy," *Business Latin America*, April 15, 1971, 118.

"Panama: The Third Force," *Nation*, CXCVIII, No. 11, March 9, 1964, 225–226.

"Panama: Two Heads for One State," *Latin America* [London], II, No. 13, March 29, 1968, 97–98.

"Panama: What Price Democracy?", *Newsweek*, LXXIV, No. 26, December 29, 1969, 34.

Pan American Health Organization. *Facts on Health Progress* (Scientific Publication No. 166.) Washington: 1968.

――――. *Health Conditions in the Americas 1965–1968*. Washington: 1970.

――――. *Report of the Director, 1969*. Washington: 1970.

Pan American Union. *América en cifras, 1967; situación cultural: educación y otros aspectos culturales*. Washington: 1969.

――――. *Directoria musical de la América Latina*. Washington: 1954.

――――. *Music of Latin America*. Washington: 1960.

――――. *Panama*. Washington: 1960.

――――. *A Statement of the Laws of Panama in Matters Affecting Business*. Washington: 1966.

Pan American Union. Departamento de Asuntos Sociales. *Datos básicos de población en América Latina*. Washington: 1970.

Pan American Union. Inter-American Economic and Social Council. *Respuestas de Panamá al cuestionario de la comisión especial de expertos para el studio de las necesidades financieras que plantea la ejecución de planes de reforma agraria*. Washington: April 6, 1960 (mimeo.).

Pan American Union. Inter-American Institute of Statistics. *La estructura agropecuaria de las naciones Américas. Análisis estadístico-censal de los resultados obtenidos bajo el programa del censo de las Américas de 1950.* Washington: 1957 (mimeo.).

Parks, E. Taylor. *Colombia and the United States, 1765–1934.* Durham: Duke University Press, 1935.

Paro, Pauline B. *Estudio de los ingresos, gastos, y costo de la vida, ciudad de Panamá, 1952–53.* Panama City: Contraloría General, 1954.

Pattee, Richard. *El Catolicismo contemporaneo en Hispanoamérica.* Buenos Aires: Editorial FIDES, n.d.

Peaslee, Amos J. *Constitutions of Nations.* The Hague: Martinus Nijhoff, 1956.

Pereira Jiménez, Bonifacio. *Historia de Panamá* (2d ed.) Panama: Agencia Internacional de Publicaciones, 1963.

"Performance Record of 41 Countries, 1960–1969," *Development Digest*, IX, No. 2, April 1971, 2.

Pick's Currency Yearbook 1970. New York: Pick, 1970.

"Political Groups in Latin America," *American Political Science Review*, LIII, No. 1, 1959.

Poor, Peggy. "A Review from the Canal," *New Republic*, CL, No. 8, February 22, 1964, 13–14.

Population Program Assistance. Washington: U.S. Agency for International Development, October 1969.

Prescott, William H. *The Conquest of Peru.* New York: Doubleday (Dolphin), n.d.

"President Kennedy Replies to Letter from President Chiari of Panama," *Department of State Bulletin*, XLV, No. 1171, December 4, 1961, 932–933.

"President of Panama Proclaims Point 4 Week," *Department of State Bulletin*, XXXVIII, No. 979, March 31, 1958, 522–523.

"President Restates U.S. Position on Panama and Canal Zone," (Statement by President Lyndon B. Johnson.) *Department of State Bulletin*, L, No. 1285, February 10, 1964, 195–196.

"President Signs Bill on Canal Zone Working Conditions," *Department of State Bulletin*, XXXIX, No. 998, August 11, 1958, 237–238.

Price Waterhouse and Company. *Information Guide for Doing Business in Panama.* Chicago: 1969.

Quiros, Jorge L. *Engineering and Economic Aspects of the Aluminum Industry* and the Potential Development of Aluminum Production in Panama (Ph.D. Dissertation.) Urbana: University of Illinois, 1966.

Ramos, Joseph R. *Labor and Development in Latin America.* New York: Columbia University Press, 1970.

"Rampaging Students," *Newsweek*, LI, No. 22, June 2, 1958, 46.

Reid, P. A. *Agricultural Development of Panama*. Washington: International Bank for Reconstruction and Development, June 1957 (mimeo.).

Republic of Panama. *Government Organization Manual*. Panama City: Imprenta Nacional, March 1961.

————. *Informe del contralor general de la Panamá*. Panama City: October 1, 1967.

————. *Memoria que el Ministro de Gobierno y Justicia presenta a la honorable asamblea nacional en sus seciones ordinarias de 1958*. Panama City: n.pub., 1958 (mimeo.).

————. *Memoria que el Ministro de Gobierno y Justicia presenta a la honorable asamblea nacional en sus seciones ordinarias de 1959*. Panama City: n.pub., 1959 (mimeo.).

————. *Presupuesto de rentas y gastos de la República de Panamá*. Panama City: Imprenta Nacional, 1959.

Republic of Panama. Caja de Seguro Social. *Boda de Plata: 1941–1966*. Panama City: 1966.

Republic of Panama. Comisión de Caminos, Aeropuertos y Muelles. *A Four-Year Program for Administrative Reorganization, Personnel Training, Rehabilitation and Maintenance of Public Highways*. Panama City: 1955 (mimeo.).

Republic of Panama. Contraloría General de la República. *Informe 1959*. Panama City: October 1, 1960 (mimeo.).

————. *Informe 1960*. Panama City: October 1, 1961 (mimeo.).

————. *Informe 1966*. Panama City: Dirección de Estadística y Censo, 1967.

————. *Informe 1969*. Panama City: Dirección de Estadística y Censo, 1970.

Republic of Panama. Editora Oficial. *Manual Electoral*. Panama City: Imprenta Nacional, 1947.

Republic of Panama. Instituto de Fomento Económico. *Facts for Investors in Panama*. Panama City: Editora Panamá América, 1956.

Republic of Panama. Instituto de Vivienda y Urbanismo. *Memoria a la asámblea nacional, 1960–61*. Panama City: Editor Panamá América, 1961.

Republic of Panama. Instituto para la Formación y Aprovechamiento de Recursos Humanos—IFARHU. *Memoria de las labores realizadas por el IFARHU, 1966–1968*. Panama City: 1968.

Republic of Panama. Junta Nacional del Cincuentenario. *Documentos fundamentales para la historia de la nación panameña*. Panama City; Junta Nacional del Cincuentenario, 1953.

Republic of Panama. Ministerio de Agricultura, Comercio e Industrias, y Administración de Cooperación Internacional Estados Unidos de América. *Memoria de seminario sobre el desarrollo del crédito agrícola en América Latina* (11–23 November 1957). Panama City: Editora Panamá América, 1958.

Republic of Panama. Laws, Statutes, etc.

Código de trabajo. Panama City: Imprenta Nacional, 1849.

Código judicial. Barcelona: Talleres de Artes Gráficas de Henrich, 1917.

La Constitución de la Repúblic de Panamá: edición extraoficial. Panama City: Editora República, 1961.

Labor Code of Panama. (Legislative Series 1947—Pan. 1.) Washington: International Labor Organization, International Labor Office, November-December 1948.

Panama 1, Act: Labour Code. (Legislative Series 1947—Pan. 1). n.pl.: International Labor Organization, International Labor Office, November-December 1948 (pamphlet).

Republic of Panama. Ministerio de Comercio e Industrias. *Panama—General Business Guide.* Panama: n.d.

Republic of Panama. Ministerio de Obras Públicas. *Memoria, 1969–1970.* Panama: Instituto Geográfico Nacional, 1970.

Republic of Panama. Contraloría General de la República. Dirección de Estadística y Censo. *Censos nacionales de 1950. Boletín informativo no. 5, lugares poblados.* Panama City: October 1954.

————. *Censos nacionales de 1950. Quinto censo de población, V, población urbana.* Panama City: 1954.

————. *Censos nacionales de 1970: VII de población, III de vivienda—cifras preliminares.* Panama City: n.d.

————. *Censos nacionales de Panamá, 1960—Compendio general de población.* Panama City: 1965.

————. *Censos nacionales de Panamá, 1960, V:* Características económicas. Panama City: 1964.

————. *Censos nacionales de Panamá, 1960—segundo censo de vivienda.* Panama City: 1965.

————. *Censos nacionales de Panamá, 1960, VI:* Características educativas. Panama City: 1964.

————. *Censos nacionales de Panamá, 1960, III:* Ciudad de Colón. Panama City: 1963.

————. *Censos nacionales de Panamá, 1960, II:* Ciudad de Panamá. Panama City: 1963.

————. *Estadística panameña, año XIX: Estadísticas vitales, año 1959.* (Series "B".) Panama City: November, 1960.

————. *Estadística panameña, año XX: Industrias, año 1960.* (Series "F", No. 1.) Panama City: April 1961.

————. *Estadística panameña, año XX: Industrias: encuesta de 1960, año 1959.* (Series "F", No. 1.) Panama City: February 1961.

————. *Estadística panameña, año XXVIII: Hacienda pública y finanzas, año 1968.* (Series "E", No. 1.) Panama City: 1969.

————. *Estadística panameña, año XXVIII: Hojas de balance de alimentos, años 1960 a 1967.* (Series "M".) Panama City: 1969.

————. *Estadística panameña, año XXIX: Anuario de comercio exterior, año 1968.* (Series "K".) Panama City: December 1970.

————. *Estadística panameña, año XXIX: Hacienda pública y finanzas, año 1969.* (Series "E", No. 1) Panama City: 1970.

————. *Estadística panameña, año XXIX: Hacienda pública y finanzas, 1er semestre de 1969.* (Series "E", No. 2.) Panama City: 1970.

————. *Estadística panameña, año XXIX: Inversiones directas extranjeras en Panamá, año 1960–1968.* (Suplemento.) Panama City: December 1970.

————. *Estadística panameña, año XXVII: Comercio exterior, año 1967.* (Series "K".) Panama City: 1968.

————. *Estadística panameña, año XXVII: Industrias, año 1968.* (Series "F", No. 1) Panama City: 1969.

————. *Estadística panameña, año XXVI: Demografía—población, imigración, asistencia social y educación, año 1966.* (Series "A".) Panama City: n.d.

————. *Estadística panameña: Indicadores económicos, años 1968 y 1969.* (Series "P", No. 4.) Panama City: 1970.

————. *Indicadores económicos y sociales de la República de Panamá, 1965–1969.* Panama City: October 1970.

————. *Sexto censo de población y vivienda (1960). Boletín informativo No. 1, cifras preliminares.* Panama City: April 1961.

————. *Unidades de medida.* Panama City: July 1952.

Republic of Panama. Presidencia de la República. Comisión Nacional de Planificación de la Salud. *Estudios sectorales: sector salud, diagnóstico, años 1960–1968.* Panama City: 1970.

Republic of Panama. Presidencia de la República. Dirección General de Planificación y Administración. Departamento de Planificación. *Diagnósticos sectorales: sector electrificación, 1960–1968.* Panama City: 1970.

————. *Estrategia para el desarrollo nacional, 1970–1980.* Panama City: Editora Lemania, Aprill 22, 1970.

————. *Estudios sobre política comercial internacional de Panamá.* Panama City: Industrial Gráfica, 1970.

De Revello, Concepción M. *La Migración interna y sus repercuciones en la economía de Panamà.* Panama City: Consejo de Economía Nacional, 1957.

Reyes, Roman B. *Origen e historia de la pollera.* **Panama** City: La Academia, 1954.

Robertson, William Spence. *History of the Latin American Nations.* New York: D. Appleton, 1930.

Robinson, Harry. *Latin America, a Geographical Survey.* New York: Praeger, 1967.

Rodriguez, Mario. "Panama and the United States," *Vital Issues,* XIV, No. 10, June 1965, 1–4.

Romero, Fernando, et al. *Vocational Education in Panama According to the Official Answer to "Preliminary Survey of the Americas, 1950."* Washington: Pan American Union, July 1952.

Romoli, Kathleen. *Balboa of Darién: Discoverer of the Pacific.* Garden City: Doubleday, 1953.

Ross, Kip. "We Drove the Darien Gap," *National Geographic,* CXIX, No. 3, March 1961, 369–381.

Rubio, Angel. *Atlas geográficao elemental de Panamá.* Panama City: Imprenta Nacional, 1947.

Rubio, Angel, and Guzmán, Luis E. "Regiones geográficas panameñas," *Revista Geográfica* [Rio de Janeiro], XXIV, No. 50, January–June 1959, 53–66.

Sandner, Gerhard. "La Costa Atlántica de Nicaragua, Costa Rica, y Panamá: su conquista y colonización desde principios de la época colonial," *Informe Semestral: Instituto Geográfico de Costa Rica* [San Jose], January–June 1964, 83–187.

Santos, Joâo Oliveira. "Latin America's Export Earnings." (Paper prepared for symposium on contemporary economic problems and issues in Latin America. Latin American Forum. Georgetown University.) Washington: November 23, 1968 (mimeo).

Saxe-Fernandez, John. "The Central American Defense Council and Pax Americana." Pages 75–100 in Irving L. Horowitz, Josue de Castro, and John Cerasse (eds.), *Latin American Radicalism: A Documentary Report on Left and Nationalist Movements.* New York: Random House, 1969.

Schott, Joseph L. *Rails Across Panama (The Story of the Building of Panama Railroad).* Indianapolis: Bobbs-Merrill, 1967.

"Second Anniversary of the New Panama—Dynamic Example for Latin America," *New York Times* (unnumbered advertising supplement), October 11, 1970, 1–18. (reprint, separate section.).

Sherman, Charles. *Roman Law in the Modern World.* New Haven: New Haven Law Book, 1922.

Sims, Grover J. "Central America Builds Up Its Livestock Industry," *Foreign Agriculture,* XXV, No. 6, 1961, 9–10.

Skinner, Ralph K. "New Deal for Bananas," *Christian Science Monitor,* July 31, 1961, 6.

Solís, Menalco. "50 años de agricultura en Panamá," *Revista de agricultura, comercio e industrias* [Asunción, Paraguay], IX, No. 6, 1953, 5–24.

Solving Latin American Business Problems. New York: Business International, 1968.

The South American Handbook, 1970. London: Trade and Travel Publications, 1970.

Statesman's Yearbook, 1971–1972. (Ed., John Paxton.) London: Macmillan, 1971.

Statesman's Yearbook, 1959. (Ed., S. H. Steinberg.) London: Macmillan, 1959.

Stein, J. Stanley, and Stein, Barbara H. *The Colonial Heritage of Latin America—Essays on Economic Dependence in Perspective.* New York: Oxford University Press, 1970.

Steward, Julian H., and Faron, Louise C. *Native Peoples of South America.* New York: McGraw-Hill, 1959.

Stokes, William S. *Latin American Politics.* New York: Crowell, 1959.

Stout, D. B. *San Blas Cuna Acculturation: An Introduction.* (Viking Fund Publications in Anthropology, No. 9.) New York: Viking Fund, 1947.

"Surveys are Begun for Panama Road," *New York Times,* July 7, 1961.

Tannenbaum, Frank. *Slave and Citizen: The Negro in the Americas.* New York: Knopf, 1947.

Tanner, James C. "Puzzle in Panama: Torrijos Brings Calm, Prosperity to Nation at Expense of Freedom," *Wall Street Journal,* CLXXVII, No. 117, June 17, 1971, 1.

Tapia, Lola C. *Panamá, donde los grandes oceanos se unen.* Panama City: Republic of Panama, Comisión Nacional del Turismo de Panamá, 1935.

Teeters, Negley K. *Penology from Panama to Cape Horn.* Philadelphia: University of Pennsylvania Press, 1946.

———. *World Penal Systems.* Philadelphia: Temple University Press, 1944.

Theel, Gustav Adolph (ed.). *Weltschiffahrts-Archive,* No. 8, Breman: Institute für Schiffahrtsforschung, 1959.

Thompson, Honorable Clark W. "Isthmian Canal Policy of the United States—Documentation," *Congressional Record,* CI, Part 3, March 23, 1955, 3611–3616.

Tomlinson, Edward. *The Other Americans.* New York: Scribner's, 1943.

"Treaty Information," *Department of State Bulletin*, LXIV, No. 1666, May 31, 1971, 720.

"Treaty Negotiations with Republic of Panama," *Congressional Record*, April 1, 1971, S4480–S4487.

"Truth About Panama," *New Statesman*, LVII, No. 1468, May 2, 1959, 598.

Turner Morales, David. "El Contrabando Zoneita," *Revista de la camera de comercio de Panamá* [Panama City], No. 180, February 1960, 7–8.

"The Uncertain Future of the Panama Canal," *U.S. News & World Report*, LXIII, No. 9, August 28, 1967, 70–71.

United Kingdom. Central Office of Information. Reference Division. *Britain and Latin America*. London: HMSO, 1968.

United Nations. *Compendium of Social Statistics, 1967*. (Series K, No. 3.) New York: 1968.

―――. "Population and Vital Statistics Report—Data available as of 1 July 1970," *Statistical Papers*, XXII, (Series A., No. 3, 1970, 1–27.)

United Nations Educational, Scientific and Cultural Organization. *World Survey of Education*, IV: Higher Education. New York: 1966.

―――. *World Survey of Education*, III: Secondary Education. New York: 1961.

―――. *World Survey of Education*, II: Primary Education. New York: 1958.

United Nations. Economic Commission for Latin America. *Estudio económico de América Latina, 1969*. New York: 1970.

―――. *Los Recursos humanos de centramérica, Panamá y México en 1950–1980 y sus relaciones con algunos aspectos del desarrollo económico*. Mexico: 1960.

United Nations. Industrial Development Organization. *El Desarrollo industrial de América Latina: Panamá*. (Simposio Internacional Sobre Desarrollo Industrial 29 Noviembre—20 Diciembre 1967.) Santiago: Economic Commission for Latin America, 1967.

―――. Small-Scale Industry in Latin America. New York: 1969.

U.S. Agency for International Development. *Latin America. Economic Growth Trends*. Washington: January 1971.

―――. *Status of Loan Agreements as of March 31, 1969*. Washington: 1969

―――. *Status of Loan Agreements as of March 31, 1971*. Washington: 1971.

―――. *U.S. Foreign Aid and the Alliance for Progress: Proposed Fiscal Year 1970 Program*. Washington: GPO, 1969.

————. *U.S. Foreign Aid and the Alliance for Progress: Proposed Fiscal Year 1971 Program.* Washington: May 1970.

————. *U.S. Foreign Aid and the Alliance for Progress.* Washington: February 1968.

U.S. Agency for International Development. Bureau of Technical Assistance. *Population Program Assistance.* Washington: October 1969, 83.

U.S. Agency for International Development. Bureau for Program and Policy Coordination. Office of Statistics and Reports. *Selected Economic Data for the Less Developed Countries.* Washington: May 1970

————. *U.S. Economic Assistance Programs Administered by the Agency for International Development and Predecessor Agencies.* Washington: May 1970.

————. *U.S. Overseas Loans and Grants and Assistance from International Organizations.* Washington: 1970.

U.S. Congress. 89th, 1st Session. Committee on Foreign Affairs. Subcommittee on Inter-American Affairs. *Hearings. Communism in Latin America, February 16, 25; March 2, 10, 16 and 30, 1965.* Washington: GPO, 1965.

U.S. Congress. 86th, 2d Session. Senate. Committee on Foreign Relations. *Latin America: Venezuela, Brazil, Peru, Bolivia and Panama* (Report of Senator George D. Aiken on a Study Mission). Washington: GPO, 1960.

U.S. Congress. 91st, 2d Session. House of Representatives. Committee on Appropriations. *Report No. 91–1134. Foreign Assistance and Related Programs Appropriation Bill, 1971.* Washington: GPO, June 1, 1970.

U.S. Congress. 91st, 2d Session. House of Representatives. Committee on Government Operations. *U.S. Economic Assistance to Transportation in Latin America. Twenty-Seventh Report.* Washington : GPO, 1970.

U.S. Department of Agriculture. Economic Research Service. *Agricultural Policies in the Western Hemisphere.* (Foreign Agricultural Economic Report No. 36.) Washington: GPO, 1969.

————. *The Agricultural Situation in the Western Hemisphere— Review of 1970 and Outlook for 1971.* (ERS-Foreign 312.) Washington: GPO, 1971.

————. *Indices of Agricultural Production for the Western Hemisphere. Revised 1961 through 1969. Preliminary 1970.* (ERS-Foreign 264.) Washington: GPO, April 1971.

————. *The Latin American Farmer.* (ERS-Foreign 257.) Washington: GPO, 1969.

————. *U.S. Foreign Agricultural Trade. Statistical Report FY 1970.* Washington: 1971.

U.S. Department of Agriculture. Foreign Agricultural Service. *The Beef Cattle Industries of Central America and Panama.* (FAS M–208.) Washington: 1969.

———. *World Agricultural Production and Trade: Statistical Report.* Washington: May, 1971.

U.S. Department of Commerce. Bureau of Foreign Commerce. *Basic Data on the Economy of Panama.* (World Trade Information Service: "Economic Reports," Pt. 1, No. 59–61.) Washington: GPO, 1961.

U.S. Department of Commerce. Bureau of International Commerce. *Foreign Business Practices.* Washington: 1968.

———. "Basic Data on the Economy of the Republic of Panama." *Overseas Business Reports.* (BR 68–41.) Washington: GPO, June 1968.

———. "Foreign Trade Relations of Panama." *Overseas Business Reports* (OBR 67–84.) Washington: December 1967.

———. "Market Factors in Panama." *Overseas Business Reports* (OBR 66–51.) Washington: 1966.

———. "Market Indicators for Latin America." *Overseas Business Reports* (OBR 67–74.) Washington: November 1967.

———. "Market Profiles for Latin America and the Caribbean." *Overseas Business Reports* (OBR 68–48.) Washington: 1968.

———. "Market Profiles for Latin America and the Caribbean." *Overseas Business Reports* (OBR 69–32.) Washington: 1969.

U.S. Department of Commerce. Bureau of the Census. *Population of Panama, Estimates and Projections: 1961–2001.* (Series P–96 No. 2.) Washington: GPO, July 1970.

U.S. Department of Commerce. Office of Business Economics. *Foreign Grants and Credits by the United States Government,* March 1961 Quarter.

U.S. Department of Health, Education, and Welfare. International Educational Relations. Division of International Education. *Bibliography: 1959 Publications in Comparative and International Education.* (Studies in Comparative Education, OE–14004–59.) Washington: GPO, 1960.

U.S. Department of Labor. Bureau of Labor Statistics. *Labor Conditions in Panama.* (Labor Digest No. 54.) Washington: 1964.

———. *Labor Law and Practice in Panama* (BLS Report No. 356.) Washington: GPO, 1970.

U.S. Department of State. *Background Notes: Republic of Panama.* Washington: GPO, 1970.

———. *Foreign Relations of the United States 1945—Diplomatic Papers,* IX: The American Republics. Washington: GPO, 1969.

————. *Lease of Defense Sites; Agreement between the United States of America and Panama.* (Executive Agreement Series, No. 359.) Washington: GPO, 1944.

U.S. Department of State. Agency for International Development. *Voluntary Foreign Aid Programs, Fiscal Year 1967.* Washington: 1968.

U.S. Department of State. Bureau of Intelligence and Research. *Research Study: Communist Diplomatic, Consular and Trade Representation in Latin America.* (RARS–11.) Washington: August 3, 1970. (Revised, October 14, 1970.) (mimeo.)

U.S. Department of Transportation. Bureau of Public Roads. *The Inter-American Highway: Linking the Americas.* Washington: 1970.

U.S. Embassy in Panama. *Activity in the Panamanian Construction Industry.* Panama City: September 18, 1969.

————. *Controls on Production, Consumption and Export of Logs.* Panama City: July 29, 1969.

————. *Incentive Decree For Panama's Tourism Industry.* Panama: April 5, 1971.

————. *Incentives for Panama's Construction Industry.* Panama City: January 13, 1970.

————. *Panamanian Fisheries—1969.* Panama: May 13, 1970.

————. *Panamanian Meat Exports to the United States.* Panama: U.S. Department of State, October 17, 1969.

————. *Sugar Situation in Panama.* Panama: March 10, 1969.

U.S. Embassy in San José. *Panama: Livestock and Meat.* San José: March 24, 1970.

U.S. Institute of Inter-American Affairs. Agricultural and Natural Resources. *Servicio interamericano de cooperación agrícola en Panamá. Annual report, 1956.* Panama City: Republic of Panama, 1956.

U.S. Panama Canal Company. *Annual Report, FY 1970.* Canal Zone: Canal Zone Printing Plant, 1970.

U.S. United States Information Service. *Communications Fact Book on Panama.* Washington: 1960 (mimeo).

U.S. War Department. OC/S, 2nd (MI) Division. *Notes on Panama.* Washington: GPO, 1903.

"U.S. and Panama Announce Results of Canal Zone Talks," *Department of State Bulletin,* XLIX, No. 1259, August 12, 1963, 246–247.

"United States and Panama Reestablish Diplomatic Relations," (Statement by President Lyndon B. Johnson) *Department of State Bulletin,* L, No. 1269, April 27, 1964, 655–656.

"U.S.-Panama Pact: A Double Gain," *Business Week*, X, No. 1883, October 2, 1965, 29.

"U.S.-Panama Plan Spurs Link for Inter-American Highway," *New York Times*, May 14, 1961.

University of Tennessee. "Report of the University of Tennessee Technical Assistance Unit in Panama to the International Co-operation Administration, United States Operations Mission to Panama, Semiannual Report, April 1960–September 1960" (mimeo.).

————. "Report of the University of Tennessee Technical Assistance Unit in Panama to the International Cooperation Administration, United States Operations Mission to Panama, Semiannual Report, October 1960–March 1961" (mimeo.).

————. "Report of the University of Tennessee Technical Assistance Unit in Panama to the International Cooperation Administration, United States Operations Mission to Panama, Semiannual Report, October 1959–March 1960" (mimeo.).

"USA Cannot Surrender its Rights in the Panama Canal," *Saturday Evening Post*, CXXXI, No. 17, October 25, 1958, 10.

Valdés, Ignacio de J. *Cuentos panameños de la ciudad y del campo*. (1st ed.) Panama City: Editorial Gráfico, 1928.

————. *Sangre criolla (nuevos cuentos panameños)*. Panama City: Imprenta "Acción Católica," 1943.

Van Olst, H. Rijken. *The National Income and National Accounts of the Republic of Panama: 1944–1952*. New York: Technical Assistance Administration of the United Nations, November 16, 1953.

Véliz, Claudio (ed.). *Latin America and the Caribbean: A Handbook*. New York: Praeger, 1968.

Wafer, Lionel. *A New Voyage and Description of the Isthmus of America*. (Reprint of original 1699 edition.) Cleveland: Burrows Brothers, 1903.

Walter Reed Army Institute of Research. *The Republic of Panama and the Canal Zone*. Washington: Walter Reed Army Medical Center, 1966.

————. *The Republic of Panama*. (Health Data Publications, No. 1, November 1959.) Washington: GPO, 1960.

Weaver, Findley. *Panama's Receipts from the Canal Zone in Relation to Her Foreign Trade and National Income*. Washington: International Monetary Fund, 1946 (typescript).

Westerman, George W. *Fifty Years (1903–1953) of Treaty Negotiations Between the United States and Republic of Panama*. Panama: Panama's Newspaper Guild, 1953.

The West Indies and Caribbean Year Book, 1961. London: Skinner, 1961.

"Who Really Owns Panama: A Source of U.S. Trouble," *U.S. News & World Report*, LVI, No. 14, April 6, 1964, 64–65.

Wilgus, A. Curtis (ed.). *The Caribbean: Its Culture*. Gainesville: University of Florida Press, 1955.

Wilgus, A. Curtis, and D'Eca, Raul. *Latin American History—A Summary of Political, Economic, Social, and Cultural Events from 1942 to the Present*. New York: Barnes and Noble, 1967.

Williams, Mary Wilhelmine. *Anglo-American Isthmian Diplomacy, 1815–1915*. Washington: American Historical Association, 1916.

Wolf, J. "Development and Structure of the World Banana Market," *Monthly Bulletin of Agricultural Economics and Statistics*, VIII, No. 2, 1959, 9–18.

Worcester, Donald E., and Schaeffer, Wendell G. *The Growth and Culture of Latin America*. New York: Oxford University Press, 1956.

"World Population Review," *Population Bulletin*, XV, No. 2, 1959.

Yearbook of Labour Statistics, 1970. (30th issue.) Geneva: International Labor Organization. International Labor Office, n.d.

Yearbook of Labour Statistics, 1960. (20th issue.) Geneva: International Labor Organization. International Labor Office, n.d.

Yearbook of Labour Statistics, 1968. (28th issue.) Geneva: International Labor Organization. International Labor Office, n.d.

Yearbook of National Accounts Statistics, 1969. II: International Tables. New York: United Nations, Department of Economic and Social Affairs, 1970.

Zárate, Manuel F. "Carnaval panameño," *Lotería* [Panama City], VII, No. 94, 1949, 22–24.

Zárate, Manuel F., and de Zárate, Dora Pérez. *La Décima y la copla en Panamá*. Panama City: n.pub., 1953.

Zimmerman, Gereon. "The Threat to the Panama Canal," *Look*, XXV, No. 16, 1961.

(Various issues of the following periodicals were also used in the preparation of this edition: *Alliance for Progress Weekly Newsletter* [London], February 1967–September 1971; *BOLSA Review* [London], December 1967–September 1971; *Business Latin America* [New York], November 1970–September 1971; *La Estrella de Panamá* [Panama City], May 1971–September 1971; *Evening Star* [Washington], July 1971–October 1971; *Gazeta Oficial* [Panama City], 1953–1960; *La Hora* [Panama City], June 1971; *Inter-American Center of Tax Administration Newsletter* [Panama City], January 1969–September 1971; *International Police Academy Review* [Washington], January 1971; *Latin America* [London], March 1968–September 1971; *Matutino* [Panama], May

1971–September 1971; *New York Times,* July 1971–October 1971; *Noticias* [New York], April 1971–August 1971; *Panama Tribune* [Panama City], May 1971–September 1971; *Quarterly Economic Review: Central America* [London], May 1968–May 1971; *Times of the Americas* [Washington], January 1969–October 1971; and *Washington Post,* July 1971–October 1971.)

GLOSSARY

balboa (B/)—The monetary unit. Official value is B/1 equals US$1. No paper balboas, only coins.

commisiones permanentes—Standing committees in the National Assembly.

criollo—Native-born person of Spanish descent.

DENI (Departamento Nacional de Investigación)—National Department of Investigation.

fiscal auxiliar—An assistant to the procurator general.

GDP—Gross domestic product.

lanchas patrulleras—National Guard patrol launches.

machismo—Literally, maleness; complex of beliefs and attitudes defining the image of masculinity.

macho—A man who exemplifies the concept of machismo.

mestizo—Person of mixed European and American Indian ancestry.

Metropolitan Area—The cities and districts of Panama and Colón, together with seven largely urban adjacent districts, including the towns of La Chorrera and Arraiján in Panama Province.

Public Ministry—An organization embracing all district attorneys, solicitors, and other individuals engaged in the legal representation of the state.

SCP—System of Classification of Positions, Wage Scales, and Compensation for civil service personnel.

terminal cities—The cities of Panama and Colón.

INDEX

cement: 295–296
censorship: 167, 170
censuses: 19, 59–63 *passim*, 66, 72, 89, 98, 100, 129, 152, 272, 299
Center for Development and Industrial Productivity: 287, 316
Center for Study, Promotion, and Social Assistance: 212
Central America: 236, 344
Central American Common Market: 210, 218, 235, 236, 243, 327
Central American Court of Justice: 235
Central American Defense Council: 236, 356
Central American Federation: 23
Central American Institute of Business Administration: 288
Central Isthmus (region): 50–51, 54, 55, 63, 83
Central Panama (region): 51, 54–58 *passim*, 64, 81, 148, 305, 312
Chamber of Commerce: 210, 218, 236, 243, 316
Chanis, Daniel: 38
Chan-Marín, Carlos Francisco: 159
Charles I, King of Spain: 13
Charpentier, Eduardo, Jr.: 164
Chase Manhattan Bank: 40, 265, 267, 308
Chiari, Roberto: 38, 39, 40, 43, 201, 202, 205, 206, 231, 232
Chiari, Rodolpho: 36, 200
Chiari family: 106, 197
Chile: 241
China, Nationalist: 241
China, People's Republic of: 240
Chiriquí Citrus Company: 283, 293
Chiriquí Electric Enterprises: 291
Chiriquí Land Company: 86, 94, 211, 280, 281, 282, 315, 342
Chiriquí Land Company Railways: 343
Chiriquí Milk Company: 292
Chiriquí Province: 51, 54–58 *passim*, 64, 83, 86, 87, 98, 101, 102, 112, 130, 148, 157, 170, 184, 185, 188, 190, 195, 208, 221, 236, 305, 342, 343, 361; agriculture, 272, 277–284 *passim*; industry, 288, 290, 294
Chitré: 338, 339
Christian Brothers: 146
Christian Democratic Party: 193, 201, 202, 210

cigarette factories: 283, 295
cimarrones: 14
cities: economy, 2; government, 190–191, 260
citizenship: 180
Civil Alliance: 39
civil service: 191–192
Clark Memorandum: 223
Clay, Henry: 22
Clayton-Bulwer Treaty: 24
climate: viii, 52–54, 277
clinics: 84, 87
coastal waters: 231, 239
Coclé Province: 51, 82, 98, 112, 157, 185, 188, 190, 272, 277, 278, 281, **282**, 284, 291, 294
coffee: 324; industry, 197, 294; production, 54, 281–282
Coffee Bank: 265
Coffee Institute: 282
Coiba Island: 49, 184, 353, 358, 360
Colegio del Istmo: 148
Colegio La Salle: 146
Colombia: 29, 103, 148, 174, 175, 179, 199, 234, 241, 326, 328, 356; canal project, 28, 30, 31, 218–219, 220; independence from, 30–33, 219, 220; relations with, 235, 237; union with, 7–8, 21, 27
Colón: 2, 8, 25, 27, 33, 34, 36, 49, 51, 53, 54, 69, 71, 86, 90, 91, 104, 105, 147, 153, 170, 184, 195, 230, 265, 284, 302, 306, 309, 345, 361; living conditions, 73, 74, 79, 80; population, 63; refinery, 41, 42, 249; trade, 319, 320, 336, 338, 339, 341
Colón Free Zone: 191, 232, 236, 249, 252, 320, 323, 326, 332; trade, 329–330, 333, 336, 338
Colón Province: 54, 55, 58, 63, 75, 83, 98, 185, 188, 190, 195, 273, 280, 288, 291, 361
communications (*see also specific medium*): ix, 320, 345
communism: 315
communist parties: 171, 202, 316, 347, 361, 362
compadrazgo: 117, 122
Condominis, Rev. Ramón María: 161
Confederation of Workers of the Republic of Panama: 211, 315, 317
Conference of American States: Sixth International, 222; Seventh International, 223

401

403

405

309; Public Health, viii, 67, 81, 83, 86, 253, 360; Public Ministry, 187, 189–190, 354, 357; Public Works, 253

Miranda, General: 20

Miró, Ricardo: 158

Miro, Rubén: 238

missions: 130

Mobil Oil Company: 289

monetary controls: 246

Monroe Doctrine: 28

Morales, Eusebio A.: 222

Morgan, Henry: 11, 16, 65

Mosquera, President (of Gran Colombia): 22, 26

motion pictures: 170–171

Movement of Revolutionary Unity: 362

municipal councils: 190–191

Muñoz, Avelino: 165

music: 164–165

Napoleon: 157

National Abbatoir: 294

National Assembly: vii, 40, 42, 107, 173–189 *passim*, 194, 198, 201–208 *passim*, 222, 226, 231, 242, 252, 348, 358

National Bank for Commerce and Industry: 265

National Bank Commission: 262

National Bank of Panama: 176, 191, 262–267 *passim*

National Brewery Company: 70, 292, 294

National Cattlemen's Association: 210

National Commission of Foreign Commerce: 326

National Commission for Health Planning: 81

National Conservatory of Music: 164

National Council of Cooperatives: 266

National Council for Foreign Relations: 218, 243

National Department of Investigation: 350, 353, 354, 357, 359

National Development Corporation: 210

National Free Enterprise Council: 210, 316, 317

National Guard: viii, x, 3, 138, 165, 173, 181, 182, 184, 186, 193, 198, 202–207 *passim*, 212, 213, 218, 227, 228, 233, 236, 253, 357, 360; admin-

istration, 354–355; awards and rank insignia, 355–356; organization and operation, 349–351, 352–354; personnel and training, 351–352; politics and power, 208–209, 214, 242, 347–348; strength, x, 352

National Guard Orientation School: 352

National Institute: 145, 148, 162, 212, 213, 362

National Institute of Agriculture: 147

National Institute of Culture and Sports: 241

National Institute of Music: 138, 165

National Liberal Movement: 42

National Liberal Party: 39, 41, 193, 201, 202, 205, 206

National Liberation Movement: 202, 206

National Minimum Wage Council: 306

National Museum: 139, 156

National Opposition Alliance: 201, 205

National Opposition Union: 201, 205

National Patriotic Coalition: 39, 40, 41, 42, 197, 201, 204, 205, 206

National Police Corps: 35, 38, 347, 348, 353

National Printing Office: 139, 169

National Products of Panama: 293

National Railway of Chiriquí: 343

National Revolutionary Party: 39, 177

National School of Agriculture: 139, 147

National School of Painting: 163

National Securities Commission: 266

National Sugar Refinery: 293

National Symphony Orchestra: 138, 139, 164, 165

National Theater: 139, 160, 162, 164

National Water Supply and Sewerage Institute: 81, 83, 253

National Welfare Lottery: 79, 81, 159, 257, 320

nationalism: 1, 2, 4, 108, 119, 155, 158, 194, 198, 199, 202, 217, 233, 243, 362

Negroes: vii, viii, 4, 8, 28, 95–100 *passim*, 109, 130, 178, 195–199 *passim*

Nentzen Franco, Col. Luis Q.: 209

Netherlands: 281, 326, 330

New Granada: 18, 20, 22, 23, 25–27; transisthmus treaty, 24

New Panama Canal Company: 219

407

Social Security Fund: 81, 86, 90, 91, 93, 191, 253, 261, 265–266
socialist bloc: 218, 241
Socialist Party: 39, 193, 202
society (*see also* lower class, middle class, status, upper class, values): character of, 1–5; mobility, 105–110 *passim*, 120, 128; structure, 4, 19, 96–97, 104–112, 127–129, 196–199
soils: 46, 54, 275, 276
Solis, Galileo: 243
Sosa, Juan: 155
Soviet Union: 171, 241, 362
Spain (*see also* cultural influences): 151, 171, 174, 241; colonial rule, 13–20; exploration and settlement by, 9–13; independence from, 20–22; trade, 14—18
Spanish (language): vii, 5, 99, 102, 103, 140, 145, 180
sports: 78–79
squatters: 73, 111, 116, 211, 269, 273, 274
standards and measures: 341
Star Sugar Refinery Company: 293, 294
status, social: 71, 74, 78, 95, 96, 97, 104–108 *passim*, 113, 119, 121, 122, 126, 127, 196
steel: 297
Stevenson, Adlai E.: 238
Stimson, Henry L.: 37, 223
Stock Brokers Association of Panama: 266
storage facilities: 336–337, 340, 341, 344
strikes: 312–313
students: 108–109, 148–150, 228; demonstrations and riots, 148, 154, 208, 227, 232; exchanges, 171; and politics, 154, 193, 212, 362
Sucre, Arturo: 173, 182, 194, 209
Suez Canal: 9, 42, 226–227, 240
sugar: 234, 324, 325
sugar industry: 197, 293–294
sugarcane: 278, 282
Superior Labor Court: 312
supermarkets: 339, 341
Supreme Court of Justice: viii, 38, 176, 182–189 *passim*, 207, 312, 348, 357, 359
Switzerland: 330
symbols, national: 57, 214–215

Tabei, Mohammed el: 241
Taboga (island): 49, 225
Tack, Juan Antonio: 234, 242
Taft, William Howard: 35, 220
Taft Convention: 37
tariffs: 220, 236, 287, 323, 332
taxes: 140, 206, 231, 232, 239, 246, 250, 255–259, 260, 282, 330, 332
teachers: 141, 142, 198, 229; training, 146, 148, 153–154
Teacher's Association: 210, 243
telegraph services: ix, 345
telephones: ix, 345
television: 138, 170, 241
temperature: viii, 52
Ten-Year Strategy for National Development: 252
textiles: 296
theater: 160–161
Third Nationalist Party: 206
Time: 169
tobacco: 28, 295
Tobar, General: 31, 32
Tocumen Airport: ix, 162, 331, 344, 349, 350, 353
Tocumen Airport Guard: 350, 353
topography: vii, 46–49
Torrijos, Brig. Gen. Omar: 2, 3, 167, 173, 186, 194, 198, 202, 208, 209, 218, 233, 242, 314, 348, 351, 352, 362, 363
Torrijos government: attitude toward, 4
tourism: 2, 80, 285, 320, 328, 332, 333, 342
tractors: 277
trade (*see also* balance of payments, exports, imports, licensing): 37, 65, 234, 236, 241, 249, 304, 319–341; agreements, 326–327; colonial, 14–18, 20; direction of, 325–326; domestic, 336–341; establishments, 336–338; foreign, 322–336; government role and policy, 319, 320–322, 323; illegal, 326
Trade Union Federation of Workers of the Republic of Panama: 211, 314, 316
transport companies: 337
transportation: ix, 249, 251, 252, 258, 281, 284, 319, 320, 341–345
treaties. *See* agreements and treaties
Treaty for Free Trade and Customs Preferences Between Panama, Costa Rica, and Nicaragua: 326

411

PUBLISHED AREA HANDBOOKS

550–65	Afghanistan		550–69	Ivory Coast
550–98	Albania		550–30	Japan
550–44	Algeria		550–34	Jordan
550–59	Angola		550–56	Kenya
550–73	Argentina		550–50	Khmer Republic (Cambodia)
550–66	Bolivia		550–81	Korea, North
550–20	Brazil		550–41	Korea, Rep. of
550–168	Bulgaria		550–58	Laos
550–61	Burma		550–24	Lebanon
550–83	Burundi		550–38	Liberia
550–166	Cameroon		550–85	Libya
550–96	Ceylon		550–163	Malagasy Republic
550–159	Chad		550–45	Malaysia
550–77	Chile		550–161	Mauritania
550–60	China, People's Rep. of		550–79	Mexico
550–63	China, Rep. of		550–76	Mongolia
550–26	Colombia		550–49	Morocco
550–67	Congo, Democratic Rep. of (Zaire)		550–64	Mozambique
			550–35	Nepal, Bhutan and Sikkim
550–91	Congo, People's Rep. of		550–88	Nicaragua
550–90	Costa Rica		550–157	Nigeria
550–152	Cuba		550–94	Oceania
550–22	Cyprus		550–48	Pakistan
550–158	Czechoslovakia		550–46	Panama
550–54	Dominican Republic		550–156	Paraguay
550–155	East Germany		550–92	Peripheral States of the Arabian Peninsula
550–52	Ecuador		550–42	Peru
550–150	El Salvador			
550–28	Ethiopia		550–72	Philippines
550–167	Finland		550–162	Poland
550–29	Germany		550–160	Romania
550–153	Ghana		550–84	Rwanda
550–87	Greece		550–51	Saudi Arabia
550–78	Guatemala		550–70	Senegal
550–82	Guyana		550–86	Somalia
550–164	Haiti		550–93	South Africa, Rep. of
550–151	Honduras		550–95	Soviet Union
550–165	Hungary		550–27	Sudan, Democratic Rep. of
550–21	India		550–47	Syria
550–154	Indian Ocean Territories		550–62	Tanzania
550–39	Indonesia		550–53	Thailand
550–68	Iran		550–89	Tunisia
550–31	Iraq		550–80	Turkey
550–25	Israel			

550-74	Uganda	550-57	Vietnam, North
550-43	United Arab Republic (Egypt)	550-55	Vietnam, South
550-97	Uruguay	550-99	Yugoslavia
550-71	Venezuela	550-75	Zambia

☆ U.S. GOVERNMENT PRINTING OFFICE: 1974 O—541–141 (PO 28)